Hemingway and Women

Hemingway and Women

Female Critics and the Female Voice

EDITED BY LAWRENCE R. BROER AND GLORIA HOLLAND

THE UNIVERSITY OF ALABAMA PRESS
Tuscaloosa and London

Copyright © 2002
The University of Alabama Press
Tuscaloosa, Alabama 35487-0380
All rights reserved
Manufactured in the United States of America

Typeface: ACaslon and Minion Ornaments

∞

The paper on which this book is printed meets the minimum requirements of
American National Standard for Information Science–Permanence of Paper for
Printed Library Materials, ANSI Z39.48–1984.

Library of Congress Cataloging-in-Publication Data

Hemingway and women : female critics and the female voice / edited by
Lawrence R. Broer and Gloria Holland.
p. cm.
Includes bibliographical references and index.
ISBN 0-8173-5150-7 (pbk. : alk. paper)
1. Hemingway, Ernest, 1899–1961—Characters—Women. 2. Feminism and
literature—United States—History—20th century. 3. Women and literature—
United States—History—20th century. 4. Hemingway, Ernest, 1899–1961—Views
on sex role. 5. Sex role in literature. 6. Women in literature. I. Broer, Lawrence R.
II. Holland, Gloria, 1945–
PS3515.E37 Z6178 2002
813'.52—dc21

2002002095

The poem "Hemingway" from *Collected Poems, 1917–1982* by
Archibald Macleish, copyright © 1985 by the Estate of Archibald
MacLeish, is reprinted by permission of Houghton Mifflin Com-
pany. All rights reserved.

Excerpts from the essay "Brett Ashley as New Woman in *The
Sun Also Rises*" by Wendy Martin from *New Essays on "The Sun
Also Rises,"* edited by Linda-Wagner Martin, copyright © 1987 by
Cambridge University Press, is reprinted with permission.

The Ernest Hemingway Foundation has generously granted permission for the use of materials from its archives.

FOR MY FAMILY:

Odes, Catherine, and
Carl Holland and Kay Holland Pearson

He was so complicated; so many sides to him you could hardly make a sketch of him in a geometry book.

Hadley Hemingway

As literary critics, we must work on the assumption that the author is a site, like the text and the reader, in which meaning is fluid and unstable rather than predetermined.

Debra Moddelmog

Contents

Introduction

Lawrence R. Broer and Gloria Holland

Susan Beegel informs us that of the seventeen women writing about Ernest Hemingway in the decade following his death, only Naomi Grant, a 1968 graduate student, discussed Hemingway's female characters, daring to challenge the "male-oriented" focus of early male critics (276). But the number of notable women Hemingway scholars doubled in the 1970s, doubled again after the publication of *The Garden of Eden* in 1986, and today accounts for nearly one-third of Hemingway criticism (Beegel, "Conclusion" 282, 290). More than numbers, it is the salubrious impact of these women upon Hemingway studies—what Debra Moddelmog calls "the most extensive reevaluation" of a writer's reputation and life "ever undertaken" ("Reconstructing" 187)—that we wish to acknowledge here. Just as Philip Young's concept of the code hero made it hard for subsequent critics to approach Hemingway in any other fashion, so the challenge by these women to forty years of often superficial or misguided interpretations of Hemingway's treatment of women and gender has infinitely deepened and expanded our understanding of the ways these complicated subjects function in Hemingway's novels and stories.[1]

Whatever other forces have attracted some of the brightest women scholars to Hemingway, the authors of these essays generally agree that the appearance of *The Garden of Eden* was their entree to "*el nuevo* Hemingway" (Comley and Scholes 146), a writer whose androgynous impulses not only contradict the machismo Hemingway of myth but also whose complex female protagonists and problematic treatment of gender relationships demand a reevaluation of Hemingway's entire literary output. Such closer readings as represented by these essays awaken readers to a Hemingway less reconstructed than rediscovered, an author whose fiction required all along that we read his women with the same care given his heroes, recognizing that the same emotional undercurrents, the same subtleties of style and technique underlying his male creations, explained his female portraits as well. Suddenly, as Susan Beegel observes, rather than reading gender in Hemingway only in relation to manhood, focusing on Young's question about "what makes a man a man," the "question was enlarged to include what makes a man a woman? what makes a woman a woman? what makes a woman a man? what makes men and women heterosexual? homosexual? bisexual? where are the boundaries of gender? and what importance does gender have in our make-up?" ("Conclusion" 290). If these questions were always there for us to ponder—if his female characters were always more central to his novels and stories and more complexly portrayed than critics had reported—how have these issues been missed or ignored, and why have his female characters been typically cited for their weakness and unreality?

As these essayists seek to answer such questions, they inquire as well into Hemingway's *other* notable women—women writers, early scholars, literary characters, wives, and lovers. Part 1, "Heroines and Heroes, the Female Presence," begins with Linda Patterson Miller's "In Love with Papa" because it illuminates the long-standing problems facing female scholars writing on Hemingway and because it expresses the personal identification with Hemingway that some women readers have always felt. Miller's "twenty-year odyssey" as a teacher and critic of Hemingway reflects the struggles of and the rewards found by scholars such as Linda Wagner-Martin, Susan Beegel, and Ann Putnam. Writing toward the beginning of the revisionist work on Hemingway's women, these scholars have, in turn, inspired such confident new voices in Hemingway studies as Lisa Tyler, Amy Strong, Hilary Justice, and Gail Sinclair.[2] Proceeding, we turn to a rich variety of readings of notable female characters and the central role of gender in Hemingway's novels and stories. Even though essayists were invited to design their own topics, their essays follow the approximate order in which Hemingway's fictional women appear. In general, these essays respond to the often simplistic interpretation of Hemingway's fictional creations by Edmund Wilson, Philip

Young, Leslie Fiedler, and a host of other primarily male critics who too often adopt the subservient view of women held by Hemingway's male characters. More specifically, these essays explore the way the author's fictional men and women deal with the complex circumstances of their lives, as well as the relationship of female scholarship to mainstream Hemingway criticism—what Tyler calls a "meta-analysis" of critical response.

From Miller to Comley, these essays demonstrate not only that gender was Hemingway's constant concern, and that his female characters are drawn with complexity and individuality equal to Hemingway's males, but that the feminine voice in Hemingway resonates throughout his work in often surprising ways. Kathy Willingham, for instance, overturns old views of the exclusive masculinity of Hemingway's male protagonists by exploring the feminized origins of the bullfight. Linda Wagner-Martin shows us that the author's concept of love as erotic desire explains both his romantic vision and, paradoxically, his spare and intense style. Tyler and Kim Moreland make clear that the psychological traumas of Hemingway's minor female characters are as complex and far-reaching as those of Brett Ashley, Catherine Barkley, or Maria of *For Whom the Bell Tolls,* and that Marie Morgan of *To Have and Have Not* and the strong-willed females of "Cat in the Rain" and "The Sea Change" enjoy a greater freedom and range of expression than once supposed. Ann Putnam, Susan Beegel, and Rose Marie Burwell point out that the questions of gender—male and female identity and sexual ambivalence—are as important to understanding Hemingway's heroes as his heroines. These authors show that Jung's "Eternal Feminine"—what Beegel refers to as a "sense of the sea as wife," is an inseparable part of young Nick Adams, as well as such later heroes as Santiago and Thomas Hudson. Moddelmog's argument that we must enlarge our definition of family to understand the emotional bonds between Hemingway's characters reflects the ongoing posture of these female critics that Hemingway's portrayal of sexual identity clearly upsets traditional notions of the author's portrayal of men and women. Focusing finally upon the novel that can be said to have started it all, *The Garden of Eden,* Amy Strong and Nancy Comley make the case toward which all these essays build: that while sexual ambiguity—androgyny, bisexuality, role transformation—has always been present in Hemingway's work, *Eden* was the text, as Comley remarks, that "brought gender issues to the foreground, not simply of that text" but of Hemingway's work as a whole. Strong and Comley complete our reexamination of Hemingway's most complex and underestimated heroines by arguing that Catherine Bourne is not only Hemingway's most interesting and complicated female but one who usurps Brett Ashley's place as the most remarkable of Hemingway's creations.

While these essays explicate specific texts and characters, their explorations of gender take us into a variety of related works and issues. Putnam's ostensible subject, for instance, may be the feminine in the depiction of nature in "Big Two-Hearted River," but she explores as well *The Green Hills of Africa, The Old Man and the Sea, A Movable Feast,* and other stories in *In Our Time.* Wagner-Martin may explicate Hemingway's concept of love as erotic desire in *A Farewell to Arms,* but she also shows us how this "erotic paradigm" relates to Maria and Pilar in *For Whom the Bell Tolls.* Maria and Pilar are discussed at greater length by Sinclair, who joins Kathy Willingham in enlarging our sense of Hemingway's code hero to include major female characters. Burwell's analysis of Thomas Hudson's suppressed androgyny in *Islands in the Stream* carries over to the gender confusion of Nick Adams of "Indian Camp" and "Now I Lay Me" and to Santiago of *The Old Man and the Sea* and Colonel Cantwell of *Across the River and into the Trees.* Moddelmog's explorations of Hemingway's queer families highlights the author's alternative family formations in "The Battler" and "The Sea Change" but extends to such stories as "The Doctor and the Doctor's Wife," "Indian Camp," "Fathers and Sons," and "The Last Good Country" and to the novels *The Sun Also Rises, The Old Man and the Sea, Across the River and into the Trees,* and *Islands in the Stream.* In short, scarcely a work in the Hemingway canon goes unremarked upon.

The second group of essays—"Mothers, Sisters, Wives"—approach Hemingway's depiction of women and gender in historical and biographical context. Hilary Justice, Miriam Mandel, Sandra Spanier, and Rena Sanderson show us that it is not only Hemingway's fictional females we must judge more carefully but also the real-life women who cared for, promoted, or competed with the author and often helped to shape his art. To use Spanier's expression, these new readings reverse the male gaze of Hemingway and Hemingway's male critics, releasing such women as Hadley, Martha Gellhorn, and Hemingway's mother, Grace—

the author's first model of the feminine—from decades of male-imposed stereotypes. We see the roles Hemingway wished these women to play and the roles they actually played in their struggles with traditional prescriptions for gender identification and sexual orientation. We see these women not as Hemingway accessories but as accomplished women, heroines in their own right, diverse and complete as individuals. Always we see how these women defy the gender myths that have formed around them, how Hemingway's relationships with them expose the author's lifelong attempts to comprehend his own conflicting feelings about gender and sex, and how Hemingway's most compelling female characters have their genesis in the real-life women whose import to his art has often been marginalized and trivialized.

While the new scholarship represented here seeks to expand and deepen our appreciation of gender issues in Hemingway's novels and stories, and in his life as a whole, these scholars do not speak in a single voice with equal sympathy for Hemingway's treatment of women nor do they respond with like readings of Hemingway's life or works. Rather they represent the diversity of interest and interpretation inspired by the destabilizing nature of the texts themselves [Barlowe (-Kayes) 25]. The polyphonic discourse that ensues includes close textual analysis, cultural criticism, and a self-appraising conversation between these women and their male colleagues and among the women themselves. While Linda Miller's essay may differ from others in this text in its markedly personal tone, Jamie Barlowe's equally lively albeit more academic discussion of how women's criticism on Hemingway has been "tokenized" and "trivialized" or refuted by male scholars, offers immediate counterpoint.[3] Such juxtaposition reflects our emphasis on the ideological complexity of Hemingway's work that inspires a rich diversity of interests and critical approaches. Whether one praises or pillories, both are ways of acknowledging Hemingway's status as a writer who speaks to everyone, to the extreme ends of the methodological spectrum and every point between.

Even as these scholars debate their differences, they argue cogently for the central role of women in the Hemingway canon, whether demonstrating their passionate presence or their disconcerting absence. They show that while Hemingway was certainly influenced by traditional perceptions of women, he was no mere conduit for the inherited prejudices of his age. Rather he recognized the importance of the struggle of the emerging new female of his era and made it a major concern of his fiction. We see that, early and late, the most central conflicts in Hemingway's work revolve around questions of gender—male and female identity, sexual ambivalence, the crossing of sexual boundaries—and that understanding these complicated gender dynamics offers vital new ways of interpreting Hemingway's fiction as a whole. In so doing, these analyses rise always to what Miller calls the demands of Hemingway's art: appreciating the author's gift for portraying life and characters in terms that are piercingly real and his genius for evoking these absences and ambivalences that account for the always-surprising hidden depths of his men and women alike.

These female voices in Hemingway criticism send an invaluable message to both new and old readers of Hemingway's fiction—that his work has always been as inclusive of and as important to women as to men. As Miller says, "If Frederic Henry cries at night, so does Catherine Barkley, and so do we all" (8). Hadley Hemingway remarked that Hemingway was "so complicated; so many sides to him, you could hardly make a sketch of him in a geometry book" (qtd. in Diliberto 115). These notable female scholars show us that the author's portraits of women and his deepest understanding of sex and love are a continuing tribute to that complexity—inclusive, open, and endlessly fascinating.

Acknowledgments

We are foremost indebted to the many female scholars whose work inspired this book. We also want to thank Jackson Bryer and Susan F. Beegel, whose encouragement and cogent criticisms helped shape and strengthen this text. Thanks as well to Professors Cherrill Heaton at the University of North Florida, and John Sinclair at Rollins College for their help with musical terms. For permission to use materials from its archives, we thank the Hemingway Foundation. Finally, we would like to express our appreciation to Mary Ann Pidick for her aid in untangling computer glitches and to Dava Simpson and Leslie Fisher for their innumerable typings, wrappings, and mailings.

Abbreviations

AFTA	=	*A Farewell to Arms*
AJ	=	*African Journal*
BL	=	*By-Line: Ernest Hemingway*
DIA	=	*Death in the Afternoon*
FWTBT	=	*For Whom the Bell Tolls*
GHOA	=	*Green Hills of Africa*
GOE	=	*The Garden of Eden*
IITS	=	*Islands in the Stream*
MF	=	*A Moveable Feast*
NAS	=	*The Nick Adams Stories*
OMATS	=	*The Old Man and the Sea*
SL	=	*Ernest Hemingway: Selected Letters, 1917–1961*
SAR	=	*The Sun Also Rises*
SS	=	*The Short Stories of Ernest Hemingway (1938–1966)*
TAFL	=	*True at First Light*
THHN	=	*To Have and Have Not*

Hemingway and Women

1
Heroines and Heroes, the Female Presence

1
In Love with Papa

Linda Patterson Miller

I little imagined two decades ago how much Ernest Hemingway would take over my life. Almost all of the writing and teaching that I do, along with the day-to-day living of my life, inevitably comes back, in some way, to Hemingway. This should not surprise me, since Hemingway had already taken over my reading life as early as my sophomore year in high school. I discovered him, by chance, after I had determined to read all of the fiction in our Chicago library by working my way through the stacks alphabetically, taking them on in rows. My system shattered, however, when I had arrived at the "H's" and read *A Farewell to Arms* for the first time. The book so unsettled me that I could not reshelve it and move on. I can still see myself reading *Farewell* in my bedroom, where the afternoon sun formed neat squares on the peach wallpaper. Outside my window an early spring had exposed our lawn in brown patches, but I was already transported to Hemingway's stark white land where I could hear Catherine's and Frederic's boots squeaking as they walked. I could see Catherine matching Frederic's strides, her walking stick puncturing the crusty snow. I did not want the book to end, and when it did I knew that my life had changed. This marked the beginning of my love affair with the father of modern American prose. Recently I took comfort in Maya Angelou's confession that William Shakespeare was her "first white love." Angelou "pacified" herself about Shakespeare's "whiteness by saying that after all he had been dead so long it couldn't matter to anyone any more" (13–14). Although some today have tried to rush Hemingway's artistic death, banishing him to that authorial graveyard of dead white males, he will not go quietly. Nor should he.[1]

A recent issue of *The Missouri Review* devoted to the subject of "Men" humorously highlights a resistance to Hemingway's prose that has persisted since his actual death in 1961. In Mick Steven's cartoon that heads up the issue, a man sits at a round table with four women who eye him suspiciously from behind their reading glasses. They all have their lips pursed, and one woman has her arms crossed rigidly over her chest. The man, a bemused and authoritarian discussion leader, voices the cartoon's caption. "Just *what* is this book-group's problem with Hemingway?" Were some of my female colleagues to answer this question, they would say—and they do—that Hemingway's world of machismo both alienates and undermines women. Accordingly, they argue that he should not be taught, either in book groups or in schools. Even my mother-in-law takes potshots, telling me that "the man was a slob." No other American writer, except for Norman Mailer, generates such venom. But what evokes the hatred? The man? The legend of the man? The Art? A little of each?

To be honest, any lover of Hemingway's art who surveys his biography feels a bit betrayed by the man. He made strong demands of his women, expecting them to remain true, even when he did not. He expected his women to anticipate and meet his needs, and he faulted them when they tried to remain independent, as did his third wife, Martha Gellhorn, herself a recognized writer. When she stood up to Hemingway, he later accused her of belligerence and mean-spiritedness. Hemingway's real life women walked a fine line, as did his fictional women. One of his women in *To Have and Have Not* asserts that men are not "built" to be monogamous. "They want some one new, or some one younger, or some one that they shouldn't have, or some one that looks like some one else. Or if you're dark they want a blonde. Or if you're blonde they go for a redhead. Or if you're a redhead then it's something else. A Jewish girl I guess, and if they've had really enough they want Chinese or Lesbians or goodness knows what. . . . Or they just get tired, I suppose. You can't blame them if that's the way they are. . . . I suppose the good ones are made to have a lot of wives but it's awfully wearing trying to be a lot of wives yourself" (244–45).

Hemingway perhaps considered himself one of the good ones since he did have a lot of wives, four to be exact; and each of his marriages unraveled when a new woman caught his eye. None of his wives, or friends, saw him as an easy man. According to Hemingway's fourth wife Mary, tension and unhappiness were inevitable with a man as "complicated and contradictory" as Hemingway, who drove women "to bitchery." She questioned why some, including herself, hung on as long as they did (qtd. in Kert 414–16). Hadley Richardson, Hemingway's first wife, gave it a softer slant. She believed that Hemingway masked his sentimental streak with an outer toughness and that his deep sensitivity and vulnerability in relationships caused him to lash out at others (Sokoloff 58). During the 1930s, and thereafter, he gained a reputation for his undue harshness to his friends, and also to his wives.

Recently, Jamie Barlowe (-Kayes) has argued that since Hemingway's real-life women (including his four wives) became "marginalized characters" in Hemingway's personal legend, they emerge in his fiction as figures that stand "outside the action, yet implicated in it." Through her "destabilizing readings" of Hemingway's texts, Barlowe (-Kayes) challenges the prevailing Hemingway legend that has emerged both apart from and integral to Hemingway scholarship so as to "expose cultural codes and attitudes about women which continue to haunt and limit their lives" (26–27, 33). Earlier feminist critics such as Judith Fetterley have argued more one-sidedly that since Hemingway created his female characters in order to destroy them (as such, he kills off Catherine Barkley in *A Farewell to Arms*) women should be resistant readers of Hemingway. More recently, and with admirable balance and breadth, Rena Sanderson illuminates the "historical and biographical contexts" (as related to gender issues) that influenced but did not inhibit Hemingway's art (171). She joins with other scholars in recognizing that Hemingway's heroines reflect their cultural and literary circumstances while also emerging as believable and even archetypal figures—larger than life but no less real.

Whether or not Hemingway saw women as they were and not as he wanted—and perhaps we want—them to be, remains the key issue. As I look at the women in Hemingway's art, I ask a basic question in keeping with Hemingway's own artistic demand (as he expressed it in *Death in the Afternoon*) that the art be true. Are his women real? Are they viable? Does he get them "out entire" so that they have "more than one dimension and . . . will last a long time?" This is how Hemingway described characterization when it is true. If the writer "has luck as well as seriousness," he said, he will "write people" and "not skillfully constructed *characters*." These people will be "projected from the writer's assimilated experience, from his knowledge, from his head, from his heart, and from all there is of him" (191).

I would argue that many of Hemingway's women reach that third or fourth dimension where true art lives, even though Hemingway's macho label continues to prohibit a totally unbiased reading of his art. Beyond this, some readers fail to recognize the truth of Hemingway's characters, because they do not meet the demands of Hemingway's art. They do not read between the lines and thus miss the emotional complexity of his art and of his heroines. Failing to allow for Hemingway's whittled style, they interpret what seems to be a sketchy treatment of the women as a weakness of character. With Hemingway's women especially, he discovered them more fully by giving them little to say. His women embody the 7/8 of the iceberg that is down under and carry much of the work's emotional weight accordingly.[2]

This occurs most powerfully in his early stories. Marjorie's relatively quiet presence in "The End of Something," for example, centers the story's emotional spin. After Nick has told her that love "isn't fun any more," she gathers herself up with great solemnity and rows out onto the lake, leaving Nick lying "with his face in the blanket by the fire" where he "could hear Marjorie rowing on the water." Her rowing back to the beginning point evokes the story's opening images of a once vital life suddenly gutted and lost. Just as "the sails of the schooner filled and it moved out into the open lake, carrying with it everything that had made the mill a mill and Hortons Bay a town," Marjorie too has taken with her all of lived life's emotional heft. With the wind suddenly knocked out of his own sails, Nick feels but does not know how to deal with his unexpected loss (*SS* 107–11).

When Hemingway's parents responded to his early stories, including "The End of Something," as crude and immoral, Hemingway replied:

> I'm trying in all my stories to get the feeling of the actual life across—not to just depict life—or criticize it—but to actually make it alive. So that when you have read something by me you actually experience the thing. You can't do this without putting in the bad and the ugly as well as what is beautiful. Because if it is all beautiful

you can't believe in it. Things aren't that way. It is only by showing both sides—3 dimensions and if possible 4 that you can write the way I want to. (*SL* 153)

As Hemingway concluded in his defensive 20 March 1925 letter to his father, "When you see anything of mine that you don't like remember that I'm sincere in doing it and that I'm working toward something. If I write an ugly story that might be hateful to you or to Mother the next one might be one that you would like exceedingly" (*SL* 153).

If Hemingway was understandably defensive in his letter to his parents, I must confess to my own defensiveness of Hemingway and his art over the past two decades. I had entered the profession at a time when women seemingly found it easier to dismiss Hemingway than to read him, and only a handful of female scholars wrote about, talked about, or read (or admitted to reading) Hemingway. When I was invited as a female scholar to speak about Hemingway and his women at the 1985 Year of Hemingway Conference (Boise State University), I suspected that the invitation came primarily by default. I also suspected that the conference organizers assumed I would castigate rather than praise the artist and his art. So, on an unseasonably hot spring morning in Idaho, I stood before a crowd of academics and some locals, including one man who said he had "come down from the mountain" in Hemingway's honor. Jack (Bumby) Hemingway, Hemingway's oldest son, sat before me in the first row, and a poster image of Hemingway, inflated the size of the wall, looked over my shoulder from behind urging caution. Refusing to feel cowed, I defended Hemingway against his detractors. "My father usually gets short-changed in these academic discussions about his life and art," Jack Hemingway told me later. "Thank you for the balanced portrait." Another female professor, herself an invited speaker at the conference, revealed that she too loved Hemingway's art but that her colleagues would not let her teach him. We acknowledged together that other women—closet readers of Hemingway—undoubtedly existed. They just needed to be heard.

"So, what is it you do when you, as a woman, 'read' Hemingway?" Jim Hinkle asked. We were at the Second International Hemingway Conference in Lignano, Italy, in 1986, and I had just finished talking on Hemingway's women, a follow-up to my talk in Idaho the previous year. "Is this some new kind of literary stance?" he asked, as we both settled into the cushioned seats that lined the tiered meeting room. The conference hall, on pilings, jutted out over the Adriatic Sea. Only a glass wall at the upper rear of the room separated us from that arc of water. Hinkle had arrived at Hemingway scholarship late in his career at San Diego State University, and he pursued with almost fanatical zeal the truth of Hemingway's art. He was not interested in theories but in the words on the page, the artistic flow. He thought that if he could memorize Hemingway's work he might "get" it whole. He told me that he had memorized, among other works, the entirety of *The Sun Also Rises*. I believed him.

Jim proceeded to tell me that he and Jack Benson were organizing a Hemingway conference to be held at San Diego State in spring, 1987. They were interested in hearing how Hemingway scholars variously approached their reading of Hemingway, and he outlined to me in a letter of 13 December 1986 the goals for the conference. "Our idea," Jim wrote, "is for each speaker to make explicit what it is he thinks he is doing in his work on Hemingway—where he is going, how he tries to get there, why he does what he does in the way he does it—and then to give a sample (or a group of brief samples) of his method in operation." Seemingly unaware of his exclusionary language when it came to defining Hemingway scholars as men only, Jim added that he and Benson had "tried to select people who take widely different approaches in their work on Hemingway" and who represented "a balance between those who are regular Hemingway meeting-goers" and those outside the field. He reiterated that he did not understand how someone might read Hemingway based on gender but that the idea intrigued him.

The twenty-one invited speakers at the "Approaches to Hemingway Conference" (27–28 March 1987) included four women (Claudia Brodsky, Barbara Lounsberry, Sandra Spanier, and myself). My talk, "'It's Harder to Do about Women': Rereading Hemingway's Heroines," reiterated my belief that Hemingway's art had been unjustly maligned for its maleness. In particular, I questioned why Hemingway criticism had repeatedly dismissed Hemingway's women as narrowly drawn, both morally and artistically. "I am a teacher, a writer, a woman," I began. "I am a woman who reads Hemingway. Women, I am told, do not read Hemingway, nor do they argue for the emotional truthfulness of his art, particularly when it comes to his women." I concluded that a misreading of Hemingway's women became almost inevitable when people failed to separate the man—or the idea of the man—from the work. Furthermore, beyond failing to allow for Hemingway's whittled style and misinterpreting a sketchy treatment of the women as a weakness of character, I suggested that misguided perceptions about his heroines have something to do with setting as well as narrative form. Many of his works build around war, which distorts and intensifies human behavior, sometimes to the point of hysteria. Herein, Hemingway's females become stereotyped as hysterics. In addition, he often writes about male/female love in its early stages, evoking the heady distortions—the giddiness—of falling in love. These women-in-love might seem superficial, exaggerated, or silly if separated from the contexts of their thematic environment. Finally, I concluded that Hemingway scholarship was only beginning to reassess Hemingway's supposed heroic code and the macho world associated with it—ideas instilled early on by Philip Young and others.

Fortunately, that reassessment continues and thrives today with both female and male scholars joining in the dialogue. Despite a residual resistance among the feminist camp during the past two decades, women have increasingly risen to Hemingway's defense, stemming and even reversing the anti-Hemingway tidewaters. Besides those scholars already mentioned, Linda Wagner-Martin wrote the first and still definitive article on Hemingway's sensitive portrayal of women in his short stories, and Sandra Whipple Spanier recognized early on that Hemingway's heroic code had its female counterpart. Barbara Lounsberry's perceptive analysis of Hemingway's lyricism—his intricate rendering of place and time and memory—further contributed to a rereading of Hemingway's art. Instead of castigating Hemingway, female scholars such as these have collectively celebrated his "muscular" prose that allows for a seductive rendering of life's emotional truths. As revisionist readings such as these continue to gain ground, they challenge those assessments that too simplistically dismiss Hemingway's women and his art. This scholarship does not for the most part make moral pronouncements, as did Edmund Wilson when he categorized Hemingway's heroines as either goddesses or bitches, and it recognizes the artistic viability and versatility of his women and his art. Hemingway's women are not all the same woman: strong, aggressive, pragmatic, independent, all somehow like Pilar, which is perhaps a more modern but equally damaging kind of stereotyping. That his

women are not all Pilars attests to their truthfulness. Catherine is not
Maria is not Brett. As there is no collective Hemingway man, there is no
collective Hemingway woman. To suppose so in either case is to deny
Hemingway's art.

The Hemingway women most often maligned and misread by readers
are Catherine Barkley and Brett Ashley. One of my female students recently summarized the typical response to Catherine as a somewhat
mindless and passive woman who allows her man to manipulate her.
What I see predominantly, though, is a woman in love. Hemingway knew
about the transcendence of being in love. He knew about the silly child-
like talk of lovers. He also knew about love's impermanence. As the girl
in "Hills Like White Elephants" realized, once they take it away you
never get it back again. If Hemingway was at his best in capturing men
and women in love—the headiness of it, the intensity of feeling that distorts everything else—he also portrayed how that headiness cannot be
sustained in any persistent and certain form. As Hemingway's art repeatedly underscores this conflict between the romantic and the real—life as
one would like it to be and life as it is—Hemingway's women, more often
than his men, understand and confront the complexities of life and of
male/female relationships. Although they too yearn for the romance of
life and all of its promise, they also see this romance less idealistically.
That is, they see the romantic view as a necessary pretense in the face of
things that are. As both sexes feel helpless in the face of life and of themselves, the women are more willing to make themselves vulnerable.

To the degree that Hemingway's women suffer and are willing to confront suffering, they are alive. His women are not silly, nor are they
glib. This was what Fitzgerald said of Catherine Barkley: she seemed
"too glib." Essentially, Fitzgerald believed that Hemingway had made
Catherine too one-dimensional. "Don't try to make her make sense," he
said, "she probably didn't!" (227). Fitzgerald was right in advising Hemingway that Catherine did not have to make sense. Indeed, she should
not make sense. People who are real usually do not "make sense" in
any formulaic way, and it is Catherine's very complications that make
her true.

The same can be said for Brett Ashley, the Hemingway woman who
also resists formulaic readings even as critics try to contain her. Neither a
nymphomaniac nor a devourer of men, Brett remains a woman who is

aware of and trapped by her beauty.[3] She knows that her appearance draws men to her, and she defines herself in relation to this. Yet, as she molds herself to what the crowd wants her to be, she also tries to shatter this image. Her skittishness, her incomplete sentences, her carelessness, her restlessness—moving from place to place and people to people, all reflect her increasing sense of unrealized relationships and of her unrealized self. She would like to believe that the beauty that identifies her is real and that it comes from within. Whereas in *Cassandra's Daughters* Roger Whitlow, not unlike other critics, argues that Brett's obsessive bathing reflects her guilt for abusing men (58), I would argue that it predominantly reveals her need to get beneath surfaces, to wash away the outer image so as to get to who she really is. She wants that, but she also fears it. Without her looks, what will she have? Brett needs the affirmation of herself that men's adoration gives her, just as, like most of Hemingway's characters, she fears being alone. Ironically, because of her beauty, Brett is more alone and alienated, from others and from herself, than anyone else in the novel. The fiesta scenes where the men dance around Brett, chanting, illuminate her isolation. "Brett wanted to dance" too, Jake says, "but they did not want her to. They wanted her as an image to dance around" (*SAR* 155).[4]

The exterior image that both disguises and reveals less tangible interiors stands at the heart of Hemingway's art, and his females, like Brett, most embody this contradictory thrust. Hemingway's females accordingly, both elusive and real, become powerful literary devices within the intricate weave of his narratives. Because Hemingway's women do not fit any one mold, they should not be contained by any one literary stance that imposes on the text its own agenda. It is the formulas I resist, and it is this resistance that most defines what I do when I read Hemingway and when I read Hemingway's women. Hemingway, more than most writers, has been oversubjected to schematic readings, probably because readers feel unsettled by the elusive layers of his work, which they would like to pin down and label.

At the risk of contradicting myself, however, I do think some generalizations can be made about Hemingway's women overall. They are feminine, intuitive, realistic, direct, quiet and principled; and they tend to be risktakers at the same time as they try to order their lives. As to how he went about getting them entire—that fourth and fifth dimension, allow me to suggest that he effectively used parallel structuring and vignettes—short, telling scenes void of talk. With parallel structuring in various forms, he established repetitive and contrapuntal motifs that build a larger emotional framework for his women. The reader begins to see these women—their emotional nuances—beyond any direct physical description of them.

This occurs quite powerfully with Brett Ashley in *The Sun Also Rises*. Before Brett enters the novel, Georgette has already set the scene. Pretty until she smiles, Georgette reveals, in parody, Brett's conflict between her idealized and her real identity. After Jake has introduced Georgette as someone other than who she is, the jokes at the bar revolve around her mistaken identity. When Robert Cohn's Frances then enters the novel, the theme of lost identity and betrayal intensifies. Frances Cohn's despair over losing her looks and her man overnight parallels Brett's desperation, both present and potential, regarding her beauty and her lost self. Hemingway adds to the parallel patterning through Brett's male counterpart, the exceptionally handsome Romero. Like Brett, Romero's appearance identifies him the first time Jake sees him, "the best-looking boy" he has "ever seen." "Standing, straight and handsome and altogether by himself, alone in the room with the hangers-on," Romero mirrors Jake's descriptions of Brett as staring or standing "straight" and "altogether alone" despite, or even because of, the hangers-on (163). Brett too notices Romero's looks immediately. "Oh, isn't he lovely," Brett says. "And those green trousers" (165). Jake often describes Brett as "lovely," with all the same sexual overtones.

Romero's bullfighting and the fact that he is "real" contrasts with Belmonte's phony imitation of self. Romero works the bull close; he does not, like Belmonte, *pretend* to work the bull close. Throughout Jake's long description of Romero's bullfighting, he repeats words like "faked," "simulated," "appeared" to emphasize the contrast between image and identity, between something idealized and sentimentalized versus something pure and primitive and true. As Romero fights the color-blind bull with integrity, the crowd does not like it, for they do not understand how his little sidesteps compensate for the bull's deficiencies. They think he is afraid. As Montoya understands, people can corrupt someone like Romero. "People take a boy like that," he tells Jake, and "they don't know what he's worth. They don't know what he means" (172). As Hemingway recognized, one no longer has himself once he has accepted and molded himself to the crowd's wishes. The crowd creates out of the real the phony image of the real, for it makes them feel more comfortable.

If Belmonte foreshadows and parallels Romero's future, especially as the crowds have already tried to mold him and contain him, he might foreshadow Brett's future as well. The boys, the dancers, and the drunks who carry Romero away at the end of the fight have done the same with Brett, who associates throughout the novel with drunks, the boys at the bar who encircle her, and the dancers at the fiesta. She understands her own desperation when she tells Jake that she has got to do something she really wants to do, which is to break free of that image. She does not want to let the crowd determine her identity and her destruction.

As Hemingway juxtaposes throughout the novel these various parallel patterns, they begin to qualify each other so as to build overall a strong emotional resonance, all as related, finally, to Brett. The subtle shifts and replications of this cubistic rendering intensify as Hemingway incorporates vignettes into the narrative weave. These quick, cameralike shots that zoom in close to freeze the moment and the character in time work particularly well to create the emotional more than the physical truth of Hemingway's women, including Brett, whose character and sense of self becomes more sharply etched when she is alone with Jake. Hemingway highlights this reality through juxtaposing a constrictive sense of the crowd against a sudden burst of intimacy, such as occurs in Brett's first cab ride with Jake.

"Well, we're out away from them," Jake says, prior to their getting into the taxi that carries them away from the crowds and the bar and "up the hill" past the "lighted square, then on into the dark, still climbing." Jake and Brett (previously "sitting apart") are "jolted close together," and he notes that her hat is "off," which reinforces the idea that Brett's taking off her hat represents self-exposure. With her head thrown "back," the physical contours of Brett's face glow in the vignette's almost lurid lighting. "I saw her face in the lights from the open shops," Jake says. "Then it was dark, then I saw her face clearly." This view of Brett, highlighted by the glare of the workmen's acetylene flares on her face and neck, emphasizes her physical beauty. Her "face was white," Jake says, "and the long line of her neck showed in the bright light of the flares. The street was dark again and I kissed her" (24–25).

As the keen darkness repeatedly shifts into a sudden and intense light, the surrealistic highlighting and distortion of Brett's physical form allows for a glimpse into her emotional interior. Brett's eyes match this movement as they shift from flatness to open exposure, like the lens of a camera: "Her eyes had different depths," Jake says, and "sometimes they seemed perfectly flat." Finally, Jake sees "all the way into them" as the moment holds transfixed in time (26). Although Jake cannot penetrate Brett physically, he can realize her emotionally, as her eyes become the windows of her soul. "She was looking into my eyes with that way she had of looking that made you wonder whether she really saw out of her own eyes," he says. "They would look on and on after every one else's eyes in the world would have stopped looking. She looked as though there were nothing on earth she would not look at like that, and really she was afraid of so many things" (26). When Brett is in the public sphere, she tries to disguise that fear such that her eyes flatten and shield, sometimes by staring "straight ahead" or by wrinkling her eyes at the corners (almost closing them up like the shuttered lens of a camera).

When Hemingway creates cameralike vignettes such as this, they usually catch his women at moments of poise—moments when they confront the darkness at the center and then gather their strength to act. I think of Brett leaving the cab and Jake as she goes back into the bar to meet the crowd. Poised there, torn between her need for exposure and her fear of it, she puts on her hat with a shaky hand, pulling this "man's felt hat down" farther on her head, almost as a disguise. I think of Margorie leaving Nick behind at the point, that point of turning at which everything both physically and emotionally shifts. I think of Catherine Barkley sitting edgewise on the bed in the hotel room that suddenly seems too red, or reaching out her hand and laughing as Henry holds a suddenly turned inside-out umbrella. Such vignettes, with their stark, sudden exposures, catch the reader off guard. To witness the vignette, the moment, is to experience it, like stepping into a self-contained room. I think of Marcel Proust's description of dipping his biscuit into his tea and then tasting it. At this moment he discovers, suddenly, his grandfather, himself. His discovery comes in a flash, a quick chain-reaction, as he steps into time and memory and knowledge (34–36). Reading Hemingway is like that.

As Hemingway used the external details in his own precise and highly selective way, he made visible those internal truths we cannot name. Ultimately these truths are universal, and they have everything to do with men and with women. Because Hemingway captured, more than any other writer has, an emotional more than a physical landscape, I have defended his art in the face of those who say it rings hollow. I would also like to defend the man, whose galvanizing presence cannot be separated from the power of his art. Hemingway's colleague Malcolm Cowley recognized this when he talked about Hemingway's "inborn gift for projecting himself." This influenced all of Hemingway's personal relationships as well as his art, and the gift reveals itself vividly today in Hemingway's photographs. Even in "the first photographs, after those in baby clothes," Cowley noted, Hemingway "looks straight at the camera, he smiles that warm smile of his, and his sisters—as later his companions in fishing or skiing—fade into the background" ("Image" 112).

I look up now, as I reflect on my twenty-year odyssey as a teacher and scholar of Hemingway, to where Hemingway's photo hangs, framed, on my office wall. There he is as a young man in Paris where it all began. The father of modern American prose looks handsome, wise, his hair parted slightly off center. How did he ever come to know what he knew, I wonder, as I look into his eyes that stare into the room, into me? His presence fills the room. Soon, one of my students comes for her conference clutching her composition and sitting down nervously. When she looks up, she stops midsentence. "Wow! Who is that?" she asks, looking at Hemingway, who now seems to smile knowingly. "That's Ernest Hemingway," I say. "He's really something, isn't he?" For the rest of that afternoon, as more students file in and out, Hemingway stays with me. I cannot shake him.

I see myself standing with other Hemingway scholars in the wine barn of Gianfranco Ivancich, the brother of Adriana Ivancich (Hemingway's "model" for Renata in *Across the River and into the Trees*). It is summer 1986. Hemingway scholars have gathered in Italy for the Second International Hemingway Conference, and Ivancich has arranged an exhibit of previously unseen photographs, many from Hemingway's early years in Paris. Each photo seems alive, and Hemingway's eyes tag us from all angles. I feel the pull of each picture, mesmerized by all these Hemingways, and I stay on longer as the others begin to file down from the barn for dinner in the garden. I can hear their voices, muted in the distance, and I can see through the barn window the white lights strung throughout the garden swaying in the darkening night.

Shortly before this Italian conference, Hemingway's *The Garden of Eden* has been posthumously published, as edited by Tom Jenks at Scribner's. I am to chair the Hemingway session at the Modern Language Association Conference in New York that December 1986, and Allen Josephs has urged me to invite Jenks to address the Hemingway session. I suspect that Jenks will not accept; after all, he has resisted talking about his role in the project up to this point. Why should he welcome the opportunity to talk openly and no doubt defensively about his work before a group of not disinterested scholars? But when I call him by phone, he seems suddenly to want to talk about his work and about Hemingway, because he has been living with it for so long, moving in and out of the manuscript, awed by its intricacy and its emotional weave. Jenks tells me that Hemingway had begun to "haunt" him. Later, in New York, Jenks admits to a large MLA gathering that Hemingway "did pass through" him in such "a powerful and intimate way" that now he needed to "declare a moratorium" on his "slight agency as a potential medium to Papa. The work, any man's work, speaks best for itself" (31, 33).[5]

During my years of research and writing on American expatriation as it revolved around life at Gerald and Sara Murphy's Villa America during the 1920s, I have found that Hemingway—his life and his work—has repeatedly taken over my critical thinking and writing, even when my focus deals with him only tangentially. I have come to realize the great degree to which his presence—within the literary history of his time and in his own art—both compels and eludes us. Malcolm Cowley recognized this when he criticized Carlos Baker's "enormous and very useful life of Hemingway" for failing, finally, to get to the essential Hemingway. "It tells us what he did and what he said to whom during his long career, but it gives hardly any notion of the immense charm he exerted on his friends, on women, and on older persons he respected," Cowley stated. "Partly the charm was due to his physical presence: he was tall, handsome, broad-shouldered, with heavy biceps, yet carried himself with a curiously diffident and reassuring air; meeting him was like being led into the box stall of a huge, spirited, but surprisingly gentle stallion" ("Image" 113).

I think suddenly of Gerald Murphy's recognition that Sara Murphy (whose love for Hemingway was intense, unqualified and lifelong) was drawn to Hemingway's animal magnetism. When she heard of Hemingway's illness and hospitalization in the spring of 1961, she wrote him one last letter that ironically reinforced the virile image of Hemingway the man and the writer that he could no longer sustain. She had hoped to will away Hemingway's illness so as to bring them all back to that moment of ripeness. She wanted to see again the young Hemingway who was learning to write by going to the museums to see the Cézannes. "Dear Ernest," Sara wrote on 24 May 1961. "We read—too often, in the papers—about your being in the Mayo Clinic,—mentioning various ailments, and please write me a card, saying it isn't so,—or at least that you are all recovered— It *isn't* in character for you to be ill—I want to picture you—as always— as a burly bearded young man—with a gun or on a boat—Just a line, please" (qtd. in Miller, *Letters* 328–29).

When Sara learned that Hemingway was dead, she did not take it well. "Sara is repairing slowly," Gerald told Calvin Tomkins, "but it's been a wretched business. Ernest's death affected her deeply. She had written him ten days before assuring him that his illness would pass and that it was unlike him to be ill. Apparently he decided he wouldn't wait to find out" (qtd. in Miller, *Letters* 270–71). Just as Sara had tried to will away the sickness of her two sons (each of whom died at the ripe age of sixteen), she tried to do the same for Hemingway. By his death, as with the other deaths, she felt betrayed.

Archibald MacLeish's poem, written upon Hemingway's death, creates the picture that Sara visualized of the "burly bearded young man." As MacLeish's poetic lens clicks in on the young Hemingway, each successive angle cubistically moves us in closer to bring us back again to the beginning, which is where Hemingway's art always takes us. "In some inexplicable way an accident," says Mary Hemingway after Hemingway's body is discovered. But MacLeish writes:

Oh, not inexplicable. Death explains,
that kind of death: rewinds remembrance

backward like a film track till the laughing man
among the lilacs, peeling the green stem,
waits for the gunshot where the play began;

rewinds those Africas and Idahos and Spains
to find the table at the Closerie des Lilas,
sticky with syrup, where the flash of joy
flamed into blackness like that flash of steel.

The gun between the teeth explains,
The shattered mouth foretells the singing boy." (482)

Now I am there also, at Closerie des Lilas, but it is too hot for Paris,
even in July. Crowds of Hemingway scholars and fans press in for this
opening night of the 1994 Hemingway/Fitzgerald International Conference. Gregory Hemingway, Hemingway's third son, is here but soon
leaves. Too many memories. Too many people. "Don't you know?" he says
to me. "I never had a mother." Gregory slips out of the terrace through
the wrought iron gateway not to be seen until the next summer, when he
and his wife Ida join a group of scholars in Cuba. We visit Hemingway's
haunts and we talk about Hemingway, and all the while Gregory is a
gentle but solid presence. When we gather at Finca Vigia, he walks
slowly up to see into the windows of the house he remembers as a boy.
"All my books are still here," he says quietly, looking in the windows of
the guesthouse wing. Later, we stand in the middle of the congested Havana airport waiting to leave. We have confronted each other unexpectedly, one of those unplanned moments, and I ask him if he has enjoyed
the week. "No," he says adamantly. Then he catches himself. "Oh, not you
people. You've been great. It's him. It's him I can't get rid of. Ida thinks
that if I go back to the places and see them again, that I can put him to
rest. But I can't. No matter how I work it over and work it over in my
head. I am always and only Hemingway's son who never had a mother."
He looks me in the eyes as he pauses and then looks away. People have
begun to gather around us wanting to take pictures. Then he turns back
to me with a sudden intensity. "You know, Linda, I just want to kill him.
I can't stop hating the bastard." The anger comes down over his face like
a hard veil before it just as quickly lifts. "If I had had a mother," Gregory

says softly, before he breaks away, "she would have been beautiful like you."

As I have tried to suggest in this essay, Hemingway was not an easy man for those who knew him personally. But if they could not shake his powerful presence in their lives, neither can we when we confront him through his times and in his art. I remember discovering, in the manuscript room of Harvard University, a previously unpublished letter (c. December 1940) of Dorothy Parker's to Alexander Woollcott, her New York pen pal. I had not anticipated finding this letter, another of Parker's characteristically long and, of course, witty letters that details her recent visit with Hemingway and his soon-to-be-wife Martha Gellhorn in Sun Valley, Idaho. Her letter, with its frank reflection on Hemingway and Parker's relationship with him over the years, surprised me somehow. Parker had not seen much of Hemingway after the late 1920s, and yet she could not shake Hemingway's hold over her, as she confessed it to Woollcott.[6] Parker here meets Gellhorn for the first time and finds her "truly fine. Even leaving aside her looks and her spirit and her courage and her decency—though I can't imagine why they should be shoved aside—she is doing such a really . . . glorious job as to Ernest." She goes on to describe how she has "heard Martha, with complete good-humor and as one telling a funny story, report on some circumstance in her daily life with him that would drive any other woman white-haired—such as, say, the presence of rats in her sleeping-bag. And Ernest has answered, serious and frowning, 'Well, look, Marty. You signed up to be tough, you know.' Well, I guess that's a statement of fact, at that. But she's being tough graciously and gaily. The others couldn't. I think this marriage will last, and keep fine." Parker does not know then that the marriage, like the others, does not keep, but she adds of herself: "I have known [Hemingway], hard and well, for fifteen years. I love him and revere him. But baby, in his personal relationships, and particularly those with his women, he can only be called No Cinch."

The continued upsurge in Hemingway scholarship, including that among women, attests to the fact that women can and do say, along with Parker, that we love him and revere him despite, or maybe because of, the unsettling complexities of his life and art. As Susan F. Beegel, editor of *The Hemingway Review*, has emphasized in her 1998 editorial outlining the robust state of Hemingway scholarship today, "the only dangerous response to Hemingway is no response" (17). In asserting that Hemingway has not, as some might believe, "fallen from grace in the contemporary academy," Beegel declares her wish to kill the "entirely unfounded myth circulating not only in the academy as a whole, but even among Hemingway scholars—that Hemingway is in danger of losing his place in the canon because he is, after all, the archetypal Dead White Male" ("Journal" 6, 8). Although this supposed "Dead White Male status" has been "one of the engines driving the remarkable productivity" and wideranging diversity of Hemingway studies, the overall response to Hemingway from whatever angle inevitably and rightly recognizes the "intrinsic value and abiding importance" of his work (9). As Beegel concludes, "whether your impulse is to shower Hemingway with flowers or punch him in the jaw, both are ways of acknowledging his status" as a writer who speaks to everyone—"to the extreme ends of the methodological spectrum and every point between," and certainly to women as well as men (17, 9).

Recently when I taught an undergraduate course on Hemingway, one woman in the class confessed at the onset that reading Hemingway "terrified" her. As a group, the class concluded that confronting Hemingway's art involves great risk. Those who teach Hemingway regularly acknowledge the emotional intensity of students' interactions with Hemingway's art, even when students initially resist reading him, or do not know quite how to read him. At the end of that course, one of the female students, Laurie Welsh Mirales, wrote in her final exam about how reading Hemingway had caught her off guard. "Maybe because Hemingway is considered the father of modern American fiction," she wrote, "I am tempted to read his work like I would read a trade novel. You can do that. All the required elements are there—love, action, adventure, intrigue, foreign locales." But she felt "unsatisfied" and vaguely like she "was missing something, until she returned to his work again "with a more critical eye." "I'm not sure how it happened," she wrote; "I think it was a cumulative effect or a slow build up, like a locomotive that chugs along at first and then when the steam starts to build, the train is just careening down the track and all of a sudden I'm on board, and I'm turning pages and Hemingway is talking to me. So, just like one of his wild, never-ending sentences I'm suddenly in the thick of his work and I'm starting to really like it." Initially she found herself too "lost in misconceptions about his work—

code heroes and nada—to ever notice his style," which is "infectious." "Whereas before I thought his work to be masculine, raw, harsh and violent," she concluded, "I found it on a second reading to be tender and insightful and very emotional."

Honoria Murphy Donnelly, daughter of Gerald and Sara Murphy, Hemingway's "Understanding Rich" in *A Moveable Feast* (208), regretted that many people seemed to overlook or fail to see Hemingway's tenderness. During the years of my research on the Murphys and Hemingway, I had the privilege of spending much time with Honoria, who generously shared with me documents, photographs and stories of her parents and their extraordinary friends, that included Scott and Zelda Fitzgerald, Archibald and Ada MacLeish, John Dos Passos, Dorothy Parker, and Ernest Hemingway. Between 1925 to 1929, Honoria's bedroom window at Villa America in Antibe, France, allowed her a bird's-eye view of these friends as they entered through the gateposts (where Gerald had affixed his original Villa America painting with its five stars representing the five Murphys) and walked up the pathway to the villa terrace. Zelda Fitzgerald invariably dazzled her with her pink shimmering dresses and her dark blonde hair "flecked with streaks from the sun," but she came to love Ernest Hemingway most of all.

Honoria's childhood memories of Hemingway when I was with her often came by chance association, striking in their clarity and primitive purity. "I remember," she said once, suddenly, "how Hemingway would talk out of the side of his mouth, like this." In her favorite photograph, she and Hemingway stand against the white backdrop of Switzerland, where Honoria's brother Patrick had been taken to fight off tuberculosis, and where Hemingway had come to visit. In the picture, she and Hemingway hold hands, look into the camera, and Hemingway is grinning. "I call this picture 'Pals,'" Honoria would say. She often recalled how Hemingway taught her to catch and gut a fish. Because he wanted to show her the fish's beauty, he slit it open and spread it wide, slowly pointing out and naming all its parts. In Hemingway's hands, in the morning sun, the fish's insides glistened like jewels.

As scholars, writers, and hangers-on gathered during an April weekend at Hemingway's 1999 centennial celebration in Boston, I stood instead at the gravesite of Honoria Murphy Donnelly. That her burial coincided with Hemingway's celebration in Boston seemed fitting, for she too throughout her life celebrated Hemingway and believed that most people, including scholars, had gotten him wrong. Honoria's internment next to her husband in Washington's Arlington Cemetery called for a military ceremony that seemed precise, hurried and somehow unlikely for someone who seemed like her own Renoir painting. A man in a dark red-trimmed uniform, his arms held out stiffly, carried Honoria's boxed ashes, his heels clicking, to place them on the chartreuse astro-turf rug that draped the gravesite. Throughout the short service, the square box sat there beside a single vase of flowers that tilted and then spilled midway through the Lord's Prayer. We stood in clumps among the surrounding graves, and behind us, in another part of the cemetery, the white markers of the soldiers fanned out until they floated skyward. In the gray morning air, I remembered Honoria turning to me and saying: "Hemingway was the most gentle and loveliest man I have ever known. When he came to see Patrick as he lay dying, Hemingway wept openly. It was the first time I had seen a grown man cry."

When Malcolm Cowley noted Hemingway's charm, his inordinate gift of self-projection that drew people to him, he quoted Hemingway's first wife, Hadley, in saying that Hemingway "was then the kind of man to whom men, women, children, and dogs are attracted. It was something." Cowley added that central to that attraction was Hemingway's ability to listen to people speak. He had "a habit of paying undivided attention to each of several persons in turn. He looked in one's eyes, then he turned his head to listen carefully. 'Most people never listen,' he used to say" (113). Because Hemingway listened and then brought to the written page that lived life, his art demands that it be read with passion, with commitment and without pretension. More than crudity or violence or exclusionary politics, tenderness and an ardor for truth inspired and sustained Hemingway's art. This is the essential and still "living" Hemingway that will sweep us into the next century to show us yet again who we are and how best to live our lives.

2
Re-Reading Women II

The Example of Brett, Hadley, Duff, and Women's Scholarship

Jamie Barlowe

Because the absence of women in mainstream literary scholarship remains all too familiar and acceptable, many literary professionals are not surprised when they do not see women included in a particular body of scholarship.[1] In fact, the absence of women's scholarship often functions as proof that they did not write or publish essays on an author like Ernest Hemingway or on such books as *The Sun Also Rises*, or as evidence that what they wrote and published was not good enough to be considered by the mainstream. Actually, a significant number of women scholars have published on this novel since its completion in Paris in 1925 and its publication in the United States in 1926. Their absence in the mainstream body of scholarship reveals its lack of awareness of or engagement with women's scholarship, but whether this omission is a deliberate slight or an oversight is not at issue in this essay. Instead, my argument rests on the assumption that no matter what was intended or not intended on the part of mainstream critics and scholars, the exclusion occurred. In this essay, then, I will demonstrate briefly the existence and continuation of this absence, focus on women's scholarship, and discuss some of its differences from the familiar, accepted critical interpretations of *The Sun Also Rises*. I am also invoking the cultural context, as well as Hemingway's particular situatedness inside that context, in order to theorize briefly about the absence and its familiarity. Finally, I am arguing that the absence, once it is exposed, confers responsibility on all literary professionals, rather than offering a site for defensiveness and further entrenchment.

Although some women's scholarship on *The Sun Also Rises* is listed in a few endnotes and in some bibliographies of Hemingway scholarship, and although some of their work appears in various collections (for example, Harold Bloom's *Brett Ashley*), most of the women who have written about this text and its contexts are generally unacknowledged, except by each other. For example, Claire Sprague's essay *"The Sun Also Rises:* Its 'Clear Financial Basis'" (1969), is neither noted nor quoted in Scott Donaldson's "Hemingway's Morality of Compensation" (1971) or in Richard Sugg's "Hemingway, Money, and *The Sun Also Rises*" (1972), even though both essays deal with the same issue of commodification. Except for some few exceptions (for example, Harold Mosher, Gerry Brenner, and Morton Ross), mainstream Hemingway scholarship has pointed to Donaldson and Sugg as having done the significant work on commodification in *The Sun Also Rises*. Nancy Comley, however, in her essay, "Hemingway: The Economics of Survival" (1970), notes not only Donaldson and Sugg but also Sprague.

When women's scholarship has been cited or mentioned in a mainstream essay or book, usually briefly, one or two women have been tokenized to speak for all women's scholarship, or their work has often been refuted or trivialized.[2] For instance, Peter Griffin's stunning omission of a reference to Bernice Kert's *The Hemingway Women* (1983) in his text *Less Than a Treason* (1990) is followed by a trivializing of Alice Hunt Sokoloff's biography of Hadley Hemingway (1973) in his section called "Sources." There, he says that Jack Hemingway allowed him to listen to the tapes of Sokoloff's interviews with Hadley. He claims that "Sokoloff *seemed* in awe of Hadley and approached her gingerly, asking only questions that could not possibly give offense" (my emphasis, 180). Continuing to trivialize women, he also names Agnes von Kurowsky as a "petty opportunist" (91) and Duff Twysden an opium addict (94) with "beautiful upturned breasts" (96).[3]

Instead, as a way to acknowledge and value the contributions of women to the body of scholarship on *The Sun Also Rises,* in the following section of my essay I will incorporate some of their critical insights about Brett Ashley, as well as about Hadley Richardson Hemingway and Duff Twysden as they function contextually. This revaluation and incorporation will occur inside my observations about the gendering of integrity and identity in the novel.

Hemingway's Jake Barnes of *The Sun Also Rises* has been examined and discussed from every possible angle and context in terms of his integrity and male identity/sexuality and in terms of the difficulty, even the impossibility, of integrity in a war-ravaged world, as well as in a world in which gender-roles were changing.

> If woman had new rights and powers, had men lost old ones? If femininity no longer consisted of cooking and sewing and tending the babies, what did it consist of? Or did it cease to exist? What about masculinity? It is surely no coincidence that the themes of sexual identity, of homosexuality, of proving one's manhood in sexual terms, of impotent and unfulfilled lives dominate the literature of the twenties in America. (Schmidt 902)

However, like women's sexuality and identity, their integrity has primarily been judged socially and literarily insofar as it bolsters, reveals, or reflects on male integrity. That is, in our patriarchal world women's integrity has had no definition aside from its oppositional or obstructionist relationship to male integrity, just as women's sexualities have only begun to be socially defined apart from the heterosexuality of men. In this world women continue to be constructed and viewed (despite claims to the contrary) as the problematic of male definitions of integrity and identity, as they tempt or deter men from their strivings for desired ontologies. Women have thus been represented as sexualized, conflicted, and deeply problematic.

Cathy and Arnold Davidson describe this thinking as it appears in *The Sun Also Rises* as "the opposition between male/female, masculine/feminine, and (more particularized, more individualized) men/women [which] is pervasive . . . (the all male ritual of the bullfight, the crucial matter of Jake's wound)." These are set against, even "undermined" by Brett's "bob and her swagger" (88).[4] In "The Great American Bitch" Dolores Barracano Schmidt discusses the opposition as it constructs and undermines Brett Ashley:

> the emancipated woman . . . was a joyous symbol: single, free, worldly, independent, confident . . . Brett with her 'hair brushed back like boys' . . . her man's felt hat, her freedom to travel, drink,

and talk like one of the chaps, is, nonetheless . . . an extremely desirable woman, whose ability to dominate every man she meets
dooms her to a life of unfulfillment. This represents, however, a
man's view of female fulfillment, explicitly sexual in nature and
based solely on the subordination/domination pattern. (901–02)

Gay Wilentz sees Brett as part of the triangle Hemingway created to
valorize Jake and denigrate Robert Cohn (188).[5] Wendy Martin argues
that if "Brett has gained a measure of freedom in leaving the traditional
household, she is still very much dependent on men, who provide an
arena in which she can be attractive and socially active as well as finan-
cially secure" (71). Thus, Brett, like the other women in the novel, "sometimes find themselves in . . . contradictory roles" (72).

Such women critics and scholars have been trying to reread and reconstruct this socially and literarily patriarchal world in terms of what has
not been noticed, not been said, not been defined, causing in Hemingway
studies what Debra A. Moddelmog has called a "thorough reconstruction
of Hemingway." This reconstruction is not based, though, on "new" information about him, because the "new," as Moddelmog argues, "does
not differ too greatly from the Hemingway we have already known"
("Reconstructing" 188). Instead, women have been rereading Hemingway,
his texts, and his life for at least three decades to provide not new information, but new insights, which are possible only when the rereadings
rest on a different set of assumptions about literature, culture, author/
reader relationships, gender, sexuality, identity, subjectivity, and integrity. In such a context, women's scholarship has exposed Brett Ashley's
textual function as the means by which Jake's integrity, particularly his
maimed heterosexual grace-under-pressure, can be measured and how
his self-insights about male sexuality and identity can occur. As Nina
Schwartz argues, "Brett is of course the perfect love *object* precisely because she affords so many opportunities for rivalry and its consequent
evocation of desire" (my emphasis, 51), or as Carol H. Smith puts it:
"[Brett] is a threat to men because she forces them to recognize the
primitiveness of their desire and the fragility of male bonding when
threatened by lust, sexual need, or competition for a woman" (132).

Lady Brett Ashley is Jake's problem in his wounded world, not his solution. As Wilma Garcia argues, "The fact is that Hemingway's characterizations of women adhere very closely to roles and functions traditionally prescribed by our society as models for the female, particularly the woman as sexual partner. . . . [I]n Hemingway's works . . . the good woman is faithful and subservient to the needs of her man; the bad woman is not . . . Brett Ashley in *The Sun Also Rises* is a woman who cannot be good, who cannot meet the needs of her man" (9). Smith echoes this estimate of Brett when she says that she "is one of Hemingway's bad women, a Circe who turns men into swine" (132); Kim Moreland agrees: "Brett is Circe, turning men not into the chivalric knights they desperately want to be but into swine," adding that Brett is "incapable of fidelity" (186).[6] Thus, as Carole Gottlieb Vopat says, "in Madrid . . . Jake at last renounces his dreams about Brett. . . . He and Brett no longer form a working 'we'" (251–52). Emily Miller Budick is more emphatic about Jake's agency in separating himself from Brett's problematic influence: "Whereas Jake was once a puppet playing out a pantomime directed by Brett, jerking back mindlessly to Brett's every pull of the threads that bind them . . . now he directs the action, as his telegram to Brett and their subsequent conversation reveals. . . . He is his own man" (333).[7] Brett Ashley is also seen as the problem in Jake's (re)self-identification, as well as the obstacle to his integrity, whether she is viewed as profoundly heterosexual, even described by that vile misnomer "nymphomaniac," or as lesbian or associated with a kind of androgyny or "bisexual image" that enhances her heterosexual lure (Gladstein 58), as "gender-bending" (Moddelmog, "Reconstructing" 194), as the "New Woman" (W. Martin and O'Sullivan), as occupying the center of the novel: "beautiful, vulnerable, and finally herself" (L. P. Miller, "Brett Ashley" 182), as Helen of Troy (Morgan), as performing an "unselfish act [in] giving up Romero" (Curtis 279), as a "girl" (DeVost), as a "nice girl" in that she "remains self-possessed and flouts decorum with a flair" (Achuff 44), as destructive to Jake (J. Wilson), as linguistically alienated inside "the dynamic of silence in Hemingway's discourse" (Barnett 164), as using "one man (Romero) to cleanse herself of another (Robert)" (Grace 124), as having a "kinship" with Marie in Henry James's *The Ambassadors* (Tintner), as the victim of her titled husband, or as the profligate drunk, whore, bitch, or sinner (Helbig).[8] Brett's failure to fulfill female roles, as well as her infidelity and always potentially castrating "bad-ness," thus provide the stage on which Jake's integrity and heterosexuality can be reaffirmed, as he frees himself from her constraining and tainting influence.

Without Brett's multiplicity of oppositional defining traits, however they might be constructed and described, Jake's traits do not signify. This insight has been exposed and probed by women scholars, while most male mainstream scholars have not even examined or problematized the binarily oppositional construct of male/female. Instead, they have mea-sured Hemingway's almost caricatured heterosexualized identity and his own self-constructed integrity and honor in terms of how he, like Jake Barnes, functioned *in spite* of the destructive women in his life.[9] The pri-mary difference I see between the critical claims of male and female scholars and critics is that most of the men are discussing Brett as a fe-male type and, thus, as Hemingway claimed about his own work, reflec-tive of the reality of women in the world outside his texts, while many of the women are exposing Hemingway's construction of women, not as reflective of real women, but as reflective of Hemingway's own psychic struggles with women. For example, Mimi Reisel Gladstein sees Brett as part of Hemingway's internalized and unacknowledged problem with "indestructible" women, for example, his mother, Agnes von Kurowsky, and Hadley Richardson Hemingway. Gladstein says, "These women pro-vided the archetypes, the primal patterns against which other women were measured" (54). She sets up a subcategory, which she calls the "de-structive indestructibles," and it is into this category that she puts Brett Ashley. She argues that "[w]hile they themselves are indomitable and en-during, association with them proves destructive for the men in their lives" (59).[10]

Duff Twydsen has also been viewed as an obstacle to Hemingway's integrity, identity, and desire. Linda Wagner-Martin and others have noted that "Brett Ashley is modeled on Duff (and was called Duff in early drafts of the book)" (Introduction 3–4).[11] Gioia Diliberto's biogra-phy of Hadley also notes Duff as "Ernest's model for Brett Ashley," de-scribing her as an alcoholic. She quotes Hadley as attributing to Duff "amazing sexual fearlessness" (110). She adds that "[a]lthough Hadley liked Duff, she was deeply distressed by Ernest's relationship with her. Sometimes he would go out alone to meet Duff at a café, and other times he would take Hadley along on their drinking expeditions in Montmartre. He'd flirt so openly with her that Hadley would start to cry" (198).

Sokoloff, too, says that "Hadley thought [Duff] wonderfully attractive, a real woman of the world with no sexual inhibitions" (81). Kert confirms this and adds that "Hadley found something else attractive about Duff, the implicit assurance that husbands were not fair game, that in spite of being a man's woman, she would respect the code" (158). Thus, while Hemingway may have based Brett Ashley on Duff, he deviated from the actual woman in order to create the fictional one who had no such notions of integrity. The revision allowed him to maintain his socially constructed notions of gender and has allowed generations of critics and scholars to assume Brett as reflective of not only Duff, but also of a category of real women. Hemingway also revised Jake's social condition from his own, from married to unmarried; thus, Jake's desire for Brett is not fraught with infidelity on the part of the male character, and is instead projected onto the female character.

In addition to the Duff-to-Brett revision, discussed by women scholars and critics, many see Hadley as the absent-presence in *The Sun Also Rises,* punished and eliminated as a "castrator" merely because, as his wife, she entered into unspoken female collusion with Duff, which prevented Hemingway from consummating his desire. How painfully ironic that Hemingway would choose to "castrate" his character Jake Barnes so that he could not sleep with Brett and would choose to eliminate Hadley from the group of real people on whom he based the novel's characters. Hemingway may not have punished his "scarlet woman" Brett Ashley in the same ways that Hawthorne punishes Hester Prynne, as W. Martin has argued. And he may not have, as Kert suggests, "substituted the condition of Barnes' impotence for his own reluctance to betray Hadley" (167). Instead, Hemingway can be seen as punishing his wife, omitting her from the book and subsequently, from his life. Whatever loss of integrity it may have cost him to leave her in order to marry Pauline Pfeiffer, it cost him nothing to eliminate Hadley symbolically in his book. How ironic that after he divorced her, he made sure she received all the proceeds from its sale. And how further ironic that he tried to make up for the omission of Hadley in *The Sun Also Rises* when he wrote *A Moveable Feast* or anytime he discussed the Paris years.

Sokoloff mentions that Hadley considered the drafts of *The Sun Also*

Rises "magnificent," although she told Sokoloff that she was "distressed" because she "didn't see anything of [her]self in it" (Diliberto 200). Kert's description reveals an even more complicated relationship to the book:

> Reading it as he handed it over to her, [Hadley] had praised him lavishly. . . . But she later admitted that subconsciously she kept a distance from the book, especially as it delineated the intensity of Jake's feelings for Brett Ashley. Perhaps as she waited for him to join her, it gave her pause that Ernest put nothing of her in the book but used Duff Twysden as the model for his first fully developed heroine. (166)

Duff's and Hadley's integrity have never been a critical or biographical issue for mainstream scholarship; the losses they suffered as a consequence of inclusion in the novel for Duff and of exclusion for Hadley have been addressed primarily by female scholars. And, as Wagner-Martin tells us, they were not the only women insulted directly or indirectly by *The Sun Also Rises:*

> The name of Georgette LeBlanc is an actual one. . . . During the 1920's, Margaret Anderson and Georgette LeBlanc, acknowledged lovers, maintained their household in Paris and, later, in the country, sometimes in company with Jane Heap, Anderson's previous lover and co-editor of *The Little Review.* . . . So his defiant treatment of an acknowledged lesbian, one of the best-loved women of this powerful homosexual culture, his abuse of her as a 'sick' heterosexual whore . . . —using her name plainly and angrily—cannot be disguised. ("Racial and Sexual Coding" 40–41)

Jake thus makes a show of masculine power, as a way "of giving dominance to the heterosexual culture in Paris . . . Jake becomes her patron, a reversal of the actual situation in Paris, where Hemingway benefited frequently from the friendship, kindness and support of . . . lesbian women [including, of course, Gertrude Stein]" (41).

Such an exploration, however brief, of Hemingway's internalized attitudes about and relationships to women, focusing on Brett Ashley of *The Sun Also Rises,* can allow us to see how those attitudes functioned in determinative but consciously unacknowledged ways in the creation of his literary characters. For example, his representation based on Duff Twysden, his omission of Hadley, and his characterization of Georgette LeBlanc indicate how Hemingway problematically understood and dealt with these particular women and then created (and revised) the characters of Brett and Georgette as a consequence. Thus, like other women scholars, whether they see Brett as a negative or positive representation, I am claiming that Brett says more about Hemingway's relationship to the women in his life than about the women in his life.

Unfortunately, though, one of the consequences of traditional mainstream literary scholarship is that despite the fact that Brett Ashley is only a metaphor of a woman created in the mind of Hemingway, she, like other female characters created by male authors, is discussed as though she is a real woman—and real women are judged similarly. In other words, social stereotypes and representations of women's identities, sexualities, and integrity continue to be perpetuated, even at the turn into the twenty-first century, often functioning as backlash against feminism—whether these women are literary characters, scholars, critics, or biographers, or whether they are women in the culture.

As I have argued in this essay and elsewhere, Hemingway scholarship has repeated these problematic relationships to women, including the omission of most women scholars from serious consideration, unless they are refuted, separated into books of their own, or recategorized as doing marginalized scholarship, e.g., feminist. Jake's and Hemingway's strengths and weaknesses, their moments of integrity and loss of it, their struggles and alienations have remained the relentless focus of Hemingway studies on *The Sun Also Rises.* Thus, rather than a war-ravaged world, women scholars, critics, and biographers are describing a woman-ravaged world in which women are constructed in terms of men in order to represent these women as conflicted, sexually problematic, suffocating, and/or crazy. Even when professional conditions for real women are challenged and/or seem to be changing, such gendered assumptions about women remain deeply imbedded and generally unacknowledged, and women writers, scholars, and literary characters remain as literary-men's binary opposite, as Difference, as Other. And, more often than not, the changes in conditions are so superficial that they are easily reversible, ignored, trivialized, or seen as threatening. If women's scholarship on

Hemingway is not taken seriously enough to be quoted, noted, or cited, if women's scholarship is not engaged at the level of argument and evidence, if women's scholarship does not inform and transform mainstream Hemingway scholarship, then the "Hemingway" we discuss will never differ much "from the Hemingway we have always known" (Moddelmog, "Reconstructing" 188). Nor will the academic world in which real women function ever differ much from the one we have already known.

3

The Sun Hasn't Set Yet

Brett Ashley and the Code Hero Debate

Kathy G. Willingham

> Every tradition grows ever more venerable—the more remote is its ori-
> gin, the more confused that origin is. The reverence due to it increases
> from generation to generation. The tradition finally becomes holy and
> inspires awe.
>
> Nietzsche, *Thus Spake Zarathustra*

With the publication of *The Garden of Eden,* Hemingway criticism has become preoccupied with such thematic concerns as androgyny, trans-sexuality, and sexual fetishism and, in turn, the scholarship is increasingly becoming more sensitive to the issue of gender politics. Very often, though, these critical forays eclipse or ignore some of the more traditional, even stereotypical, motifs in Hemingway's *oeuvre.* This is particularly true of the code hero, yet this need not be the case. In fact, heightened insight into the psychosexual dimensions of Hemingway can enhance and expand our understanding of his code hero, enabling us to see not only a much more feminized creation but, moreover, one which actually includes women, and while this may be true of a number of Hemingway's protagonists, it has particular relevance to Brett Ashley. Of his many characters, specifically females, she has provoked the most disagreement, controversy, and, perhaps, interest, as evidenced by her inclusion in Harold Bloom's prestigious series, Major Literary Characters. As numerous critics from Wolfgang E. H. Rudat to Jackson J. Benson have suggested, interpretations of *The Sun Also Rises* inevitably (or necessarily) center on Brett's characterization.[1] Because of her importance to the plot, or her notoriety, or even sensationalism, Lady Brett captivates readers and critics alike. To extricate Brett, then, from some of the more unfavorable interpretations is to simultaneously help destigmatize those women in general who resemble her. In effect, Brett provides a model no less significant, important, or romantic than any of the male code heroes who have inspired or influenced countless readers, hence contributed in large part to Hemingway's endurance. In an age where thousands of men and women admire the pop culture icon Madonna, and precisely for her brazen individuality and independence, it is difficult to understand persistent negative criticisms of Brett.

For many decades, Hemingway and the code hero have been synonymous, and the numerous historical revisions focusing on his psychosexuality, gender politics, and the like, have done little to erode this association in the minds of many readers—both the general public and scholarship alike. My experience both within and outside academe has convinced me that information about Hemingway's "sea change" is not as pervasive as those advancing such theories might presume. It appears that the code hero motif is as firmly entrenched as ever, yet, importantly, this does not necessarily do a disservice to Hemingway, his authorial intentions, or to those readers enamored with the general concept of a code hero. In fact, quite the contrary seems true, and for this reason, a renewed look at the motif is warranted, though it seems that a revaluation needs to occur among some Hemingway scholars much more than with the general reading public.

The idea of the code hero was born out of necessity, as a means of coping with an unsettling or absurd world, and as we now grapple with the postmodern condition, the concept is not only relevant but, perhaps, more necessary than ever. Because the code hero is grounded in the existential be-ing in the world, in contradistinction to a world of absolutes, it offers the potential for transcendence beyond or escape from arbitrary and restrictive cultural and ideological conventions. In short, the code hero has much to offer to readers today and particularly to any woman who resists criticisms or pressures to perform according to an other's standards and insists on defining her own authentic self, as does Brett Ashley.

The significance of Brett's characterization can best be realized by utilizing some long overlooked and sadly undervalued sources. By returning to an early, pivotal study of the code hero, Lawrence R. Broer's *Hemingway's Spanish Tragedy,* we can recognize that his thesis concerning *particularismo* has profound and direct bearing on Brett's characterization. Moreover, that she embodies the characteristics associated with the matador, hence qualifies as the code hero, becomes further evident if we reassess bullfighting in light of its more feminized tradition, namely the folklore of tauromachy. In doing so, an overdetermined trope with important political implications emerges. That is, the bullfight, the matador, and the code hero, as understood and interpreted by Hemingway, can no longer be defined as strictly symbols of *masculine* dominance, mastery, or sovereignty. However, to equate these entities (the bullfight, matador, or code hero) with stereotypical definitions of femininity such as passivity, modesty, weakness is equally misguided, for my usage of the term *feminized* stems from a metonymic chain originating from pagan, not contemporary, associations. The signifying links of which I speak include some of the earliest conceptions about Dionysus and this god's relationship to androgyny, the sun, the eternal return, and the bull, but with a continual eye on a poststructuralist perspective that sees the Dionysian space as a site of disruption from which marginality can survive and even flourish.

For far too long, a great many critics have viewed Brett (and, unfortunately, influenced generations of readers of their studies) as merely an emasculating bitch, slut, nymphomaniac, or Circe who turns men into some sort of debilitative or dehumanized state. And far too often those who do take a somewhat favorable view toward her do so in an apologetic and equivocal manner, intimating a lack of conviction and signifying that perhaps there is indeed something wrong with her. Such negative or anemic defenses, however, reveal much more about certain critics, the ideologies constructing such formulations, and interpretive communities (what in this case I would term phallocentric critical legislators) than they do the character herself. For as Wendy Martin has pointed out, widespread denunciation of Brett ironically exists in the face of a portrait by Hemingway that is actually "sympathetic" (69). As Martin explains:

> much critical reaction has mirrored traditional values. Allen Tate calls her "hard boiled"; Theodore Bardake sees her as a "woman devoid of woman hood"; Jackson Benson says that she is "a female who never becomes a woman"; Edmund Wilson describes her as "an exclusively destructive force"; and John Aldridge declares that Brett is a "compulsive bitch." In a somewhat more generous inter-

pretation, Roger Whitlow describes Brett as self-destructive, and Delbert Wylder sees her as a Janus-like character. (69)

Martin writes that Brett's behavior "is not validated by the social world in which she lives" (69). This leads to an important question: What about Hemingway's world?

The failed recognition of Brett is all the more troubling when coupled with our understanding of what Nancy R. Comley and Robert Scholes term "el nuevo Hemingway" (146). That is, the many recent studies alerting us to Hemingway's profoundly complex and thoughtful consideration of gender from a myriad of perspectives demand a paradigmatic shift and radical rethinking of not only the code hero but of Brett in particular. As Comley and Scholes argue, the "sexual truths, for Hemingway, lie not at the center of "'standard' heterosexual practice" but "at the margins: in what the society of Hemingway's parents" would have thought taboo or perverse (77). The "margins" are where we need to look for a better understanding of other such issues and motifs central to *The Sun Also Rises,* including our assessment of Brett and her relationship to the code hero debate. We can begin to appreciate better the value of both a code hero in general and Brett in particular if we look at those areas of critical marginalization such as: Broer's study, the less conventional but nevertheless valid history of the folklore of tauromachy, and certain textual considerations in light of a Dionysiac hermeneutic. In addition, it is important to remember that Hemingway himself rarely occupied a space (either psychologically or socially) that could be interpreted as the "norm" or conventional. That he lived a psycho-sexual and experiential life quite remote from the one embraced by mainstream Americans—from his unorthodox and androgynous upbringing to his fascination with lesbianism, homosexuality, transsexuality, hair fetishism, sexual transgression, and other related topics—has been explored in varying degrees by Kenneth S. Lynn, James R. Mellow, Mark Spilka, Carl Eby, Rose Marie Burwell, Debra A. Moddelmog, and others. If Hemingway did not occupy a centrist position in these matters, then it is safe to presume that he also entertained a rather unconventional viewpoint concerning other areas of interest to him—the bullfight included.

According to Broer, in the bullfight Hemingway found an "objective correlative," which informed not only his aesthetics but his definition of existential authenticity as well. Broer argues that "in the image of the matador" Hemingway "found a symbol of the best a man can be in a violent and irrational world—a model of manhood and integrity after which he would pattern his fictional heroes" (vii). If, however, Hemingway radically identified with the idea of the androgyne, then it is only fitting that we substitute "a model of manhood" with that of "personhood." Critics would be wise to take into careful consideration Robert E. Gajdusek's observations in "The Mad Sad Bad Misreading of Hemingway's Gender Politics/Aesthetics," for as he notes, Hemingway has long suffered the same "unremitting message to his male reader: that the individuated male consciousness must be purchased through a daring act of surrender to the feminine" (37). Gajdusek adds, "and that only through the *effiminization* of his consciousness and psyche does a boy become a man" (my emphasis, 37). Importantly, no polemical discrepancy exists when shifting the focus from the code hero to bullfighting, for folkloric traditions of tauromachy reveal a ritual not as straightforwardly masculine as previously supposed.

In his study of the bullfight, John McCormick turns to Spanish folklore not only to corroborate the conventional belief linking the bull to fertility and sexual virility but additionally to demonstrate the role of marriage and other aspects of human sexuality. McCormick argues that much Spanish folklore on the bullfight indicates that "the emphasis, significantly, is upon marriage and hopes of fertility in marriage, not upon the torero" (12). Drawing upon Angel Alvarez de Miranda's studies from *Ritos y juegos,* McCormick writes:

> the modern corrida derives from an association in the naïf or un-scientific mind between vegetable and human fertility, symbolized totemically by the bull in many cultures and countries, and drama-tized in Spain for centuries in a "corrida" involving a hobbled bull and the bridegroom and his friends for the benefit of the bride. (12)

Notably, McCormick also comments on the reception of this tradition, arguing that "thus we may understand the lack of interest on the part of the historian who would emphasize man's valor, rather than woman's hopes for children, danger rather than domesticity. After all, there is nothing glamourous about a hobbled bull" (12). Ironically, here McCormick may be only slightly mistaken, particularly if we adhere to one of the mainstream interpretations of *The Sun Also Rises* as just that—a glamorous tale about a hobbled bull (i.e., Jake Barnes). Based on a number of factors, it appears that Hemingway not only offered a far more honest account of the aspects of the corrida but, moreover, one which does not deny, repress, or ignore its more feminized origins.

Further explorations of the folkloric aspects of the bullfight, namely the tale of "the bull with the golden horns" or "La narración del oricuerno," offer important insight into two of the novel's major thematic concerns: the unconventional portrayal of gender (usually inversion) and the preoccupation throughout with marriage, coupling, unions, and domesticity (or the failure thereof). According to McCormick, this fable of the golden horns involves a young woman who assumes the guise of a man (Carlos), in order to avoid detection for her revengeful murder of a former suitor who, in turn, had killed her own preferred or chosen lover. Circumstances force Carlos into a marriage with a woman most smitten with her, yet, interestingly one who has no trouble accepting Carlos's true sexual identity. When no child results from the marriage, Carlos's father-in-law forces her to forego various tests of manhood. During one such trial Carlos, while standing naked in a river, is touched in the genital area by a bull with golden horns and magically transformed into a man. McCormick elaborates on the significance of the legend:

> In a Mexican version, "Carlos," after undressing plays the bull (black in color) with her clothing in the manner of a modern matador; the bull is then transformed into a cow and "Carlos" into a man. The theme of the change of sex is as old as folklore, particularly in the Orient, while that of the transvestite is even more widespread. More than a hundred versions exist in Spain alone. (13)

In addition to these more feminized and transsexual aspects of the folklore, let us not overlook the androgynous implications of the matador's unique costume: the ornate and highly decorative suit of lights—in essence, what McCormick terms the overall "effeminate" design (197). Equally noteworthy is, of course, the coleta or pigtail worn by the matador, and it has particular significance in light of Hemingway's much discussed hair fetishism. We should finally listen to Allen Josephs's long ignored observation, namely that "there is no more androgynous male in western culture than the wasp-waisted, lace-fronted, pink-stockinged, ballet-slippered, gold-bespangled killer of bulls" (63). That Hemingway recognized in the corrida manifestations of his particular sexual interests from transsexuality and androgyny to hair fetishism is overtly evident in the seemingly unrelated interpolations in *Death in the Afternoon.*

One particularly telling section pertains to Waldo Frank's *Virgin Spain,* which Hemingway terms "erectile writing" and "full of *pretty* phallic images *drawn in a manner of sentimental valentines*" (my emphasis, *DIA* 53). Hemingway was, however, disturbed by Frank's prose and not the actual content, for in this same section he talks at length about writing without fakery or without the "mysticism" of Frank. In spite of such criticisms, though, Hemingway obviously noted Frank's book and, moreover, its sexual overtones, and two of Frank's observations about the corrida are worth reviewing. Speaking of Belmonte's performance, Frank refers to the torero's contact with the bull as a "marriage," saying that "they are joined more closely, more terribly than love. He plunges" (235). Frank elaborates on this "rigorous dance," writing:

And now another change in the beauty of their locked encounter. The man becomes the woman. The dance of human will and brutish power is the dance of death no longer. It is the dance of life. It is a searching symbol of the sex act. The bull is male; the exquisite torero, stirring and unstirred, with hidden ecstasy controlling the plunges of the bull, is *female.* (my emphasis, 236)

Although Hemingway may have cringed at Frank's prose, he was certainly both familiar with and accepting of the idea of the torero as female, for in addition to the folkloric links between woman and corrida (as well as modern manifestations such as Frank's), such a treatment also exists in the visual art—in works by Goya, Manet, and Picasso.

As Keneth Kinnamon in "Hemingway, The *Corrida,* and Spain" explains, the bullfight "had become a profound spiritual experience, perhaps the most profound of all" (46). Hemingway himself acknowledges the religiosity of the bullfight in *Death in the Afternoon* when he speaks of the faena and its ability to make man feel "immortal" as well as provide him with "an ecstasy, that is, while momentary, as profound as any religious ecstasy" (207). As an aficionado, surely Hemingway was aware of the significance of the bull in ancient, pagan worship, and an overview of some of these very same traditions will better enable us to appreciate these motifs in the novel as well as glimpse the complexity of associations.

As Herodotus explains, the god Dionysus or Bacchus was an offshoot of the Egyptian sun god, Osiris (58). According to the *Dictionary of Symbols,* the Egyptians made no distinctions between the bull as a "symbol of fertility and a funeral-god associated with Osiris and his resurrections" (Chevalier and Gheerbrant 134). With the Greek appropriation of Osiris and subsequent transformation into Dionysus, the traits most commonly associated with this vegetative god of the vine and all of its transgressive implications become firmly entrenched. Such characteristics include intoxication, ecstasy, divination, frenzy, madness, chaos, destruction, and rebirth, and other forces typically attributed to the unconscious. Notably, the Greeks perpetuated the link established by the Egyptians between the bull and a god, for as James G. Frazer explains in *The Golden Bough,* Dionysus was often represented in the shape or form of a bull who was ultimately sacrificed in a bloody rite.

One of the most interesting aspects regarding the genealogy of Dionysus, however, is this god's ambiguous gender distinctions. While Dionysus is almost always referred to as a masculine deity, the strict designation as masculine or with masculinity becomes, at best, problematic. As Frazer's study attests, the vegetative gods from Osiris to Dionysus inevitably become entwined, interrelated, and, in essence, inextricably linked to nature goddesses such Isis and Demeter or other corn goddesses or corn mothers. In other words, the history of these myths points to the collapse of strictly male/female assignations and suggests, instead, a much more fluid, androgynous, even hermaphroditic genealogy of the vegetative god/goddess.

And let us not forget Nietzsche's model of Apollo and Dionysus (as interpreted by numerous poststructuralists and their precursors ranging from Georges Bataille to Hélène Cixous), which aligns Apollo with a strictly masculine economy while Dionysus is seen as a representative of both the masculine and feminine, with emphasis on the latter. What the genealogy of Dionysus appears to reveal, therefore, is a highly overdetermined trope linking the sun, the slaying of bulls, intoxicative and transgressive behavior, and gender ambiguity in one associative chain.

This signifying chain, in turn, has direct and overt relevance to Hemingway's *The Sun Also Rises* with its play and treatment of these same motifs. In this respect, Sibbie O'Sullivan's reading of the novel in "Love and Friendship/Man and Woman in *The Sun Also Rises*" proves insightful, as evidenced, for example, in her observation that Ecclesiastes, rather than Stein, provides "the more applicable epigraph for his novel" (95). She explains:

> If this novel exhibits traits of Stein's lost generation, it also exhibits the cyclical nature of friendship, its rhythm of disintegration and renewal. Brett's and Jake's relationship may have been dealt a cruel blow by fate or the First World War, but it is anything but lost, sadistic, and sick. It, and the bullfights, are the only lasting things in the book. Contrary to what many readers believe, Brett Ashley is a positive force, a determined yet vulnerable woman who makes an attempt to live honestly. (95–96)

Another important source for appreciating the complex aspects of the corrida and therefore for better assessing Brett and the novel as a whole is Vincente Blasco Ibáñez's classic, *Blood and Sand.* That the work represents a rich source for reading and understanding much of Hemingway has been suggested by Susan Beegel in "'The Undefeated' and *Sangre y Arena:* Hemingway's *Mano a Mano* with Blasco Ibáñez" (83). She also claims that the affair between Brett and Pedro Romero owes much to Ibáñez's novel (83).

In passages in *Blood and Sand* featuring the dressing of the protagonist/matador, Gallardo, Ibáñez offers not only highly sensual details but clearly effeminate ones as well. Gallardo's toiletries for both shaving and preparation of the coiffure are stored in "a feminine looking" box, and as for his person, Gallardo emanates "a smell of clean manly flesh" that is "combined with the strong odor of feminine perfume" (21). Everything about his actual donning of the suit of lights exudes a soft, sensual femininity, from his care to avoiding any wrinkling of the pink stockings to the stringing of the machos, which is likened to the stringing of a corset (22). In essence, the portrait of Gallardo is quite androgynous.

Ibáñez also strongly suggests bisexual activity when he tells of Gallardo's first patron "who had a weakness of handsome young bullfighters, and whose intimacy" with Gallardo triggers such outrage in his otherwise staid, religious mother that she voices her objections to their relationship with "obscene expressions" (60). During his association with the old patron, Gallardo wears "a double gold chain like a woman's. This had been lent to him by his elderly friend; it had already been worn by other young men at the outset of their careers" (61).

Most interesting, perhaps, is the introduction into the plot of Doña Sol, aristocrat, former wife of a foreign ambassador, who is known all over the European courts for her promiscuity and scandals. Ibáñez says that she "was a wild eccentric creature" with a highly "original and independent character" (100). She handles horses and riding "with the agility of a boy" and even dons a riding habit that includes "a man's shirt with a red tie" (105). She is athletic and fond of the rough and dangerous sport of "bull baiting" (99). And Ibáñez tells us, "She can fence, box like an English sailor, and has even learned ju-jitsu" (100). Doña Sol and Gallardo, in effect, demonstrate inverted gender characteristics with the woman assuming the more stereotypically masculine traits and the matador feminine ones. In this respect, the representation is not unlike that of Brett and Jake. Interestingly, both Ibáñez's and Hemingway's play with gender inversion is sociologically validated by one of Hemingway's favorite authors, the sexual theorist Havelock Ellis.[2] In *The Soul of Spain,* Ellis includes information that would have certainly intrigued Hemingway. Ellis speaks of one "thoughtful observer" of Spanish culture who noted that Spanish women display a "masculine boldness," and in the mating ritual "they wish to choose and not be chosen . . . they play the man's part, and it is for him to yield and sacrifice himself" (84).

As Ibáñez's novel unfolds, this independent, freethinking, and opium smoking woman seduces the younger Gallardo, eventually ruining his entire career and life. Clearly, the parallels between this and aspects of Hemingway's *Sun* are readily apparent, but, importantly, Hemingway did not merely rewrite Ibáñez's novel. While Brett, like Doña Sol, may be construed by some as merely a destructive force, with critics privileging this slant rather than noting her acutely androgynous traits, as much evidence exists to say that Hemingway actually celebrated or endorsed Brett's behavior. According to William Balassi, for instance, in "The Trail to *The Sun Also Rises,*" Hemingway initially attempted a book about bullfighting, and in the work the narrator "'Hem' tells the story of how he endangered the . . . promising young bullfighter by exposing him" to the vice of the expatriate life in general (35). Importantly, Balassi also explains that not Duff, but rather one "Mrs. Carlton" was the "nymphomaniac" that signified the destructive temptress (36).

The more feminized tradition of the corrida and Spanish mating rituals, as articulated by neglected aspects of folklore and corroborated by the more recent commentators such as Ibánez, Frank, Ellis, and even Hemingway's own original manuscript, should lead us to view the plot and characterization of *Sun* in a different light—that is, that the novel is much more concerned with love, bonding, and mating, as opposed to machismo sport or masculine sensibilities, than previously assumed. In addition, both the folkloric link with androgyny and the genealogy of Dionysus should enable us to understand better the gender inversion of the novel's central couple and to see that it is an idea grounded in a valid, historical, ancient context, one, moreover, that is not incompatible with some of Hemingway's own psychosexual fantasies and interests. In this respect, it could be said that Jake and Brett constitute a symbolic couple or union, a hermaphroditic pair, and as such, one that closely resembles the kind Hemingway himself sought to create or realize in his private life. That Brett and Jake relate to and understand one another at such deep levels (not to mention like, love, and consistently respect one another) is an overriding element throughout both the original drafts and the finished novel. As O'Sullivan points out, much criticism of the novel as merely a treatise on the wasteland or lost generation theme "undervalues Hemingway's intuitive awareness of cultural and historical forces and the impact they have on personal relationships" (76). She adds that these sorts of critical approaches contribute to "the harmful propagation of sexist stereotypes," and they disregard as well Hemingway's approval of the "New Woman" (76). O'Sullivan urges that we read the novel as a treatise not on "the death of love," rather "as a story about the cautious belief in the survival of the two most basic components of any human relationship: love and friendship" (76). What is most notable about Hemingway's treatment of relationships is, however, its deviation from orthodox renderings and expectations. Much of the book works to displace or disrupt convention to allow for a space where an(other) can thrive. Speaking of Hemingway's portrayal of Jake and Brett as an antithesis to the norm, O'Sullivan offers many examples. She argues:

What is striking about these role reversals is how easily and naturally they appear and reappear throughout the couple's interactions. Brett's behavior, especially, flows back and forth between being soft and caring, and hard and straightforward. Jake has the ability to snap back after painful relapse. Such flexibility is unthinkable in traditional relationships where sex roles are rigid. (85)

W. Martin too explores the novel's play with inversion of roles, and she notes that:

> the emotional challenges of Brett and Jake are antithetical: Jake must learn to escape the discomfort and uncertainty that comes with loss of authority, and Brett must learn to make choices for herself and to take responsibility for those choices. In this reworking of traditional psychological patterns, Jake becomes more nurturing and *responsive,* Brett more decisive and *responsible.* This role reversal reflects the changing definitions of gender in the jazz age. In *The Sun Also Rises,* men cry and women swear; Brett aggressively expresses her sexual desires, while her lovers wait to be chosen; she likes action—noisy public gatherings, large parties, the blood and gore of the bullfight—whereas the men appreciate the pleasure of sipping brandy in a quiet café. (75)

Martin's insights here should not be underestimated, for Brett's smoking, screwing, and swearing are not conventionally feminine traits. Neither are Jake's pandering for and pining over Brett, which is what one typically expects from a man in relation with one woman he deeply loves.

When speaking of coupling and marriage at a more literal level, we must not overlook the amount of plot devoted to this subject, and this is true for both the manuscript and the published versions. In many respects, Brett's marital life, past, present, and future, form the core of the novel, from information about her previous husbands to intense interest (bordering on obsessive) by all her male friends and acquaintances concerning whom she will marry, or mate, next and why. Early drafts indicate a most thorough examination of her marital history (as well as reveal Hemingway's intention at one point to make her the hero of the book). That Brett's relationship with men, be it romantic, sexual, or social, signifies a major thematic concern in the novel is indicated at the very outset and persists until the very end.

Our first introduction to Brett involves Jake's reaction to her homosexual companions followed immediately by his description of Cohn looking at Brett as though he has glimpsed "the promise land" (22). From Jake's declaration of love for her, to the Count's pursuit, to the Cohn affair and subsequent anticipation of Mike Campbell's reaction to it, to the liaison with Pedro Romero and Cohn's reaction to this, and then full circle back to Jake's love for Brett and his coming to her aid—the novel unequivocally sets Brett at center stage, thus making a strong case that *she* is the central protagonist as well as hero of the book. While Jake may be the narrator, Brett provides the overriding subject of interest.

When the plot does not delve into Brett's love life and issues of marriage or mating, it comments on a wide range of other couplings, including even the more unconventional or socially unacceptable ones: Cohn and his first wife, Cohn's affair with Frances, Frances and her unnamed ex-husband, Jake and Georgette (whom he introduces as his fiancée), the Count and Zizi, the wedding announcement Jake receives for Katherine Kirby, and the homosexuals at the bal musette. The subject of marriage and domesticity comes up repeatedly in seemingly unrelated or odd contexts as well. Bill Gorton, for instance, suggests playfully to Jake that instead of going off with Cohn, Brett should pair up with him: "Why didn't she go off with some of her own people? Or you . . . or me? Why not me?" (102). He jests that "every woman ought to be given a copy of this face as she leaves the altar" (102). During the fishing trip, Gorton sings "Oh, Give them Irony and Give them Pity" to the tune of "The Bells are Ringing for Me and My Gal" (114). Hemingway includes further references to marriage in the sequences when he introduces the American couple on the train who "had always wanted to get over" but chose to "See America First" (85), when the old Basque on the bus explains that he "was going to go back [to the States] but" his wife does not "like to travel" (107), when Jake reads the A. E. W. Mason novel about a bride who planned to wait twenty-four years for her husband's "body to come out of the moraine, while her true love waited too" (120), and, finally, when we learn of the death of Vincente Girones, a farmer with a wife and two children (196).

In addition to a literal concern with coupling, marriage, or unions, the novel has much to say on a metaphorical level as well. Gajdusek offers numerous instances of such concerns, from Bill and Jake's talk of the Civil War to their play on William Jennings Bryan with its myriad of inter-related binaries: drumstick/egg, male/female, Creationism/Darwinism, Apollo/Dionysus (43). In an attempt perhaps to include even those unions thought to be taboo at the time, Hemingway also employs in this same section numerous references to homosexual couplings as well, as in Gorton's drunken expression of friendship:

> You're a hell of a good guy, and I'm fonder of you than anybody on earth. I couldn't tell you that in New York. It'd mean I was a faggot. That was what the Civil War was about. So was Jefferson Davis. . . . Sex explains it all. The Colonel's Lady and Judy O'Grady are Lesbians under their skin. (116)

It is important that we understand that the novel's preoccupation with marriage and coupling is central to the subject of bullfighting from the perspective of its ancient, folkloric tradition. Notably, Hemingway's in-clusion and, moreover, strong emphasis of this leitmotif in its numerous manifestations certainly contradict both the traditional criticism and in-terpretations such as those hurled by Leslie A. Fiedler and others re-garding Hemingway's avoidance of the subject of women, love, and do-mesticity and, in turn, simplistic preoccupation with male bonding and homoerotic love. In addition to assessing both plot and characterization from the folklore of tauromachy, it is imperative that we also critique Brett's portrayal from another vantage point as well, namely the notion of *particularismo*.

In addition to literally embodying *particularismo* (the characteristics epitomized by the matador, and by association, the code hero), Brett is also symbolically likened to a matador in the novel. Drawing upon the assessment of Spanish culture by such writers as Angel Ganivet and Ortega y Gasset, Broer concludes that the idea of *particularismo* best signifies key aspects of the Spanish sensibility, and ones specifically asso-ciated with the matador. The qualities most often identified with this label include a radical independence bordering on anarchy, pride, defi-ance, resistance to authority, arrogance, and courage to the point of recklessness (even to the degree of potentially self-destructiveness). Broer argues that prior to Hemingway's attraction to *particularismo*, he drew characters (male) who demonstrated neurosis, weakness, "vulnerability and helplessness in the face of life's uncertainties" (vii). After his adoption of *particularismo*, however, a radically different character emerges:

> [They] are distinctly aggressive and bellicose in nature. These later heroes seem to derive unmistakably from Hemingway's sympathetic portraits of Pedro Romero, Juan Belmonte, and Manuel Garcia Maera—those figures whom Hemingway apotheosizes in *The Sun Also Rises* and in his Spanish manifesto, *Death in the Afternoon*. These, Hemingway felt, were men worth emulating—men in the throes of perpetual conflict, who nevertheless were erect and proud looking, possessing a seemingly indomitable spirit and sardonic carelessness. (vii)

This description describes Brett as succinctly as it does those characters whom Broer and others have repeatedly labeled the code hero.

From the concierge's claim that Brett is "*tré, tré gentille*" to the Count's comment, "You got class all over you," Brett captivates people with her presence and stature. Her proud carriage and charisma make her an inevitable icon or image around which to dance or to seat upon a wine cask as if enthroned in a pagan court, adorned with her garland of garlic (an item typically linked with Dionysus). Her self-possessed stature clearly aligns her, and aptly so, with the very bullfighter she admires, making the description Hemingway gives to Romero equally applicable to Brett: "Romero had the old thing, the holding of his purity of line through the maximum of exposure, while he dominated the bull by making him realize he was unattainable, while he prepared him for the killing" (168).

As Broer explains, the bullfight signified "an antidote to the feeling of inner helplessness experienced" by a number of Hemingway's earlier characters (59). According to Broer, Hemingway believed that "violence, suffering, and death constitute the reality of life" and that once he became convinced of death's sovereignty, he turned to the Spanish sensibility as a means of coping (57). Hemingway, says Broer, admired the rebellious attitude inherent in the bullfight: "Here is the chief motivating force in the character of the matador—this strained spirit of rebellion and prideful individualism . . . that both Jake Barnes and Ernest Hemingway found so attractive" (61).

A thoughtful assessment of Brett's life reveals a number of trials no less traumatic than those experienced by certain male characters. These include the death of her first true love, the constant and immanent danger each night from her second husband's psychosis, her futile sexual love for Jake, and Cohn's and Romero's insistence on remaking her into their own image of a woman. In fact, Brett's past and potential suitors should force us to understand that she simply is not provided with many favorable options, hence should lead us to see the validity of that old cliché: "Just what's a woman supposed to do?" The answer seems to be that she must do what is expected of any other existential hero, namely make choices that are self-authenticating in contexts that are absurd, alienating, and painful. And this is precisely what Brett does throughout the novel.

Speaking of Brett's valor, W. Martin writes, "Brett's affairs represent the kind of risk taking for her that the confrontation with the bull represents for Romero; by exercising sexual freedom she risks disease, pregnancy, or ostracism" (77). Martin also comments on Brett's milieu, reiterating the potential dangers a woman such as Brett would have actually faced:

> Along with the opportunities created by the dissolution of polarized spheres came increased vulnerability for women. Because public space is defined as male, women were often seen as interlopers or "fair game" undeserving of respect or safety. Frequently a woman who left the sanctity of the home was automatically defined as disreputable or dangerous. (67)

In effect, everything about Brett's behavior is in strict accordance with the idea of *particularismo*. If Brett is a hard-hearted bitch, as so many critics have believed throughout the years, then this trait too is befitting the matador's (and Hemingway's) code, for as Broer explains, Hemingway in his later years increasingly began to think that "the universe [was] endlessly hostile and unjust," and that he "adjudged the matador's aggressive stance to be a correct and necessary one for survival" (21). While Broer does not demonstratively praise Brett, or at least overtly label her a code hero, he nevertheless acknowledges or credits her with as much by saying that "the two matadors in [*Sun*] provide an image of integrity against which" Jake's "friends, with the exception of Brett, are measured and found wanting" (51).

It is very important that we disassociate *particularismo,* however, with masculinity as defined by modernity, for *particularismo* has far more in common with the ancient traits of Dionysus and this god's more ambiguous distinctions. For those who have trouble reconciling the traits of *particularismo* with what I term a more feminized or Dionysiac code hero, Georges Bataille's idea of sovereignty is helpful, for he offers a paradigm that can help us transcend strict textual and interpretive taxonomies and grasp more completely the complex and multifarious archetypal associations. That Bataille can provide us with an appropriate and important interpretive lens is aided by his own insightful critique of both Hemingway and Brett herself.

In his assessment of Hemingway's relationship to games, Bataille includes love in this category, remarking: "Love is but the complement or flowering of life mercilessly risked or life's excellence making a sport of itself. Love is the excellence of the person loved. Worthy of its name, love is sovereign; nothing counts more, and its object must somehow have the same value the master assumes for himself" (10). Bataille believes that a woman as an object of a man's love in both life and in Hemingway's fiction has two options. First, she "can maintain her sovereignty by a pact with the master, with whom she becomes identified to the point of no longer existing" (10), and Bataille says that Catherine of *A Farewell to Arms* and Maria of *For Whom the Bell Tolls* exemplify this choice (10). Bataille writes, "instead of backing out with resistance, she can maintain her sovereignty on her own in a game of rivalry pitting herself against the master. Henceforth, she no longer plays the master's game like Maria . . . but a personal game like Brett" (10).

Bataille finds Brett to be a "fascinating character," one which exceeds all others in the novel in terms of "prestige" (6). Bataille quarrels with Carlos Baker's comparison of her with Cohn and the label "of evil (of neurosis, which is evil)" (7). Bataille says, "Quite the contrary, intoxication, in her personality, is sovereignly seductive. And Carlos Baker ought not to forget that Hemingway's whole life is the effect of that intoxication" (7). As for her drinking and self-destructive behavior, Bataille believes that "the sensual freedom often attained through games would be for those women [like Brett] who have freely chosen it, the equivalent of what the havoc of battles is for men" (10).

Bataille acknowledges that Brett does reflect a neurosis; however, he insists that such a condition is inextricably linked with the struggle involved in "feminine sovereignty" (10). According to Bataille, "masculine supremacy" is a "monstrosity," and therefore a certain amount of neurosis inevitably results when battling with male supremacy and struggling to be an autonomous human being (9). Bataille offers interesting insight into the contrast between such a sovereign character like Brett and an "amoeba" by arguing that what Hemingway's work reveals is that "contradictory situations yield the same result: either man is sovereign, and the woman he loves—and who loves him—is his reflection; or only the woman is sovereign, the man she loves—and who loves her—being impotent. Frederic Henry and Robert Jordan cancel out Catherine and Maria, but, when equated against Lady Brett, Jake Barnes's existence is annulled, by impotence" (9–10).

Bataille's label of Brett as sovereign is not only complimentary, it is, significantly, a term that he uses with both "nobility," "dignity," and "mastery" to explain the profundity of the Spanish bullfight. He writes:

> The bull itself, attacked, then put to death, is admired for its nobility. It is not a worthless creature, and nobody would picture an arena-bull pulling a plough. In addition, the game is based on the noble beast's blindness and stupidity. The intelligent bull, sniffing out the trap, is hissed. . . . When bullfighting became part of history, in Spain, it was the sport of princes, and paid matadors mark the decline, transition to politeness, and eventual impotence of the nobility. Nevertheless, bullfighting remains the reflection in present times of the bygone world of masters: man braves death not only by merely fighting the monster or bull. He makes a game out of confronting it, grazes it, and gains prestige by rubbing against it. If, in a moment of unhoped for risk, he comes close to not believing it, the old flash of sovereignty sparks once again before our eyes.
>
> Starting with . . . the Hegelian notion of "master," I have defined the world of archaic values illustrated by Hemingway's work. His

> heroes excel in hunting or fishing, their only other occupation being war. . . . Of all games, bullfighting is the one that suits them. . . . Or, to put it another way, nothing suits them which is not a game, on the condition that, in some way, the game is one of life and death. (10)

Notwithstanding Hemingway's own protestations when questioned once by a staffer at the *New Yorker*, the fact remains that *The Sun Also Rises* is structured like a bullfight and, once again, Brett is central to such a reading. Not only does she literally embody qualities of a matador and *particularismo*, her involvement with Cohn and then Romero metaphorically parallel the situation in the corrida where the matador takes on two bulls. While some readers may have much difficulty imagining Brett in this light, it is important to remember that the corrida does indeed allow for the participation of women in the role of a matador, and two examples include the famous Spanish torero Doña Maria de Gaucin of the nineteenth century and the *rejoneadora* Conchita Cintrón who frequently appeared in corridas in Arles in the 1940s and 1950s.

In order to interpret Brett as symbolic matador, it is important to return to Hemingway's early drafts and rethink his possible authorial intentions. With his consideration first to open the book with Pedro Romero dressing in preparation for a corrida, and then with Brett, and finally with Cohn, Hemingway appears to be establishing associative links. The published version of the novel merely reinforces this, for the plot is highly centered around Brett's manipulation of these two men who are, in the manner of bulls, strong, virile, and potent.

As for Jake, he faithfully assists Brett in her engagements with these men; moreover, he does so in a manner similar to that of a picador—the one who piques and baits the bulls for the benefit of the matador. Speaking of the relationship between the matador and the picadors, Hemingway explains in *Death in the Afternoon* that their job is to wear down the bulls while the matador is able to size up and then efficiently manipulate the opponent (155). Moreover, it is important to note that to compare Jake to a picador does not detract from his character in any way, for as Hemingway himself makes quite clear, the picador is an invaluable, yet underesteemed and underpaid component of the corrida. In his glossary, he writes that "of all ill-paid professions in civil life I believe it is the roughest and the most constantly exposed to danger of death, which, fortunately, is nearly always removed by the matador's cape" (*DIA* 436).

Therefore, in the context of the novel as a symbolic bullfight, Brett and Jake form an important union. Not only do they signify the matador/picador coupling, they also represent an interpersonal fusion, which, with Jake's support, allows Brett to aggressively pursue her own sovergnity (existential, sexual, and social) and in doing so to subvert rigidly defined conventions concerning the passivity of women. Moreover, Brett's *particularismo* is Dionysian and, as such, it entails behavior and character traits that defy logic, reasoning, moderation, and other such Apollonian characteristics commonly identified as masculine, such as socialization and civilization. She is the pagan maypole around which merry mounters dance their orgiastic revelries or the Dionsysiac force that signifies life and death, regeneration and destruction, creativity and chaos, the bull and man, and male and female. In any event, she is not passive, safe, predictable, nor totally intelligible.

The profile of Brett, of matadors, and of code heroes, as defined and endorsed by Hemingway, signifies an aspect of his aesthetic that is truly pagan, primitive, and archetypal, hence closely approaches the Bataillian notion of *informe* or that which resists exact or precise limits, understanding, or classification. Perhaps this helps explain why the novel tends to separate those in the "know" from persons like Cohn who cannot enter into nor understand the sensibilities of Brett and her friends. It is important to note that none of the characters in the novel dislike, disrespect, nor ultimately reject Brett, even when they perceive that they have been hurt by her or when she refuses to adhere to their expectations. Her failure to meet appointments on time or not at all, her total disregard for managing money, and, above all, her forthright control of her own sexuality—that is, her determination to sleep with whom she wants, when she wants, and under what circumstances she chooses—are traits that all of her friends ultimately accept. Moreover, with the exception, perhaps, of Robert Cohn, they do so without sniveling. All the other whining, complaining, and disapproval comes, ironically, from critics.

Just as the negative critical reception of Brett can be linked to arbitrary social conventions and prejudices as well as rigid, modernist definitions or understandings, so too can the unfavorable response to the novel's rendering of relationships in general (i.e., as a story of a lost or misguided generation). For throughout *The Sun Also Rises* Hemingway offers a myriad of combinations and contrasts, both literally and symbolically, involving partnerships, couplings, or unions—gay/straight, married/divorced, promiscuous/impotent—perhaps without intending to privilege one expression over another. In doing so, he further enhances the spirit behind the religious text inspiring the novel's title: namely "the thing that hath been, it *is that* which shall be; and that which is done *is* that which shall be done: and *there is* no new *thing* under the sun" (my emphasis, Eccles. 1:9)

4

The Romance of Desire in Hemingway's Fiction

Linda Wagner-Martin

As we learn more and more about Hemingway, the self-created macho man's man, we start to understand why he worked so hard to show his sexual prowess. Part of being macho was being sexually adept, being able to satisfy women (who were, in turn, only sex partners rather than people). We come to see that Hemingway was a product of his times—and those times were marked with a nearly obsessive interest in sexuality and erotica.

Otto Weininger, Havelock Ellis, and Edward Carpenter were on the scene long before Sigmund Freud (at least in English translations), and for Hemingway, judging from his book orders, Ellis seems to have been of continuing interest at least until the late 1930s. One of Ellis's most important works, to Hemingway the writer, was his 1906 *Erotic Symbolism* (which Bill Smith borrowed and returned to Hemingway in March of 1920). Hemingway also seems to have owned Ellis's *The Dance of Life* and his four-volume *Studies in the Psychology of Sex*, published in the mid-thirties (Reynolds, "Supplement" 101).[1] What had happened in the early twentieth century to make sexuality a topic deserving of attention and study was the recognition that sex was pleasure, that sensuality was healthy, and that human relationships benefited from sexual exploration. The underside of this recognition was that some people learned that knowing how to pleasure their lovers was a means to power; we see Hemingway in this role in the love letters he wrote Hadley, where it also seems clear that their reading lists to each other comprise a kind of erotic pedagogy.[2] When Hemingway began to write seriously a few years later, what he felt he knew most about—the "subject" he had studied, discussed, and explored—was eroticism. As he said somewhat coyly to F. Scott Fitzgerald in 1925, "Love is also a good subject as you might be said to have discovered" (*SL* 177).

There are several qualifications here to be made about Hemingway's use of the word "love." What he seems to have meant by "love" was erotic desire, sexuality, blended with the chivalric concept of courtly love; he seems to have wanted both, synthesized into some all-encompassing, completely satisfying, unquestioned and unquestioning emotion. Perhaps he had not understood that eroticism need not depend on love, but again, perhaps he had. What he *had* understood, as his fiction shows, was that the world wanted to read erotic books. Even as he praised Stein's *The Making of Americans* and Cummings's *The Enormous Room*, Hemingway knew that the general reader was never going to rave about Pound's poems or Dorothy Richardson's *Pointed Roofs*—or even Joyce's *Dubliners* or Anderson's *Winesburg, Ohio*, though the latter came closer. What the general reader wanted was a good love story, and Hemingway learned increasingly to write that. Whether in the guise of war novel or bullfight adventure, Hemingway's real subject was eroticism. And the form he needed to tell that story, to entice the general reader, was the romance.

The contradiction here is immense. Hemingway wanted, at least once he landed in Paris and found himself being tutored by both Stein and Pound, to be an important serious writer—but he also wanted to be self-supporting, successful, and famous. Literary fame, at least, was given only to the truly innovative and ultimately serious writers—Henry James, T. S. Eliot, Flaubert, Turgenev. As John Raeburn has shown in *Fame Became of Him*, Hemingway wanted more than literary fame; he wanted celebrity status, power, and fortune. Mark Spilka has shown how Victorian Hemingway was in his alliances, Gertrude Stein called him a Rotarian (though today she would more likely have used the designation Yuppie), and others have written of the influence of medieval romance on both Hemingway and Fitzgerald: much of Hemingway's reading was conventional romance, and even though he paid homage to Pound and Eliot's poetry, his own was nothing like theirs.[3] He was from the first trying to combine a popular mode with modernism's elitist models. What he managed to do in the process was learn to replicate the conventions of popular romance in his own spare and intense writing. Though his style seemed remote from the romantic, Hemingway very subtly mastered the classic romance plot, the age-old narrative of the discourse of desire.

According to John G. Cawelti, the most significant qualities of romance are these: (1) "its organizing action is the development of a love relationship, usually between a man and a woman," and, unlike the adventure story, which has a male protagonist set against an adversary, the romance may *include* elements of adventure, "but the dangers function as a means of challenging and then cementing the love relationship." (2) Such intense focus on the love relationship supports the "moral fantasy" that love is all-sufficient. The structure of the work, all conventions of the work, reinforce this premise. "Though the usual outcome is a permanently happy marriage, more sophisticated types of love story sometimes end in the death of one or both of the lovers, but always in such a way as to suggest that the love relation has been of lasting and permanent impact." In fact, as Cawelti points out, in the stories of Romeo and Juliet, Tristan and Isolde, or *Last Tango in Paris*, "the intensity of the lovers' passion is directly related to the extent to which their love is doomed." (3) Accepting this moral stance means that both writer and reader have accepted that women characters play a traditional female role, that of love object (39–42). As Linda Kauffman describes that role, "the heroine is defined by the lover she addresses," and she "always locates herself—spatially"; these are essentially affirmations of the ideals of monogamous marriage and feminine domesticity (35).

Maurice Charney notes that "desire is the energizing element of all sexual fiction—not gratified desire but desire that is blocked, frustrated, and diverted; in other words, desire that has become part of imaginative projection" (124). Thus, Charney extends the discussion from the pattern of romance to the concept of a narrative embodying explicit passion and desire, the sexual narrative, which is a more important element in Hemingway's kind of romance than had been noticed until the recent publication of *The Garden of Eden*. The intent of fiction of desire is not to bring the reader the sense of idealization and completion that the romance form might deliver, but to deal in a more hesitant, a more titillating way, with the primary focus of desire. "Desire evokes an eroticized reality; desire seeks correlatives, gestures, and rituals of satisfaction; desire creates a world that is the object of desire" (124). With Hemingway, fiction existed in part to spin the fantasy of some idealized sexual union.

His fictional worlds were increasingly peopled with characters—not only male characters—for whom sexual realization was paramount, and even in his early writing, ritualized eroticism was a primary means of creating narrative. We have long talked about the movement in a Hemingway fiction, the detail-to-detail attention that focuses the reader's eye, and mind, on the activity of the character. What we perhaps have not said, or said clearly enough, is that much of that movement, much of that activity, is sexual.

Let me add this personal aside: twenty years ago at the first of these Hemingway conferences I presented an essay called "'Proud and friendly and gently': Women in Hemingway's Early Fiction," in which I tried to claim that Hemingway was really OK as a man and a writer, that he had clearly drawn women characters who were intended to be positive, to be superior to the male characters in their respective fictions. But—and this is not a recantation, more of an elaboration—I chose to ignore what was, always, in Hemingway's fiction, the crucial element: that his female characters exist mostly in relation to the male. If the women are superior, they are that because the male will eventually learn from them: the process is symbiotic. Women are never central to any Hemingway work on their own terms. For all our interest in both Catherine and Marita in *The Garden of Eden*, David Bourne is the narrative center of that novel, and the women are key only in their relationship to David.

And that is one point of this essay. All his life, Hemingway was creating idealized women, who played their narrative roles in his romances, and, one assumes, in his life. A corollary to this is that all his life, Hemingway was writing romances—not only in his fiction but in his letters, his journalism, and *A Moveable Feast*. His writing proves that, indeed, Hemingway seems to have believed in the simplicity of the all-sufficiency of love, the chivalric ideal of knightly love, purity, sacrifice, the private world—where time does not exist—set against the public (and the private so often either "the Cave of Lovers" or a garden, a bower of roses, and in another country), lovers trading locks of hair and other trophies, the couple aided by a nurse or magician figure, the lovers giving up identities (at least the women give up their identities, become absorbed into the male), renouncing all other interests for the supremacy of the lovers' world and relationship, the symbolic tears when the beauty of the union is realized. But he was also giving these romances a heavily symbolized sexual text, filling those lovers' worlds with phallic and womb imagery, creating dialogue that was sexual in implication even if not literally so, and writing fiction that was subliminally more erotic than that of either James Joyce or Henry Miller.

The full force of this method appears in *A Farewell to Arms,* the novel he wanted to be seen as his "war" novel. Sheer erotic romance, this fiction is propelled narratively by the Frederic-Catherine story, and every chapter in the book anticipates, and then supports, that narrative. From the first, in which the "we" narrator observes troop activity ("Sometimes in the dark"), the concept of imminent death either in battle or, ironically, with cholera is introduced through the sexual imagery of the "wet" rifles and the "six months gone with child" soldiers; through the second chapter with its bawdy discussion of male sexual needs and the five-fingered baiting of the shy priest; to the third where Frederic describes his sexual leave as "Magnificent" and lists his conquests as if running through a "timetable." Even the usually encouraging Rinaldi becomes cynical about his prowess, and reminds him that he is "dirty" and "ought to wash," at the same time introducing the notion of Miss Barkley as someone to marry, saying that he, Rinaldi, is considering "marrying Miss Barkley—after the war, of course" (12).[4] While one might suppose the opening of this novel would be "about" military action, and it is set amid men who are connected with the war in one way or another, its focus is entirely sexual. Frederic thinks to himself in his next meeting with his friend the priest not about the war or peasant life in Abruzzi but rather about:

> the smoke of the cafes and nights when the room whirled and you needed to look at the wall to make it stop, nights in bed, drunk, when you knew that that was all there was, and the strange excitement of waking and not knowing who it was with you, and the world all unreal in the dark and so exciting that you must resume again unknowing and not caring in the night, sure that this was all and all and all and not caring. Suddenly to care very much and everything sharp and hard and clear and sometimes a dispute about the cost. (13)

That passage, if you remember—and most readers do—continues for another half page. The idealization of the sexual act, the nameless and faceless female partner thoroughly subordinated to the male pleasure, becomes the dominant trope of the novel. Psychologically, it is meant to endear Henry to the reader, who is drawn in to the rhythm of the sexual experience only to be jolted with the realization that this is a purchased "love"—"sometimes a dispute about the cost." Hemingway plays on the reader's middle-classedness: the sympathetic reader thinks, this man deserves someone to love him. And since the only desirable woman in the text so far is Catherine, the reader replaces these faceless women with her. Long before Henry meets Catherine, *Farewell* plays intensely and intently on the concepts of romance as the way to fulfill life. That it is a coded message, opening fully only to readers who have experienced full sexual initiation, is also implied as Frederic says, "I cannot tell it now. But if you have had it you know" (13). (The obscurity of the source of Hemingway's title serves him too, because his 1920s readers equated the "arms" of the title with the arms of embrace, of love.)

Once the reader meets Catherine, all elements of conventional romance come into play. The meeting occurs in a garden; Catherine—dressed in white, aristocratic, educated, later described as a "goddess"—is protected by a nurse, Fergie; and Rinaldi as magical introducer suggests the *Song of Roland*'s second of the same name—a greater lover than Roland himself (Wagner-Martin, "Hemingway's Search" 60–61). Catherine calls attention to the *game* of romance, a trope Hemingway uses frequently, and pretends to undercut it; she carries a stick, the memento of her previous (and one assumes, because the courtship lasted eight years, only) lover; and the beauty, and length, of her hair becomes an important topic of conversation. Catherine also instructs Frederic about the war, being privy to its non-picturesque qualities. But immediately, lest the reader become too interested in the tough British woman, Hemingway begins the sexual attack, and gives the reader play-by-play details—placing his hand where? French kissing? Rough handling? Although Catherine has said that the nurses are not "cloistered," she then acts out the prudery such a verb suggests—slapping him, her disgust alternating with desire, and in succumbing, crying: "'Oh, darling,' she said. 'You will be good to me, won't you?' / What the hell, I thought. I stroked her hair and patted her shoulder. She was crying. / 'You will, won't you?' She looked up at me. 'Because we're going to have a strange life'" (27). Throughout even this scene, however, Hemingway diminishes the singularity of the experience by stressing the heat, the weather and its effects on everyone, and Rinaldi's insults about Henry's being a "dog in heat."

Two pages further on, Hemingway includes a long passage about Frederic's trying to "master the jerk of the ridiculous short barrel" of his Astra 7.65 caliber, concluding that, with it, "there was no question of hitting anything" (29). Meeting Catherine once again—this time surrounded by the deathlike marble busts, indistinguishable one from the other, that foreshadow her image in death, Frederic leaves for action—and the next segment of his idealization of her includes this scenario. If one reads a phrase at a time, the sexual coding becomes plainer:

> I would like to eat at the Cova and then walk down the Via Manzoni in the hot evening and cross over and turn off along the canal and go to the hotel with Catherine Barkley. Maybe she would. Maybe she would pretend that I was her boy that was killed and we would go in the front door and the porter would take off his cap and I would stop at the concierge's desk and ask for the key and she would stand by the elevator and then we would get in the elevator and it would go up very slowly clicking at all the floors and then our floor and the boy would open the door and stand there and she would step out and I would step out and we would walk down the hall and I would put the key in the door and open it and go in and then take down the telephone and ask them to send a bottle of capri bianca in a silver bucket full of ice and you would hear the ice against the pail coming down the corridor and the boy would knock and I would say leave it outside the door please. Because we would not wear any clothes because it was so hot and the window open . . . and when it was dark afterward and you went to the window very small bats hunting over the houses and close down over the trees and would drink the capri and the door locked and it hot and only a sheet and the whole night we would both love each other all night in the hot night in Milan. (38)

The sexual agenda as fantasized here could move forward without the reader's being at all interested in Catherine Barkley. Hemingway's unnamed characters are faceless manikins; and Catherine's one great personal loss—the death of her lover—is here diminished by Frederic's reference to him as "boy," the same epithet he uses for the hotel bellhop. Nakedness, heat, the step-by-step movement into the clandestine room —these are the elements of the fictional passion the author creates. In these explicit scenes, as in Frederic's conversations with both Rinaldi and the priest, the reader's attention is held by a random sexuality, a privileging of the male sexual experience that exists quite separate from its ostensible love object.

It may look as if *A Farewell to Arms* is "about" war, but even the war scenes exist to prepare the reader, to reinforce the message of the conventional romance—that the deepest, the greatest, loves are doomed—to death. As Hemingway creates that doom in the early sections of the novel, he also assures the reader that the doom is not war-related. Henry says explicitly, "I knew I would not be killed. Not in this war. It did not have anything to do with me. It seemed no more dangerous to me myself than war in the movies" (37). What would be dangerous to Frederic Henry, by this textual suggestion, was his feeling for Catherine, his relationship that could not be made impersonal, that did have something to do with him. Immediately Hemingway provides the scene of Catherine as lady to Henry's knight errant, giving her suitor the medal before battle, and he in turn kissing her hand in gratitude. To see his love for Catherine as somehow more dangerous than battle twists the normal narrative of romance, as does Hemingway's continuing translation of "love" into sexual passion.

The most-often-quoted scene from this novel, Frederic Henry's wounding, has been described as an "out-of-the-body" experience, marvelous prose, evocative writing (Josephs, "Experience" 11–17); but it is as well descriptive of sexual orgasm, even to its emphasis on the words *dead* and *died*. As Hemingway writes this passage, he makes the final movement into a kind of advance description of Catherine Barkley's death—of hemorrhage after childbirth, the ultimate sorrow with which the novel contends. All the description of Henry's wounding, care, and blood-letting anticipates Catherine's death (of which there is almost no description). Here is the central image of Henry's wounding, which begins this compelling sequence:

> on and on in a rushing wind. I tried to breathe but my breath would not come and I felt myself rush bodily out of myself and out and

out and out and all the time bodily in the wind. I went out swiftly, all of myself, and I knew I was dead and that it had all been a mistake to think you just died. Then I floated, and instead of going on I felt myself slide back. I breathed and I was back. (54)

Henry's wounding is necessary, so far as narrative goes, because Hemingway wants to give the reader the hospital scene, the full import of death and the frustration of medical knowledge that cannot save lives; and to create the mood of inexorable death, complete with its blood, relentless blood, the blood that readers who focus on the white purity of chastity, innocence, and military honor would like to deny. The reader cannot avoid the recognition of blood as Hemingway describes Passini's dreadful death—after the futile tourniquet attempt, and Henry's own "warm and wet," repeated as "wet and warm," wounds, and his careful planting of the word *hemorrhage* ("there was so much dirt blown into the wound that there had not been much hemorrhage" [57]). Once Henry is on the operating table (in a rite of privilege that accords with his elevated status as an American man), we are told again, with careful repetition, about the blood, this time the "sweet smell of blood." And after the cleaning and suturing, the doctor closes his cynical and distant monologue with the comment, "Your blood coagulates beautifully."

There are many ways to describe wounds and operating rooms. With all the skill Hemingway had acquired in his writing by 1929, his use of scenes and words and images that would both foreshadow and ironically comment on Catherine's later hospital scene seems more than accidental. He is careful to avoid describing Henry's wound as *leg* wounds so that the reader can think of all that the dark wounding passion can bring to the mortal body. And the doctor's flippant inquiry also contributes to extending Henry's experience to Catherine's. The doctor asks, "How did you run into this thing anyway? What were you trying to do? Commit suicide?" (59). The reader thinks later, what was Catherine trying to do? To procreate, to give life, to allow the great passion she had experienced with Frederic Henry to come to fruition. But her blood, the reader assumes, did not coagulate beautifully.

Hemingway uses carefully ambiguous language throughout the operating scene: "The captain, doing things that hurt sharply and severing tissue. . . . Me—trying to lie still and feeling my stomach flutter when the flesh was cut. . . . Captain doctor—(interested in something he was finding). . . . Sweat ran all over me. 'Good Christ! I said. . . . The pain . . . had started and all that was happening was without interest or relation" (58–60). By the end of the novel, Hemingway provides very little description of Catherine's ordeal, but the reader has already experienced it. And his description is relentless, because here it continues with the pain and agony, but with complete suppression of the word *blood*. As Henry is being transported by ambulance, his stretcher is placed under that of another wounded man. Again, the words *hemorrhage, warm,* and *dead.*

> As the ambulance climbed along the road, it was slow in the traffic, sometimes it stopped, sometimes it backed on a turn, then finally it climbed quite fast. *I felt something dripping. At first it dropped slowly and regularly, then it pattered into a stream.* I shouted to the driver. He stopped the car and looked in through the hole behind his seat.
>   "What is it?"
>   "The man on the stretcher over me has a hemorrhage."
>   "We're not far from the top. I wouldn't be able to get the stretcher out alone." He started the car. *The stream kept on. In the dark I could not see where it came from the canvas overhead. I tried to move sideways so that it did not fall on me. Where it had run down under my shirt it was warm and sticky.* I was cold and my leg hurt so that it made me sick. *After a while the stream from the stretcher above lessened and started to drop again and I heard and felt* the canvas above move as the man on the stretcher settled more comfortably.
>   "How is he?" the Englishman called back. "We're almost up."
>   "He's dead I think," I said.
>   *The drops fell very slowly,* as the fall from an icicle after the sun has gone. It was cold in the car in the night as the road climbed. At the post on the top they took the stretcher out and put another in and we went on. (my emphasis, 61)

The complete absence of the word *blood*—in its place, *something, the stream, the drops,* and particularly the innocent *it*—achieves terrible force. As an isolated scene, coming to close the one episode of war wounding

Henry experiences, it is remarkably powerful; but as a foreshadowing of the romance denouement, the proof of medical inability to save life, the randomness of hemorrhage and death, it is superb.

Hemingway's art of omission here, and in his treatment of actual sex between Catherine and Frederic, also feeds into the romance tradition. It is almost possible for the reader to believe that this "love" is chaste, and that is the intention of most romances, to keep the possibly offensive details of sexual experience out of the narrative. But as this look at the early sections of *A Farewell to Arms* has shown, erotica is more suggestive than explicit; and by the time of *For Whom the Bell Tolls* in 1940, Hemingway was even more skillful at embedding sexual imagery within his innocently descriptive opening. Drawing from Ellis's *Erotic Symbolism*, the reader may be alert for those many objects that have implicit phallic meaning—jets of water, knives, pears, garden hose, sticks, the lobe of the ear, teeth, tongues, ships, water, worms and snakes, horses, dogs, railway engines, trees, bananas, fish, a flower's pistil, catkins, arrows, bolts, poles, upright stones, stumps, crosses, obelisks, T's, giant leeks, carrots, and so on. *For Whom the Bell Tolls* is, accordingly, scaffolded with pine trees and "pleasantly rigid" carbines and dynamite sticks. Through the steep mountains, Jordan could see "the dark of the oiled road winding through the pass." Cut and bruised into hollows, the terrain formed shelters, and those bowls of earth mirrored the bowls of wine ("a deep stone basin full of red wine"), dipped into and into again by all the men around the table: the group living in the cave (of lovers), centered as it is with the life-giving fire—and dominated by the Earth Mother Pilar, whose name means bowl, basis, and pillar, the synthesis of androgynous power (1, 20).

But before Robert Jordan gets to the camp—the cave, hidden like a bear's den—he must wrest his power from Pablo, and he does this through the challenge of identifying weaknesses in the stolen horses. As Jordan, Anselmo, and Pablo observe the five beautiful animals, Hemingway recounts a litany of masculine knowledge—of battles as well as animals, strength as well as pride. Pablo's great love is his captured horses, and Jordan—seeing their importance to him—thinks, "I wonder what could make me feel the way those horses make Pablo feel" (16). Again, drawn into the text through this rhetorical strategy, the reader is prepared for Jordan's attraction to Maria, even before reading that she moves awkwardly, "as a colt moves." Interchangeable as power objects, horses,

women, riches, and political allegiance all become sources of conflict between Pablo and Jordan.

In this novel the camaraderie of Rinaldi and Frederic Henry has become the competition of Pablo and Jordan: just as Fergie's protection of
Catherine has changed into Pilar's more aggressive protection *cum* competition of Maria. The romance plot, if not transmuted, is doubled, and
the reader has more trouble keeping track of the narrative line. But as in
A Farewell to Arms, most of the scenes among the male characters in *For
Whom the Bell Tolls* also point to the acquisition of sexual booty. Golz
begins the pattern when he questions Jordan about his technique ("You
really blow them?" a question that is repeated in quick succession before
Golz's query about his women, and before the triple tease about Jordan's
hair cut). The gypsy extends the sexual text with his prowess in carving
the cross bar for a trap for foxes (Pablo's totem), which is really a trap for
rabbits (Maria's totem). And Pablo is a constant reminder of sexual power
gone bad, as he yearns for the possession of both Maria's body and Pilar's
control.

At several places in this sexual text, Hemingway fuses the separate
symbols into a scene that blends passional and political power. Rafael's
story of the rescue of Maria, through sheer animal strength and endurance, leads to his telling the story of the victory of the dynamited train, a
text rife with phallic imagery:

> Never in my life have I seen such a thing as when the explosion was
> produced. The train was coming steadily. We saw it far away. And I
> had an excitement so great that I cannot tell it. We saw steam from
> it and then later came the noise of the whistle. Then it came chu-
> chu-chu-chu-chu-chu steadily larger and larger and then, at the
> moment of the explosion, the front wheels of the engine rose up and
> all of the earth seemed to rise in a great cloud of blackness and a
> roar and the engine rose high in the cloud of dirt and of the wooden
> ties rising in the air as in a dream and then it fell onto its side like
> a great wounded animal and there was an explosion of white steam
> before the clods of the other explosion had ceased to fall on us (29).

If this is the orgasmic rite of the exploded engine, Rafael's next segment
—when Pilar slapped him so that he would fire the machine gun, its

barrel burning so that "it was very hard to hold my gun steady"—is his more personal account of sexual responsibility. Anselmo's acknowledgment, "It must have been something very hard. . . . Of much emotion," reifies the passional importance of the event. Again, through Hemingway's imagery, events of war are described as if they are events of sexual power.

Once again, the reader is prepared by foreshadowing for Jordan's reaction to Maria. The thickening in his throat (which, after several mentions, becomes a stiffening elsewhere that interferes with his walking) is his inexplicable response to the young girl's purity—despite her victimization at the hands of the enemy. The regenerative power of true love is what Pilar wishes for Maria, and what Hemingway provides for the reader. Although the earth moving has become a fetishistic image for that all-encompassing passion, *For Whom the Bell Tolls* insists that sexual intercourse epitomizes experience both compassionate and passionate. The novel concentrates on that narrative line, and by the final scenes, the reader cares very little for the blowing of the bridge—and the resulting deaths of Anselmo, the saint from Avila who has transcended gender in his peasant smock and charitable existence, or the men of El Sordo's band. Once again, narrative attention focuses almost entirely on the Maria-Jordan relationship; the battle becomes secondary, as Robert meditates: "He had never thought that you could know that there was a woman if there was battle; not that any part of you could know it, or respond to it; nor that if there was a woman that she should have breasts small, round and tight against you through a shirt; nor that they, the breasts, could know about the two of them in battle. But it was true and he thought, good. That's good. I would not have believed that" (456). The primary ending is Maria's leave-taking of Robert Jordan. She bears his spirit, his identity, his child; and in that union he maintains his existence. Yet the way Hemingway's narrative works is that Maria's last scene with Jordan serves the same purpose Catherine Barkley's death scene did: to make the reader care more about Frederic/Jordan.

It goes without saying that much of the language of sexual love, of courtship, of romance mimics the language of war. Perhaps that is one reason so much of Hemingway's ostensible "war" fiction can easily be read as fiction of desire, and his unpublished stories of World War II also continue the paradigm. Three stories housed at the University of Texas

Harry Ransom Humanities Research Center, "A Room on the Garden Side," "The Monument," and "Indian Country and the White Army," show again this pattern of male camaraderie given heart, and center, through its focus on sexual acquisition. A central narrative line in the "Garden" story concerns Red, one of the soldiers, who gets a letter every day from a girl he had met the night "we'd come into town. She was some sort of oriental dancer, Red said, and she had a very impressive torso and Red said she really loved him. But he had never been able to remember where he met her and had never found her again although Claude had looked for her very seriously for him. It was someplace on a big hill, Red said, but they couldn't find her" (9). The fantasy elements—exotic woman, beauty, dedicated love—are here set into a seriocomic frustration, as the men cannot find the woman. There is more fantasy as the stories continue, and soon only Onie and Red are left alive out of a force of some two thousand soldiers.

Perhaps the reader will not be surprised that much of the early 1950s correspondence between Hemingway (as self, not as character) and Adriana Ivancich also re-creates this paradigm. Hemingway, older than the beautiful Adriana by more than thirty years, writes his insistent letters for more than five years, loving her, pursuing her, inviting her to the States, and, obviously and chivalrously, idealizing her. These are fragments from the three letters he wrote between 10 April and 15 April of 1950: in the first, he addresses her as "Hemingstein" and notes that they are the same person, speaking "our own language." He refers to her as "Daughter," signs the letter "A. Ivancich" and makes two comments that mark the text as chivalric: "I missed you every minute of all the time since Havre and you can imagine what it was like to have the letters. How do you like it now, Gentlemen," and—about Patrick's coming wedding, "I am a sad son of a bitch if I will go to any weddings at which you are not present." This letter concludes, "I love you very much. . . . I will write you very much if you do not mind." The other two letters continue in this vein, and that of 15 April becomes a litany of expressions of love: "I do not, and cannot, ever love anyone as I love you . . . I love you however you are . . . you and I are very alike, however it is. . . . In these things we are alike. . . . We love our families and the Sea," and that letter concludes, "I love you so much" and is signed "Papa."

By 27 June 1950, after several letters that are signed "A. E. Hemingstein-

Ivancich," Hemingway in a sense apologizes for his intensity: he will always love her but he will not write it if she prefers. He then continues, "I get terrible lonely for you; sometimes so it is unbearable. . . . I work hard but after I work I am twice as lonely. On the sea I get so lonely for you that I cannot stand it." That restraint lasts less than two weeks, however, and by 8 July he is writing, "To hell with the rules: I love you very much and the longest period of epoca that I could ever give you up (renunciar) was one hour and a half." One surmises that Adriana has decided that less writing might do the trick, and by 30 August 1950, Hemingway writes a pleading letter, "If you could find any time to write it would be wonderful because I get so lonely I could die. (I mean this literally and exactly)."

The pathos that accrues from these letters, which Baker avoided including in the *Selected Letters,* is evidence of the human response to pain, and to the continued power of Hemingway's sexual text, writer as earnest and dedicated lover, crushed by the disdain of his "lady." In a more vicious model, in a manner the reader cannot pretend to sympathize with, Hemingway also structures *A Moveable Feast* to complete his erotic paradigm.[5] The opening scene of a montage that was to erase all old wounds and debts, or at least attempt to repay them, focused on the idealized male writer, young and hungry in Paris, drawing energy and vitality from his unsatisfied sexual desire as he studies an unknown beautiful woman in the cafe. "I looked at her and she disturbed me and made me very excited. I wished I could put her in the story, or anywhere" (5). The writer speaks silently to her, "I've seen you, beauty, and you belong to me now, whoever you are waiting for and if I never see you again, I thought. You belong to me and all Paris belongs to me and I belong to this notebook and this pencil" (6).

Forgotten once the "heat" of his writing takes over, however, the woman vanishes from the care and from the story—never named, never missed, but used as a sexual object, a "starter" for the really important work of the great male writer. *A Moveable Feast* is filled with such use of recognizable people, most of them Hemingway's "friends." Indeed, the entire structure is shaped to be the narrative of sexual encounter, so that the memoir closes, in effect, with the tawdry "A Matter of Measurements." This chapter effectively demolishes both F. Scott Fitzgerald (in that he has so little common sense, so little real masculine resourcefulness that he cannot battle Zelda; and, further, and perhaps worse, that Georges the bartender at the Ritz does not even remember him, even though he drank at the Ritz regularly) and Zelda, whose impropriety was that she challenged and criticized her husband rather than supporting and encouraging him. Assuming the moral stance of traditional romance, Hemingway levels these detractors from the ideal; without qualms, he destroys any deviants in his fictional realm. Zelda Fitzgerald would never have assumed the roles of a Catherine Barkley or a Maria (and as Hemingway was to learn, most of his wives would not assume those roles either). For that refusal, any deprecation was fair.

As a powerful and inventive male romance, Hemingway would—in fiction—end his narratives. He would kill off troublesome women, leave them pregnant, erase them to imaginary and idealized images, or label them deviant in ways that Otto Weininger or Havelock Ellis or Sigmund Freud would have understood. But troublesome wives, and troublesome readers, are less easily handled, although even the most cantankerous of the latter must give Hemingway—as inventive writer of erotica—his well-earned applause.

5

"I'd Rather Not Hear"

Women and Men in Conversation in "Cat in the Rain" and "The Sea Change"

Lisa Tyler

"Women have served all these centuries as looking-glasses possessing the magic and delicious power of reflecting the figure of man at twice its natural size," Virginia Woolf writes in *A Room of One's Own.* "That serves to explain in part the necessity that women so often are to men" (35). But how do men respond when women begin to resist serving as reflectors? How do men react when women tell the truth, and the figure in the looking-glass shrinks? As the male character in "The Sea Change" responds, "I'd rather not hear."

In both "Cat in the Rain" and "The Sea Change," Ernest Hemingway dramatizes the ways in which women reflect—or more accurately, resist reflecting—men. In each of these stories, the "girl" (and Hemingway uses the term advisedly) wants something different than her male companion wants, and in each case, the male character is disturbed by this jarring experience of difference.[1] These troubled couples engage in conversations that do not satisfy either participant. In part, their unhappiness indicates conflicting expectations about male/female relationships and especially the woman's role in a romantic relationship with a man.

Because the critics who have analyzed these stories have traditionally been writing from a male viewpoint, the critics often seem to side with the male character rather than recognizing the complicated gender dynamics at work in the stories. My essay is thus simultaneously an analysis of these fictional men and women in conversation and a meta-analysis of critics' responses to these conversations.[2] In it I draw on the object relations psychology of Nancy Chodorow and Jessica Benjamin, the linguistics research of Deborah Tannen, the cultural analysis of Adrienne Rich, and the feminist theory of Virginia Woolf's *A Room of One's Own*.

What the woman seeks in "Cat in the Rain" is recognition and attention; George is either unwilling or unable to provide them. She wants to change her hair to gain his attention, but he remarks blandly, "I like it the way it is" (*SS* 169). It's significant that the narrator had earlier described her hair as "clipped close like a boy's" and that she then goes on to say "I get so tired of looking like a boy" (169). Clearly, she wants to be recognized for herself, not as a mere reflection of her husband and his desires.[3] Wanting to change her hair and clothes surely reflects a wish to gain his attention; the candlelight dinner she describes, complete with silver, would very likely require the oblivious George to put down his book and sit face to face with her. It would thus presumably force him to pay her at least a little of the attention she craves. "Oh, shut up and get something to read," he says—as he himself reads. He wants her to reflect his behavior, as well as his appearance; he insists on her sameness, while she insists on her difference. His irritation is reminiscent of Henry Higgins's testy question in *My Fair Lady:* "Why can't a woman be more like a man?"

George is thus "a stereotypical male who sees little benefit in taking his wife seriously" (Prescott 154). George's reading, too, is stereotypically masculine: "Women's dissatisfaction with men's silence at home is captured in the stock cartoon setting of a breakfast table at which a husband and wife are sitting: He's reading a newspaper; she's glaring at the back of the newspaper" (81). For the woman, Tannen points out,

> Telling things is a way to show involvement, and listening is a way to show interest and caring. It is not an odd coincidence that she always thinks of things to tell him when he is reading. She feels the need for verbal interaction most keenly when he is (unaccountably, from her point of view) buried in the newspaper instead of talking to her. (81–82)

And George is consistently buried in his book, if not his newspaper, as Hemingway makes clear through repetition: "The husband went on reading" (167), "George was on the bed, reading" (169), "George was reading again" (169), "He was reading again" (170), and "George was not listening. He was reading his book" (170). When George takes a break, "putting the book down" for a moment, he is described as "resting his eyes"—which suggests he has closed his eyes. He only looks at his wife once—when he praises her boyish haircut (169).

When the maid asks her (in Italian), "Have you lost something, Signora?" the answer should be yes. Joseph DeFalco suggests that the Signora has lost her "intimacy with her husband" (160), but in her troubled relationship with her husband, Signora has also lost herself. She identifies with the kitty she sees in the rain presumably because like her, it feels abandoned and alone, its suffering unrecognized: "It isn't any fun to be a poor kitty out in the rain" (*SS* 169).

To be fair, it is possible that George is not as disengaged as he appears. Tannen points out that men tend to spend time working side by side with friends rather than gazing into their eyes; their idea of a good time together might be silently performing parallel activities. A direct look can seem too much like a challenge or a sexual advance, and conversation can seem too much like a game of one-upmanship. The fact that "He looked up from his book" in response to the knock on the door indicates that George is not completely oblivious, and that his silent reading may simply indicate that he is comfortable with his wife.

> For many men, the comfort of home means freedom from having to prove themselves and impress through verbal display. At last, they are in a situation where talk is not required. They are free to remain silent. But for women, home is a place for talk, with those they are closest to. For them, the comfort of home means the freedom to talk without worrying about how their talk will be judged. (Tannen 86)

The disjunction between what George wants and what "the American girl" wants may, therefore, be related to their socialized gender roles.

It is intriguing that so many male critics have maintained that this story is about the woman's desire to have a child.[4] There is no mention of a child or pregnancy in the story, and it is surely more plausible to see the cat as a symbol of the woman than as a symbol of an imaginary child. It's possible that the reading is biographical; Carlos Baker writes that "'Cat in the Rain' was derived from a rainy day spent with Hadley that February at the Hotel Splendide in Rapallo" (*Life* 133). In his notes, however, he admits, "Identification of EH and Hadley with the persons of the story is my surmise" (*Life* 580). Hemingway himself explicitly denied this identification in a letter to F. Scott Fitzgerald: "Cat in the Rain wasnt about Hadley" [*sic*] (*SL* 180). Michael Reynolds concedes, "when Hemingway wrote 'Cat in the Rain,' a story set in a Rapallo hotel about a dissatisfied American wife and her uninterested husband, *we wanted* it to be about that February in Rapallo when Hadley was pregnant with a child Ernest did not want" (my emphasis, Reynolds, *Paris Years* 113). Yet what David Lodge calls the "gynecological reading" persists (16; see also Barton). Men see the wife's desire for attention as a desire for a child, because they recognize (perhaps unconsciously) that George is both unwilling and unable to fulfill his wife's emotional needs. It is instructive to turn to object relations theory for an understanding of the dynamic at work here: "Men grow up rejecting their own needs for love, and therefore find it difficult and threatening to meet women's emotional needs. As a result, they collude in maintaining distance from women" (Chodorow 199). "Women try to fulfill their need to be loved" and "are encouraged both by men's difficulties with love and by their own relational history with their mothers to look elsewhere for love and emotional gratification" (Chodorow 199–200). A woman's first alternative is often to seek friendships with other women, although in this case, the isolation of the couple makes that choice impractical: "They were the only two Americans stopping at the hotel. They did not know any of the people they passed on the stairs on their way to and from their room" (*SS* 167). Her second alternative is to have a child of her own (Chodorow 200).

Thus many of the male critics (with the notable exceptions of Warren Bennett and Clarence Lindsay) implicitly assume George's inability to respond to his wife's need for attention and suggest that what she really needs is a child. Indeed, they seem to regard her need for attention with the same resentfulness George does. For example, the usually phlegmatic Carlos Baker complains of her "irrational yearnings" (*Artist* 136), while James Barbour and Clarence Lindsay both accuse her of "narcissism" (Barbour 102; Lindsay 23). Thomas Strychacz acknowledges that the problem is her "complete lack of emotional and physical contact from

George" but then later seems to suggest that the wife's desire for emotional and physical contact is unrealistic when he refers to her "romantic
fantasy of being treated like a princess" (78).

Women apparently read the story differently; one female critic points
out that the wife's needs "seem uncomplicated, even meager" (Prescott
154), and another, Linda W. Wagner (-Martin), writes of George's choice
against "giving his wife the love she so apparently needs" (123). It is hardly
coincidental that it is another female critic, Gertrude M. White, who,
while not disputing the traditional reading, contends of the sought-after
kitty: "It is the symbol not only of the child she wants but of the child
she is; the child in her which her husband refuses to indulge" (243).

The cat serves obviously in the story as symbol for the wife and her
feeling of being shut out of her husband's life—of being dripped on.[5]

> Juxtaposed to the image of the cat's coldness and isolation is
> the image of the husband, self-sufficient and comfortable on the
> bed. . . . The wife makes an appeal, a statement of the cat's (and her
> own) need for warmth. The husband only plays at responding to
> this appeal. The appeal is rejected and the wife is on her own. (Has-
> bany 235)

It is when she begins to look for the cat that she ceases to be "the American wife" or "the wife" and becomes "the American girl" or "the girl"—
ceases, that is, to be a possession and becomes a being in her own right
(albeit perhaps an immature one).[6] Her husband changes at this point
from "the husband" into "George"—the name giving him an identity and
a social legitimacy that are never granted to the female character.[7] The
ending thus becomes doubly ironic, for instead of bringing in the female
kitty that the Signora identifies with and seeks to aid, the maid hauls in
a "big" (and presumably male) "tortoise-shell cat"—one more false reflection of the woman for her to confront.[8]

"The Sea Change" is a story about the breakup of a couple when the
"girl" leaves the relationship for another woman. Baker writes that the
story "examines at its crux the problem of an otherwise satisfactory liaison" (*Artist* 139), but it's clear that the relationship is "otherwise satisfactory" only to Phil. Near the beginning of the story, the unnamed woman
tells Phil in exasperation, "You have it your own way," and he responds,

"I don't have it my own way. I wish to God I did." Her response is telling: "'You did for a long time,' the girl said" (*SS* 397). Clearly this couple has had an unequal relationship for a long time, at least from her vantage point.[9] The fact that she is dumping him, temporarily anyway, gives her the upper hand for a change—a change he clearly finds unpleasant.

She actuates his nightmare: "[M]en really fear . . . that women could be indifferent to them altogether, that men could be allowed sexual and emotional—therefore economic—access to women only on women's terms, otherwise being left on the periphery of the matrix" (Rich, "Compulsive Heterosexuality" 43). Phil is left on the periphery of the matrix in the course of "The Sea Change." What Judith Roof writes of another fictional character applies equally well to Phil: "The lesbians' independence and disregard for phallic power and efficacy threaten his own shaky identity grounded entirely in the powers of the penis" (108).

It's interesting that Warren Bennett, who sees the story's theme as "the relinquishment of masculine power," later describes its ending as "the death of the 'brown young man' who believes that he had *the* power and authority" (my emphasis, "That's Not Very Polite" 226, 240). It's as if Bennett, like Phil, envisions the relationship as a zero-sum game, in which only one partner can dominate, leaving the other to submit. Such a relationship indicates that Phil, as the dominant partner, has (like the wife in "Cat in the Rain") a longing for recognition, for attentive love, from the woman with whom he is in a relationship, but that dependency on her love becomes such a threat that he has chosen to subjugate her rather than recognize her in return (Benjamin 54, 220). It's not surprising that she turns the tables on him:

> The subjugated, whose acts and integrity are granted no recognition, may, even in the very act of emancipation, remain in love with the ideal of power that has been denied to them. Though they may reject the master's right to dominion over them, they nevertheless do not reject his personification of power. They simply reverse the terms and claim his rights as theirs. (Benjamin 220)

The couple's relationship is, to judge by their conversation, superficial. Phil focuses primarily on the woman's physical attributes, suggesting that what he will miss is her beauty. While she knows he is not sincere when he tells her, "Go on, then," she nevertheless chooses to ignore the under-tone and take his words at their surface value. Like the American in "Hills like White Elephants," she wants both to get her own way and to secure the forgiveness and approval of the lover she has hurt.[10] She leaves him briskly and apparently without regret: "She stood up and went out quickly. She did not look back at him" (*SS* 400).

Phil's reactions alternate between aggressive hostility and resentful self-pity, and his angle of vision changes accordingly. He looks at her and says, for example, "I'll kill her" (397). When she says, "Please don't," he looks down at her hands—apparently a sign of his intense resentment. When he confesses he does not really know what he will do, she ostensibly tries to comfort him by saying, "Poor old Phil" (398). He looks down at her hands again, and it is clear he does not care for what he perceives as her condescending tone. Tannen notes that men are particularly likely to interpret gestures of sympathy as "reminders of weakness" (28); the wom-an's gesture of putting her hand out to him adds insult to injury by (prob-ably inadvertently) framing him as a child in need of her protection (Tan-nen 35). He later looks at her once more when he resorts to aggression again, telling her sarcastically, "I'll understand all the time" (*SS* 398).

His aggressive behavior may be an attempt to re-establish their rela-tionship; Tannen notes that men are likely to use conflict to accomplish connection (150). Women, on the other hand, are taught to avoid direct confrontation and "make nice" (Tannen 158, 165). They sometimes "sacri-fice sincerity for harmony" (Tannen 158). Thus the woman repeatedly at-tempts to reassure him that she loves him, that he can trust her, that she will come back to him—all of which sound insincere, incongruous, and ironic, given that she is leaving him. She seems to want to preserve har-mony at the expense of directness—a preference that is emphasized when she primly tells him that asking her to prove her love "isn't polite" (*SS* 398), says the word "vice" is also "not very polite" (399), and admonishes, "There's no necessity to use a word like that" (400). Like many women (Tannen 231–34), she repeatedly apologizes, adding after "I'm sorry" the comment, "That's all I seem to say" (*SS* 398). Perhaps like many women in unequal relationships (Tannen 184–85), she finds it easier to leave him than to openly oppose his will. It's entirely possible that the liaison with another woman is a convenient fabrication to enable her to escape from what has become an untenable relationship with Phil.[11] It is, after all, the one unanswerable reason for breaking off the relationship. If she mentioned another man, Phil would fight him; if she broke it off without another partner in the offing, Phil presumably would either try to compel her to return to him or refuse to countenance her defection. A lesbian rival leaves him with no conventional, face-saving response.

Phil's final action is to gaze at his own reflection, which he does three times in the space of three paragraphs: "As he looked in the glass, he saw he was really quite a different-looking man. . . . The young man saw himself in the mirror behind the bar. 'I said I was a different man, James,' he said. Looking into the mirror he saw that this was quite true" (401). Why is Phil suddenly so obsessed with his appearance?

Phil and the woman look alike; both are brown, attractive, and young. The two were described as even more alike in an earlier draft (qtd. in Comley and Scholes 85–86). He has long assumed that her desires were identical to his, refusing to recognize her as having separate desires. It is important to remember that she tells him that he has had it his way for a long time. Apparently she has given way to his wishes whether she agreed or not. Now suddenly she has turned the tables on him: she desires something and is unwilling to recognize that what she wants is not the same as what he wants.

"The looking-glass vision is of supreme importance because it charges the vitality; it stimulates the nervous system. Take it away and man may die, like the drug fiend deprived of his cocaine," Virginia Woolf tells us, adding elsewhere, "That serves to explain in part the necessity that women so often are to men. . . . For if she begins to tell the truth, the figure in the looking-glass shrinks; his fitness for life is diminished" (*Room* 35). Phil sees himself as diminished because (as Woolf helps us understand) he no longer has a "girl" to reflect him back to himself at twice his natural size. It's no coincidence that Hemingway's narrator, who has referred to Phil as "the man" throughout the story, abruptly calls him a "young man" twice in the six paragraphs that follow the girl's departure. In putting her hand out to him twice, calling him "poor old Phil," and instructing him on what is and is not polite language, the woman treats him as a child, not a lover. In one fragment not included in the published story, Hemingway acknowledges this change: Phil asks to have what the "punks" drink (qtd. in Bennett, "That's Not Very Polite" 237); a "punk" is a "young inexperienced person" ("Punk"). When the woman leaves, she thus robs him of the chance to continue to see himself reflected in the eyes of a beautiful "girl" whose highest value seems to be politeness (e.g., "making nice" and not using words that people do not want to hear). He is left with the sorry substitute of a literal mirror, in which he looks like a very different (and ordinary) man indeed.

The point is made again in *The Garden of Eden,* when Catherine tells David,

"You can't fool a bar mirror."
"It's when I start looking quizzical in one that I know I've lost," David said.
"You never lose. How can you lose with two girls?" Catherine said. (*GOE* 103)

No wonder H. Alan Wycherley repeatedly calls Phil "a loser" (67): He no longer has any girls at all.

Phil's anguished reaction is—in the words of Virginia Woolf—"a protest against some infringement of his power to believe in himself" (35). His girlfriend's decision to leave him for another woman is important to him not because he loves her or because she has found herself, but for what it reveals to Phil about himself.

The insidious threat of the representation of lesbian sexuality in nineteenth- and twentieth-century literature is its disruptions of the symmetry of displaced identity, of the male projection of self-unity onto the woman. Predictably, the representation of lesbian sexuality by male authors during this period is more concerned with the male anxiety created by its disturbing presence. Rather than representing sexual encounters between women, male authors represent lesbian sexuality as a male reaction to it. (Roof 107)

Interestingly the word "punk" can also mean a passive homosexual or catamite, and Hemingway typically uses the word in stories with homosexual themes ("The Light of the World," for example, and "A Lack of Passion").[12] In the scene in the unpublished fragment in which he asks what the punks drink, Phil is associating himself with punks and therefore with homosexuals. Fully (if irrationally) convinced that his girlfriend is a reflection of himself, he comes to the disturbing realization that his heterosexuality is now in question. If his (human) reflection is homosexual, then he must inevitably be gay. He describes himself bitterly to the barman as "a recent convert" (qtd. in Bennett, "That's Not Very Polite" 237).

This reading raises a curious question: Why do so many critics of this story—including Paul Smith, Nancy R. Comley and Robert Scholes (88), H. Alan Wycherly (67), J. F. Kobler (321–22), and arguably Joseph DeFalco (177)—agree with Phil in supposing her lesbian desire implies his homosexuality? Kobler is perhaps the bluntest when he asserts of Phil, "There can be no question that he is moving toward a homosexual affair" (322). There's precious little evidence in the story itself to indicate such avid homosexuality on Phil's part; his comment about embracing vice might well mean that he is afraid he will take her back eventually, not that he is afraid he will himself become homosexual.[13]

Although there has been some speculation that the two men he joins at the bar are gay, there is no evidence of that—much less that they are male prostitutes, as Warren Bennett contends ("That's Not Very Polite" 241). On the contrary, when they hear Phil mention the word "perversion" in his quarrel with the woman, they react with predictable alarm, striking up an empty and nonsensical conversation with the barman specifically so that they will not have to overhear anything else Phil says. They really do not want to get involved: "The two at the bar looked over at the two at the table, then looked back at the barman again. Towards the barman was the comfortable direction" (399). Moreover, they react with homophobic discomfort to Phil's mention of vice, edging away and comically rationalizing their behavior as intended purely for his benefit rather than theirs: "The other two moved down a little more, so that he would be quite comfortable" (401).

When Phil tells the woman, "I understand," he suggests that he knows what it's like to desire a woman as she does. As Warren Bennett points out, Phil may also be acknowledging that he has participated in sexual acts that he feels link him to her lesbian lover—not that he necessarily knows what it's like to be homosexual. His own words suggest he does not know; when she says she "can't" come back to him, he insists she "won't" (*SS* 397). He believes that her lesbian desire is chosen, not innate.

Like Phil, however, several critics apparently accept without question the girlfriend's role as a reflection of Phil. If she is homosexual, he must be as well; if she gives in to "vice," so must he. Yet Adrienne Rich cautions us, "To equate lesbian existence with male homosexuality because each is

stigmatized is to erase female reality once again" ("Compulsive Heterosexuality" 52). Like Phil, the critics refuse to see the "girl" as the separate
human being she is.

Both of the "girls" in these stories attempt to assert their own identity
in opposition to their roles as mere reflections of the men they are with,
but they are not equally successful. The American wife in "Cat in the
Rain" never frees herself from her role as a reflector; her husband seems
incapable of recognizing her as a separate person in her own right. The
girl in "The Sea Change" manages to break away, thus forcing Phil to
recognize her emotional independence, but he remains mired in the ego-
centric (and chauvinist) impression that her unorthodox behavior says
more about him than it does about her.

Reading Hemingway's work through the lens of feminist theory and
criticism enhances our understanding and appreciation of these "marriage
stories," which have sometimes been unfairly dismissed as slight or as
weaker efforts. His dissections of the sexual politics of heterosexual relationships are dazzling in their precision and accuracy. They are in fact so
lifelike that his critics have all too often read them in ways that reveal the
fault lines in their own sexual politics.

6
To Have and Hold Not

Marie Morgan, Helen Gordon, and Dorothy Hollis

Kim Moreland

Ernest Hemingway's *To Have and Have Not* (1937) has received comparatively scant critical attention. The novel has been widely regarded as a failure from its time of publication. Those critics who have discussed it typically have seen it as a roman à clef and focused on identifying the historical counterparts for fictional characters,[1] or they have explored whether it is Hemingway's attempt at a proletarian novel designed to deflect criticism that he was out of touch with contemporary sociopolitical realities.[2] The most charitable critics have regarded it as a "transitional" text, bridging Hemingway's nonfiction of the 1930s with his monumental 1940 novel *For Whom the Bell Tolls*.[3]

Surprisingly, comparatively little criticism focuses on the narrative experimentation of *To Have and Have Not*, which includes varying points of view, notably frequent interior monologues that sometimes veer into a sort of stream of consciousness.[4] This narrative experimentation may represent a precursor to Robert Jordan's interiority. But another experimental aspect is still less remarked. In his brief discussions of *To Have and Have Not*, Mark Spilka acknowledges "Hemingway's first stylistic attempts to think his way into the minds and hearts of women" (*Quarrel* 245), and he describes the novel as "much more sympathetic to women than anything else Hemingway ever wrote" ("Dying" 216). As Lisa Tyler observes, "This novel presents an intriguing collection of female characters, about whom next to nothing has been said" (57).

To Have and Have Not includes three very different female charac-

ters—Marie Morgan, Helen Gordon, and Dorothy Hollis—who are
among the most sympathetically drawn and psychologically complex of
Hemingway's women. Not beautiful but one-dimensional ideals like Maria
or Countess Renata, nor compelling but repudiated bitch-goddesses like
Brett Ashley or Margot Macomber, these characters are simultaneously
psychologically rounded and sympathetic, simultaneously realistic and
compelling. Physically and socially diverse, each is revealed to have a rich
interior life that enables the reader to sympathize and identify with her.
And each is failed by her husband, whose ultimate absence occurs variously as a result of death, divorce, or disinterest. Each survives this devastating absence, though in different ways. Their strength in the face of
the absence of their men renders them yet more sympathetic and admirable—indeed, more even than the novel's hero, Harry Morgan, the character who has absorbed most of the critical attention.[5]

Appearing only briefly at the very end of Part One and not at all in
Part Two, Marie Morgan increasingly takes over the heretofore male narrative in Part Three (which comprises more than half the novel); its final
chapter, a powerful interior monologue exclusively from her perspective,
offers her the novel's final word.[6] Whereas Harry's centrality in Parts
One and Two effectively overwhelms all other characters (virtually all of
whom are male), in Part Three Marie becomes an important character in
her own right rather than a mere foil for Harry. The portrait of Marie is
constructed from multiple perspectives, like a cubist painting. Most powerful are her own interior monologues, but she appears also from the
third-person omniscient perspective and from the perspectives of Harry
and Richard Gordon, these multiple layers adding to the complexity of
her characterization.

Though Marie Morgan is the most significant of the female characters, Helen Gordon and Dorothy Hollis are also important. Both appear
only in Part Three, Helen several times and Dorothy only once. Helen is
presented exclusively from the outside, the omniscient narrator describing her appearance and recording her comments when she appears briefly
at the end of chapter 15, even more tangentially in chapter 19, and then
centrally in chapter 21, which is devoted exclusively to her bitter argument with her husband. Dorothy Hollis garners the least narrative attention, appearing only once, but her position as the last in the series of
portraits comprising chapter 24 intensifies her importance. The narrative

modulates from third-person omniscient to interior monologue, giving us extended if one-time access to Dorothy's thoughts.

Marie Morgan is in one sense the most unlikely of Hemingway heroines. Middle-aged, overweight, and badly dressed, her dyed blonde hair showing its dark roots, Marie is the lower-class wife of the smuggler Harry, a woman who worked as a prostitute before her marriage.

Helen Gordon is far more conventionally cast as a Hemingway heroine. "The prettiest stranger in Key West that winter" (138), Helen is the young and lovely wife of novelist Richard Gordon. Though not rich, the couple has sufficient income to stay at resorts in Switzerland, the French Riviera, and Key West, while Richard writes his novels.

Dorothy Hollis seems perfectly cast as the Hemingway bitch-goddess, given that she is the wife of a "highly paid Hollywood director" and the mistress of "a professional son-in-law of the very rich" (241). A woman of a certain age, she is still "extraordinarily pretty" (243), though she must take care to get enough sleep, always remembering "how terribly bad it is for the face to sleep . . . resting on the pillow" (246). Though Dorothy worries that she will "end up a bitch . . . [or] maybe [is] one now" (244), she is actually the third in Hemingway's unlikely triptych of heroines.

By contrast, the novel does include a bitch-goddess in the character of Hélène Bradley, who "collect[s] writers as well as their books" (150), engages in sexual activities with various men while her husband looks on voyeuristically, and slaps a man who is not "man of the world" enough to be able to perform sexually in this kinky scene (190).

Though all three women are married, their marriages, like their socioeconomic statuses, are significantly different. Spilka asserts that Marie and her husband enjoy "the only middle-aged love affair in [Hemingway's] fiction—perhaps in all modern American fiction" (*Quarrel* 243). Though neither Marie nor Harry evinces any moral squeamishness about her past (regarding it from a pragmatic economic point of view), they seem to have been sexually faithful to each other during their nineteen or so years together. Their sexual bond is strong and passionate, despite their obvious physical flaws, which include not only Harry's amputated arm but also Marie's recent hysterectomy, which is alluded to indirectly (103, 114). Each feels less than whole, and each reassures the other as to their continuing desirability. The love-making scene so prominent in Part Three is remarkable for its intensity and realism. Not Maria and Robert

Jordan feeling the earth move as they explore each other's beautiful young bodies in a sleeping bag during their brief time together, nor Renata and Colonel Cantwell engaging in forbidden and enigmatic sexual practices in a Venetian gondola, Marie and Harry lie together in their bedroom, reassuring each other, joking with each other, and deeply satisfying each other, while remaining aware of the need for quiet so as not to awaken their three daughters. This portrait of marital sex realistically represents the familiarity, intimacy, and passion experienced by long-married partners who love each other. While the sex act itself is narrated by unmediated dialogue between the two, afterward the focus shifts to Marie, whose interior monologue reveals her sense of satisfaction, sexual and otherwise, in her marriage with Harry. Indeed, her sexual desire, needs, and satisfaction are the focus of the entire episode, both the sex act itself and the aftermath.

Helen's marriage to Richard Gordon, on the other hand, is in the process of disintegrating. Because she is one of the "good little girls," Helen's sexual experience has been limited to her marriage (139). However, her husband neither remains faithful to her nor has the grace to be embarrassed by his indiscretions. At the mention of Helène Bradley, who interests Richard "both as a woman and as a social phenomenon," Helen pointedly asks, "Do people go to bed with a social phenomenon? . . . I mean is it part of the homework of a writer?" to which Richard pompously replies, "A writer has to know about everything. . . . He can't restrict his experience to conform to Bourgeois standards." He does not respond to Helen's dangerous question, "And what does a writer's wife do?" (140). Too self-involved to notice Helen's unhappiness, he also misses the emotional significance of her interest in her friend John MacWalsey. Though she ultimately allows MacWalsey to kiss her, she does so out of anger and frustration with her husband's behavior rather than passion for MacWalsey.

Richard Gordon's obtuseness is demonstrated most powerfully by his misreading of Marie Morgan, a stranger to him. When he passes her on the street, he is appalled by her appearance, thinking she looks like a "big ox" (176). His imagination stirred, he decides to include her in his novel, determining that "he had seen, in a flash of perception, the whole inner life of that type of woman." The "inner life" that he ascribes to Marie, knowing it to be "true," runs completely counter to the inner life revealed in her interior monologues as well as in her dialogues with Harry: "Her early indifference to her husband's caresses. . . . Her lack of sympathy with her husband's aims. Her sad attempts to simulate an interest in the sexual act that had become actually repugnant to her." Richard's failure of imagination leads him to assume that "her husband when he came home at night hated her, hated the way she had coarsened and grown heavy, was repelled by her bleached hair, her too big breasts" (177). Richard's inability to enter sympathetically into Marie's inner life bodes ill for his novel, with its trite characterizations, but it also bodes ill for his marriage.[7]

Dorothy and John Hollis seem to have reached a separate peace in their marriage, whether explicitly articulated or not. Dorothy is free to be Eddie's mistress, so long as she behaves with a modicum of discretion—for example, staying with her lover in Key West rather than Hollywood, and leaving her maid behind in California. In her long stream-of-consciousness passage, Dorothy reflects on her continuing affection for her husband as well as her affection for her lover, both "sweet" men who bear a striking resemblance to each other (242). Dorothy and John's understanding seems to be grounded in John's impotence—a result of his terminal alcoholism—and his earlier history of affairs, which Dorothy accepts more or less philosophically: "I suppose the good ones are made to have a lot of wives but it's awfully wearing trying to be a lot of wives yourself, and then some one simple takes him when he's tired of that. . . . There must be men who don't get tired of you or of it. There must be. But who has them? The ones we know are all brought up wrong" (245).

Of course, the man who does not "get tired of you or of it," the man who was not "brought up wrong" in the effete confines of middle- or upper-class America, is Harry Morgan. No wonder he is hailed by some critics as an archetypal Hemingway hero whose vital presence casts into the shadows the female characters. The oft-cited proletarian message of this novel is Harry's final pronouncement: "A man alone ain't got no bloody fucking chance" (225). This message strikes a false note, however, given the "frontier individualism" so central to Harry's characterization (Baker, *Writer* 211). "It would be better alone, anything is better alone," he thinks as he plans his final smuggling adventure (105). His sudden "some kind of epiphany" about human solidarity seems a strange, unearned response (Sylvester, "Sexual Impasse" 184). But what of the women, each of whom is left, after all, alone?

Harry's smuggling, by which he supplements his charter boat fishing business, inherently puts him at risk, but his final adventure carries a special danger, as Marie realizes despite the few details he shares. When he asks for his submachine gun, she begs, "Don't take that," asking, "You aren't going on that kind of a trip?" and then proclaiming, "Oh, God, I wish you didn't have to do these things" (127). She kisses him, to which he responds, "Leave me alone" (127), and she "h[o]ld[s] him tight against her," to which he responds, "Let me go" (128). As Harry departs, she weeps, begging him to be careful. Marie's unusual behavior signals her recognition that Harry may not return from this adventure, and her attempts to dissuade him—phrased as negated assertions or in the unarticulated language of the body—are feeble because she recognizes their futility. Perhaps, too, she knows her place in this marriage, knows not to object too strenuously once Harry, who advises Albert to "smack" his wife when she "talk[s]" back, has made up his mind (144).[8]

Like Marie, however, Harry has doubts about this smuggling operation. Smarter than the intermediary lawyer known as Bee-lips, he knows that the Cuban revolutionaries he smuggles into Cuba will try to kill him and all other witnesses; even if they fail to kill him, Harry will surely face legal questions and possible prosecution by American authorities if he returns. No wonder he stares at "the picture of Custer's Last Stand on the wall" (123). He briefly contemplates abandoning the operation: "I could stay right here and I'd be out of it" (147). But he decides to continue despite the unfortunate odds of four to one (briefly amended to four to two when Albert unwittingly accompanies Harry, only to be immediately killed), and his own physical disability. In an interior monologue, Harry persuades himself that he must undertake this foolhardy task because of his need to provide for Marie and his three daughters. But this motive does not quite hold water, given Harry's recognition that the operation will likely fail and he will be either killed or jailed. In such a case, Marie and the girls will clearly be worse off, their economic jeopardy yet more intense. Indeed, Harry's repeated thoughts and assertions that he must participate in order to save his home are undercut by his willingness to put up his house as security for a boat on which to undertake this ill-starred adventure.

Instead, his unrecognized motive is to reinforce his own sense of identity as a man: "What can a one-armed man work at? All I've got is my *cojones* to peddle" (147). His injury implies a metaphoric castration that calls into question his masculine identity, just as the lack of work in Depression-era America does for a whole generation of men. Though Harry represents his motive to himself as a selfless sacrifice designed to protect his family and home, his real motivation is to prove to himself that he is still a man: "'A man's still a man with one arm or with one of those.' . . . Then after a minute he says, 'I got those other two still'" (97). As such, the success or failure of the smuggling operation is irrelevant. Indeed, he seems not to expect to succeed, thinking "I'm doing better than I expected" (164) when he manages to push overboard a submachine gun belonging to one of the revolutionaries. It is his behavior during the adventure, not its conclusion, that is all-important. In order to encourage himself to begin firing upon the four revolutionaries, he rebukes himself, "Where're your balls now? Under my chin, I guess" (170). He proves that his balls are in the right place when he succeeds in killing all four revolutionaries single-handedly, even though he is mortally wounded—a failure of luck but not manhood.

As Harry lies dying on the boat, his thoughts revert to Marie:

> I wonder what Marie will do? . . . She'll get along, I guess. She's a smart woman. I guess we would all have gotten along. I guess it was nuts all right. I guess I bit off too much more than I could chew. I shouldn't have tried it. . . . I wish I could do something about Marie. . . . I wish I could let the old woman know what happened. I wonder what she'll do? I don't know. . . . I guess what a man like me ought to do is run something like a filling station. Hell, I couldn't run no filling station. Marie, she'll run something. She's too old to peddle her hips now. (174–75)

Though Harry at one level regrets his choice and its results, at another level he recognizes that his particular definition of manhood—"it was nuts allright"—renders any other choice impossible.

The final chapter of *To Have and Have Not* is composed almost exclusively of an interior monologue during which Marie revisits a powerful scene from early in her marriage. Her recollection of the first time she dyed her hair blonde evokes "the powerful bond between this pair, their sexual excitement over her transformation, her discovered beauty, which is still there for them when she is forty-five and he is forty-three, and which returns now at his death as a memory of appreciative love" (Spilka, "Dying" 220). While providing comfort, this memory also sharpens Marie's pain as she confronts the implications of Harry's death.

So emotionally devastated that she was unable to attend his funeral, Marie nonetheless knows that she must go on. Harry's dramatic action, undertaken superficially to protect Marie yet in actuality to protect his own sense of himself as a man, and undertaken despite Marie's attempt to dissuade him, will result for Marie in a life of economic deprivation and hard work and profound loneliness. Though he undertook the dangerous smuggling operation ostensibly to save their house, she knows that "first thing I've got to do is try to sell the house" (257). Though Harry was so "tired" at the end that "he never woke up even," the tired Marie envisions no possibility of rest or happiness as she looks twenty years into the future. She will persist, "big now and ugly and old and he ain't here to tell me that I ain't"—a noble if unglamorous portrait of stoic endurance. Unlike Harry's, her epiphany is earned: "Now I got to go on the rest of my life. . . . It ain't what happens to the one gets killed. I wouldn't mind if it was me got killed" (260). Marie knows that it is harder to live than to die heroically.

Helen's disintegrating marriage receives its final blow when her husband accuses her of having an affair with MacWalsey, slaps her, and calls her a bitch, then does so again after her warning that "if you call me that I'll leave you." Richard Gordon, proceeding on the assumption that the best defense is a good offense, makes his accusations after his wife challenges him about his affair with Helène Bradley: "You reek of that woman" (182). While Helen is right that Richard has just come from a sexual encounter with Helène, Richard is wrong about Helen, who did not kiss MacWalsey, admitting only to allowing him to kiss her, but also admitting that she "would have [kissed MacWalsey] if [she]'d known what [Richard] w[as] doing" (183). The similarity in the names "Helène" and "Helen" draws attention to the difference between these two women. While Helène never appears directly as a character, but only indirectly when other characters allude to her or recall her, Helen has a tour-de-force scene that is arguably the most powerful in the novel, one of only two episodes that Hemingway cites in defense of *To Have and Have Not* in a 1948 letter to Lillian Ross: "It has a nice part in it where the girl denounces the writer" (*SL* 649).

The "girl" is not the "bitch" that Richard calls her in an identification that dooms their teetering marriage, but neither is she a one-dimensional idealized woman. Having unknowingly edged out the middle-aged "famous beautiful Mrs. Bradley" (139) as the most beautiful woman in Key West, Helen rejects a competition with her as the novel's bitch-goddess: "I'm not a bitch. I've tried to be a good wife" (183). But her harsh and merciless attack on Richard reveals her depths of anger and pain, a psychological complexity that is articulated rather than merely asserted:

> Love was the greatest thing, wasn't it? Love was what we had that no one else had or could ever have? . . . Love is just another dirty lie. Love is ergoapiol pills to make me come around because you were afraid to have a baby. Love is quinine and quinine and quinine until I'm deaf with it. Love is that dirty aborting horror that you took me to. Love is my insides all messed up. It's half catheters and half whirling douches. I know about love. Love always hangs up behind the bathroom door. It smells like lysol. . . . Love is all the dirty little tricks you taught me that you probably got out of some book. All right. I'm through with you and I'm through with love. Your kind of picknose love. You writer. (185–86)

Helen's bitter words reveal a woman he has never known, never tried to know, never wanted to know. In sorrow at the failure of their marriage, she expresses her regret, "If I hadn't of said some of that, or if you hadn't hit me, maybe we could have fixed it up again," but he rejects her appeal: "No, it was over before that" (191).

Richard's hard-boiled response to the end of their marriage, "You're not such a star [in bed]," is belied by his self-pitying late-night tour of Key West's bars (191). Despite Helen's final plea, "Oh, don't go out," he responds, "I've got to"—an exchange that parallels Marie and Harry's (192). And like Marie, Helen is left at home alone.

Ironically, Richard ends up in the same bar as MacWalsey. The two men talk, engage in a pathetic fist-fight that Richard inevitably loses, and then share a cab ride during which MacWalsey attempts to take care of his "brother" (221). MacWalsey's romantic and pugilistic victories over Richard are problematic, not least of all because the outcome of his relationship with Helen is unpredictable. He has asked her to marry him, and she may say yes. He has already failed one wife, and he hopes to be a better husband to a second. Yet this marriage too would seem to be doomed, not only because of her acknowledged lack of love for MacWalsey, but because of his alcoholism. He knows that "it all may turn out badly" (222). Should Helen marry MacWalsey, she will likely still end up alone. Her marriage to Richard is ended by infidelity and inattentiveness; a practical marriage with the good-hearted but alcoholic MacWalsey would likely place her eventually in the situation of Dorothy Hollis.

Like Helen, Dorothy rejects the label of "bitch." She worries about its potential accuracy, however, not wanting to become another version of Helène Bradley. Most critics indeed identify her as such, manifesting remarkably little sympathy for her lonely plight.[9] Yet Dorothy is painfully alone, without Marie's comforting memories of her marriage and without Helen's comforting hope that a different marriage will fix her problem: "I wonder how Eddie would be if we were married. He would be running around with someone younger I suppose" (244). Dorothy would like to remain faithful to one man, but neither her husband nor her lover has remained faithful to her, teaching her that men want what no woman can be:

> I suppose they can't help the way they're built any more than we can. I just want a lot of it and I feel so fine, and being some one else or some one new doesn't really mean a thing. It's just it itself, and you would love them always if they gave it to you. The same one I mean. But they aren't built that way. They want some one new, or some one younger, or some one that they shouldn't have, or some one that looks like some one else. Or if you're dark they want a blonde. Or if you're blonde they go for a redhead. Or if you're a redhead then it's something else. A Jewish girl . . . [or] Chinese or Lesbians or goodness knows what. . . . The better you treat a man and the more you show him you love him the quicker he gets tired of you. (244–45)

The alcoholic Eddie having again passed out, Dorothy's response to her sexual frustration is to masturbate, though "she would obviously prefer intercourse—both conversational and sexual—with him" (Tyler 58): "I didn't want to, but I am, now I am really, he *is* sweet, no he's not, he's not even here, I'm here, I'm always here and I'm the one that cannot go away, no, never. You sweet one. . . . And you're me. So that's it. So that's the way it is" (246). Dorothy's masturbation is evidence for many critics of sexual deviance, an overwrought critical response that denies Dorothy's right to sexuality.[10] Were she to take many casual lovers, she would become Helène Bradley, an identity that she rejects. She would most like a faithful marriage with a sexually active man—a marriage like that of Marie and Harry Morgan, in effect. But Marie, too, is left alone, with no prospects of marriage to another, and no desire "to hire a man to do it" (260). Given Marie's own intensely sexual nature, it is reasonable to expect that her reaction to her lonely fate will be, like Dorothy's, to masturbate: "There ain't nothing now but take it every day the way it comes. . . . But Jesus Christ, what do you do at nights is what I want to know" (261). The unlikely Hemingway heroine and the seeming bitch-goddess thus come to the same end—an end to which the youthful Helen may also come, if she marries the alcoholic MacWalsey and it "turn[s] out badly too" (222).

Each of these three female characters is last pictured alone. In each case, their men have left them, whether through death, incipient divorce, or disinterest. Like Marie, they all know that "good men are scarce" (261). And each responds to her loneliness in a psychologically complex way that subverts the easy binary opposition between flat ideal and bitch-goddess. Superficially dissimilar, these women share a common fate that is identifiably female and that Hemingway presents in a complex and sympathetic fashion that also calls into question the actions of his male characters.

To Have and Have Not is in this regard certainly unusual in the Hemingway canon, where women are more typically presented superficially —that is, without interiority (with the final exception of the female protagonists of the unpublished *Garden of Eden* manuscript) and as representative of either a positive or negative type. Perhaps the complicated events of Hemingway's life during the period of the novel's composition influenced his more complex and sympathetic characterizations. His marriage to Pauline Pfeiffer had reached the breaking point, not least because of his public infatuation with the beautiful Jane Mason, but ultimately because of his new fascination with Martha Gellhorn, soon to be his third wife. While excoriating the now-rejected Jane Mason by portraying her as Helène Bradley, thereby displacing his own guilt onto another in a psychological maneuver characteristic of Hemingway, he also expressed his guilt about leaving Pauline by his sympathetic portraits of Marie, Helen, and Dorothy. Marie is the long-time wife who dyes her hair blonde to please her husband (as Pauline did for Hemingway); Helen is the wife betrayed by her husband's primary commitment to his writing (a commitment whose personal costs to Hemingway are explored brilliantly by Burwell in *Hemingway: The Postwar Years and the Posthumous Novels*) and his involvement with another woman; Dorothy is the wife who experiences the ways that alcoholism inhibits emotional and sexual intimacy, and who accepts that "the good ones are made to have a lot of wives" (245). And each of the husbands leaves—regretful, perhaps, but nonetheless gone. *To Have and Have Not* is Hemingway's apologetic valedictory to Pauline Pfeiffer (functioning as does *A Moveable Feast* with regard to Hadley Richardson), wherein he simultaneously expresses, disguises, and expiates his guilt at once again breaking his marriage vows, at having and holding not.

7

Revisiting the Code

Female Foundations and "The Undiscovered Country" in *For Whom the Bell Tolls*

Gail D. Sinclair

The blurring of gender distinctions and androgynous emphasis is central to current Hemingway scholarship and has been since *The Garden of Eden*'s 1986 posthumous publication. This novel's release shed light on the canon's previously unfamiliar or unnoticed thematic terrain and created repercussions dramatically altering critical response to the earlier works. On their surface, texts such as *For Whom the Bell Tolls* had established Hemingway's manly hero and offered versions of his standard female types: the submissive dream girl or the castrating (though sometimes maternal) bitch. But far more complicated views were also working here. As Mike Reynolds suggests, "Any novel that has an androgynous older woman, a rape-scarred younger woman, and an odd assortment of men working out male-identity problems ought to provoke something more than a knee-jerk response from those interested in gender studies" (14). While his quick categorizing seems to pigeon-hole a bit too, Reynolds's central emphasis is clear. *For Whom the Bell Tolls* offers a rich field of revisionist study, and the novel's two women are far more complex figures than many formulaic earlier responses have allowed.

Initial reaction to both Maria and Pilar as categorically Hemingway-esque female portraits is understandable. The stereotypic images seem so blatant that even as a prefeminist teenager reading *For Whom the Bell Tolls* for the first time, I was disturbed by Maria's seeming dissolution into Robert Jordan, by her soap opera–like dialogue: "I die each time. Do you not die? . . . And then the earth moved. The earth never moved before? . . . But we have had it now at least. . . . And do you like me too? Do I please thee?" (160). In direct contrast, Pilar was singularly unattractive for her crudity and coarsely unfeminine demeanor. I found both women unpalatable for polemic reasons and instead focused attention on Robert Jordan's plight and his development toward the code hero image. Twenty-five years later, however, I find these two women enormously fascinating for the interpretive depth they offer. Maria and Pilar have been largely undervalued, each in different respects, but Hemingway's iceberg principle applies to them as profoundly as it does to any other character or novel in the canon. Further, "The Undiscovered Country," as one of the considered titles of *For Whom the Bell Tolls*, offers fuller analytic implications than he might have intended, but that we surely cannot dismiss.[1]

Stereotyped assessments of Maria and Pilar are clearly reductive for both women, though the latter suffers less critically. Pilar escapes denigration borne by females such as *The Sun Also Rises*'s Brett Ashley, whose public self-assurance and sexual aggressiveness foster misogynist hostilities. Pilar's character does not invite such negative backlash perhaps because of her more advanced age, lack of attractiveness, and maternal qualities. Though according to her own revelations she is highly sexed, Pilar largely escapes being labeled as sexually dangerous. She usurps Pablo's manhood by wresting command of the gypsy band, but we fault the war and his own actions for making him "a ruin." Pilar shares Pablo's depression without his defeat and remarks, "All my life I have had this sadness at intervals. . . . But it is not like the sadness of Pablo. It does not affect my resolve" (90). With Pilar, we emphasize desirable maternal strength, not emasculating force.[2] Robert observes, "Look at her walking along with those two kids. She is like a mountain and the boy and the girl are like young trees" (136). Pilar stands in the difficult middle ground occupied by the very few Hemingway women. She possesses an ultimately complementary character, at once thoroughly gentle and maternal, and constrastingly dominant and powerful though not necessarily threatening to the men with whom she associates.

Maria, on the other hand, does suffer the traditional criticism. She is generally lumped with the other Hemingway fictional women into the two disparate but equally maligned categories. The list of critics following this approach is a long one, but Roger Whitlow's *Cassandra's Daughters:*

The Women in Hemingway provides a representative summary of the general tone. To wit, Philip Young describes the women as "either vicious, destructive wives like Macomber's, or daydreams like Catherine, Maria, and Renata (*Hemingway* 81)." "Hemingway's women either caress or castrate," says Arthur Waldhorn (123). John Killinger simplifies them as "the good and the bad, according to the extent to which they complicate a man's life" (89).[3] I would add to this list Leo Gurko's specific reference to Maria as Hemingway's "undeveloped, blank, embryonic" female whose idealized selflessness fulfills male sexual fantasy (118). Further, Colin Cass believes, "We identify her femininity with helplessness. . . . She is a passive victim of the war, in contrast to Jordan" (231–32). And male critics are not alone in their pejorative assessment. Certain feminists like Judith Fetterley and Millicent Bell tend to read all seemingly passive Hemingway females as negative. Specific to Maria, Pamella Farley calls her "submissive and flat" and Sharon Dean labels her as "lost" (qtd. in Whitlow 11–12).

One does find it easy to view Maria as Hemingway's typically submissive female if only looking at the exposed tip of the iceberg. She willingly becomes a sexual partner to the American bridge-blower, Robert Jordan, only a few hours after his arrival, and her dialogue throughout much of the novel is similar to that of Catherine Barkley's, the also idealized and sexually willing female from *A Farewell to Arms*.[4] Both women speak of themselves as nonexistent without the man's completion. Catherine says to her lover, Frederic Henry, "There isn't any me. I'm you" (115). Maria says of herself, "There isn't any me. I am only with him" (450). We develop the impression that Hemingway was writing with a rubber stamp, and critics' past responses suggest they were often doing the same.

One scholar steps too far in the other direction, however, in crediting Maria with strength. In "The Other War in *For Whom the Bell Tolls*: Maria and Miltonic Gender Battles," Wolfgang E. H. Rudat offers a misogynist reading and places her in the camp of Hemingway "bitches" viewed as dangerously aggressive. He states, "In the battle of the sexes Maria is going for the jugular vein" (9) and further believes that "Hemingway is also endowing Maria with a slightly satanic touch" ("Other War" 17). There is clearly no textual evidence to promote such a reading, and Rudat backtracks, saying he is not implying Maria is "evil or destructive." Instead, he wants to present her as an instrument for good, because she "helps Jordan change from a sexually selfish male-chauvinist . . . into a considerate human being" (17). Rudat makes the distinction that she is not a *femme fatale,* but a *femme savante* having been trained by Pilar, the "Pillar, of Knowledge for Maria" (17–18). His interpretation, though he tries to soften it, has instead merely shifted her from one standard polarity to its opposition without any validity. He presents Maria's autonomy as essentially adverse, only finding value in her as a catalyst for Robert Jordan's emotional growth.

In the past decade or so, however, a few scholars have made inroads toward rescuing Hemingway's previously maligned or shallowly viewed fictional women from circumscribed positions. Specifically, Linda Patterson Miller effectively argues Brett Ashley's strengths in *The Sun Also Rises,* and Sandra Whipple Spanier cogently presents Catherine Barkley as the real code hero in *A Farewell to Arms.*[5] The females in *For Whom the Bell Tolls* are largely missing from this list, however. In particular, critical attention to Maria's character is sparse though she deserves the same kind of intensive revision given to Brett and Catherine, among others. To a lesser degree, views of Pilar also need expansion from a mainly positive, but nonetheless limiting position, to a more fully realized assessment.

The two women of *For Whom the Bell Tolls* represent endurance. Hemingway writes of Pilar: "The woman of Pablo could feel her rage changing to sorrow and to a feeling of the thwarting of all hope and promise. She knew this feeling from when she was a girl and she knew the thing that caused it all through her life. It came now suddenly and she put it away from her and would not let it touch her" (58). Pilar later reiterates that same toughness, confirming that "neither bull force nor bull courage lasted, she knew now, and what did last? I last, she thought. Yes, I have lasted" (190). Maria also lasts and downplays her own trauma to show generosity for another. She allays Joaquín's concern that he has refreshed her pained memory when she responds, "Mine are such a big bucket that yours falling in will never fill it. I am sorry Joaquín, and I hope thy sister is well" (139). Maria is able to bear her own pain as well as ease and comfort what Joaquín suffers. Both Maria and Pilar exhibit a stoic courage we might hold up to that of the young male Hemingway protagonists— Robert Jordan, Jake Barnes, Frederic Henry. The women exhibit greater inner fortitude while participating in the same essentially male-dominated world waged in brutal war and rugged survival.

In a very real sense we might view Maria and Pilar, if not independently, then collectively, as bearers of the Hemingway code.[6] Sandra Spanier argues for Catherine Barkley's role as code hero in *A Farewell to Arms,* and her contention could be applied to the women of *For Whom the Bell Tolls* as well. Maria and Pilar offer models for living simply within the confines of one's circumstances, but acting courageously under those constraints. They ultimately survive a nomadic existence in a war-ravaged world that has broken many men. Pilar's determination to endure extends beyond herself to the guerilla band she mothers, and most especially to Maria, whom she literally saves from certain death. The gypsy Rafael relays circumstances of the harrowing escape from the train explosion, Maria's traumatized state, and Pilar's role in rescuing the girl. He says:

> We would have left her after the train. Certainly it was not worth being delayed by something so sad and ugly and apparently worthless. But the old woman tied a rope to her and when the girl thought she could not go further, the old woman beat her with the end of the rope to make her go. Then when she could not really go further, the old woman carried her over her shoulder. When the old woman could not carry her, I carried her. We were going up that hill breast high in the gorse and heather. And when I could no longer carry her, Pablo carried her. But what the old woman had to say to us to make us do it! (28)

Pilar's place in saving Maria, and Maria's recovery from such severe trauma make both women worthy heroic paradigms, the older one for the power of her resolve and the younger for coming back from the brink of psychological dissolution to a place of sanity for herself. Both, in the style of the code hero, also later provide a means of strength for others beyond themselves.

Maria especially bears connection to other of Hemingway's walking wounded through her own initiated position into the postwar wasteland. Like Brett Ashley and Catherine Barkley, she enters the novel having lost loved ones because of war. Unlike these two women, Maria experiences violence firsthand when she is audience to her parents' murders immediately followed by her own brutal degradation and rape at the fascists' hands. During this act they cut Maria's ear, and she describes seeing blood coming from the small wound. Generally this slight blood-letting would be a rather insignificant detail considering the far more horrific acts she goes on to disclose. However, Maria bears a small scar that she points out to Robert. As she relays the story of her brutalization, Maria says:

> At that time I wore my hair in two braids and as I watched in the mirror one of them lifted one of the braids and pulled on it so it hurt me suddenly through my grief and then cut it off close to my head with a razor. And I saw myself with one braid and a slash where the other had been. Then he cut off the other braid but without pulling on it and the razor made a small cut on my ear and I saw blood coming from it. (351–52).

Added to the sign of blood that can relate to both the traditional show of loss of virginity and blood from castration, this visible mark signals Maria as a brutally initiated member of the sexual world. Her violators retort, "This is how we make Red nuns. This will show thee how to unite with thy proletarian brothers. Bride of the Red Christ!" (352). The wound on Maria's ear now represents the more serious and intimate genital scaring produced by violation as well as the visible sign of emotional injury, which the experience initiates.

The resultant wounds created by Maria's trauma pair her with Hemingway's male heroes such as Jake Barnes and Frederic Henry who also bear physical reminders of their war injuries. Significantly, Maria is the only Hemingway female with such distinction. Debra A. Moddelmog notes this exception but feels, "Maria's physical scars are either too small to notice or hidden from view. Her body and skin are smooth; she has a perfect figure and no disabling or distracting disfigurements" (*Reading Desire* 129). While this is generally true, I would argue that neither Jake nor Frederic's wounds are publicly visible either, but that does not lessen the degree to which these men suffer.[7] Maria's scars, like theirs, validate her initiated state, and she too exists in the nightmarish, existential world in which Jake and Frederic must learn to live.

Maria must also learn to live in that same world. The outward scars she shares with male protagonists are significant beyond representing tangible signs of membership in Hemingway's fraternity of wounded.

They are more importantly a symbolic manifestation of psychologic effects she must overcome. To a certain degree Maria initially bears at least more emotional vulnerability than the war-wounded men, because she lives with memories not only of her own torture, but also of violence to others she loves. While Jake and Frederic ostensibly suffer immediate personal pain directly correlated to the war, Maria's own is multiplied by seeing her parents killed before her eyes and knowing that lifelong girl-friends are about to receive the same savage and humiliating treatment she has just endured, and by the knowledge that she will suffer most by living. She relates:

> My father was the mayor of the village and an honorable man. My mother was an honorable woman and a good Catholic and they shot her with my father because of the politics of my father who was a Republican. I saw both of them shot and my father said, "*Viva la República*," when they shot him standing against the wall of the slaughterhouse of our village.
>
> My mother standing against the same wall said, "Viva my husband who was the Mayor of this village," and I hoped they would shoot me too and I was going to say "*Viva la República y vivan mis padres*," but instead there was no shooting but instead the doing of the things. (350)

By the end of the novel she also experiences as Brett, Catherine, and Frederic do the death of their lovers. In a sense, Maria is an amalgamation of all the worst kinds of suffering in Hemingway. She sustains a physical wound like most of the male heroes, shares with many of the women the death of a lover, and carries the psychological damage with which all Hemingway characters live.

Maria achieves some measured triumph over hellish circumstances, however, by not remaining the emotional "ruin" she was initially. She has certainly not gained this ascendancy in isolation, though, and Pilar must be given proportional credit for that victory. Her role as mentor is important to Maria's ultimate success and later extends to Robert Jordan through Pilar's own accord and vicariously through her young protégé. Beyond physically rescuing Maria, Pilar has nursed her back from emotional collapse. By the time Robert Jordan appears on the scene some three months after the train explosion, Maria seems stable and even resilient. Robert observes, "Maria was sound enough now. She seemed so anyway. But he was no psychiatrist, Pilar was the psychiatrist" (137). Maria is now able to joke about being rescued, and she teases Joaquín, the young man who helped carry her after the train explosion. She chides him for perhaps enjoying her belly on his shoulder and her legs down his back. When Pilar chastises her for not being grateful enough Maria responds, "Allow us to joke. I do not have to cry, do I, because he carried me?" (133). Watching this scene, Robert describes Juaquín and Maria looking "as fresh and clean and new and untouched as though they had never heard of misfortune," and Pilar is "like a mountain" of strength between them (136).

Pilar is further instrumental in Maria's emotional recovery through concrete means that help explain the young woman's sexual readiness with Robert Jordan. Maria's flirtatious nature seems quite surprising here, given the short distance from such a debilitating history; and as readers we are hard pressed finding logical explanation for her eagerness to become a stranger's lover, even if he is handsome and working on their side to defeat her heinous attackers.[8] Partly because of this scene traditional assessment labels Maria one of Hemingway's vapid dream girls whose self-will is dissolved in order to provide male gratification. Such a reading is a misinterpretation, however, because to a large extent Maria controls the encounter rather than submits to it. She speaks to Robert first, and in terms of body language even exhibits confidence and invitation when she "looked at him and laughed, then slapped him on the knee" (24). Maria further exercises her position of authority by asking Robert not to stare at her shorn hair, an immediately visible sign of her previous trauma.[9] She then sits directly opposite him with hands folded on her knees, and through the rest of the meal smiles and watches him. Her demeanor does not present an emotionally broken and withdrawn victim, but instead a coquettish air suggesting comfortable familiarity. It is Robert who is more ill at ease, more incapacitated with the swelling of his throat that inhibits his speech. Maria blushes, perhaps recognizing what several critics have called Hemingway's self-censored substitution of body parts to represent male arousal, and she tells him not to make her blush again. In this playful exchange, Maria establishes a mutual physical attraction setting the stage for an emotionally healthy gesture Pilar has encouraged her to initiate.

The scene immediately prior to Robert and Maria's first sexual encounter, and a few hours after their first meeting, seems to offer her as a rag doll, or more fittingly as Robert's docile pet. Hemingway writes, "The girl came over and Robert Jordan reached his hand out and patted her head. She stroked under his hand like a kitten" (68). The next two lines shift the focus, however, and possibly shed light on Maria's actions. She appears as though she will cry, but draws herself up emotionally, looks at Robert, and smiles. Her actions are almost coquettish here, an unspoken invitation. Maria does have a purpose, though, and a psychologically wholesome one. Pilar has counseled Maria "that nothing is done to oneself that one does not accept and that if I loved some one it would take it all away" (73). Maria makes a conscious decision, encouraged by Pilar's advice, to give herself sexually to erase choice having been so brutally seized from her before. She is not a submissive woman whose will is nonexistent or twined around a man's, but instead acts positively to assert her own force and to free herself from others' intrusion upon her. I certainly would not argue that Maria is sexually aggressive or dominates her first experience with Robert, but she does initiate the action by going to his sleeping bag on that first night. She hesitates before getting in at his request, but Maria ultimately makes the decision for consummation and says, "And now let us do quickly what it is we do so that the other is all gone" (73). She answers a fierce "Yes, yes, yes" to Robert's verbally truncated question, "You want?"

The second sexual experience, the first *la gloria* scene in the high mountain heather, is also at Maria's initiation and furthers her healing process and Robert's development toward emotional maturity. Again, Pilar is partially instrumental in staging this encounter, both through sexual instruction she offers Maria, and by providing a chance for intimacy after leaving them alone in the mountain heather. In what is likely a pre-arrangement between the two women, Pilar takes her leave from the young lovers even though Robert tries to resist and encourage all three to continue toward camp together. The ensuing conversation makes Maria's determination clear:

> "Wait," Robert Jordan called to her. "It is better that we should all go together."
> Maria sat there and said nothing.

> Pilar did not turn.
> "*Qué va,* go together," she said. "I will see thee at camp."
> Robert Jordan stood there.
> "Is she all right?" he asked Maria. "She looked ill before."
> "Let her go," Maria said, her head still down.
> "I think I should go with her."
> "Let her go," said Maria. "Let her go!" (157)

She refuses to follow Pilar down the mountain nor to let Robert persuade them both to do so, and Maria's desire wins over his concern. She becomes an autonomous partner with Robert, sharing in the right to decision-making. This mutual position of power enhances the lovemaking that follows, and they enter the realm of the mystical when each experiences the earth move beneath them. From that point onward Maria's self-determination is unshakable.

Maria has moved from victimization three months earlier, to a seizing of her will and her sexuality. She is still apprentice to Pilar's more solidified autonomy, but she is gaining ground, and Maria has already demonstrated her innate strength when she has the power to exercise it. During her rape, in which she alludes there were multiple perpetrators, Maria stresses, "Never did I submit to any one. Always I fought and always it took two of them or more to do me the harm. One would sit on my head and hold me. I tell thee this for thy pride" (350). She offers this information to Robert as testament to her will. Maria is a source of power, and not by emasculating the male, but by gaining ascendancy in her milieu.

Still further, in an emotional sense she will become a mentor for Robert. Maria inspires strength in Jordan, helping him draw courage to face his imminent death. As he muses about the possibility, Jordan surmises that one's own danger could be ignored for "he himself was nothing, and he knew death was nothing. He knew that truly, as truly as he knew anything. In the last few days he learned that he himself, with another person, could be everything" (393). Completion is achieved only through joining with another, but that was a rare exception, which he and Maria had achieved in the compressed space of three days. Robert confesses to himself that "Maria has been good. Has she not? Oh, has she not, he thought. Maybe that is what I am to get now from life. Maybe that is my life and instead of it being threescore years and ten it is forty-eight hours" (166)

Even Robert's death could not rob him, because he has gained an ascendancy through his varying relationships with Maria and Pilar. *La gloria* represents a mystic other-worldly union with a lover by offering a symbolic "alliance against death" (264), and through this sexual union and emotional bond Maria has helped Robert feel that same transcendental quality's ability to overcome actual annihilation. Robert and Maria's last conversation is certainly romanticized and partly affected to give her courage, but in doing so she vicariously returns the same to him. He wills himself into her by saying, "The me in thee. . . . There is no good-by, *guapa*, because we are not apart" (464). When left alone in his final moments Robert's words to Maria offer him hope as well. He assures himself with, "Try to believe what you told her. That is the best. And who says it is not true? Not you. You don't say it, any more than you would say the thing did not happen that happened. Stay with what you believe now. Don't get cynical" (466). Jordan finds a calmness that has much to do with having lived and loved fully in the last three days. At the novel's end, he achieves the "masculine maturity" (Boker 85) that all code heroes come to, and his mentors, beyond a brief remembrance of his grandfather's heroics, have been predominantly Maria and Pilar.

Pilar mentors the lovers' relationship because she knows its restorative value for Maria and its saving grace compensating for Robert's shortened life. Struggling with the two women's roles in the last few days, Robert muses to himself:

> It hit you then and you know it and so why lie about it? You went all strange every time you looked at her and every time she looked at you. So why don't you admit it. All right, I'll admit it. And as for Pilar pushing her onto you. All Pilar did was be an intelligent woman. She had taken good care of the girl and she saw what was coming the minute the girl came back into the cave with the cooking dish.
>
> So she made things easier. She made things easier so that there was last night and this afternoon. She is a damned sight more civilized than you are and she knows what time is all about. (167–68)

Robert understands Pilar's beneficial role in his own development and notes to himself, "When you get through with the war you might take up the study of women, he said to himself. You could start with Pilar" (176).

Finally, during his last hours to fortify himself with courage under fire Jordan reminds himself, "I'll bet that Goddamn woman up above isn't shaking. That Pilar" (437). Jordan owes much of his final courage to Pilar, and through her from Maria much of his emotional growth. Maria has become "all of life and it was being taken from him. He held her feeling she was all of life there was and it was true" (264). Both women contribute significantly to Jordan's achieved heroic status by novel's end.

The possibility of female code heroes is a rather radical departure from the standard bullfighter, boxer, hunter models previously embraced in traditional criticism. But more current analysis of the Hemingway canon and contributing biographical factors has allowed for this shift. Androgynous qualities in Hemingway's characters, though clearly relevant to *The Garden of Eden* and other seemingly less typical works, is perhaps even more elucidating when investigating bedrock texts that have made the code hero legendary. Assessing Maria and Pilar from a revisionist perspective inevitably moves us into areas of new scholarship where gender is not so oppositional or limiting, and even works to align these women with male counterparts in the code paradigm. Since the 1980s critics have been posing arguments concerning ambiguous gender lines in Hemingway texts. Posthumous publication of *The Garden of Eden* spawned Mark Spilka's *Hemingway's Quarrel with Androgyny* and countless revisionist articles thereafter. More recently, Nancy R. Comley and Robert Scholes published *Hemingway's Genders: Rereading the Hemingway Text* with exclusive attention to sexual construction.[10] Spilka and others have made much of Grace Hemingway's androgynous practices in raising her children. She dressed Ernest and his sister Marcelline as twins in the early years of their lives, and pictures show not only identical outfits, but identical haircuts and styles as well. Biographies of Hemingway as an adult also suggest a twinning, which he and his first wife Hadley enacted—she by cutting her hair short and he by growing his longer. Similar scenarios are reported with all three subsequent wives, and *The Garden of Eden* undeniably presents a fictionalized version along those exact lines. That Hemingway had a hair fetish, as Carl P. Eby labels it in his book-length psychoanalysis, is hardly deniable. What this means contextually has generated much critical fervor.

Androgynous interest evokes a sense of fear and taboo for certain traditionalists, because it connotes a desexing rather than an equalization of sex. For Hemingway, though, the subject offered certain desirable qualities. The twinning of hairstyles was a positive indication, almost a symbolic shorthand for movement toward gender blurring, and Pilar, Maria, and Robert all possess androgynous aspects. These qualities help establish their similar status as incipient or achieved code heroes; but most especially, the young lovers' twin hairstyle symbolizes two important issues. First, Maria is androgynized by the cropped three-months' growth that elicits Pilar's comment, "You could be brother and sister by the look" (67).[11] Hair serves as an outward sign of their symbiotic relationship where they are no longer two separate identities, but one unified person. Maria declares that she and Robert are the same, specifically because both fathers have died in tortured ways, though for very different reasons. But their similar physical appearance furthers the symbolic autonomy that develops in their love affair. They dream of going to Madrid together after the war, and Jordan says, "we could go together to the coiffeur's and they could cut it [Maria's hair] neatly on the sides and back as they cut mine" (345). He sanctions her androgynous look, though he also speaks of her beauty as she becomes more feminine looking. Robert seems equally aroused by Maria's mannish cut as by the prospects of a more womanly look. For Hemingway, hair becomes a unifying feature and an important joining of kindred souls.

Maria's shorn hair also serves as a mark carrying important sexual connotations. Freudian critics cannot ignore the symbolic image her hair suggests both in its pre- and post-ravished condition. Before the rape, and the incidental rape of the lock, Maria's braids may be presented as a visual phallic substitute.[12] Their removal becomes a symbolic removing of the phallus and an effort to seize power as any brutalizing act represents psychologically. Ultimately for Maria, however, a positive result may have arisen from her decoiffing (if we can coin such a term as being useful to Hemingway analysis in a similar way that "defrocking" was to Victorian psychoanalysis.) Shearing her hair moves Maria to an androgynous position where she possesses more power, not less. She becomes less feminized, and therefore for Hemingway, a more potent and equal force with his male protagonists. Shortly after their third and last lovemaking, Maria's second experience of *la gloria*, Robert confesses, "You have taught me a lot *guapa* . . . I have learned much from thee" (380). Largely resulting from his relationship with Maria, and tangentially with Pilar, he moves from Pilar's description of a man "cold in the head," independent, and emotionally distanced, to an incorporation of all intimate possibilities. He identifies Maria as "my true love and my wife. I never had a true love. I never had a wife. She is also my sister, and I never had a sister, and my daughter, and I never will have a daughter" (381). Jordan composes this list to which we might add mother, and his connection to these female roles adds to, rather than diminishes his manhood.

Jordan does leave out the masculine position, which Maria's clipped hair circumspectly qualifies her for as well, and this omission raises questions. Gerry Brenner sees Jordan's attitude toward Maria as potentially inimical, though offering no contextual evidence as to why. In Brenner's fictitious interview of Maria, filled with tones of feminist hostility, he brings up two issues, the first related specifically and the second connected peripherally to the subject of hair. Brenner points out one of numerous references throughout the book to Maria in animal imagery. In the following passage, which Jordan offers just before they make love for the last time, he describes her cropped head against his cheek as "soft but as alive and silkily rolling as when a marten's fur rises under the caress of your hand when you spread the trap jaws open and lift the marten clear and, holding it, stroke the fur smooth" ("Once a Rabbit" 378). Immediately after this reflection, Jordan's throat swells again, and they make love at Maria's coaxing after he hesitates because of her previous pain. This description comparing Maria's hair to the fur of an animal painfully killed is no doubt startling for its violent imagery given the circumstance. However, a view of Jordan as a hostile participant in the coupling is not merited. Brenner correctly points out the unusual choice for Jordan's comparison, but nothing in the text that follows shows open animosity toward Maria. If Jordan possesses a fear of latent homosexuality because of her androgynous appearance, or if he resents her for some other sexual offense such as moving him to emotional, rather than purely physical response, Hemingway clearly offers us no context for these readings. Instead, the more likely operative emotion is a frustration with the potentially impending death Pilar has warned them both to expect.

The second issue with hair is Robert's nickname for Maria, which he uses throughout their three-day relationship. Several critics—Arturo Barea, James R. Mellow, Wolfgang E. H. Rudat, Allen Josephs, Carl P. Eby, and Gerry Brenner—argue the point that his calling her "rabbit" creates a critical problem in the text. Spanish translation of the word is *conejo,* a derogatory slang term for female genitalia. As a college instructor in Spanish, Robert Jordan would certainly have known this, critics argue, and so should Hemingway given his experience with Spanish and Cuban bars. Textually, the term seems one strictly of endearment and not derogation. I see little chance of solving this issue in terms of authorial intent. Though Eby writes a largely convincing argument equating "rabbit=hare=hair," I would disagree with his final conjecture. Eby states that "Jordan's tender feelings for Maria mask an element of hostility that is somehow bound up with 'the strange thing about her'" (*Hemingway's Fetishism* 113).[13] If latent hostility exists in Jordan, Eby seems to suggest that it may in fact be because Maria is sexually potent, able to call forth mystical powers as few could. But her abilities seem only to make Jordan more sexually potent also, and he dies feeling that he has lived fully and well in his final three days. Eby goes on to interpret Maria as a positive influence by discussing Jordan's use of her to satisfy his psychological needs. He says:

> Jordan's merger with Maria, who according to Pilar looks enough like him to be his own sister, testifies to his fluid ego boundaries and satisfies his narcissistic desire to recapture the world of primary identification and blissful twinship. But this merger, facilitated by Jordan's plans for identical haircuts, also probably satisfies Jordan's and Hemingway's urge to identify with the "castrated" woman (since *conejo* meant "cunt"), while simultaneously managing to ward off the castration anxiety implied by such an identification through identifying the phallic (hare/hair) woman and literally becoming the phallus (hare/hair) himself. (114)

Maria, in code hero fashion, can be credited with offering Jordan physical, emotional, and psychological comfort. Eby furthers this notion by citing Phyllis Greenacre's view that the "search for identical partners ('twins') can involve a 'taking in' of 'a similar person' to intensify one's sense of identity" much as the African custom of drinking the blood of one's kill is done to incorporate the slain animal's power (Eby 115, Greenacre 119). In Robert's weakness he reaches out to assimilate Maria's strength. Psychologists might argue that finding power through another does not automatically engender kindness toward the source of strength, especially if it is a male drawing from an autonomous female. This is not the point. That Maria is a source of strength and not a vapid, submissive sex-kitten made to order for Jordan's mountain idyll is the germane argument.

Maria, and Pilar as her mentor, are not subsidiary characters in *For Whom the Bell Tolls*, but women who deserve more critical attention than they have received. These women are not easily reducible, nor should they be, to the traditional polemic extremes critically assigned to Hemingway's fictional women. In light of ongoing gender reexamination in the canon, both Maria and Pilar deserve a more stringent and positive reading and a championing such as Catherine Barkley and Brett Ashley have been given. To view the women of *For Whom the Bell Tolls* in a more powerful and important role, even to read them as code heroes, of a sort, does not reduce Hemingway's males but broadens our understanding of the writer's more complex vision and its ability to reach beyond the formulaic, restrictive code. This revisionist perspective only enhances Hemingway's significance as one of this century's preeminent artists.

8
On Defiling Eden

The Search for Eve in the Garden of Sorrows

Ann Putnam

Nicholas Adams drove on through the town along the empty, brick-
paved street . . . on under the heavy trees of the small town that are a
part of your heart if it is your own town and you have walked under
them, but that are only too heavy, that shut out the sun and that
dampen the houses for a stranger.

Ernest Hemingway, "Fathers and Sons"

In *The Green Breast of the New World: Landscape, Gender, and American
Fiction* Louise H. Westling examines Hemingway's story "Big Two-
Hearted River" in the context of both feminist and eco-critical theory, an
approach that is beginning to open up Hemingway's works in new and
invigorating ways.[1] Eco-critical approaches to Hemingway are long over-
due, and her work is a fine example of the richness of this synthesis. Her
reading of "Big Two-Hearted River," for example, places Hemingway's
treatment of nature within a paradigm of the use of the feminine in the
depiction of nature from antiquity to the present.

But finally she concludes that "at least half of us are not likely to see
ourselves" in works by Hemingway, because he has "pared away so much
of the world from his fiction, retreating into such a narrow and primitive
masculinity, that there was nothing left for him [or the female reader] but
death" (100–101). This world is too narrow, too exclusionary, too hostile
to the feminine presence, to speak to the lives of both men and women.
Of course it's the old familiar complaint.[2] But reading it this time I'm
stopped in my tracks. Suddenly theory and feeling, sense and sensibility
collide in disturbing, complicated ways I have never articulated before.
Where was my female sensibility? My feminist edge? What contradictions have blindsided me just now? The synthesis of these theories is so

rich and has been so useful that I wonder if there is a way to acknowledge the power of the theory and the text as well as the response of many female readers of Hemingway to this apparently masculine, stripped-down world edged so precariously and uncompromisingly against death.

But it brings me to the question this essay seeks to answer: how do female readers who have always been moved by Hemingway's works—for whom those trees have never shut out the sun—negotiate theories that insist upon the exclusionary quality of the Hemingway world? How does the female reader locate herself in a landscape where there are no women? If, as Westling and others before her have claimed, the feminine is identified with the entanglements and entrapments of culture on the one hand, and an eroticized landscape to be mastered on the other, where do female readers find themselves in these works set in the natural world? What do they do with this theory and the ways it insists these works be read? This theory, which has been so useful, has left something unaccounted for, something left unsaid.

But what perhaps is left out is the abiding pleasure in Hemingway's work that many female readers have always found. That shock of recognition—that sense of seeing the familiar in those plain, everyday words placed as they are edge on edge like two stones striking, making such light and such surprise that you are always coming home to places you have never been. But there it is, pleasure and a strange sense of recognition. Is there any way to account for this compelling connection many female readers have felt to these seemingly exclusionary texts? Is there an accounting that goes beyond an impressionist description of one's own secret reading pleasures?

Perhaps female readers have always been able to identify so readily with this world, because no matter our gender we are a true product of our culture. Feminist film theory maintains that in order to participate in the plot of most works by men, women learn early on "to identify against themselves," as Jane Tompkins explains in *West of Everything.* Tompkins posits that "since stories about men (at least in our culture) function as stories about all people, women learn at an early age to identify with male heroes. . . . Feminist theories have shown how movies force women to look at women from the point of view of men . . . forcing them to identify against themselves in order to participate in the story" (17). In her introduction to *Female Spectators,* E. Deidre Pribram writes that the

"Filmic gaze, in terms of both gender representation and gender address, also 'belongs' to the male, leaving the female audience to identify with either the male-as-subject or the female-as-object" (1).

Is this what female readers must do in order to enter those works by Hemingway that depict the struggles of a solitary male hero in his confrontation with the natural world? Must we efface ourselves so surely and silently that we disappear altogether? In these works what is there to hold on to? Is there any abiding presence that speaks our name?

I believe that the feminine in Hemingway can be found in compelling ways not only in works with female characters, but also in those works with a solitary hero journeying across those paradisal landscapes found in such works as "Big Two-Hearted River," *Green Hills of Africa, The Old Man and the Sea,* and the elephant tale of *The Garden of Eden,* to name several. So I would like to suggest a way of reading that accounts for both the usefulness of the theory as it applies to these texts as well as the way many female readers have responded to them.

I want to focus on "Big Two-Hearted River" specifically because it establishes, as Westling points out, the "modern American hero in an emblematic Great Good Place" for generations of readers (91). But it is also a work that is wonderfully prescient, presenting in an almost uncanny way the conflict at the heart of so many works by Hemingway set in the natural world. Though for many readers "Big Two-Hearted River" is Hemingway's greatest short story triumph, it has always confounded interpretation. Yet its utter resistance to paraphrase is the source of both its difficulty and greatness. Explaining it is like trying to describe the wonder or terror of a dream, for what we remember most about it is its dreamlike quality and our own sense of astonishment that this simple story could have produced such power.

Readers first knew "Big Two-Hearted River" in the Paris magazine *This Quarter* published in May of 1925 before it became part of *In Our Time.* This is important to remember, because although it has been widely anthologized, most readers know it in the contexts of the stories of *In Our Time,* and such stories as "Now I Lay Me" and "A Way You'll Never Be," and have felt that it does not achieve coherence outside of this context. Indeed, it is almost impossible to give the story a genuinely pure reading after having first read it as the last story of *In Our Time.* And it is true that it both informs and is informed by those other stories in rich as well as complicating ways. Reading it in the context of *In Our Time*, "Big Two-Hearted River" holds the accumulation of all the sorrows from the stories that came before it—a rich reading to be sure, but one often merged with biography, and the backstory provided in "On Writing."

But the allegorical, metaphorical shape of the story becomes clearer, more resonant when it is read independently. My own sense here is to attempt to read it independently first and then see how the story plays out the patterns of gender and the natural world that emerge in works to come.

But what is the conflict in this story where nothing seems to happen? Where is the story? What is the trouble? What is the progression? And indeed, read on its own, "Big Two-Hearted River" would seem to be a story utterly without any conflict at all until the last page, when a shadow gathers over Nick's heart. "He did not feel like going on into the swamp. . . . Nick did not want to go in there now. . . . In the swamp fishing was a tragic adventure" (*SS* 231).

In order to satisfy our need for a sense of storiness, there must be a progression of some sort. The events must cohere at some place and point toward a pattern of meaning. The challenge "Big Two-Hearted River" presents is whether it is possible to discover this from the text alone. At any rate, an independent reading highlights the extraordinary achievement this story represents. In this long account of a single character to whom nothing at all extraordinary happens, who talks to no one, not even himself, and who does not allow himself even to think, Hemingway stretches the concept of story to its very limits. Using only narration, relieved briefly by interior monologue and a few lines of speech, Hemingway creates a story that carries more risks than any story he ever wrote.

Writing about it in 1926, F. Scott Fitzgerald said that he had read it with "the most breathless unwilling interest" (qtd. in Baker, *Writer* 36). But it was not until Malcolm Cowley's exploration of the murky regions of the story, that its depths were acknowledged. Since Cowley, no critic could afford to ignore the possibility of the story's underside. Yet he reads "Big Two-Hearted River" in the context of "Now I Lay Me," the war story in which fishing is the dream. Following Cowley's lead, critics have worked the dark parameters of "Big Two-Hearted River" and have caught some pretty strange fish. Lost in the murkiness they often miss the story's compelling sense of wonder. Carlos Baker suggests that "if we read the river-story *singly* looking merely at what it says, there is probably no more effective account of euphoria in the language" (Baker 125). If so, then where in the story's *underside* is the "nightmare at noonday?" (Cowley 41).[3] A number of recent readings of the story have suggested that there is no nightmare at all: that the story is a magnificent rendering of just what it seems—the story of a day's fishing.[4] In his classic study of Hemingway, Philip Young states that the story "cannot be read with comprehension unless one understands the earlier stories. One would think it no more than . . . a story about a man fishing—and it would be, as readers have often complained, quite pointless" (*Hemingway* 2–3).

And readers have interpreted that vague sense of foreboding or dread in a number of ways, depending on the context. One of the more recent and more controversial readings has been Kenneth Lynn's, in which he acknowledges the tension in the story, but attributes it to the antipathy between Nick and his mother, not the war: "Not a single reference to war appears in the story, and it is highly doubtful . . . that panic is the feeling that [Nick] is fending off" (104).[5] The trouble here is that there are no specific references to the mother either. Lynn stumbles into the biographical fallacy, reading the story in the context of Hemingway's strained familial relations in 1919, the summer of his trip to the Fox River, ignoring the fact that Hemingway *wrote* the story some five years later when the memory of those touchy months may very well have faded in importance.

In addition to the threat of the maternal that Lynn proposes, other readers have found entanglements, feminine and otherwise, in the swamp —that place which, for whatever reason, the hero Nick cannot face.[6] For Westling the swamp is fearful because it "epitomizes the feminine characteristics" (98–99). For other readers, coming at the story through the context of *In Our Time*, it has been the threat of impending fatherhood, marriage itself, familial strife, the war and its wounds both physical and psychic. Is the swamp—that confounding, bewildering metaphor that suggests everything and guarantees nothing—the dark place that holds the entanglements of the feminine? Is it all things "fearful, gloomy, [and] entangling" (Westling, 99)? In general, is there a repudiation of the feminine in Hemingway's works that are set in the natural world? Particularly, is there such a repudiation in this work? Or is the feminine erased altogether?

These readings describe the encounter with the feminine as an encounter with a fearful otherness and not the feminine as reflection of some aspect of the self. But there are two senses of nature in Hemingway's fiction that always compete in strange and complicated ways. There is the sense of nature as bountiful mother, which leads to the pastoral moment, and there is the sense of nature as mistress, as an eroticized other who must be mastered, which leads away from the pastoral moment and toward the "tragic adventure." For Hemingway, however, both senses of nature ultimately come to reflect desires of the self—desires that conflict in ultimately tragic ways. And the collision between these two senses forms the heart of this two-hearted story. For the feminine is not erased at all, but is ever-present in both the idyllic surface story set in the pastoral landscape and the buried story with its well-guarded secrets that dare not be told outright. It is here, in the collision between these two, that the tension of "Big Two-Hearted River" lies.

Even so, we get the sense that the narrator is always measuring life's terror and dread against its wonder and beauty. But in this story it is a paradox presented imagistically rather than through a dramatic progression. Hemingway uses image clusters to construct two opposing sets of values—one fraught with complications and sorrow, the other ordered and compellingly beautiful. *What happens* in the story is that this paradox is revealed to the reader, slowly, intuitively, as it is acknowledged by the protagonist. But this conflict is not presented through action. It is given in a description of a journey across a landscape, which contains images of both wonder and dread. For the basic structural principle underlying "Big Two-Hearted River," as many readers have noted, is not linear, but imagistic. Hemingway's strategy was to let the reader supply the things left out, though always guided by a careful structure of repetition, image clusters, juxtapositions, oppositions, and strange, mysterious silences. Increasingly it becomes clear that if we are to find meaning it will not come from plot but from the story's configuration of images, and from the mysterious intensity of this story in which "nothing happens."

The structure of the story itself invites multiple and conflicting interpretations, an iceberg that dazzles readers with its glittery surface yet hides its meanings within impenetrable depths. Hemingway's theory of omission describes not only the way his stories are constructed, but also the way we read them. For one thing, it points out how much he depends upon his readers to supply the things he left out. He put his theory to the supreme test in "Big Two-Hearted River," which he later said was about "coming back from the war" but with "no mention of the war in it" (*MF* 76).

This story, which in Baker's words is so "oddly satisfying" (*Writer* 126), carries a vision of order and beauty so powerful that it unfolds in strangely compelling ways. It is important to recall that Hemingway remembers the writing of the story, not in terms of exorcising unspoken terrors, but with love and a sense of wonder at the country he was trying to render like Cézanne:

> When I stopped writing I did not want to leave the river where I could see the trout in the pool, its surface pushing swelling smooth against the resistance of the log-driven piles of the bridge. . . . Some days it went so well that you could make the country so that you could walk into it through the timber . . . and feel the weight settle on your back and feel the pine needles under your moccasins as you started down for the lake. (*MF* 91)

In "Big Two-Hearted River" the landscape carries the sole burden of meaning. For Nick the landscape provides a sense of order; for the reader it represents the only way to meaning that the story offers. There is a natural order, which Nick finds with his wondering eye, and there is a created order, in the familiar sequence of details Nick follows in making his camp and fishing the river.

Right from the beginning Hemingway positions the images that are the paradox at the center of the story. Although Seney is burned, Nick knows "[it] could not all be burned. He knew that" (*SS* 210–11). If he walks far enough, he will come to the green hills again. This positioning of landscapes gives the story a *progression,* and it defines the values that are juxtaposed. At the beginning of the journey Nick finds the "fire-scarred hill" and the blackened earth. At the end he finds the dark, mysterious swamp. In between, Nick comes to the middle ground of the pastoral landscape.[7] It is this vision of nature as beckoning and maternal, the source of both salvation and rapture, that is also the vision of the perfect self. It is where he needs to go in order to hold steady in fast current. But the progression and meaning of the story is bound up in the juxtaposition of all *three* places and the values they represent.

The whole point of the journey has been to reach a place that had not changed, a place beyond the spread of the fire. Nick has earned the right to occupy such a place through the hard conditions that he had set for himself—going as far as he could go, carrying as heavy a pack as his endurance would allow. Nick sees that the grasshoppers have turned black from living in the burned-over country. And it is clear to any reader that Nick too has been burned by some kind of fire, although we cannot discover its source, not from the text, not from biography, nor from the other stories to which it seems allied. By going unnamed, it becomes the sorrow of all those who have one way or the other been broken by the world. Yet Nick comes to this middle ground where nature is generous, where good fish can be caught through skill, order, and love, where he can feel "all the old feeling" (*SS* 210).

This is the vision at the center of all works set in the natural world— that middle ground, edged on one side by civilization, on the other by wildness and haste. It reappears again and again—in the green hills of Africa and the blue waters of the Gulf; it is always strange and familiar, a landscape given in such luminous images that they shimmer with the power of the dream. For in the landscape of the dream, one can repeat the sequence of action across familiar terrain, and get "all the old feeling." The pastoral landscape is washed over with a radiant ever-presentness over which the hero journeys with a stillness of soul, and a "first chastity of sight" (*AFTA* 239 qtd. in Tanner 242).[8] Read purely by itself this is a narrative so wished for, so desired that it becomes the universal dream of reverence and stillness of heart. It becomes a landscape anyone can know.

The journey across the paradisal terrain becomes also the search for order and for meaning—some way of getting things to have "a definite end" (*SAR* 167), to have a meaning in themselves that will offer a stay against the darkness of the vision of *nada*, which is the unspeakable part of the story. But Hemingway insists that his protagonists search for meaning in the same world that holds both the wonder *and* the dread. The story moves from the town of Seney, across the landscape, but it ends with the swamp. Here there would be none of the clarity and light of the grove or the order of the camp. Here branches hang low in tangled knots

and the sun comes through only "in patches" (*SS* 231). Hemingway introduces the swamp as part of a general description of the landscape, but
through repetition it becomes an image of great power, drawing to it
other dark images. It is the place insects come from, a place where the
mist hovers:

> He did not want to go in there now. He felt a reaction against deep
> wading with the water deepening up under his armpits, to hook big
> trout *in places impossible to land them.* In the *swamp* the banks were
> bare, the big cedars came overhead, the sun did not come through,
> except in patches; in the fast deep water, in the half-light, the
> fishing would be tragic. In the *swamp* fishing was a tragic adventure.
> Nick did not want it. He did not want to go *down stream* any further
> today. (my emphasis, 230–31)

For now, the "tragic adventure" must be avoided. "There were plenty of
days coming when he could fish the swamp" (232).

In *The Old Man and the Sea* Hemingway shows what it means to have
the "tragic adventure," what it means to hook fish in places impossible to
land them. But here it is important to note that Hemingway avoids a
tragic telling by blunting the impact of the story through a structure that
submerges the dread in the presentation of a landscape full of light and
vague, mysterious shadows.

Yet perhaps one of the reasons this story seems so satisfying is because
the details the narrator so lovingly gives are so costly. The pastoral moment, which is wrapped in a luminous sense of timelessness, includes also
the pull and tug of longing. In fact for both writer and protagonist, the
intensity of the present moment is fueled by desire. "All I wanted to do
was get back to Africa," Hemingway writes in *Green Hills of Africa*. "We
had not left it, yet, but when I would wake in the night, I would lie,
listening, homesick for it already" (72). For Hemingway every country is
the "last good country." Every landscape is washed over with a sense of
both timelessness and impending loss. It is a paradox at the heart of this
story and of all Hemingway's fiction. This poignancy and discontent is
played out again and again in the figure of a solitary protagonist travelling
across paradisal landscapes. Memory itself is hunger, Hemingway explains in *A Moveable Feast*. Thus it is the hunger that comes from the past

that Nick cannot bear. He denies himself the poignancy of memory and instead intensifies his physical hunger only to satisfy it at last with exquisite deliberateness. It is the way longing itself is beckoned that creates such intensity in those seemingly simple descriptions of landscapes at once new and familiar, wrapped in timelessness and steeped in time.

By controlling sensation through parceling out experience, Nick creates a stay against the chaos that lies on either side of this middle ground he occupies. Nick employs a conscious deliberation, an exquisite sense of timing, such that he knows just when to eat, sleep, cast the next line. It involves a careful management of deprivation and satisfaction, a deliberate heightening of sensation by withholding gratification for as long as possible. The temptation is always to rush things, but by holding back, the sensation can be exquisitely controlled. So Nick deliberately parcels out his pleasures, saving and then spending them with compelling care. Life holds many pleasures, which can be heightened through a meticulous sense of timing, but perhaps its delights are numbered. In this, Hemingway reveals how fragile is the sense of wonder and how close at hand the sense of dread.

This exquisite sense of timing that all Hemingway protagonists know is rendered in prose rhythms so piercing and deliberate that each gesture becomes an incantation against unspoken things and proof of the narrator's "first chastity of sight." It is a vision rendered so lovingly it is removed from all ego and self-interest, captured by the "wondering, wandering eye" and rescued from the rush of history (Tanner 240). The cadence of the narration, emphasizing the integrity of each separate gesture, results in a sequence so incantory it finally gather him into perfect sleep.

> Nick knew it was too hot. He poured on some tomato catsup. He knew the beans and spaghetti were still too hot. He looked at the fire, then at the tent, he was not going to spoil it all by burning his tongue. For years he had never enjoyed fried bananas because he had never been able to wait for them to cool. . . . He was very hungry. Across the river in the swamp in the almost dark, he saw a mist rising. He looked at the tent once more. All right. He took a full spoonful from the plate. "Chrise," Nick said. "Geezus Chrise," he said happily. (*SS* 216)

As I'm writing this I cannot help but remember the heated exchange between Mary Gordon and Frank McCourt during an appearance at *Seattle Arts and Letters* over whether Nick Adams in "Big Two-Hearted River" ate spaghetti or beans for dinner. Gordon said it was beans absolutely, and McCourt said no I think it was spaghetti, or it might have been the other way around. Of course they were both right and both wrong. But it was an intriguing commentary on the power of Hemingway even on those female readers like Gordon who said she could not stand to read him yet believed so strongly in her memory of what a single character ate for dinner. Which Hemingway had she read, I wondered? The Hemingway of popular myth, or the Hemingway on all those pages?

Yet the pursuit of pleasure in Hemingway always comes with an ethical dimension. Sensation grounds the hero in the timeless present, and must neither be hurried nor prolonged. Doing things too long is a theme of a number of stories such as "Snows of Kilimanjaro," "Cross Country Snow," and "An Alpine Idyll" to name only a few. If these pleasures are always in danger of loss, if the lessons these heroes learn over and over is the impermanence of all things, then life's pleasures must be held for safekeeping against chance, misuse, neglect, and dullness. On the other hand, a sense of hurry inevitably leads to the tragic adventure. As David explains, Catherine burned his manuscripts out of a sense of hurry. The sense of hurry finally wears away the pastoral vision at the heart of *Green Hills of Africa* and plunges the narrator into the heart of the tragic adventure, just as it provokes the revenge hunt of *The Garden of Eden*, and the deliberate assault on nature that was a product of Santiago's 84 fishless days.

In the pastoral setting, through an imagination fired by longing, every landscape becomes a clean, well-lighted place, luminous and ever-present. But in the end it is only a temporary stay for those protagonists driven by restlessness and a discontent they do not understand, which forces them out of the pastoral moment and toward the "tragic adventure." But it is a discontent that electrifies those descriptions with a shimmering sense of place. The deliberate slowness of the pastoral world, with its sense of timelessness and mysterious silences is edged against the sure knowledge that the lesson of the past is the certainty of loss.

But where is the past, in this story of a man alone in nature who experiences no challenges from without? In such a story wouldn't any writer include internal conflicts of some kind? Yet, what is obviously left out are all those things we might expect, memories, dreams, and recollections given in narrative flashbacks if not character reminiscences. In other words, what is missing is the *past,* which holds the memory of loss, which holds the hunger that would devour him, which is present through its brooding absence. Thus the search for the *story* becomes a reader's search for the past. Instead we are given one long, glorious rendering of the *present* in all its stunning immediacy. Nostalgia may be wonderful for the narrator of *A Moveable Feast* who recollects the pleasure in writing "Big Two-Hearted River," but for Nick its hero, remembering is full of menace. "Big Two-Hearted River" is a story about the balancing of present and past, wonder and dread, mastery and reverence, sound and silence. The absence of the past is signaled by the absence of words, by the interior silence of the main character.

The overwhelming beauty of the world is balanced against terrors that must not be told. Because Hemingway refuses to name them they become more terrible yet, for we feel their presence in the prose rhythms, and in the jarring of image against image. We sense that there are hidden stories lurking in the shadows throughout "Big Two-Hearted River," and the reader must be like Nick as he watches the stream for the big trout at the bottom, sometimes seeing them, sometimes not.

But Hemingway gives us clues in several ways: in a few direct but puzzling references to the past, through imagaic equivalents, and through an implied sense of the past in the overriding emphasis given the present. The story begins with a sense of loss and change. The first image we notice is the town of Seney, blackened from fire such that "even the surface had been burned off the ground" (*SS* 209). Nick is first seen watching the train behind "one of the hills of burnt timber." "Nick looked over the stretch of hillside *where he had expected* to find the scattered houses of the town" (my emphasis, 209). In coming to the river Nick is attempting to re-create a part of the past that had nourished him. But the country is black, not green, and it presents as devastating an image as any scene of war could provide. The whole point of the journey is to find a place, a landscape, which has not changed. So in a real sense the story is about the search for permanence in an impermanent world—the search for the green hills, a pastoral landscape impervious to time, and perfect reflection of a self wrapped in a transcendent and abiding present.

Nick walks to the bridge and looks down at the river. "*The river was there*" (my emphasis, 209). That short sentence contains all of Nick's joy for this return to a place that has not been burned away. Nick looks into the water, watching the trout. Again, Hemingway gives the astonishment and joy of his return, and by inference the deprivation of the past. "It was a long time since Nick had looked into a stream and seen trout" (210). Here as always, the present moment gains in intensity refracted as it is through the images of loss, the shadow of time. Though Hemingway packs great poignancy in that simple line, we do not know where Nick has come from or why he has been so long from the river. But through the use of incremental repetition, Hemingway begins to build images of the emotions that are left out of the story and define its emotional curve:

> Nick looked down into the clear, brown water . . . and watched *the trout keeping themselves steady in the current.* . . . As he watched them they changed their positions by quick angles, *only to hold steady in the fast water.* At the bottom of the pool were the big trout. Nick did not see them at first. Then he saw them at the bottom of the pool, big trout looking *to hold themselves* on the gravel bottom. . . . A big trout shot upstream . . . and then he *tightened* facing up into the current.
>
> Nick's heart *tightened* as the trout moved. (my emphasis, 209–10)

Here Hemingway identifies Nick with the fish at the bottom of the stream, heart touching heart in the striving required to hold steady in fast current. It is part of the iceberg strategy that we are never told why holding steady is so difficult, yet we know that it is. As Nick puts on his pack and sets off across the land, we sense that holding steady is part of what this story is about. But the pack is heavy. So he takes some of the pull off his shoulders by "leaning his forehead against the wide band of the tump-line" (210). In the heat, up the "fire-scarred hill," Nick's solitary figure against that blackened landscape creates an image so wrenching it becomes a mythic journey any reader knows.

"Big Two-Hearted River" is a story wrapped in silence. It depicts an Edenic world—a prelapsarian world that exists before the need for words. Nick moves through a beckoning silence, a passive, maternal landscape, which requires nothing but perfect assent. It is a world wrapped in mystery and wordlessness, a universe where every breath is a prayer of gratitude. But in the description of Nick making the coffee toward the end of Part I, Hemingway creates the odd presence of a story that is never told. It is the solitary excursion into words and the solitary journey into the past. Nick cannot remember the way he makes coffee. What he can remember is "an argument about it with Hopkins, but not which side he had taken. He decided to bring it to a boil. He remembered now that was Hopkins's way. He had once argued about everything with Hopkins. They said good-bye and all felt bad. It broke up the trip. They never saw Hopkins again. That was a long time ago on the Black River" (216–17). It is the only extended memory Nick allows himself, and just at the end of it the narrator reveals that it has made Nick's mind begin to work.

But who is Hopkins and what is he doing in this story that does not mention a single other character besides Nick? Hemingway leaves out the war, perhaps, or whatever terrors hold him, but includes a long description of someone named Hopkins and how he made coffee. So we bump into Hemingway's iceberg—the tip of it, anyway. By describing at length what seems to be a trivial anecdote, Hemingway brilliantly reveals the paucity of memory Nick allows himself, and how quickly he stops even such an innocuous-seeming recollection as this. This one excursion into the past is pleasant enough, yet even that becomes too dangerous and Nick must finally "choke it." The coffee turned out to be bitter anyway. Better to stay with ritual that re-enacts the past through action rather than thought. This is the only narrative offered in this seemingly plotless story, and Nick must stop it before he comes to the part that makes his "mind [start] to work" (218). Yet this narrative fragment shows just how dangerous telling can become.

Words are dangerous; things are safe. In *West of Everything*, Tompkins addresses this very issue. Although she is speaking of the Western in film and novel, her comments provide an intriguing commentary on the way many of Hemingway works are sometimes read. Language as opposed to action, is "false, or at best ineffectual; only actions are real" (51). Language is "an inferior kind of reality;" it "creates a kind of shadow world" (52). The "position represented by language is always associated with women, religion . . . culture" (55). And that is why "[n]ature is what the hero aspires to emulate; perfect being . . . in itself . . . " (57). For language is in danger of taking away the "mystery of an ineffable self that silence preserves" (60). Rose Marie Burwell makes just this point in her discussion of the *African Journals,* now published as *True at First Light.* Here she quotes Hemingway's own description of, in Burwell's words, the "inadequacy of male language": "that odd short-hand of understatement which was our legal tongue. There were things I wished that I could ask him that it was impossible to ask" (*Postwar Years* 139). That Hemingway was not only aware of both the limitations of "male language" but also the intricacies of female language is illustrated everywhere in his fiction, but nowhere more clearly than in such lyric short stories as "Hills Like White Elephants" and "Cat in the Rain." In story after story Hemingway explores the pain and anguish of silence and the inability of language to tell the tale, and finally the cost to those who try to tell what is ultimately untellable.

But is the tightly controlled, laconic narration that characterizes "Big Two-Hearted River" part of the "narrowness" a number of readers have felt? Is Nick's silence exclusionary? And is he the prototype of all those other supposedly tough-talking heroes throughout Hemingway's fiction? In so many stories "*I did not say anything*" reads like a refrain. In *A Farewell to Arms,* Hemingway had described the danger of certain words that tried to tell what never could be told, words that were "obscene" when placed next to "names" and "numbers" and "dates" (177–78). You had to be afraid of words.

In his essay, "Reading Hemingway Without Guilt," Frederick Busch describes "how [Hemingway] listened and watched and invented the language—using the power, the terror, of silences with which we could name ourselves." Westling, however, insists that "Busch is wrong to assert that Hemingway's is the language with which we can name ourselves." Or "at least [for] half of us" (100). I would like to push beyond the description of the "silence[s]" Busch praises and the sound Westling dismisses to ask: what is this wordlessness for? Is it presence or absence? And what does it mean to speak? What does it mean to tell?

In "Big Two-Hearted River," it is clear that Nick must hold his tongue. Like the fish at the bottom of the fast moving current, he must hold on tight. At any moment words can slip free of the tongue and rush into dangerous places. The past is held in words that once spoken conjure it up. Better to stay with things, better to stay with masculine rituals enacted in sacramental places in ways that avoid words altogether. Better to create narratives of silence, wordless landscapes washed over in golden light and struck with green, landscapes shimmering in that original stillness. Better to remain in the paradisal world where no words are necessary and everything is bathed in an ever-present and luminous reality.

But one of the progressions of "Big Two-Hearted River" is the journey from speechlessness to sound. In one sense the story is a journey through a pastoral silence toward the rush of words, which, in this story, is a rush into the swamp and toward the tragic adventure. Perhaps what is in the swamp that for now must be avoided is words. But words are what Nick most fears and most desires. It is the world he must both avoid and ultimately enter, when silence finally erupts into the dangerous rush of sound. For in the end it is the sacred obligation of the writer to tell the tale no matter the cost the universe exacts. For the act of telling breaks the male code of silence and surrenders to words truths too fragile to hold.

In the coda, "On Writing," Nick tries to explain the passion of fishing. "They were all married to [it]," he says, "It wasn't any joke" (*NAS* 214). Some readers over the years have suggested that it is fishing and its exclusionary male world that is threatened by adulthood, by marriage, by the feminine. It is fishing that is the real marriage, perhaps a better marriage, particularly in those works that depict an eroticized landscape as feminine terrain to be taken. In this view, the feminine is always an "other" that threatens the essential male self, depicted in this story as the lure and danger that lurks in the swamp. It is an immaturity, in Leslie A. Fiedler's view, a literature of adolescence, of boys who do not want to be men.[9]

But I'm going to suggest a different way to interpret what it means to fish the swamp, looking at the text alone. Nick said, "he felt he had left everything behind, the need for thinking, the need to write, other needs" (*SS* 210). The "other needs" that he refers to but does not name remain in the iceberg, though readers over the years have gained an intriguing sense of the possibilities from the biography and many of the other works, as I have mentioned earlier. The two things Nick cannot think about doing in this story are fishing the swamp and writing. In this story they are the same thing. Here is the first example of what was to become Hemingway's gathering metaphor for the life of the writer. In work after work, the story of the hunt becomes the writer's story. The metaphor of the hunter-artist—or here in "Big Two-Hearted River," the artist as fisher— is firmly established by the time he wrote *Green Hills of Africa,* and reaches its most allegorical expansion in *The Old Man and the Sea,* which becomes almost a parable of the writer's quest. In *Green Hills of Africa* Hemingway writes,

> The way to hunt is for as long as you live against as long as there is such and such an animal; just as the way to paint is as long as there is you and colors and canvas; and to write as long as you can live and there is pencil and paper or ink . . . or anything you care to write about. (*GHOA* 12)

Both hunter and artist seek to enter the timeless world of the pastoral dream in order to stop the remorseless rush of time, yet both are finally "caught by time" (*GHOA* 12), as they enter the time-driven narratives of the hunt. The hunter's story is the story of the writer's struggle to know and fix the truth, fought against the remorseless rush of time that would only destroy it.

But is writing, like fishing and hunting, the exclusively male activity always threatened by incursions from the feminine? What about this way of talking about writing? Does this metaphor of the writer as hunter necessarily exclude the feminine? Is this metaphor as exclusionary for women as the authorial, pen/phallus metaphor or as problematic as the birth metaphor?

Women have historically found it difficult to express the dangers that creation has meant to them. The difficulties with the former are perhaps self-evident, but as for the second metaphor, the act of writing framed in images of giving birth has always been too literal a metaphor for women not to be fraught with complications—both in terms of the writing process (the act of giving birth and the potential for suffering and death), as well as the uncertainties and insecurities of authorship itself. America's first woman of letters, Anne Bradstreet, addresses her poetry as "Thou ill-form'd offspring of my feeble brain. . . . I cast thee by as one unfit for light" ("The Author to Her Book" 88). For Mary Shelley, her protagonist's monstrous creation is a mirror of her own.[10] It becomes a "hideous progeny," not only abhorrent, but fatal to everything the creator [the female writer] has called beloved. By the end of the novel, the creator's entire family has been sacrificed to his dark desires. Perhaps the most natural metaphor for the female writer remains the most problematic.

But what about writing as a killing out of season? To be sure, there are other ways to speak of writing, but I believe that Hemingway's metaphor does not exclude women and that it points to a certain sense many writers of both genders have felt to be true. For example, in her essay "Becoming a Writer," Gail Godwin describes the writing process this way as well. She is trying to write the story of her mother's life and wonders what kind of bargain with the devil she must make in order to tell a certain kind of truth: "But what about the other truths you lost by telling it that way? You ask. Ah, my friend, that is my question too. The choice is always a killing one. One option must die so that another may live. I do little murders in my room every day" (qtd. in Sternburg 303).

In *Writing Past Dark*, Bonnie Friedman discusses the same issue. She explores the anguish many women feel about writing, invoking the image of Mary Shelley's monster.

> *Frankenstein*, Mary Shelley's myth about bringing the dead to life, is in fact a parable about sacrificing family for the sake of artistic ambition. It reads like a transcript of our fears. . . . His work requires exhuming bodies; writers' work requires unburying events and emotions which have been suppressed. In both cases real people become mere material for the creator's ends. And what happens when the work is done? I am looking not for objective truth but for emotional truth. I am looking for the way writing about the living feels when we feel its dangers most forcefully. . . . At 4 A.M. the light shines straight through, showing the stalker in all its clarity. (29–33)

The violence is the same either way. It is a killing every time. The dark, which is Friedman's gathering metaphor, is the swamp that Nick, whose heart has broken apart, cannot face. Nick knows there is something dangerous in the swamp—something forbidden and fraught with potential sorrow.

Earlier in the day, Nick had hooked a huge trout, a trout "broad as a salmon," "the biggest one [he] ever heard of" (*SS* 227). But the leader finally breaks under the strain and he loses him.

> There was a long tug. Nick struck and the rod came alive and dangerous, bent double, the line tightening, coming out of water, tightening, all in a heavy dangerous, steady pull. . . . He had never seen so big a trout. There was a heaviness, *a power not to be held.* (my emphasis, 226)

It is a presentiment of what would happen if he fished the swamp, how he would "hook big trout in places impossible to land them." In the treacherous light, where the "sun did not come through, except in patches . . . the fishing would be tragic" (231). This fish, both caught and lost, is a *type* of other animals in other stories, too brave and strong and beautiful to be taken, but pursued nonetheless by other Hemingway protagonists who become figures of the hunter-artist. The spirit animal is what the writer is always seeking to catch, pursued finally, into dark, tangled places —the swamp, the deep forest, the sea beyond all people. The vision the hunter seeks to capture is embodied in an animal so elusive and unearthly it is a vision seen only in flickering light and mysterious shadows—the visionary kudu, the mythical elephant, the otherworldly marlin. This animal is always taken against the rules, slain out of season by trick and by treachery, caught in forbidden places, in forbidden ways.[11]

And what of that moment of tightening, that sudden, cool detachment as one takes aim? What of that pulling away, that of taking notes on the scene before the release of words? The imagery is unarguably masculine. In *Green Hills of Africa* Hemingway describes exactly how the hunter does it: "I was watching, freezing myself deliberately inside, stopping the excitement as you close a valve, going into that impersonal state you shoot from" (76). Santiago shows the same tightening, the same hardening of spirit: "Now is no time to think of baseball, he thought. Now is the time to think of only one thing. That which I was born for" (*OMATS* 40). And so finally he gathers himself and lifts "the harpoon as high as he could and [drives] it down with all his strength. . . . He felt the iron go in and he leaned on it and drove it further and then pushed all his weight after it" (*OMATS* 93–94). It is how the writer, Jane Smiley, describes that sense of the self splitting off, dividing into halves, "Even if my marriage is falling apart and my children are unhappy, there is still a part of me that says, 'God! This is fascinating'" (qtd. in Shaughnessy 80).

It is just as Santiago had said it was—a "trick" and a "treachery" and a betrayal every time. The writer sacrifices the living vision—the miraculous elephant by moonlight, the fish's purple-stripes flashing in the sun, the unearthly kudu glimpsed in the flickering light—the living reality out of which both trophy and text are made. The writer takes from the lives of those most loved the tale not meant to be told and tells it anyway. Snapshots of life are caught and ferreted away, the eye going where it has no right to go, remembering what ought to be forgotten, hearing what ought not to be heard, seeing what ought not to be seen. And whatever was sacred about the reality that was lived must be transformed in order to see it whole, in order to bring it out of the tangled dark and into the light. For the artist must forever enter a fallen world where what is most loved must always be slain, where the conversion of vision to text will always bring sorrow. There are casualties everywhere.

Does this explain why the metaphor of the hunter-artist has always seemed to catch, if not the whole truth, a certain truth? Or does it simply mean that there are others of us who have yet to escape the cultural metaphors that have trapped us in ways we still do not know? Yet, maybe it is as Virginia Woolf describes it, that the "incandescent" mind must be truly androgynous, as Shakespeare's was.

> [I]t is fatal to be a man or woman pure and simple; one must be woman-manly or man-womanly . . . for anything written with [a] conscious bias is doomed to death. It ceases to be fertilised. . . . Some marriage of opposites has to be consummated. The whole of the mind must lie open if we are to get the sense that the writer is communicating his experience with perfect fullness. (*Room* 107–08)

Perhaps the tightening I have been describing is the masculine mind taking aim; the feminine mind is the release of words that must tell the tale no matter how untellable. Isn't this the very mingling of the masculine and feminine we see in *The Garden of Eden* that fuels David's art such that what was once feared, that dark moon of the self, is finally brought into the light? And isn't this what Rose Marie Burwell means when she speaks of David's experiments with androgyny as the "fluid gender alignment that would cross-fertilize the creative imagination?"—a conclusion she believes is unfortunately negated by the Scribner ending (*Postwar Years* 98).

But what if the writer is not Adam, the one who names, after all? What if the writer is Eve? Hemingway played with this idea himself. In *The Garden of Eden,* David uses the feminine to create the androgynous honeymoon narrative as well as provide the creative energy for the African stories, those dark, exclusionary tales of fathers and sons. But unlike the honeymoon narrative, the elephant tale becomes the masculinist text, which David finally protects from the influence of the feminine. So he locks away this privileged text, product of his masculine side, from all influences of the feminine, this Other, now that he no longer needs it, or so he thinks.

Yet I would argue that the elephant tale is itself a feminine tale. This elephant is one that has a light side and a dark side that Davey has betrayed through a telling he cannot take back. What happens in that moonlit forest is Eve's story. Hers was always the greater knowledge, the greater sorrow. Hers was the tale of betrayal and the suffering and awareness that came from it. She is the one who, like Lot's wife, must always turn back to see what must not be seen; she, however, would tell it if she could. It is a kind of knowing that becomes betrayal through a telling of the forbidden, and with it expulsion from the garden, and the final knowledge that only comes from the loneliness that follows. The time-driven adventure that awaits the narrator of "River," and all hunter-artists, will propel him out of silence into sound, and the solitary sin of art. For once set loose these words cannot be called back.

I fear the pleasures are all dark ones. Would that we could stay in the pastoral dream forever—that timeless moment that is the rush and stillness of love, the rush and stillness of death flung forever into a luminous ever-present. But Nick cannot, Santiago could not, the narrator of *Green Hills of Africa* could not, Davey, watching the elephant in the moonlight, could not.

It seems like such a dark tale, a world rendered with such precision and love, a world so defiled, and the divided heart that has created them both. The ecological implications are enormous. But the pull of the swamp, in all its contradiction, is so strong, so irresistible that it is where I have to go. My response to the dividedness at the center of Hemingway's work is complex, disturbing, and rich in ways impossible to say. How to explain this beauty at the heart of loss, this beauty in the shadow of violence, this heart touching heart? There is a poignancy here that draws me in, over and over, and becomes the closest thing to an explanation of how theory reconciles with feeling that I know. Yet I go as no stranger to these parts. The heavy old boughs of those trees have never shut out the sunlight for me.

9

Santiago and the Eternal Feminine

Gendering *La Mar* in *The Old Man and the Sea*

Susan F. Beegel

"Hemingway is always less embarrassing when he is not attempting to deal with women," Leslie A. Fiedler writes, with some smugness, of *The Old Man and the Sea*, "and he returns with relief (with what we as readers at least feel as relief) to that 'safe' American Romance of the boy and the old man" ("Adolescence" 108). Like Fiedler, most critics of this novella overlook the fact that *The Old Man and the Sea* has a powerful feminine persona in a title role. Hemingway tells us that Santiago "always thought of the sea as *la mar* which is what people call her in Spanish when they love her. Sometimes those who love her say bad things of her but they are always said as though she were a woman" (29). If the novella is an "American Romance," it is not the love story of Santiago and Manolin but of the old man and the sea, conjoined in the title like Hero and Leander, Troilus and Cressida, Antony and Cleopatra, Tristan and Isolde. Given the nature of the sea in Hemingway's novella, this is not a "safe" romance at all but a story about the tragic love of mortal man for capricious goddess.

I propose a reading of *The Old Man and the Sea* that abandons the anthropocentric critical practice of relegating nature to the role of setting—of thinking like the novella's young fishermen, who consider the sea to be "a place" rather than a living being (30). When we recognize that the sea, as the novella's title suggests, is a protagonist on an equal footing with Santiago, we see how Hemingway—using a rich tapestry of images drawn from mythology, folklore, religion, marine natural history, and literature—genders the sea as feminine throughout the text, thereby raising key questions about the right relationship of man and nature.[1] Although one strand of ecofeminist thought argues that men characteristically gender nature as female to justify treating the land in a dominating, exploitative way (virgin land), while expecting unending forgiveness (Mother Earth), Hemingway argues that the true sin is masculinizing nature, treating nature as an enemy or contestant to be met in combat. Examining the role played by the feminine sea in this story may reveal that *The Old Man and the Sea* has a stronger ecological ethic than previously supposed.

Santiago genders the sea early in the novella as he rows out to fish in the early morning darkness. He begins by "feeling sorry for the birds, especially the small delicate dark terns that were always flying and looking and almost never finding" (29). Then he wonders, "Why did they make birds so delicate and fine as those sea swallows when the ocean can be so cruel? She is kind and very beautiful. But she can be so cruel and it comes so suddenly." This is the moment when we learn that Santiago "always thought of the sea as *la mar*, which is what people call her in Spanish when they love her." We learn further that

> [T]he old man always thought of her as feminine and as something that gave or withheld great favours, and if she did wild or wicked things, it was because she could not help them. The moon affects her as it does a woman, he thought. (30)

These few sentences propose a complex persona for the sea that resonates throughout the novella. I want to begin by examining how they suggest the sea's connection to a spiritual and biological principle of the Eternal Feminine. The sea's kindness, beauty, and generosity—the zenith of the natural cycle involving fecundity, copulation, birth, and nurture— offer important suggestions about right relationship to nature. Next, I want to look at the sin of masculinizing the sea instead of honoring her feminine nature, then examine the "bad things" said about the sea as though she were a woman—that she is cruel, wild, and wicked, and represents the nadir of the natural cycle—the inexorability of the death and decomposition that nourishes life. Throughout, I want to refer not only to published criticism on *The Old Man and the Sea* but also to the voices of those women students who seem less culturally conditioned than men to accept this as a story of contest and who are more likely to question the novella's violence. Finally, I will consider how gendering the sea relates to the tragedy of Santiago and its redemptive message.

Those, like Santiago, who gender what is supremely dangerous in nature as feminine (hurricanes, for instance, were traditionally called by women's names before the National Hurricane Center decided this folkloric practice was "sexist") and especially as maternal (the Tibetan name for Everest is Jomolungma, Mother Goddess of the World) do so in part as a form of appeasement. They hope if they approach with love, understanding, and respect, nature will treat them with feminine gentleness and especially with the unconditional love of a mother. Walt Whitman provides an example in "As I Ebbed with the Ocean of Life" that illuminates Santiago's professions of love for *la mar:*

Ebb, ocean of life, (the flow will return,)
Cease not your moaning you fierce old mother,
Endlessly cry for your castaways, but fear not, deny not me,
Rustle not up so hoarse and angry against my feet as I touch you
or gather from you.
I mean tenderly by you and all,
I gather for myself. (186)

Santiago's hope that the sea will not rise up angry against him as he gathers for himself explains in part his need to gender the "cruel" sea as feminine.

Santiago begins his consideration of *la mar* from a pagan or "primitive" viewpoint. The words "why did *they* make" imply his belief in a pantheon of gods responsible for natural creation. At once kind and beautiful, cruel and capricious, the sea is goddess and member of that pantheon—"they" know this "she"; "they" should have considered "her" cruelty when they made terns. Associated with the creative and destructive forces in nature, the sea in this novella represents the Eternal Feminine. She might remind us of a figure from Greek or Roman mythology—Tethys, wife of Oceanus and daughter of Uranus and Gaia, or Aphrodite, daughter of Zeus and Dione. Santiago, however, knows her as "*la mar.*"

The novella also draws from Catholic imagery in representing the sea as the Eternal Feminine. A devotional picture of the Virgin of Cobre, the patroness of Cuba, hangs next to an image of the Sacred Heart of Jesus on the wall of Santiago's shack.[2] The Virgin is a feminine icon, relic of his dead wife (16). During his agon at sea, he promises to make a pilgrimage to the Virgin of Cobre's shrine if he should catch his fish, and the prayers that he offers are "Hail Marys," which he finds "easier to say" than "Our Fathers" (65). She too is a sea goddess. Santiago acknowledges this when he prays to her for a great favor—"the death of this fish" (65). Bickford Sylvester recounts the Cuban legend of how this small statue of the Virgin, now enshrined in a sanctuary at Cobre, arrived from the sea. She was "floating on a wooden board off the coast . . . in 1628, when . . . found by two Indians and a Creole in a rowboat" ("Cuban Context" 252).

The Virgin Mother of Christ is most familiar to us in her medieval roles as Mater Dolorosa and mediatrix: kind and beautiful, meek and mild, sorrowing for the suffering of man, compassionately interceding for him, offering clemency "at the hour of our death," in the words of the Ave. But mariologists remind us that she is also the descendant of the pagan Magna Mater and Eternal Feminine (Katainen) and of Old Testament figures including Eve and the bride of the erotic "Song of Songs" (Johnson). Her biblical foremothers are tricksters Tamar and Ruth, the prostitute Rahab, and the adultress Bathsheba—brave and holy women, to be sure, but scarcely meek and mild (Shroer). Mary functions "as a bridge between cultures and traditions" (Johnson), linking both paganism and Judaism to Christianity. Ben Stolzfus notes that "the effect of the christological imagery" in *The Old Man and the Sea* "is essentially non-Christian," that the novel is less "Christian parable" than "pagan poem," and this is certainly true of the Virgin of Cobre (42–43).

Insofar as she represents the Eternal Feminine and *la mar*, the Virgin of Cobre's origins reside deep in humanity's primitive past. In *The Log from the Sea of Cortez*,[3] John Steinbeck and Edward F. Ricketts suggest how the Virgin may be more pagan than Christian as they describe the Virgin of Loreto. Patroness of a Mexican fishing village on the Sea of Cortez, she is a sister to Hemingway's Virgin of Cobre:

> This Lady, of plaster and wood and paint, is one of the strong ecological factors of the town of Loreto, and not to know her and her strength is to fail to know Loreto. One could not ignore a granite

monolith in the path of the waves. Such a rock, breaking the rushing waters, would have an effect on animal distribution radiating in circles like a dropped stone in a pool. So has this plaster Lady a powerful effect on the deep black water of the human spirit. She may disappear, and her name be lost, as the Magna Mater, as Isis have disappeared. But something very like her will take her place, and the longings which created her will find somewhere in the world a similar altar on which to pour their force. No matter what her name is, Artemis or Venus, or a girl behind a Woolworth counter dimly remembered, she is as eternal as our species, and we will continue to manufacture her as long as we survive. (207–08)

In the *la mar* passage, Santiago continues to gender the sea in a pagan vein when he considers that "The moon affects her as it does a woman" (30). Now he invokes the ancient personification of the moon as a feminine principle in nature, the monthly lunar changes affecting both the tides of the sea and woman's cycle of ovulation and fecundity, her provision of "the nutriment, the catamenia, or menstrual blood" (Merchant 13, 18–19), the nourishing matrix from which life grows. "[M]oon and sea and tide are one," write Steinbeck and Ricketts, and:

The imprint [of tidal forces] is in us and in Sparky and in the ship's master, in the palolo worm, in mussel worms, in chitons, and in the menstrual cycle of women. The imprint lies heavily on our dreams and on the delicate threads of our nerves. . . . (37, 39)

The disciplines of oceanography and marine biology both supply a scientific basis for Santiago's mythologizing the sea-as-matrix, a Mother Goddess obeying the cycles of the moon, with "changing woman" her acolyte. In *The Sea Around Us*,[4] Rachel Carson explains in a chapter titled "Mother Sea" how all life evolved from the sea and how the development of the human embryo recapitulates this evolutionary history.

Fish, amphibian, and reptile, warm-blooded bird and mammal— each of us carries in our veins a salty stream in which the elements sodium, potassium, and calcium are combined in almost the same proportions as sea water. . . . [O]ur lime-hardened skeletons are a heritage from the calcium-rich ocean of Cambrian time. Even the protoplasm that streams within each cell of our bodies has the chemical structure impressed upon all living matter when the first simple creatures were brought forth in the ancient sea. And as life itself began in the sea, so each of us begins his individual life within his mother's womb, and in the stages of his embryonic development repeats the steps by which his race evolved, from gill-breathing inhabitants of a water world to creatures able to live on land. (*The Sea Around Us* 28–29)

Carson postulates that man's love for and desire to return to "mother sea," his mythologizing and gendering of the sea as female, springs from his evolutionary history and longing for "a world that, in the deepest part of his subconscious mind, he ha[s] never wholly forgotten" (29).

Santiago knows the maternal, womblike space the fishermen call "the great well," a sudden deep hole teeming with life, where the current stirs a nutrient upwelling and brings "all the wandering fish" to feed on "shrimp and bait fish and sometimes schools of squid" (28). He also experiences the sea-as-matrix when he looks at plankton and feels happy because it means fish:

The water was a dark blue now, so dark that it was almost purple. As he looked down into it he saw the red sifting of the plankton in the dark water and the strange light the sun made now. He watched his lines to see them go straight down out of sight into the water and he was happy to see so much plankton because it meant fish. (35)

"Plankton," Thor Heyerdahl explains in *Kon-Tiki*,[5] "is a general name for thousands of species of visible and invisible small organisms which drift about near the surface of the sea. Some are plants (phyto-plankton), while others are loose fish ova and tiny living creatures (zoo-plankton)" (138). Where there is plankton, Steinbeck and Ricketts write, the sea "swarms with life." Plankton water is "tuna water—life water. It is complete from plankton to gray porpoises" (54). "These little animals, in their incalculable numbers, are probably the base food supply of the world"— their disappearance would "eliminate every living thing in the sea" if not "all life on the globe" (256).

Hemingway's sparing lines hint at all of this when Santiago experiences the plankton as a "red sifting" in the water (35). It's a "strange light" that makes translucent zooplankton and greenish phytoplankton appear red. But this coloring aligns the plankton with all of the blood of life spilled in the sea throughout the novella, and especially with the nutritive blood of the womb. Heyerdahl calls it "plankton porridge . . . the squashy mess . . . magic gruel" (140). From it, Mother Sea brings forth life.

The sea, Herman Melville reminds us in *Moby-Dick,* has its "submarine bridal-chambers" as well as its nurseries (400), and of this, Santiago is well aware. To him, "a great island of Sargasso weed that heaved and swung in the light sea" looks "as though the ocean were making love with something under a blanket" (72). In the night, two porpoises come around his boat, and Santiago "could tell the difference between the blowing noise the male made and the sighing blow of the female." He identifies with and values the porpoises for their mated love: "They are good. . . . They play and make jokes and love one another. They are our brothers . . ." (48). Later, he dreams of "a vast school of porpoises that stretched for eight or ten miles and it was in the time of their mating and they would leap high in the air and return into the same hole they had made when they had leaped" (81).

Asked in class how Hemingway's seemingly simple and objective prose could achieve such poetic quality in *The Old Man and the Sea,* a woman student gave this explanation: "It's the difference between a man taking a photograph of a woman and a man taking a photograph of a woman he loves." Throughout the novella, the images selected to represent *la mar* establish that she is indeed "very beautiful," and that Santiago is a lover, engaged in what Terry Tempest Williams has called an "erotics of place," a "pagan" and "primal affair" (84). The sea itself is sublimely beautiful, with its deep blue waters and shafts of sunlight, as is the sky with its canyons of clouds. All of the sea's creatures except the *galano* sharks are beautiful, even the mako and the poisonous jelly fish, and some are exceptionally so, like the dorado that takes Santiago's bait from beneath the erotically heaving blanket of Sargasso weed: "He saw it first when it jumped in the air, true gold in the last of the sun and bending and flapping wildly in the air" (72).

Always the prose seeks what Hemingway called "the action that makes the emotion" ("Monologue" 219), and the emotion is love: "In the dark

the old man could feel the morning coming and as he rowed he heard the
trembling sound as the flying fish left the water and the hissing that their
stiff wings made as they soared away in the darkness" (29). Or, "as the old
man watched, a small tuna rose in the air, turned and dropped head first
into the water. The tuna shone silver in the sun and after he had dropped
back into the water another and another rose and they were jumping in
all directions, churning the water and leaping in long jumps after the bait"
(38). "Listen to Hemingway write!" responds another woman student.
"Gorgeous!" (Gensler). Most "gorgeous" of all is the giant marlin that is
the sea's great gift to Santiago:

> The line rose slowly and steadily and then the surface of the ocean
> bulged ahead of the boat and the fish came out. He came out un-
> endingly and water poured from his sides. He was bright in the sun
> and his head and back were dark purple and in the sun the stripes
> on his sides showed wide and a light lavender. (62)

Although *The Old Man and the Sea* may seem to be about "men without women," the figure of a man *wedded* to a feminine sea is omnipresent
in our culture, from ancient myths of Venus rising from the foam of the
sea to be given as bride to Vulcan, to a contemporary rock ballad such as
E. Lurie's "Brandy," where a sailor tells his human lover, "[Y]ou're a fine
girl. What a good wife you would be. But my life, my lover, my lady is
the sea." Santiago is no exception. He is a widower and feels his loss—
"[T]here had been a tinted photograph of his wife on the wall but he had
taken it down because it made him too lonely to see it" (16)—and his loss
gives him empathy and compassion for the marlin. "The saddest thing
[he] ever saw with them" was the reaction of a male to the capture of his
mate. "He was beautiful, the old man remembered, and he had stayed"
(50). But now the beauty of the sea assuages Santiago's loneliness for his
flesh-and-blood wife: "[H]e looked ahead and saw a flight of wild ducks
etching themselves against the sky over the water, then etching again and
he knew no man was ever alone on the sea" (61).

In the course of the story, Santiago becomes wedded to the marlin. His
angling uses the language of seduction: "'Yes', he said. 'Yes.'" (41). "Come
on . . . Aren't they lovely? Eat them good now and then there is the tuna.
Hard and cold and lovely. Don't be shy, fish" (42). "Then he felt the gentle

touch on the line and he was happy" (43). Even after the marlin is firmly hooked and Santiago's ordeal begins, his developing sense of connectedness with the fish is expressed in language from the sacrament of marriage: "Now we are joined together" (50) and "Fish . . . I'll stay with you until I am dead" (52).

This sense of the sea-as-wife is not incompatible with Santiago's calling the marlin his "brother." Porpoises and flying fish of both sexes are Santiago's "brothers," too (48), and the word "brother" is neither gender-specific nor used only of humans in Hemingway's work. In "The Last Good Country," Nick's sister Littless looks like a "small wild animal" (*SS* 101), and wants to be both his "brother" (95) and his "wife" (104). In *The Garden of Eden,* Catherine Bourne tells David that he is "my good lovely husband and my brother too" (29), and David comes to understand that the elephant also is his "brother" (197).

Brothers are children of the same mother, living together in an implied state of equality and fraternity, depending on one another for mutual support. In *To Have and Have Not* Captain Willie says, of the human community at sea, "Most everybody goes in boats calls each other brother" (83). In *The Old Man and the Sea,* that marine community expands to include sea creatures. The man o' war bird is "a great help" to Santiago in locating fish (38), and Santiago in his turn aids the exhausted migrating warbler, "Take a good rest, small bird" (55). Hemingway's signature use of the word "brother" reflects longing for an Eden where men and women, husbands and wives, as well as birds, beasts, and fish might live together on such terms. Such an Eden would bring male and female principles, as well as man and nature, into harmony and balance.

How then may Santiago ethically "live on the sea and kill [his] true brothers" (75)? To render sea creatures as children of the same mother raises vital questions about right relationship to nature. Hunter-philosopher Ted Kerasote proposes some answers. "Hunting," he writes, should be a "disciplined, mindful, sacred activity. . . . hav[ing] much to do with kindness, compassion, and sympathy for those other species with whom we share the web of life. . . . based on the pre-Christian belief that other life-forms, indeed the very plants and earth and air themselves, are invested with soul and spirit" (191). Here we recognize the "primitive" Santiago who fishes with unmatched physical and mental discipline and with prayers, the Santiago who hits the landed tuna on the head "for kindness"

(42), who begs the female marlin's pardon and butchers her promptly (50), and who understands that the great marlin not only is his "brother," but suffers as Santiago himself suffers (92). In his introduction to *Atlantic Game Fishing*, Hemingway writes that "Anglers have a way of . . . forgetting that the fish has a hook in his mouth, his gullet, or his belly, and is driven to the extremes of panic at which he runs, leaps, and pulls to get away until he dies" (qtd. in Farrington 11). Santiago never forgets the "fish's agony" (93).

Ethical killing, Kerasote tells us, is not for "the cruel delight that comes at another's demise," but for "the celebratory joy inherent in well-performed hunting that produces a gift of food" (190). The blood of life may only be spilled to nourish life. Here we recognize the Santiago who sacramentally partakes of the flesh of every fish he kills—dolphin, tuna, marlin, and even tiny shrimp from the floating blanket of Sargasso weed. This is the Santiago who seeks a fish to feed "many people," and who hopes to repay his indebtedness to his human community with "the belly meat of a big fish" (20). He is drawn in part from Hemingway's Cuban boat-handler, Carlos Gutiérrez, who unlike the trophy-hunting sport fishermen always calls the marlin "the bread of my children," relating it to the staff of life—and the continuity of life: "Oh look at the bread of my children! Joseph and Mary look at the bread of my children jump! There it goes the bread of my children! He'll never stop the bread the bread the bread of my children!" (Hemingway, "On the Blue Water" 242). "Everything kills everything else in some way" as Santiago observes (106), and is ethical so long as the killing is followed by eating, the act of communion, of sharing the blood of life.

Aldo Leopold writes that all ecological ethics "rest upon a single premise: that the individual is a member of a community with interdependent parts. His instincts prompt him to compete for his place in the community, but his ethics prompt him also to co-operate" (239). Glen A. Love feels that *The Old Man and the Sea* lacks a fully developed ecological ethic, because Santiago perceives some creatures of the sea, such as sharks and poisonous jellyfish, as "enemies." Hemingway, Love argues, does not understand that all of the sea's creatures "are members of a community which man is not privileged to exterminate for real or assumed self-benefits" (208). Yet Love's is an environmental sensibility that places man outside of the food web, forgetting, as Leopold does not, that survival demands an ethic that includes the necessity of competition as well as of cooperation.

Santiago, as a subsistence fisherman, knows that he is part of the web of life. His community is truly "the great sea with our friends and our enemies" (120). He loves to see big sea turtles eating the jellyfish, and then he in turn eats the eggs of the turtles that eat the jellyfish in order to be strong "for the truly big fish" he himself hunts (36–37).[6] Others do not like the taste, but Santiago drinks "a cup of shark liver oil each day from the big drum in the shack where the fishermen keep their gear" to sharpen his eyesight (37). Indeed, Santiago's eyes, "the same color as the sea . . . cheerful and undefeated" emblematize that the sea and its creatures are the well-spring of his own life—"with his eyes closed there was no life in his face" (10, 19). He understands that the lives of his "enemies" too are part of the "celebratory gift," part of his fisherman's communion with life.

A woman student who does not accept the primitive hunter's communion of blood, the pagan appreciation of the intimate proximity of life and death, objects to Santiago's slaying of the marlin in gendered terms:

> Ultimately, while I pity Santiago and mourn his defeat, I can't relate to his struggle. I do not share his need to defeat the marlin, or his desire for conquest. This type of battle is common to Hemingway, I've come across the same one in *Islands in the Stream* and I know he's restaged it with bulls and matadors in other books. What I wonder is what form these epic battles would take if Hemingway had been a woman. How would she describe childbirth? Imagine, these arduous, protracted ordeals produce nothing but dead fish, but what magic, what power would be imparted to a two-day struggle to produce a screaming new human being? (Betancourt)

In one sense, *The Old Man and the Sea* may already fulfill this student's wish for a Hemingway who places the male values of strength and endurance in the service of the Eternal Feminine, of bringing forth rather than taking life. To *la mar*, Santiago owes his disciple, the boy Manolin who is more to him than a son. Santiago has no child by his mortal wife, but has delivered Manolin from the sea in a violent birthing. "How old was I when you first took me in a boat?" the boy asks Santiago, in the manner of a child asking a parent for the legend of his birth. "Five and you were nearly killed when I brought the fish in too green and he nearly tore the boat to pieces. Can you remember?" (12). Manolin responds:

> I can remember the tail slapping and banging and the thwart break-ing and the noise of clubbing. I can remember you throwing me into the bow where the wet coiled lines were and feeling the whole boat shiver and the noise of you clubbing him like chopping a tree down and the sweet blood smell all over me. (12)

Fish and boy are elided here, as man-midwife Santiago forcibly ex-tracts the flapping, struggling fish from the sea and throws the child slicked in "sweet blood" into the bow. "Can you really remember that or did I just tell you?" asks Santiago. Manolin insists that he can, but the scene is so primal that readers may share Santiago's doubt, wondering whether the boy remembers it any more than he would remember the scene of his birth.

In an essay titled "Forceps" that is in part a history of masculine in-volvement in obstetrics, Hemingway's doctor father writes that for cen-turies men were not permitted to attend or witness normal births. "Men midwives," he mourns, "were not allowed at confinements . . . except in cases where an extraction by *force* [his emphasis] of a dead fetus was re-quired." He celebrates the eventual inclusion of men in the process of normal birthing: "to help and share the responsibility" of the "sacred trust" (C. Hemingway 3). In the "birthing" scene from *The Old Man and the Sea*, where Santiago acts as a man-midwife, we do see how his great strength and heroism might serve the cause of life.

On the positive side of the ledger, then, Santiago's gendering the sea as *la mar* underlies this novella's strong ecological ethic. To gender the sea as female or as a mother goddess implies reciprocal obligation. The man who approaches nature as his lover, wife, or mother, expecting "great fa-vours" and kindness, must also, as Whitman phrases it, "mean tenderly" by her. The concept of the sea as a feminine, living being ought to serve, as Carolyn Merchant has pointed out on behalf of the earth, "as a cultural constraint restricting the actions of human beings. One does not readily slay a mother, dig into her entrails . . . or mutilate her body. . . . As long as the earth [is] considered to be alive and sensitive, it could be considered a breach of human ethical behavior to carry out destructive acts against it" (3).

There is no more potent example in American literature of a book that genders the sea as masculine than Herman Melville's *Moby-Dick,* celebrating its centennial the year Hemingway composed *The Old Man and the Sea.*[7] "To and fro in the deeps, far down in the bottomless blue," Melville writes, "rushed mighty leviathans, sword-fish, and sharks, and these were the strong, troubled, murderous thinkings of the masculine sea" (543). No character more obviously treats the sea as masculine contestant and enemy than Captain Ahab, or is more closely associated with man's self-destructive technological assault on nature: "Swerve me? The path to my fixed purpose is laid with iron rails, whereon my soul is grooved to run. Over unsounded gorges, through the rifled hearts of mountains, under torrents' beds, unerringly I rush! Naught's an obstacle, naught's an angle to the iron way!" (172).

Santiago seems to uphold an ecological ethic diametrically opposed to Ahab's "iron way" when he recognizes that those who gender the sea as masculine treat the sea more violently than those who think of her as *la mar:*

> Some of the younger fishermen, those who used buoys as floats for their lines and had motorboats, bought when the shark livers had brought much money, spoke of her as *el mar* which is masculine. They spoke of her as a contestant or a place or even an enemy. (30)

These two sentences are dense with environmental history. Aligned with technology, Santiago's young fishermen are not only the workaday descendants of Captain Ahab, they are the ancestors of today's long-liners. Dr. Perry W. Gilbert, a shark expert familiar with the Cuban fishing village of Cojimar where Hemingway based *The Old Man and the Sea,* explains the fishing rig described above:

> [F]ishermen put out from Cojimar in their small boats, only eighteen to twenty-four feet over all, and head for the deep water. . . . [T]wo men comprise the crew, and their boat carries ten to fifteen floating fishing rigs of three hooks each . . . The hooks of one set hang at different intervals in the water, usually at twenty, fifty,

and eighty fathoms. . . . The wooden buoys, spaced forty to fifty feet apart, are joined to each other by a three-quarter inch manila rope, attached at one end to a square wooden float bearing the name of the boat . . . and a four foot mast carrying a lantern and flag. . . . After the sets are all placed and the lanterns lit, they are patrolled until dawn. At daybreak the catch of dolphin, marlin, broadbill, and sharks is removed, and if the weather is fair, a set may be rebaited. . . . The 'Old Man,' of course, did not have this set. His lines were off his boat or in his hands. (qtd. in Farrington 28–30)

The young fishermen fish not so much for the "celebratory gift of food," Gilbert tells us, but for the "shark factory" mentioned at the beginning of *The Old Man and the Sea* (11), an industry processing their catch for the Oriental soup fin trade, for an Ocean Leather Company in New Jersey converting shark skin to wallets, belts, and shoes, and for the vitamin A in shark liver oil (in Farrington 30–31). Their motorboats are the fruits of war. "Shark livers had brought much money" during World War II, when German submarines in the North Atlantic cut off the Grand Banks and the world supply of cod liver oil for pharmaceuticals (R. Ellis 45); the Cojimar shark factory would remain profitable until 1958, when vitamin A was synthesized (Gilbert in Farrington 31).

Santiago sees in the young fishermen the death of his way of life, the end of putting to sea in small boats powered by oar and sail, of locating fish only with his own intimate knowledge of the sea and her creatures, and of catching them with the unaided strength of his body. In part, *The Old Man and the Sea* is Hemingway's elegy for the subsistence fisherman, and perhaps, as when Santiago wonders what it would be like to spot fish from airplanes (71), or to have a radio in the boat that would bring him the "baseball," but distract him from "thinking much" about the sea (105), a prophesy of things to come. Mary Hemingway recalled:

Our habit was to anchor *Pilar* in the little bay of Cojimar. . . . The town's population was almost entirely fishermen who went out as Santiago did in those days with their skiffs and were carried by the Gulf Stream, which flows from west to east across the northern part of Cuba's coast. They would then put their baits down and drift. . . . When they had their fish, or when the day was finished . . . they'd stick up their sails and come sailing back against the Gulf Stream, the wind being stronger than the current. . . . [B]efore we left, the fishermen . . . were able to add outboard motors to their boats. (qtd. in Bruccoli, "Interview" 193)

Neither Santiago nor Hemingway could predict the modern fleet of Atlantic swordboats—long-liners assisted by global positioning systems, weather fax, down temperature indicators, Doppler radar, color sounders, video plotters, radiofrequency beeper buoys, and hydraulic haulbacks for lines twenty-five to forty miles long, indiscriminately cleansing the sea of swordfish, sharks, sea turtles, tuna, and other deep oceanic fish (Greenlaw 137). Nor could they predict a generation whose most successful fishermen would be "fishing gear engineers and electronics wizards," ignoring birds and clouds to "study data and base decisions on statistics" (Greenlaw 137–38).

But Santiago does know that the fishermen of the future will follow the "el mar" ethos of treating the sea as a masculine enemy or contestant. Contemporary swordboat captain Linda Greenlaw, ironically a woman, bears him out when she describes her work as "Man vs. Nature." She uses words like "warrior," "relentless beast," "fight," "monstrous sword," "war," "forces," and "combat" to describe a losing contest with a commodified "$2,000 fish," and then, when the line snaps and the swordfish gets loose, leaps to the rail with her men to give the animal, perceived as "gloating" in "victory," the phallic upraised finger, and to scream "Fuck you" until her throat is raw (Greenlaw 173–75). If Carolyn Merchant is correct that gendering nature as female and as the mother-of-life acts as a cultural constraint against destructive acts, then the converse appears to be true, that gendering the sea as a masculine opponent enables destructive and violent behavior. Since the first swordfish took bait on an American longline in 1961, Santiago's "young fishermen" have swept the Atlantic of 75 percent of its bluefin tuna and 70 percent of its breeding-age swordfish (Safina, Chivers), carrying us ever closer to the "fishless desert" of Santiago's nightmare (2).

Santiago rejects those who masculinize the sea. But against his view of Mother Sea as a beautiful, kindly, and generous feminine provider—a belief that in many respects does temper his behavior toward her—he sets an opposing view of feminine nature as cruel and chaotic—spawning poisonous creatures, sudden storms, and hurricanes. Although early in the novella Hemingway tells us that Santiago "no longer dreamed of storms, nor of women, nor of great occurrences, nor of great fish, nor fights, nor contests of strength, nor of his wife," *The Old Man and the Sea* is a dream of all such things, and here we learn that Santiago includes the feminine principles of "women" and "wife" with "storms" and "great fish," natural things that might be fought or engaged in "contests of strength" (25). As Merchant points out, such views of nature as a disorderly female force call forth the male need for rationalistic or mechanistic power over her (127).

Critic Gerry Brenner labels the *la mar* passage "a litany of sexist aggressions" in part for Santiago's "metaphoric equation" of woman and the sea "as dependent on the moon or some power over which she has no control" (*Story* 84). However, the point of Santiago's "and if she did wild or wicked things it was because she could not help them," may be that women and the sea are not *under* control, but *beyond* control. Carson writes that man may approach "mother sea only on her terms. . . . He cannot control or change the ocean as . . . he has subdued and plundered the continents" (*Sea Around Us* 29–30). When Santiago thinks "the moon affects her as it does a woman," he betrays male fear of female power, of the menstruous or monstrous woman, whose wildness and wickedness challenges his rationalism and control, and whose cruelty provokes his attempts at dominance. In *The Garden of Eden*, Catherine Bourne (who needs to "go up to the room" because "I'm a god damned woman"), speaks for menstruous woman, and perhaps for *la mar*, when she overrides David's effort to silence and control her: "Why should I hold it down? You want a girl, don't you? Don't you want everything that goes with it? Scenes, hysteria, false accusations, temperament, isn't that it?" (70).

Santiago believes that, in his great love for and understanding of *la mar*, he has accepted "everything that goes with" her femininity. He knows the months of the "sudden bad weather," and is not afraid to be out of sight of land in hurricane season, because he "can see the signs of [a hurricane] for days ahead" in the sky (61). He endures the painful sting of a ray hidden in the sand, and of the Portuguese man o' war jellyfish he genders as female and calls "Agua mala [evil water]" and "You whore." Although the jellyfish strike "like a whiplash," he loves to walk on them on the beach after a storm and "hear them pop when he step[s] on them with the horny soles of his feet" (82). While Brenner finds Santiago's "vilification of the jellyfish" the novella's most "blatant" example of "hostility or contempt towards things female" (82), Katharine T. Jobes believes the old man's epithet—"You whore"—is familiar, affectionate, a reflection of Santiago's "intimate at-homeness in nature" (16).

Yet despite Santiago's apparent acceptance of the sea's wild and wicked nature, ultimately he sins against her, and she bitches him. Gendering the sea as feminine does not resolve the problem of man's violence toward nature, but raises even more disturbing questions about right relationship than gendering the sea as *el mar.* Our culture generally accepts male-on-male violence—such as the cock-fighting and arm-wrestling in *Old Man* —provided it conforms to the rituals of warfare, chivalry, or sportsman-ship. We perceive such violence as the "natural" outcome of male compe-tition for territory and sexual prerogative, although neither instinct bodes well when directed against nature. Conversely, male-on-female violence is taboo, "unnatural" because the biological purpose of male-female rela-tions is procreation, not competition.

As Melvin Backman has noted, *Death in the Afternoon* provides an interpretive key to the problem of sin in *The Old Man and the Sea:* "[W]hen a man is still in rebellion against death he has pleasure in taking to himself one of the Godlike attributes; that of giving it. . . . These things are done in pride and pride, of course, is a Christian sin and a pagan virtue . . . " (233). The old man is surely in rebellion against death. His eighty-four days without a fish, the mockery of the young fishermen, the pity of the older fishermen, the charity of his village, the role reversal that sees his much-loved apprentice Manolin taking care of him ("You'll not fish without eating while I'm alive" [19]), and perhaps most of all the loss of Manolin, forced by his parents into a "luckier" boat, conspire to make Santiago feel his proximity to death. These things send him out to sea, beyond all other fishermen, to seek "a big one" (30), and the struggle with the marlin becomes in part a struggle with the "treachery of one's own body" (62), with his spells of faintness and blurred vision, with his cramped hand: "Pull, hands. . . . Hold up, legs. Last for me, head. Last for me" (91). Santiago's rebellion against death draws him first into sin, and then into an orgy of violence against the sea he loves.

In Christian iconography, both the sea and the Eternal Feminine are associated with death and resurrection. *The Book of Common Prayer* makes of the ocean a vast graveyard, and, strangely for a Christian text, feminizes the sea: "We therefore commit his body to the deep, to be turned into corruption, looking for the resurrection of the body, when the Sea shall give up *her* dead" (my emphasis, 552). The Virgin of Cobre places Santiago in this cycle of death and resurrection. Opus Dei scholar Dwight Duncan opines: "Christianity is the celebration of Christ as a man, one of us. So it is natural to approach it through the perspective of the mother. Mary is the guarantor of Christ's manhood" (Kennelly). Phrased somewhat differently, this means that the Virgin is the guarantor of Christ's suffering and death—and Santiago's. As his mortal progenitor, the Mother makes Christ subject—as all humanity is subject—to the immutable laws of biological nature.

Santiago kills the marlin with the most masculine of weapons, the harpoon, driving it deep into the fish's heart, the organ of love and the seat of life:

> The old man dropped the line and put his foot on it and lifted the harpoon as high as he could and drove it down with all his strength, and more strength he had just summoned, into the fish's side just behind the great chest fin that rose high in the air to the altitude of the man's chest. He felt the iron go in and he leaned on it and drove it further and then pushed all his weight after it.
>
> Then the fish came alive, with his death in him, and rose high out of the water showing all his great length and width and all his power and his beauty. (93–94)

Three times Hemingway tells us that the old man's target was the heart: "I must try for the heart" (91); "the sea was discoloring with the red of the blood from his heart" (94); "I think I felt his heart. . . . When I pushed on the harpoon shaft the second time" (95).

The heart of the marlin recalls the Sacred Heart of Jesus, the other devotional icon that hangs on the wall of Santiago's shack next to the Virgin of Cobre (16). That heart symbolizes the love and suffering of Christ, and his sacrifice—his death that man might live. By suggesting that the marlin too might have a sacred heart, Hemingway asks us to contemplate the passion of the natural cycle, or, as Kerasote puts it, to "fac[e] up to this basic and poignant condition of biological life on this planet—people, animals, and plants as fated cohorts, as both dependents and donors of life" (191). Hemingway invites us to understand that the marlin, in the words of Santiago's "Hail Mary," is the "fruit of the womb" of the Eternal Feminine (65). Coming "alive with his death in him," the marlin conjoins the principles of life and death implicit both in natural cycles and in the iconography of resurrection that arises from them. Santiago sees the eye of the dead fish looking "as detached as mirrors in a periscope or as a saint in a procession" (96), suggesting that the marlin should remind us of our own mortality, and our own mortality should remind us to have compassion for all living things.

Santiago's harpoon, probing the sacred heart, probes again the essential question of male-on-female violence, of right relationship of man and nature. When may man ethically kill the thing he loves? "If you love him, it is not a sin to kill him," Santiago thinks of the great marlin. "Or is it more?" (105). Santiago cannot bear to pursue the question—"You think too much, old man"—he tells himself, but the text would seem to argue "more." Too late, he recognizes that "You did not kill him to keep alive and to sell for food," the only allowable answers, "You killed him for pride and because you are a fisherman" (105). Despite knowing that the marlin is "two feet longer than the skiff" and cannot be landed (63), despite believing that it is "unjust" and that he is doing it to show the marlin "what a man can do and what a man endures" (66), despite feeling that "there is no one worthy of eating him from the manner of his behaviour and his great dignity" (75), the old man proceeds to kill the marlin anyway. When sharks attack the fish, as Santiago knows they must, his tragedy will be to recognize that he was wrong: "'Half fish,' he said. 'Fish that you were. I am sorry that I went out too far. I ruined us both'" (115).

Sylvester has argued that Santiago's "slaying of the marlin and his responsibility for its mutilation are sins," but "tragic precisely because they are a necessary result of his behavior as a champion of his species" ("Extended Vision" 136). Sylvester sees "opposition to nature as paradoxically necessary to vitality in the natural field" ("Extended Vision" 132), and perhaps it's true that a man "born to be a fisherman as the fish was born to be a fish" (105) could not conceive, as Hemingway himself could conceive, of releasing a marlin and "giv[ing] him his life back" (G. Hemingway 73). Perhaps a man who fishes for his living cannot say, as young David Hudson says in *Islands in the Stream* about a marlin that escapes him after a gruelling fight: "I loved him so much when I saw him coming up that I couldn't stand it. . . . All I wanted was to see him closer. . . . Now I don't give a shit I lost him. . . . I don't care about records. I just thought I did. I'm glad that he's all right" (143). Yet if Sylvester's concept of "necessary sin" is correct, then the text violates Santiago's own philosophy—that it is wrong to gender the sea as *el mar* and to treat it as a contestant or enemy. A woman student proposes instead that Santiago's sin is both unnecessary and the direct result of the "masculine" thinking he himself has deplored:

> The code of manhood that gives Santiago the strength for his battle and even the reason to begin it is completely foreign to me. He doesn't *have* to do this—a fisherman can make a living on the tuna and dolphin that Santiago uses only for bait and sustenance. . . . When Santiago says he has not caught a fish in eighty-seven [*sic*] days, he does not mean fish, he means Krakens, sea monsters. The bravery involved in just wresting a living from the sea is nothing . . . Santiago has to be a saint and fight dragons. . . . I guess what it comes down to is greatness. . . . Killing a 1500 lb. Marlin puts him on the same level with the magnificent fish, giving him a power as great as the ocean's. There is nothing about this that's hard to understand; a man wishes to be strong and so he tests himself against the strongest thing he can find (Betancourt).

Nature's punishment for the harpoon in the heart is swift and inexorable. The heart pumps the blood of the stricken fish into the sea—"First it was dark as a shoal in the blue water that was more than a mile deep. Then it spread like a cloud" (94). The heart's blood summons the first shark, a mako, and Santiago recognizes the consequences of his own actions: "The shark was not an accident. He had come up from deep down in the water as the dark cloud of blood had settled and dispersed in the mile deep sea" (100). Indeed, the mako almost seems like the marlin's avenging ghost: "His back was as blue as a sword fish's and his belly was silver and his hide was smooth and handsome. He was built like a sword fish except for his huge jaws" (100). Like the marlin too, the mako is "beautiful and noble" (106). His teeth "shaped like a man's fingers when they are crisped like claws" (100–101), recall Santiago's left hand cramped "tight as the gripped claws of an eagle" (63). The mako comes as a grim reminder that marlin, shark, and man—all predators—are brothers, children of the same mother.

Yet "the shadow of sharks is the shadow of death," as Peter Matthiessen has observed (5), and when Santiago sees the mako, he curses the mother—"*Dentuso*, he thought, bad luck to your mother" (101)—and who is the Mother of Sharks if not *la mar*? Santiago assaults the shadow of death "without hope but with resolution and complete malignancy" (102). He harpoons the mako with a precision so reminiscent of the bullfight, one wonders whether Hemingway knew that the ancient Hawaiians built marine arenas in shallow water, where men armed with shark-tooth daggers fought sharks to honor Kama-Hoa-Lii, the shark god (Cousteau 205). Harpooning the mako, Santiago sins a second time, and explicitly partakes of the matador's sin from *Death in the Afternoon*. "You enjoyed killing the *dentuso*, he thought" (105), and this is both the Christian sin of pride in taking pleasure in the Godlike attribute of giving death, and the pagan sin identified by Kerasote, of taking "cruel delight" in another's demise (109). Again Santiago's sin sends a blood message of life wrongfully taken into the sea: "Now my fish bleeds again," he thinks after the dead mako sinks with his harpoon, "and there will be others" (103). Santiago's rebellion against death, which has, from the start of the novella, underlain his quest for the marlin, now assumes crisis proportions.

Sharks begin to arrive in numbers, and they are a different species—not the "beautiful and noble" mako, *Isurus oxyrinchus*, that like the marlin preys on tuna and dolphin (Bigelow 23–25), but *galanos*, probably oceanic whitetip sharks, *Carcharhinus longimanus*, but certainly—and significantly—members of the family *Carcharinidae*,[8] commonly known as the "Requiem sharks" (R. Ellis 130). These sharks are not only biologically apt (whitetips are well-known to whalemen and big game fishermen for feeding on their kills, and notorious for attacks on victims of shipwrecks and air disasters), but for a marine naturalist like Hemingway they also allude to the introit of the Roman Catholic mass for the dead. Santiago truly vilifies the *galanos* as

> hateful sharks, bad smelling, scavengers as well as killers, and when they were hungry they would bite at an oar or the rudder of a boat. It was these sharks that would cut the turtles' legs and flippers off

when the turtles were asleep on the surface, and they would hit a man in the water, if they were hungry, even if the man had no smell of fish blood nor of fish slime on him. (108)

Rising from the sea as from the grave, their evil smell a reminder that the body is destined "to be turned into corruption," the scavenging *galanos* are the ultimate reminder of death as the reabsorption of the individual into the matrix of life. When Santiago sees them, he makes "a noise such as a man might make, involuntarily, feeling the nail go through his hands and into the wood" (107). "Old men should burn and rave at close of day," Dylan Thomas writes (942), and Santiago does indeed rage against the dying of the light, stabbing, hacking, and clubbing at the sharks with everything he has, although he knows that the fight is "useless" (118). "'Fight them,' he said. 'I'll fight them until I die'" (115). Like the mako, the *galanos* too are sent by the mother, and Santiago seems to perceive himself as sending a message of defiance to her when he says to a shark he has killed: "Go on, *galano*. Slide down a mile deep. Go see your friend, or maybe it's your mother" (109).

The "evil" of the shark, emblematizing the inexorability of suffering and death in nature, has long constituted a theological problem, calling into question the benevolent intentions of God toward man, and suggesting instead cruelty and indifference. "Queequeg no care what god made him shark," pronounces Melville's savage, "wedder Fejee god or Nantucket god; but de god wat made shark must be one dam Ingin" (310). Even a marine ecologist such as Philippe Cousteau, who recognizes that it is risible to "qualif[y] one animal as 'good' and another as 'bad'" (133), can write of the same oceanic whitetip shark that Santiago finds hateful:

> [O]ne of the most formidable of the deep-sea sharks, a great *longimanus*. . . . this species is absolutely hideous. His yellow-brown color is not uniform, but streaked with irregular markings resembling a bad job of military camouflage. . . . He swims in a jerky, irregular manner, swinging his shortened, broad snout from side to side. His tiny eyes are hard and cruel-looking. (89)

Cousteau also recognizes that his fear of sharks is related to his fear of an indifferent, inhuman creator: "The shark moves through my universe like a marionette whose strings are controlled by someone other than the power manipulating mine" (70).

The Old Man and the Sea suggests, through its twice-repeated reference to the "mother" of sharks, that "de god wat made shark" must be one damn woman—cruel, wild, wicked, irrational, beyond control. Santiago's battle with the sharks, his rage and rebellion against *la mar,* is his most Melvillean moment. Like Ahab, Santiago seems to say:

> I now know thee . . . and I now know thy right worship is defiance. To neither love nor reverence wilt thou be kind; and e'en for hate thou canst but kill; and all are killed. . . . I now own thy speechless, placeless power; but to the last gasp of my earthquake life will dispute its unconditional mastery in me. In the midst of the personified impersonal, a personality stands here. (512)

Santiago puts it more simply, spitting blood coughed up from his chest into the sea when the last of the shark pack leaves the ruined marlin, saying "Eat that, *galanos,* and make a dream you've killed a man" (119). The life that burns in him, the will to survive, is the source of his proud individualism and refusal to submit tamely to annihilation. Ahab proclaims "[O]f thy fire thou madest me, and like a true child of fire, I breathe it back" (512).

Ahab's defiance of a masculine god places him outside of nature and against nature, a crime for which he will be executed with a hempen cord of whale line around the neck. Santiago's defiance of the feminine "mother of sharks" places him inside nature and outside of nature. Like the turtle whose heart beats "for hours after he has been cut up and butchered" (37), like the great marlin who comes "alive, with his death in him" (94), and especially like the shark who is dead but "would not accept it" (102), Santiago is a true child of *la mar.* Her law proclaims that "all are killed," but her law also proclaims that all—turtle, marlin, shark, and man—will dispute their deaths. The sea punishes Santiago for the wrongful deaths of marlin and mako, but for the final battle with the sharks—for breathing back the fire of life—she forgives him.

When the battle with the sharks is finally and irretrievably lost, Santiago achieves a kind of serenity born of acceptance that Ahab never knows. Ahab neither repents nor relents—"for hate's sake I spit my last breath at thee" (574–75). Santiago does both, apologizing to the marlin and acknowledging that he has been "beaten now finally" by the sharks (119). This the old man experiences as a lightening, a release from a great burden:

> He settled the sack around his shoulders and put the skiff on her course. He sailed lightly now and he had no thoughts nor any feelings of any kind. He was past everything now. . . . In the night sharks hit the carcass. . . . The old man paid no attention to them and did not pay attention to anything except steering. He only noticed how lightly and how well the skiff sailed now there was no great weight beside her. (119)

Eric Waggoner reads this passage as a restoration of harmony, citing the *Tao-te Ching:* "Return is the movement of the Way; / yielding is the function of the way" (102). Waggoner's Taoist perspective prompts us to understand that by yielding to the sea, by accepting his place in nature, "[Santiago] can re-place himself in the balance of his fishing life and sail his skiff 'well'" (102). Still more important, however, is the end of Santiago's rebellion against death, and the beginning of his acquiescence.

Now Santiago is "inside the current," and the text restores him to his original love and reverence for the sea with all her vagaries and caprices. In this key passage, *la mar* is aligned not with an enemy wind that sends great storms, but with the friendly wind that carries an exhausted fisherman lightly home. The sea is associated not with the cruelty of a watery grave and its scavenging sharks, but with bed, where a tired man may find rest:

> The wind is our friend, anyway, he thought. Then he added, sometimes. And the great sea with our friends and enemies. And bed, he thought. Bed is my friend. Just bed, he thought. Bed will be a great thing. It is easy when you are beaten, he thought. I never knew how easy it was. (120)

Now, in Whitmanian rather than Melvillean fashion, Santiago hears the word up from feminine rather than masculine waves, the word of "the sweetest song and all songs," the word "out of the cradle endlessly rock-ing," the word whispered by the sea—death (184).

Santiago's acquiescence is not Christian. Earlier, Santiago has con-fessed that he is "not religious" (64); there is no hint that he believes in resurrection. But if he believes in the sea as both friend and enemy, cradle and grave, life and death, and accepts her cycles, then he may partake in the "natural" consolation of Ecclesiastes slightly revised—"One genera-tion passeth away and another generation cometh: but the [sea] abideth forever" (1.6). The pagan—and the naturalist—both draw spiritual com-fort from material immortality in the Eternal Feminine. As Carson puts it in *Under the Sea Wind:* "[I]n the sea, nothing is lost. One dies, another lives, as the precious elements of life are passed on and on in endless chains" (105).[9]

A text that masculinized the sea might end with Santiago "destroyed but not defeated" (103), the existential hero with the trophy of his pyrrhic victory, "the great fish . . . now just garbage waiting to go out with the tide" (126). But *The Old Man and the Sea* ends instead not only with San-tiago's acceptance of death as natural as sleep—but with the cycle of life turning upwards once more. Hemingway reunites Santiago with Mano-lin, the boy who is more-than-son to him, the child of Santiago's man-midwifery, delivered from the sea. Theirs is what Claire Rosenfeld calls a "spiritual kinship" (43); the sea as wife-and-mother joins them as father-and-son. Manolin cares tenderly for the old man, allowing him to sleep undisturbed, bringing him coffee, food, newspapers, and a clean shirt, and making cheerful talk about the future. When Santiago cannot see him, the boy weeps for the old man's ordeal and shows his understanding: he weeps for Santiago's suffering when he sees the bloody stigmata of the rope on the old man's hands (122), he weeps for the ruin of the great fish when he sees the skeleton lashed to the skiff (122), and he weeps for his mentor's heartbreak and imminent death after Santiago tells him that "something in his chest [feels] broken" (125).

Manolin will carry Santiago's legacy forward, insuring the continuity of life in the face of destruction. The boy asks for and receives the spear of the great marlin from his mentor (124), a gift that represents not only Santiago's greatness as a fisherman, but the dignity and courage and beauty of the fish himself and the lesson of his loss. The spear is also a gift from the sea that binds man and boy and fish together, a true family heirloom, and a pagan devotional icon. Having received the bequest of the spear, Manolin promises in his turn to leave the boats of the young fishermen where his other "family" has placed him, to follow Santiago for "I still have much to learn" (125). If Santiago is dying, then Manolin's discipleship may be more metaphorical than literal, but the passage of the marlin's spear to him affirms the continuation of Santiago's values, the perpetuation of a line of fishermen who gender the sea as *la mar* because they love her. That Manolin is a worthy heir, we know. From the beginning of the text, when he tells Santiago—"If I cannot fish with you, I would like to serve in some way" (12)—this filial boy has met the test of love as defined by the priest in *A Farewell to Arms:* "When you love you wish to do things for. You wish to sacrifice for. You wish to serve." (72). We expect Manolin to honor both Santiago and the sea by fishing in the disciplined, mindful, sacred way.

Making his bequest, accomplishing this transition, brings Santiago final serenity and this text full circle. We leave him asleep, the boy keeping vigil beside him, dreaming the recurrent dream of lions that has been with him from the beginning of the story (25, 127). The dream lions, we know, come to a long yellow beach to play like young cats in the dusk, and Santiago "love[s] them as he love[s] the boy" (25). "Why are the lions the main thing that is left?" (66), Santiago has wondered, and we may wonder too. Perhaps his dream of innocent predators, allied with the boy and the continuity of life, carries him to a Peaceable Kingdom, an Eden unspoiled by sin where men no longer need to "live on the sea and kill our true brothers" (75), to a place where viewing nature as a contestant or an enemy is no longer possible, and love alone remains.

10
West of Everything

The High Cost of Making Men in
Islands in the Stream

Rose Marie Burwell

In cowboy jargon "to go west of everything," means to die—a euphemism that was probably borrowed from Indians, for whom *to travel the three-day road* was to take the westward journey walked by the dying. Jane Tompkins, in her little jewel of a book *West of Everything: The Inner Life of Westerns* (1992), examines the exposure of Americans to the Western genre. Tompkins contends that from 1900 to 1975 a large portion of the adolescent male population spent Saturday afternoon at the movies watching Westerns, concluding that in the afternoon kids saw Roy Rogers, Tom Mix, Lash LaRue, Gene Autry, and Hopalong Cassidy—while on Saturday night many of their parents saw John Wayne, Gary Cooper, Steve McQueen, and any number of Sam Peckinpah's heroes and villains in slightly more sophisticated versions of the Western genre.

Although Tompkins does not explore the transposition of Westerns from movie to television, it is interesting to note that five of the most popular and long-running early TV series were Westerns: *Gunsmoke, Have Gun Will Travel, Bonanza, The Rifleman,* and *The Virginian.* Among the conventions of the Western novel and film that have come to define what makes a man a man in American popular culture, Jane Tompkins ranks linguistic choice first, a priority that Hemingway recognized early he shared with Owen Wister, the writer on whose work *The Virginian* was based.[1] Tompkins's list continues: (1) language devoid of abstraction or emotion, (2) centrality of landscape, (3) importance of horses & cattle,

(4) unquestioning commitment to a goal, and (5) acceptance of the reckoning or entrapment that dispenses death.

How well most of us know, even without having consciously internalized it, that the Western is laden with codes of conduct, standards of judgment, and habits of perception that shape our sense of the world and govern our behavior. Westerns play to a Wild West of the psyche in the same way that *the West* functions as a symbol of freedom that offers an escape from life lived in a world of social entanglements and meaningless proscriptions, the world that Hemingway fled in 1939 and of which he wrote to Maxwell Perkins soon after:

> It's so much more fun living here than in Key West that it's pitiful. You see the bridges put KW all on the bum. You couldn't shoot anymore. The government took over all the Keys and put bird wardens on them. . . . If you did a good day's work (a miracle with people bothering all the time, with people always comeing to swim in the pool and you hearing every word they said . . .) there was nothing to do except go down to Mr. Josie's place and drink. . . . (28 January 1940)

Inherent in Hemingway's complaints about what drove him from Key West is ratification of another comfortably and deceptively simple element of the vision offered by the Western—the assumption that reality is *material* and that the spheres of women and men are easy to separate, for certainly it is a woman who issues the invitation for noisy socializing around the pool while the writer tries to work. The Western gives little space to the life of women; her world is repetitious, unexciting, exhausting, and often painful—if she is a good woman. It is filled with bearing and raising children, with making do, with entertaining the preacher. Religion, books, and ideas are abstractions that belong in the world of women—if they have a place at all—for they interfere with the work of men.

Not that the work of men is easy or painless, but *it* has at center a clearly defined goal—which, when it is accomplished, stays accomplished. Men's work is always recognizable because it is so easily presented in action-filled material images. How easy it is for the devoted viewer of western movies, projected at twenty-four frames per second, or the reader of its plot-driven and page-bound counterpart to ignore that a crucial element of men's work is, if not more dangerous than women's, dangerous in ways difficult to render in material images. The heroic male figure who offers vicarious satisfaction to viewers and readers of both sexes is dominated by his need to dominate, and the code he embodies both elevates and limits him. Set apart by the very material nature of his representation—his garb, his walk, his verbal frugality—he is also dehumanized. The cowboy cannot alternate between his code hero role and participation in that part of humanity that carries on the tasks necessary to existence back at the ranch where life is just one damned thing after another. Consider for a moment the viewer/reader reaction to the cowboy who, on his triumphant way home from disposing of bad guys, stops for a conference with the school teacher about his child's lack of progress in arithmetic or who slows his lope from corral to house to take dry clothes from the line.

In Louis L'Amour's novel *Heller with a Gun* there is a paradigm of the self-imprisoned state of the Western hero. L'Amour's hero is alone, in a blizzard, with a murderer on his trail. And it is forty below zero. He overpowers the man who was trying to kill him, and after thirty-six hours in the saddle he rides into a supply station. The chapter ends with this: "His mind was empty. He did not think. Only the occasional tug on the lead rope reminded him of the man who rode behind him. It was a hard land, and it bred hard men to hard ways" (15). The paradigm says that the hero is tough and strong, that the West made him that way, that it is his ability to endure pain that saves him, and that the only qualities required of the hero are self-discipline, unswerving purpose, the possession and exercise of knowledge, skill, ingenuity, excellent judgment, and the capacity to continue in the face of total exhaustion and overwhelming odds. These are important qualities; who would not identify with such a man? But they are also the qualities of a workaholic, a terrorist, and a religious fanatic. Further, for the individual of whom these are the *only* qualities required, they provide an escape from the messy, boring demands that constitute life back at the ranch where unheroic jobs abound and the preacher may ride in to visit without warning.

What the Western does—whether the hero is on land riding a horse, or at sea commanding a fishing boat converted for submarine chasing—is to simplify, and thereby to transform, the effort and the struggle of daily

life, giving exhausting and painful work an overriding purpose that satu-
rates the activity with meaning. Unfortunately the transformation of the
daily routine comes at tremendous cost to the hero and to those left back
at the ranch.

Biographer Michael Reynolds has said that from 1928 onward every
novel Hemingway wrote was a Western,[2] and in 1992, working with the
manuscripts of *Islands in the Stream,* it became clear to me that Ernest
Hemingway recognized the high cost of living in the dichotomized world
he had often occupied, the world of the Western relocated to Bimini,
Havana, and the islands around Cuba.[3] This is the area where, in 1942 and
1943, Hemingway had carried on submarine hunting activity that his wife
Martha Gellhorn dubbed "The Crook Factory," and that he later referred
to as "a sea-borne comic strip."

Hemingway possessed from early childhood a Wild West of the psyche
that had probably been formed not only by Saturday matinees but also by
national adulation of Teddy Roosevelt and by living out his own parents'
vision of frontier life during long summers in upper Michigan. He happily carried that Western vision into his adult life, spending as much time
as possible each year in Wyoming, Montana, and finally, in Idaho—
sometimes on a dude ranch, and always engaged in those single-minded
endeavors that can be materially reckoned by the weight of an antelope,
the length of a fish, or the massive carcass of a bear.

Although Hemingway's attempted pilgrimage into the past reversed
the compass of the Western—he had gone from Oak Park and Toronto
to Paris, and when he returned after more than seven years in Europe he
settled at the southern-most tip of the United States before fleeing to
Havana a decade later—his letter to Max Perkins documents that lighting out for a new territory (with all that Twain implies) was his intention.
Further, Hemingway's unpublished correspondence reflects the same aver-
sion to the social obligations of being in New York that he expressed
toward Key West, and he complains ritually about the stream of visitors who track him down and interfere with work at the Finca. Despite
the direction of his own journeys, Hemingway knew and embedded in
Islands in the Stream the linguistic trope that makes "west of everything"
an epithet for dying, and that appears in this novel repeatedly in cryptic
orders from the base at Guantanamo as "CONTINUE SEARCHING CARE-
FULLY WESTWARD."

Hemingway began the ur-text that contained *Islands* in October 1946, seven months after returning from reporting the war in Europe. But he was unable to develop it into what he referred to in letters as the "Land, Sea, and Air Book," and in 1948 he carved out the "Land" segment and incorporated it into *Across the River and into the Trees.* Three years later he excised the story of the old fisherman who had gone out too far (which he had begun in 1936),[4] and shaped it into *The Old Man and the Sea.* What remained of the ur-text, which is largely what was published in 1970 as *Islands in the Stream,* he worked on intermittently through December 1951 and then put it in the vault of the Bank of Boston in Havana. Mary Hemingway brought the manuscript from Cuba a few weeks after Hemingway's death, and in 1969 Carlos Baker edited from it the book that Hemingway had referred to as *The Islands and the Stream.* Baker did not want his part in the editing disclosed, and it was therefore attributed to Mary Hemingway and Charles Scribner Jr. Not until 1990, when Scribner published his memoir *Among Writers,* did we learn of Baker's role. The shaping force of Carlos Baker's work will be clear by the end of this essay when we see how that very eastern biographer, a distinguished professor at Princeton, ignored and obscured the western elements of the book.

Islands is a triptych of a novel: Hemingway had written the "Bimini" section in 1946–47, and then put it aside as he began cannibalizing the ur-text for *Across the River and into the Trees.* When he took it up again in May 1951, he made significant changes: the painter Thomas Hudson acquired two ex-wives; the three male children, who had earlier belonged to writer Roger Davis, became Hudson's; and the ending was changed completely to add the deaths of the two younger sons, David and Andy. Finally, he added a chapter (much reduced by Baker) that reveals Hudson's refusal or inability to grieve as he travels to France for David and Andy's funeral.

At first blush, "Bimini," which takes place during six weeks of the summer of 1936, seems very different from the later sections, "Cuba" and "At Sea," which take place during seven or eight days in February of 1943. But the difference between the early and the later sections is actually the inevitable working out of the ethos of the Western novel once the domestic ties have been severed by the death of Hudson's sons.[5] In these sections, as in the Western, landscape becomes a text that must be read, while the action is driven by the same unquestioning commitment to a goal and an unspoken acceptance of its ending in a fatal entrapment.

The middle and final sections of *Islands* also differ from the opening "Bimini" story in another way that significantly reveals the western nature of the novel. Despite the fact that the Bimini household has no resident females (even the staff is male), there is much factual domesticity in the lives of the men and the boys: concern with food, sleeping arrangements, clean clothing, and the great affection of Thomas Hudson for his house. Although the boys' mothers are relegated to Hudson's past, he and Davis parent Hudson's sons almost as if they were a married couple, and the western ethos that comes to the foreground in "Cuba," and dominates in "At Sea," lies just under the surface in "Bimini." We first realize this when Roger Davis reveals to Hudson the burden of guilt he has carried for his entire adult life, because his younger brother was drowned in a canoeing accident from which he thinks he should have been able to save him. Roger was 12 at the time and has always believed that his father blamed him for the accident and for surviving. Like Nick Adams in "Indian Camp," Roger learned while still too young about death and the flawed nature of parental love. The conventions of the Western are also latent in Hudson's contempt for the "Christers" on the island and in his resistance to his sons' concerns about his and Roger's drinking. In "Bimini," there is an endurance contest between twelve-year-old David Hudson and an enormous fish during which Roger coaches David, trying both to minimize the toll the long struggle with the fish is taking on David's body and to remind the child that he can honorably give it up. But here Hudson establishes his unquestioning commitment to western assumptions about how men are made, for throughout most of David's six-hour battle with the fish, Hudson stands aloof on the flying bridge, denying the injuries to the boy's back, hands, and feet by seeing in them images of the bleeding icons that infest Latin American churches (*IITS* 136). When young Tom, the oldest of Hudson's sons, voices his concern with the punishment David is taking, Hudson responds, "[T]here is a time boys have to do things if they are ever going to be men. That's where Dave is now" (131).

In "Bimini" Hudson is mute about his own childhood, except to establish that he, like Roger, is from Oklahoma. But he makes a significant revelation in "Cuba." His disclosure comes seven years after Roger has disappeared from the story and all three sons have died unmourned.

Hudson is entertaining Lil, the hooker at his favorite bar, telling her of his boyhood brush with death when he was trapped beneath logs in brown water. He makes a joke of the terror, keeping Lil in suspense, and answering her final "And *then* what happened?" with "I drowned." Lil is superstitious and she scolds him for joking, so he goes on to tell that he pushed his way between two logs: "I had an arm over each log. I loved each log very much" (278). This is gallows humor, but it is the first evidence that an essential part of Hudson did perish sometime back in his western boyhood where there was a dark underside to the endurance rituals by which boys became men. He goes on to tell Lil that the water from the stream where he nearly drowned was as brown as her whiskey drink —which is also as brown as the water in the channel where Hudson runs fatally aground in the final section.

From Hudson's indifference to David's injuries in the fishing scene of "Bimini," the reader can predict the price he is willing to pay when he begins the paramilitary activity in the two later sections. In "Cuba," the middle section, Hudson learns that his remaining son, young Tom, has been killed in action. For two weeks he has told no one—although these weeks were spent at sea with eight men who are his friends. He is drunk when he finally discloses young Tom's death and becomes angry when his drinking partner offers sympathy. It is as if having such feelings as grief, loss, and sorrow attributed to him is an attack on his manhood.

The only love relationship that Hudson admits to (aside from that with Boise the cat) is his continuing attachment to young Tom's mother, the first wife—who is beyond needing him in any reciprocal way. When she arrives unannounced in Havana, he beds her (quite improbably, after a day of marathon drinking), then tells her of their son's death in a single syllable, "Sure," when she asks, "Tell me. Is he dead?" (319).

A phone call ordering Hudson back to sea spares him the messiness of Tom's mother's tears. Leaving his home for the last time, Hudson tells himself: "Love you lose. Your sons you lose. Honor has been gone for a long time. Duty you do" (326). The narrative of "Cuba" covers about twenty-four hours, but it establishes that some time ago Hudson abandoned the work of the artist that sustained the domestic tenor in "Bimini" and replaced it with the submarine hunt that requires him and his crew to dedicate themselves to the pursuit of a murderous, and ultimately suicidal, material goal. Duty you do.

Hemingway seems to offer the deaths of David and Andy as the blow that loosed Hudson from his life of monastically disciplined creativity and inclined him toward a failed third marriage and his present Hobbesian existence. But the lost younger sons have no part in Hudson's memories in "Cuba" except as refracted through a time when Boise, the cat, had been happy (204, 210). And in the final section, "At Sea," they appear only once, nameless in Hudson's dream, and are not again remembered (343). Nor is it the death of his remaining son, Tom, that causes Hudson to give up painting, for his work as an artist ceased some time earlier.

The near obliteration of David and Andy from Hudson's memory after "Bimini," the silence of the text on his relationship with young Tom during the seven years that have passed, and the disappearance of Roger from the narrative, cause a textual lacuna that leaves Hudson's creative decline unexplained and his alternating self-hatred and grandiosity unconvincing. For many of Hemingway's protagonists the response to irreparable loss was work, often creative work. But Thomas Hudson moves from creation to destruction, admitting to himself as he travels west of everything: "We are all murderers. . . . We are all on both sides, if we are any good, and no good will come of any of it" (356). In the final section of the novel we see Hudson and his mates, whom he calls "half-saints and desperate men" consumed by the hard work and overriding purpose that elevates the action in a Western.

Hudson's home outside Havana, with its unused bedroom, empty larder and undisciplined servants, contrasts sharply with the well-ordered life of companionable males in "Bimini." As Thomas Hudson considers moving the best of his paintings from his bedroom, because he is never in that room any more, he is a descendant of Jake Barnes—with the disturbing difference that Hudson made this suicidal, talent-wasting choice when, as he admits later, he could have chosen his art over the murderous duty that he is involved in. It is a choice that Hemingway recognized he had made himself when he published no fiction from 1940 to 1950.

However, in drawing on his own experiences to create the narrative, Hemingway does not consistently use Thomas Hudson to shrive or mythologize himself. This is a distinction missed by many readers, and by Baker in his editing of the novel. For example, in "Bimini" we were given evidence that Hudson's sons are concerned with both his and Roger's drinking. Young Tom, who is fifteen, brings drinks for the men during the epic fish struggle; and he plans to make cork insulators that will protect the ice in the adults' drinks. In "Cuba," Thomas Hudson "fondly" uses "a sheet of molded cork that came to within a half-inch of the rim of the glass" to hold a drink as his surly chauffeur drives him into Havana (240, 241–42, 244). The accoutrements of drinking survive the eager-to-please oldest son who made them just as Boise the cat survives the two younger boys who found him—at a bar in Cojimar where they spent Christmas morning with their father.

Like drinking habits, the patterns of dangerous and dehumanizing behavior learned from older males usually survive those who instilled them. When Hudson implicates Tom, David, and Andy in his drinking routines, he is entrapping them like his own father entrapped him in the killing of ducks he recalls in "At Sea." One of the ways in which the ethos of manhood-made-by-ordeal is transmitted is through the father-son bond. In the powerlessness of childhood, a son often wants either to please, or is compelled to obey, a parent, and in the process he becomes implicated in parental actions that are cruel and/or frightening, for example, Nick Adams's exposure to a caesarean section performed without an anesthetic and to a suicide in "Indian Camp" and David Bourne's implication in the death of the elephant his father is hunting in *The Garden of Eden.*[6]

Hemingway had held the potential pain of emotional relationships at a distance in his early work by denial or stoicism; but like Roger Davis, Thomas Hudson, David Hudson, and David Bourne, he had known many forms of entrapment as a child, and he was terminally wary of permanent emotional relationships. His more than a quarter of a century of refusing to deal with them—in his life as well as in his work—is clearly related to Thomas Hudson's inability to sustain the human relationships he needs in order to create.

When Hudson leaves his home at the end of "Cuba," he knows how far westward he is traveling, for he gives the letters and pictures of Tom to the boy's mother and plans to deposit at the embassy a will making the finca hers. Many images of the section prepared for this—the empty house, with the wind blowing under doors, the bartender at the Floridita who looks like a death's head, Ignacio Revello's toast ("I hope you die"), and Hudson's statement that he has no use for money. His only consolation during the last days and nights of his life is that he has something to do and is doing it in the company of good men.

Six days of chasing the German submarine crew provide the structure of "At Sea," and although the details of the pursuit are excessive and repetitive, they contain some of the best writing Hemingway offers in this uneven novel. He must have believed this too, for the only part of *Islands* Hemingway exposed during his life was a reading from "At Sea" that was not released until 1965 (*Ernest Hemingway Reading*).

Although most of "At Sea" is given to Hudson's command decisions and—in true western fashion—to thinking himself into the heads of his quarry as he pursues them, the natural world where he searches for clues directs him back to the painting he knows could have been a way to continue his life instead of becoming a murderer: "Because we are all murderers, he told himself. We are all on both sides, if we are any good, and no good will come of any of it" (356). Here the novel re-evaluates the cause that justifies any sacrifice, and Hemingway seems to deliberately undercut the conventions of the Western as Hudson argues with himself:

> He had been thinking so long in their heads that he was tired of it. Well, I know what I have to do, so it is simple. Duty is a wonderful thing. I do not know what I would have done without duty since young Tom died. You could have painted, he told himself. Or you could have done something useful. Maybe, he thought. Duty is simpler. (418)

The resonances of life on Bimini that appear near the beginning of "At Sea," along with Hudson's memories of life in Paris that appear in this final section, are Hemingway's effort to connect Hudson's present life of destruction to some earlier damage to his creativity; but the connection was obscured by the deletion of two long episodes from near the center of "At Sea." Those episodes (*IITS*, Kennedy Library, files 112 and 113) deal with the conflict of rigid gender roles and creativity; and they tell of the experiments of Hudson and his first wife (Tom's mother) with androgynous hair styling, clothing, and lovemaking. The deleted material suggests that the damage to Hudson's creativity came from another form of entrapment, one inherent in the life of men without women that he had sought in "Bimini," for they establish Hudson's attraction to, and fear of, a more fluid gender alignment than the conditioning of his western childhood could accommodate.

The first echoes of "Bimini" occur as Hudson lies on the beach at the unnamed Cay where the massacre is discovered. There he sees with a painter's eye the gray, sanded driftwood he had collected, cherished, and hated to burn in the house on Bimini; and his attention to the shape and texture evokes both the impossibility and the consequences of that di-chotomized, exclusively male world in which he had found creativity and lasting relationships with women incompatible. As he admires the drift-wood, which he would like to paint, his pistol lies between his legs. A moment later he thinks: "A beach tells many lies but somewhere the truth is always written." The truth written on this beach concerns not just the German submarine he is pursuing; it is also a reflection of what Hudson has excluded from his life, for as he moves closer to the driftwood that he will never paint and that will not warm his home, he addresses the pistol lying between his legs: "How long have you been my girl?" Don't answer. Lie there good and I will see you kill something better than land crabs when the time comes" (338–39).

Later, we learn that the sheepskin machine gun covers, which are im-pregnated with oil to protect the guns from rusting at sea, are like cradles and the guns are called niños [male children]. So Hudson has come to think of his penis as a gun and of consummation as killing. And guns, not paintings or books, are the well-cared-for progeny in this life where crea-tivity has ceased. The impossibility now of living a life where men and women can work and love together comes to Hudson in a dream on the sand by the driftwood. In the dream the dead sons are alive; Tom's mother lies on top of Hudson, as he used to love her to do, and he penetrates her with the moistened .358 Magnum!

But then with the wonderful, treacherous, possibilities of dreams, the girl says, "Let me take the pistol off and put it by your leg. The pistol's in the way of everything." And the dreaming Hudson replies, "Lay it by the bed, [a]nd make everything the way it should be" (344). What follows is that mysterious erotic exchange of sex roles that so many other of Hem-ingway's lovers seek, in which there is no need to dominate and the penis does not have to be a weapon, either lover can give or can take, and all distinction between taking and giving disappears. But the deletions of the

Kennedy Library files 112 and 113 clarify that the blurring of sexual differences posed a danger against which Thomas Hudson chose to protect himself in his first marriage.

Of course, androgyny is frightening—venturing from any place where the authority of culture both defines what one should be and evaluates how well one meets its standard is likely to be frightening. But the artist is by definition a cultural critic, and to be rendered unable to create by reluctance to explore the creativity of gender-blurring is an entrapment of the adult artist within the narrow vision of his childhood, a constraint that Ernest Hemingway knew well.

The reader cannot know the origin of this anxiety about feminization that Hudson experienced in his younger years with his attraction to androgynous sexual positions and hair styles, but it is somehow connected with his later déjà vu recognition that all his life he had felt both in command and a prisoner of his need to be in command (414).

In Hudson's late frontier youth, an inclination toward androgyny—or even a reluctance to adopt the gendered behavior of male dominance—would have elicited the epithet applied to Peters, the radio operator, whom the men call a "half-cunt." What the reader *can* deduce is the toll Hudson's need to be in command has taken on his relationships with women, for Thomas Hudson's sons die in the grip of the two most dangerous forces Ernest Hemingway could imagine: a talented, ambitious mother intent upon having her own way and an indifferent war machine.

The two deleted episodes, files 112 and 113, which shed light on Hudson's creative struggle with his masculine cultural heritage, were a part of the manuscript following the third paragraph of chapter XI in the novel. It is not clear who made the decision to delete them, but their manuscript format indicates to me that the decision was not Hemingway's. The deletions are typed, double-spaced, with triple spaces between words; and they bear holograph corrections in Hemingway's hand. This was Hemingway's usual format before the final typescript was done. Further, across the cover sheet of file 113 is written in Mary Hemingway's hand "Discarded mss (Removed from The Sea Chase ["At Sea"])".

The initial revelation of Hudson's earlier years came in the dream of androgynous lovemaking with his first wife that remains in the novel—but which the resistant reader in 1970 could interpret as "normal," female superior heterosexuality. However, the deleted episodes about gender experiments are waking memories (hence, under the control of the conscious mind) in which Hudson carries on an argument with himself about his early ability to yield control and how well he painted under the conditions in which he did not have to pretend to be a human Torpex device:[7]

> So now you spend your life hunting people to kill them which is surely as low as a man can be. So think about her and how she always made you do things while now you make others do them. . . . [D]o not think like that, you son of a bitch, because you still have work to do. . . . It will be nice when you get back to that [painting], he thought. Maybe you will have a better idea how to do it. At least you have seen the sea. . . . By now you can almost say that you have seen her and if you could do her and the mountains the way they should be done that would make up, maybe, for the lost murder years and the un-successful and successful homicides. (Kennedy Library, file 113, p. 87)

This interior monologue comes just after Hudson has been cleansed by a drought-breaking rain and is lying on the deck trying to avoid thinking of the manhunt to come. And it has been evoked by a resurgence of his creative drive; for a short time earlier he watched his crew bathing on the stern and told himself that he should be painting the scene rather than seeing it as Cézanne's bathers or wishing Eakins had painted it (382). From the deleted memories, Hudson falls into the sleep that produces two very significant dreams (348).

The deleted episodes tell of experiments at a time when some mediation between the masculine and feminine seemed possible to Hudson. Consequently, the removal of the two episodes obliterated the context of Hudson's two dreams of childhood, which follow immediately in the published text (384). Those dreams direct the reader both backward to "Bimini" and the damage done to Roger Davis and David Hudson by knowing too much, and forward to Thomas Hudson's recognition near the end of the novel that he too had a childhood over which the skin of memory has grown as over a wound. Let us recall the dreams that remain in the book (but whose context has been destroyed by the deletion of the two files): in the first dream Hudson is a boy again, riding beside a clear river where trout rise. Then one of his crew wakes him with the second of two identical orders that are the only communications he ever receives

from the Sinailike voice of the naval command station at Guantanamo—
"CONTINUE SEARCH CAREFULLY WESTWARD." Hudson sleeps again and
dreams that he is carrying out those orders, smiling at how far west he
has gone. But the dream turns on him: his home is burned, his dog and
the fawn he had raised are slaughtered, and Hudson wakes to continue
searching carefully westward.

From the end of these dreams until the fatal ambush behind Cayo
Guillermo, the natural world of the westward search reminds Hudson of
the childhood he had chosen to forget and the patterns of his adult life
that grew out of it. His childhood (like those of Roger Davis, David
Hudson, and David Bourne) included the entrapment of pleasing an adult
and becoming implicated in adult cruelty. When Hudson is aground in
the channel, we focalize through him, and the boy who killed to please
looks out through the eyes of the man who has chosen killing over creativity:

> He watched the shore birds . . . and he remembered what they had
> meant to him when he was a boy. He could not feel the same about
> them now and he had no wish to kill them ever. But he remembered
> the early days with his father in a blind . . . and how he would
> whistle the flock in as they were circling. (417)

This revelation is kindred to the connection Nick Adams makes in "Now
I Lay Me" between the dangerous combat in his parents' marriage and
the dangers of military combat, and it comes just before Hudson approaches the channel where he will be trapped. Entering that channel, he
thinks:

> He had the feeling that this had happened before in a bad dream.
> They had run many difficult channels. *But this was another thing
> that had happened sometime in his life. Perhaps it had happened all his
> life.* But now it was happening with such intensification that he felt
> both in command and at the same time the prisoner of it. (my em-
> phasis, 414)

Once they are aground, Hudson experiences his misjudgment in command "as a personal wound . . . [that had] all happened before. But it had
not happened in this way . . . " (416).

Hudson has no history of commanding anything other than his life until this intelligence mission began: he is a failed artist, a thrice-married man who buys his sexual companionship, and a parent who, when his sons were alive, did not hear their anxiety about his drinking. Therefore, Hudson's sense of being both in command of a situation and at the same time the prisoner of it can only be a reflection of his personal life. That, of course, is why the grounding comes as a personal wound. Until this moment Hudson's conduct of his life has been a disaster or he would not be here, seeking to lose it in a cause from which he knows no good will come. He would be painting. And he would be with his first wife.

In his inability to reconcile creativity with domestic life, Hudson has fled all the places and relationships where mediation between them might have occurred. He has metaphorically followed the directive to continue searching carefully westward, which is the only sound from Guantanamo —and is as cryptic as the echo in Forster's Marabar Caves. Hudson connects what he has been doing with what has been done to him: this is clear when Henry (who has his creative basis in Hemingway's frequent hunting companion Winston Guest) asks Hudson if his wound hurts, and Hudson replies: "It doesn't hurt any worse than things hurt that you and I have shot together" (402).

Baker sees the order from Guantanamo—CONTINUE SEARCHING CARE-FULLY WESTWARD—as Hudson's "unstated and largely unplanned program of self-rehabilitation" and as Hemingway's moral directive to himself (*Artist* 408). But Baker's reading is in the tradition of the Hemingway Code that can only be supported at the cost of ignoring portions of the text that are dense with meaning:

(1) the Huck Finn immaturity of Hudson's attempt to create a world of men without women,

(2) the parental failures glimpsed in the fact that Roger Davis and David Hudson know too much, too young,

(3) the sons' anxiety about the adults' drinking,

(4) the images that link Hudson to the phony Ignacio Revello with whom he drinks in Havana and to the half-mad Willie who is his closest companion on the boat,

(5) Hudson's linking the childhood memory of the logs to the whiskey brown water,

(6) his dream of the burned cabin and the slain dog and fawn, and,

(7) his abandonment of his art and his surety that no good will come of the murderous pursuit that has taken its place.

In editing *Islands in the Stream,* Baker shaped the "At Sea" section to support his own inclination to see the narrative as following what he called "The Narcissus Principle"; and in so doing he treated Hudson only as an uncritical reflection of the author. To do this Baker had to ignore the complex musings on the problems of gender and creativity that are embodied in the deleted episodes of Hudson as a younger artist. And he did. Fortunately, Baker left a record of the precedence he gave westwardness and separation of the sexes over gender-blurring in sustaining the creative imagination. One folder of the *Islands* manuscripts at Princeton contains discards. On it, in Baker's handwriting, is: "Some Montana material near end of this batch might be rescued for Miscellany volume" (catalog no. 0365, box 25, folder 3; Firestone Library). The Montana material is from "Bimini," and in it Roger tells of a curative winter spent at Hudson's ranch—away from women and on a short ration of whiskey. But the folder also contains, without comment, the two long episodes about Hudson's concern with gender and creativity in his youth, which I referred to earlier as the Kennedy Library files 112 and 113.

It is possible that Baker was uncomfortable with these episodes, and perhaps Charles Scribner and Mary Hemingway were also. Further, their connection to *The Garden of Eden* manuscript, which, during the period when *Islands* was being edited, both Baker and Mary thought unpublishable, may have made the episodes seem extraneous. Certainly they would have given Hemingway's readers a jolt in 1970. But even without knowing of the deleted episodes or of the existence of *The Garden of Eden,* one cannot read *Islands* today as an exhortation to frontier stoicism in the face of male duty. Hemingway has written a western novel that is its own critique of that genre's conventions, for in Thomas Hudson he created a failed artist who has already searched so far westward that the clear trout stream is a muddy brown channel—and who has burned his own cabin three times over.

11

Queer Families in Hemingway's Fiction

Debra A. Moddelmog

... even when you have learned not to look at families nor listen to
them and have learned not to answer letters, families have many ways
of being dangerous.

Ernest Hemingway, *A Moveable Feast*

Over the years, a number of critics have noted the lack of traditional
families and stable home life in Hemingway's fiction.[1] As Frank Shelton
put it as early as 1974, "Hemingway's books may seem to lack entirely that
most primary group to which every individual belongs, at least initially,
the family" (303). Two years later, Roger Whitlow wrote, "It is interesting
to observe in the fiction of Ernest Hemingway the virtual absence of
an organically successful family relationship" ("Family Relationship" 5).
More recently, Michael Reynolds has taken up this same line of criticism,
arguing that "With one exception, the characters [Hemingway] invented
[are] essentially homeless men, not only without family but without a
town to call home" (*Young Hemingway* 53).

I agree that Hemingway's stories and novels lack an extended portrayal
of the procreative biological family and the establishment of a permanent
home, which has such symbolic value for this family in the United States.
However, in this essay I will argue that a portrayal—even, sometimes, a
sympathetic portrayal—of the family is not missing from Hemingway's
fiction but is present in a form different from the one readers expect to
find. My argument hinges on the definition of family. It alleges that blood
ties, marriage licenses, heterosexual sex, and children are not the only, or
the definitive, indicators of family. In fact, if we view family as two or
more people who share interests and ideas, who care for and support each
other emotionally and materially, and who create a sense of belonging for
those involved, then it becomes clear that biological families often fail the

test. The individuals who have been the most outspoken about the frequent failures of these families are the survivors of incest or child abuse, children of an alcoholic parent or parents, and/or children who grow up to identify as gay or lesbian. For many of these individuals, the blood family is often not supportive, to put it mildly, nor does its household provide a haven of understanding and security. If family is to have positive meaning for these individuals, then it must be found elsewhere.

Hemingway's works are rife with alternative families, but this is not the ultimate point I want to make. Other critics have noticed the presence of such "substitute" families, proposing, for example, that the guerrilla group in *For Whom the Bell Tolls* serves as a family (Adair) or that *The Sun Also Rises* is structured around a family unit in which Jake is the father, Brett the matriarch, Bill the uncle, and Robert Cohn "an awkwardly immature son who spends too much of his time interrupting the grown-ups" (Whitlow 10). Conceding that substitute families exist in Hemingway's fiction, I believe that many of these families should be identified as "queer families." What I mean by this is not only that such families stand in for the biological family, providing the community that it often fails to establish, but also that they often stand in opposition to this family, challenging in particular the ideal that has developed around it. In addition, these families are made queer not simply because they are chosen rather than inherited but also by virtue of their transience and the ways they blur the boundaries between non-erotic and erotic, sanctioned and taboo bonds.

Although I could make my case with a number of Hemingway's narratives, to meet the space restrictions of this collection, I will concentrate on three: "The Battler," written early in Hemingway's career, and *The Garden of Eden* and "The Last Good Country," both written late.[2] I will argue that "The Battler" shows how family bonds can be forged outside the authority of both biology and the state. *The Garden of Eden* extends this exploration of family kinship and relations by demonstrating that the traditional family and the symbolic apparatus that gives it such powerful leverage in our nation—for example, biology, the natural, kinship, marriage, and the lawful—are socially constructed. Consequently, the lines between the queer family and the blood family can shift. The limits and ethics of this shifting are prominent in my third example, "The Last Good Country," where Nick and Littless Adams separate themselves from the other members of their immediate family to form their own family, a queer family that is, simultaneously, inside and outside the biological family. The point I hope to make with these three analyses is that queer families in Hemingway's fiction denaturalize the traditional, biological family by exposing its shortcomings, revealing its perversions, and refuting its claim to primacy as the emotional center of its members' lives. Crucially, this process of denaturalization is not merely oppositional or denunciatory. Hemingway's queer families pose challenges more than threats. As they reconfigure the bonds of belonging and bring substance to relationships of care, particularly in fragile contexts, they challenge the traditional family to do the same. As they target various norms of that family—especially norms of sexuality and power—they challenge queer theorists to delineate the ethics of our paradigms.

"The Battler," a story Hemingway wrote in 1925 for inclusion in his book *In Our Time,* presents one of Hemingway's most visibly queer families, Bugs and Ad Francis. The men are misfits among conventional society: they both served time in jail, Bugs for knifing a man, Ad for beating up people after his wife, whom many believed was his sister, left him. Ad and Bugs's coupling increases their difference from mainstream society. It joins two men, one white, one black, in a domestic situation that is, quite literally, transient: Ad and Bugs roam the country, setting up camp wherever they can. Also adding to the queerness of their family arrangement is the fact that Ad's wife continues to send Ad money, thereby serving as an *in abstentia* member of their family. From a conventional perspective, the union of Bugs, Ad, and Ad's wife calls up multiple meanings of queer: unconventional, eccentric, bizarre, strange, unusual, suspicious.

The queerness of the two men is marked physically as well as socially. We see them through the eyes of Nick Adams, who reflects a normative viewpoint, even though he too is a liminal character: thrown from a moving train into the sometimes dangerous woods, on the border between youth and adulthood, about to discover what it's like to be crazy, and, as we will discover in "The Last Good Country," familiar with incestuous feelings. From Nick's perspective, Ad's beat-up prizefighter body is queer. His face is so "queerly formed" that Nick must study it to make sense of it: "In the firelight Nick saw that his face was misshapen. His nose was sunken, his eyes were slits, he had queer-shaped lips. Nick did not perceive all this at once; he only saw the man's face was queerly formed and mutilated. It was like putty in color. Dead looking in the firelight" (55). In addition to resembling the living dead, Ad has only one ear. Looking at the stump where his other ear used to be makes Nick a "little sick" (55). In contrast to the detail that Nick provides about Ad's battered face, he tells us nothing about the way Bugs looks, except that he is "Negro" and can be identified as such by his walk and his voice (57). Thus, the only feature that Nick registers about Bugs's face and body is that both are black. By collapsing Bugs's personal traits and humanity into the single marker of race, Nick reduces him to his racial identity. This point is driven home through repeated references to Bugs as "the Negro" and "the nigger." Nick's reduction of Bugs to the racialized Other is a way of conventionally queering him, a pattern of dehumanization that Bugs seems used to by this point in his life. When Ad reports Nick has never been crazy, we can hear the experience in Bugs's voice as he announces, "He's got a lot coming to him" (57).

In telling his and Ad's stories to Nick, Bugs reveals how social displacement frequently ends in other kinds of displacement. Bugs claims that Ad's mental trouble has been caused by societal presumption more than by physical trauma. Ad may have taken too many beatings in and out of the ring, but he was finally driven crazy by the pressures that mounted over the relentless public speculation that his wife was also his sister. Individuals that the dominant society cannot control, accept, understand, embrace, stand to look at, or change are removed: to a prison, a mental asylum, the woods, the streets, or the constant punishment of their own internalized self-hatred. But while Bugs and Ad have been rejected by and excluded from mainstream society for many reasons, they have found comfort, support, and care in each other's company. Their treatment of each other makes us eventually question the judgment of a judgmental society, and it reverses the negative connotations of their "queerness," implying that the queer overcomes conventional condemnation by revaluing what societal norms reject.

First and foremost, Bugs and Ad show genuine affection for each other. Bugs tells Nick that when they met in prison, he liked Ad right away—liked him enough, in fact, to look him up when Bugs was released. Bugs prepares their meals, prevents others from hurting Ad, and cares for Ad when he is unconscious. Unlike Nick, Bugs is not repulsed by Ad's face and body. After thumping Ad, Bugs pulls gently on his ears to make sure he is all right (60), thus touching tenderly the ear-stump that made Nick nauseous. He claims that Ad would not be bad looking if his face were not "all busted" (61). Bugs also discredits the story that Ad committed incest, asserting that although Ad and his wife looked enough alike to be twins, "they wasn't brother and sister no more than a rabbit" (61). Moreover, Ad likes Bugs too. As he tells Nick, "This is my pal Bugs" (57).

This is not to say that the relationship between Bugs and Ad is unproblematic and completely admirable. Most troubling are Bugs's methods for keeping Ad out of trouble and thus out of jail. Whenever Ad turns combative and seems about to start a fight, Bugs taps him at the base of the skull with a cloth-wrapped blackjack. Such methods are extreme, and for anyone who knows about the head trauma suffered by boxers, it appears that Bugs is actually adding to Ad's problems. Moreover, the implications of Hemingway's portrayal of a black man repeatedly knocking out a white man are complex and stereotypical at the same time. On the one hand, Bugs's violence could be regarded as perpetuating the racist-derived stereotype of black-on-white assault in America; on the other hand, it also suggests Bugs's underlying anger toward white men. But both of these suggestions are offset by the fact that Bugs works hard to prevent confrontations in the first place: "I hate to have to thump him," he says, but "it's the only thing to do when he gets started. I have to sort of keep him away from people" (62). Bugs also knows exactly where and how hard to hit Ad to minimize his violence. After knocking out Ad to avert his growing hostility toward Nick, Bugs admits that this time he hit him a bit too hard, but with Bugs's aid, Ad will recover (60).[3] In addition, were Bugs to allow Ad to act on his sudden hostility,[4] the consequences could be serious. Ad might actually hurt someone. This result might return him to prison, which would expose him to further harm and leave Bugs on his own. But despite all these qualifications surrounding Bugs's assault of Ad, domestic violence of any kind should not be condoned, and I wish that Bugs might have found a more resourceful and less physically debilitating way to prevent Ad from hurting others.

Another potentially troubling aspect of Ad and Bugs's relationship is its financial foundation. Indeed, given that Ad's most noticeable contribution to their relationship is the money his wife sends, it might be argued that Bugs is simply Ad's salaried caretaker. This impression finds support in the way that Bugs refers to Ad as "Mister Francis," a form of address that denotes a hierarchy in their relationship. But in many families, the responsibilities are delegated, with one partner taking charge of finances, another of the domestic duties. And, in contrast to many women who historically have been unhappy with or unfulfilled by their domestic responsibilities, Bugs seems satisfied with his role in the relationship. His formality with Ad might be a consequence of racial relations of the time, with the black man pressured to show his place by addressing white men as superiors rather than equals. After all, Bugs also refers to the youthful Nick as "Mister Adams." Yet it also seems possible that Bugs's apparent deference to his white companions is one way that he lives out his imagined position as a gentleman or that it's part of how he makes the mentally fragile Ad feel important in a world that has too often made him feel less than human. In any case, I see no reason not to take Bugs at his word when he says, "I like to be with [Ad] and I like seeing the country and I don't have to commit no larceny to do it. I like living like a gentleman" (61). In fact, wherever Bugs and Ad camp is home, a metaphor made literal by the delicious food they cook and share with Nick and by Bugs's regret that they cannot extend their hospitality and ask Nick to stay the night (62). As Nick retreats from their camp, the last thing he hears is Bugs tending to the recovering Ad, protecting him in a harsh world in which they both have taken too many beatings.

The queer family presented in *The Garden of Eden* is quite different from the one found in "The Battler." I employ this obvious transition not simply to move to the next text of my analysis but to underscore the fact that queer families frequently differ from one another. Were they identical, they would no longer be queer. By making difference and plurality a part of their character, I am suggesting that queer families implicitly critique the mythology surrounding the family in the United States, which has insisted for much of this century that all families are, relatively speaking, alike: headed by a bread-winning father, nurtured by a stay-at-home mother, and blessed with one or more children. The reality of this definition has crumbled in the last twenty years under the weight of statistics that demonstrate that very few American families (only 7 percent in 1986) fit that description (Thorne 9) and under the penetrating criticism of scholars who have argued that such a definition is based in white, middle-class desire rather than in the experiences of many Americans of color and/or of the working class.[5]

Although few readers of *The Garden of Eden* will resist my characterizing David and Catherine Bourne's family situation as queer, significantly the novel opens with the couple looking very much like the husband-wife duo that forms the nucleus of the nuclear family. Newly married, Catherine and David seem poised to take their place in this conventional family formation. For instance, as David aligns himself with the masculine role of writer, Catherine resigns herself to the feminine space of serving as his inspiration. Both partners are also aware that their active sex life may eventually result in pregnancy. Finally, they both seem equally fond of each other, their marriage based in affection and mutually satisfying sex, as was expected of the so-called companionate marriage of the time. Beginning in the 1920s, these bonds of affection were seen by many Americans as the core of the family relation.[6] However, Catherine and David's story proves that appearances can be deceiving, that what looks like a so-called normal family arrangement might actually be queer, and vice versa.

Catherine's introduction of the sex-changing, identity-altering transformations sets in motion a series of deviations and deceptions. As Catherine changes into the boy "Peter" and David into the girl "Catherine," they upset the dominant ideology that requires clear distinctions between men and women, male and female, an ideology central to the traditional family. But even before undertaking this change, Catherine and David's marriage threatens the ideology that surrounds this family. The narrator tells us early in the story that they look so much alike that most people mistake them for brother and sister until they say they are married. Even then, some people do not believe they are married (6). This situation resembles that of Ad and his wife in "The Battler," and the repetition of the error suggests that it is fairly easy for outsiders to mistake a state-approved family for a queer one, to misconstrue lawful relations as taboo. Such confusion insinuates that family relations are socially constructed; the lines between normalcy and abnormalcy are contrived, capable of being redrawn. As we have seen, the redrawing of these lines by an unrelenting public ruined the marriage of Ad Francis and his wife. However, unlike the Francises, the Bournes thrive on the allegation that they are brother and sister. The narrator tells us that Catherine is pleased by the misidentification (6). In the manuscript located in the Kennedy Library, she elaborates, "It's fun without sin. . . . But sin does give it a certain quality." "I like it either way," David replies (ser. 422, folders 1–1, p. 4).[7]

After the change, in which they reverse sexes and roles in bed, Catherine and David call each other "brother" and further explore their theory that transgressing a taboo is sexually exciting (21–22). Catherine identifies this altered relationship when she says to David, "you're my good lovely husband and my brother too" (29). Lest we presume that Catherine is simply talking about brother in the sense of "comrade" or "close friend," the manuscript reveals the complexity of her allusion. Here Catherine insists, "you're my good lovely husband . . . and I love you even if you are my brother too maybe more I guess" (ser. 422, folders 1–2, chap. 4, p. 1). By becoming the male sibling of her husband, Catherine engages in homosexual incest, an act that deepens her desire and her marital bond. To put this another way, Catherine's transgendered relations with David "refamiliarize" their relationship, symbolically imposing a tabooed homosexual incest onto their licensed marital union. This inscription of brotherly bonds onto their husband-wife connection queers the marriage, but at the same time, it highlights the repressed incestuous desires that circulate within the traditional family unit. The incestuous lines that run through David and Catherine's union are thus complex, but the net effect is that they challenge the distinction between the natural and the queer.[8] In one instance, the public imposes brother-sister incest onto their relationship, and thereby queers a socially approved and state-mandated marriage. In the other instance, Catherine and David invoke brother-brother incest to heighten their pleasure, even though this act of incest goes unnoticed by the outside world. They have queered their union but can still present themselves to others as legitimate heterosexual spouses.

This game of appearances plays out in another crucial way. As I have argued elsewhere (*Reading Desire*), Catherine and David's transgendered role-switching is, in part, a way to explore same-sex desire within the context of a heterosexual marriage, even though they resist acknowledging that such desire is part of their pleasure. When Catherine first cuts her hair, the narrator reports that she has possibly crossed an important societal boundary: "No decent girls had ever had their hair cut short like that in this part of the country and even in Paris it was rare and strange and could be beautiful or could be very bad. It could mean too much or it could only mean showing the beautiful shape of a head that could never be shown as well" (16). What Catherine's haircut might mean—to society, to Catherine and David, or to the reader—is obscured by her formal identification as "wife," an identity that entitles her to the presumption of decency, until proven otherwise. Catherine and David's marriage, then, serves as a kind of cover for queer activities, a function that hints at how the legitimate often conceals the transgressive, as when married couples bring their queer desires and fantasies to bed. However, in Catherine's case, the cover is completely blown with the arrival of Marita, who pushes the repressed homosexual desire into the open. As Catherine tells David after she kisses Marita, "It started with us and there'll only be us when I get this finished" (114). But when she makes love with Marita, she discovers that "this" is not finished, that making love with a woman is what Catherine wanted all her life (120).

When David, at Catherine's urging, also sleeps with Marita, the lawful twosome has willingly and visibly become a queer family. Catherine and Marita work out a time share plan, wherein each woman alternates every two days acting as David's wife: "We're going to take turns," Catherine says. "You're mine today and tomorrow. And you're Marita's the next two days" (170). But as queer as this plan might seem to most Americans, Catherine and David point out that their situation would be normal and accepted were they living in Africa where David might register as "Mohammedan" and take three wives (144). Once again, we are reminded that families are socially constructed: the queer family in one culture is the norm in another.

Admittedly, the success of the husband-sharing plan is minimal, although all three characters accept it for a while.[9] Further, the destructive end of Catherine and David's marriage as well as David's apparent reluctance to engage in Catherine's sexual surprises would seem to qualify the success of their queer family. I even suspect that some readers will argue that Catherine's queering of their marriage is responsible for destroying it. But I would challenge this objection on two grounds. First, I question the sincerity of David's reluctance to engage in Catherine's plans. After all, he does go along with everything she suggests, including a fairly hearty consent to making love with Marita. As Catherine frequently points out, David's resistance is often a posture (e.g., 196), and during one insightful and self-aware moment, David actually confesses to his willing participation: "All right. You like it [having his hair cut and bleached the same as Catherine's]," he says. "Now go through with the rest of it whatever it is and don't ever say anyone tempted you or that anyone bitched you" (84). If this transgendered, polygamous family fails, David, and Marita, must be held accountable as well. The second reason why I resist blaming Catherine for the failure of her and David's marriage is that it is difficult to make judgments based on the published text since the manuscripts provide much more detail about Catherine and David's relationship, motives, and consequences. I have outlined some of these crucial differences in print (see my *Reading Desire*), but here I simply note that in a chapter which Hemingway labeled "Provisional Ending," Catherine and David stay together (ser. 422, folder 21). In this ending, David cares for Catherine after her return from a sanitarium in Switzerland, and both partners profess to love each other and actually contemplate a suicide pact should Catherine's mental state grow worse.[10]

If Catherine and David's relationship, and their attempt to enlarge their family with the inclusion of Marita, thrives only for a while, they nonetheless experience a happiness during that time that neither has felt previously. Significantly, both Catherine and David have conflicted relationships with their biological families. For instance, David seems obsessed with the urge to write autobiographically inspired stories about his cruel and wayward father. When Marita reads the story in which David's father slaughters African natives, she asks, "Was this when you stopped loving him?" to which David replies, "No. I always loved him. This was when I got to know him" (154). As Peter L. Hays remarks, David has affection but not respect for his father ("Nick Adams" 37). The published novel is cryptic about Catherine's biological family, with the most detailed information coming from Colonel John Boyle, who says Catherine's father was a very odd type and her mother very lonely (61). But in the manuscript, Catherine provides more significant background when she tells David, "If we'd had the damned baby I wouldn't want to have it around anymore than my parents wanted me around. They were honest enough about it" (ser. 422, folder III, p. 12).

Catherine's criticism of her parents serves as a useful reminder that although Hemingway's fiction might lack an extended portrait of a successful biological family, the biological family is not completely absent from his writing. A few members of what I am calling Hemingway's queer families have retained loving connections to their blood relatives; many others reveal—through their energetic descriptions of tyrannical mothers, weak-willed fathers, or indifferent parents—that family ties have become a kind of psychic bondage.[11] Still, the blood family is very much a factor in the estranged individual's psyche and life. Because the traditional family is often an absent presence in Hemingway's works, I am not suggesting that his fiction ignores it. Rather, as I stated earlier, his stories more often work to denaturalize this family. In "The Battler," this process of denaturalization consists of portraying the queer family in a positive light. In *The Garden of Eden*, it takes the form of a series of reversals between the traditional and the queer family, revealing the instabilities of both and the perversions of the former. This process of denaturalization assumes yet another guise in "The Last Good Country."

It might seem contradictory that I include Nick and Littless in my list of queer families in Hemingway's fiction since, unlike the other characters discussed in this essay, they are related by blood. Indeed, Nick Adams is the only male protagonist in Hemingway's fiction whose biological family and upbringing are sketched in some detail (through a series of stories, including "Indian Camp," "The Doctor and the Doctor's Wife," "Ten Indians," "Now I Lay Me," and "Fathers and Sons"). However, in "The Last Good Country," Nick and Littless deliberately separate themselves from their other family members: "[Littless] and Nick loved each other and they did not love the others. They always thought of everyone else in the family as the others" (56–57).[12] In essence, Nick and Littless form a family outside their family, although they need their immediate family to provide the negative example that defines their difference and delineates, by contrast, the contours of their own family unit. This separation creates paradoxes: Nick and Littless are a family that rejects the family; they are kin who choose each other. These paradoxes emphasize a point made earlier in regard to other Hemingway works: the most sustaining kinship is that which is chosen.

Littless maintains that she and Nick differ from their other family members, in part, because "crime comes easy" for them (99), a distinction that spotlights their status as outlaws. Obviously, Nick and Littless are outlaws in the sense that they are running from the law, as the warden and the "down-state man" attempt to "make an example" of Nick for killing a deer out of season and want to send him to reform school (57).

But they are also outlaws of the family; that is, they are moving away, both literally and symbolically, from the traditional family and the space it occupies in society. As Mark Spilka puts it, "If the game wardens overtly threaten [Nick's] freedom, his mother and the 'others' are from the first the essential threat from which, along with Littless, he wishfully flees" (*Quarrel* 268). Nick and Littless are not, however, simply fugitives of the traditional family; they are also moving toward a new kind of family. When they begin to argue over whether Littless should have come along, she demands, "Are we going to be like the others and have fights? . . . I'll go back or I'll stay just as you want. I'll go back whenever you tell me to. But I won't have fights. Haven't we seen enough fights in families?" (70). Out there, in "the last good country," one can create a new family, one that gets along and does not fight; back there, in their home in town, is the bickering, dysfunctional family.

We might regard Littless's dream of a fightless family as naive, but her determined idealism sets the stage for her and Nick's revision of family. As they move deeper into the wilderness, Littless and Nick continue to set the ground rules for their new family formation. Some of these rules consist of enacting the behavior that they expect, but fail to receive, from members of their traditional family. For example, although we never observe Mrs. Adams interacting with her children, the information we do receive points to her inadequacies as a mother. Not only does she feed the game wardens who are chasing her son and allow them to spend the night in the Adams's home, but she also tells them where they might find Nick. Littless wonders whether "our mother" intended to disclose Nick's whereabouts: "I don't think she meant to," she says. "Anyway I hope not" (61). Whether Mrs. Adams's disclosure was deliberate or merely an indiscretion, she fails to do what mothers are supposed to do: protect her children. In fact, she fails to take responsibility for both her actions and her son's fate, breaking down in the middle of the family crisis with a "sick headache like always" and retiring to her bedroom (64, 90).

The failures of Mrs. Adams stand in stark contrast to the way Nick cares for Littless on their journey as he endeavors to meet her physical and emotional needs as well as to provide moral guidance. After they set up their lean-to in "Camp Number One," Nick asks whether Littless finds her browse bed comfortable and offers to "feather in some more balsam" (91). He fixes them a tasty dinner of trout, rye bread, bacon sand-

wiches, and tea with condensed milk, then advises Littless to eat an apple
(99). Later, when she is asleep, he spreads his Mackinaw coat over her
and thinks, "I must take good care of her and keep her happy and get her
back safely" (101). Nick's loving solicitousness contrasts with the way his
mother has treated him. He has fed and sheltered his family; she has fed
and sheltered her son's pursuers, and would even lead those men to her
son. By conventional definitions of mothering, Nick is a better mother
than his mother.

The thoughtful care that Nick gives Littless is fully reciprocated, suggesting that the primary rule guiding their family formation will be extending kindness and love to each other. Littless claims that she cannot
rest, as Nick asked her to, because "all I could do was imagine things to
do for you" (96). She also tells him amusing stories and offers to share her
chocolate. Most important, she is determined to prevent Nick from killing the Evans's boy, who might be tailing them. She will be Nick's moral
counsel and conscience, just as he will be hers. At one point, she declares
that she is glad she is not ruined morally because then she could not
"exercise a good influence" on him (97). A section of the story's manuscript that was omitted from the published version summarizes Littless's
hope for their relationship. She states, "I thought we'd go away together
and I'd take care of you and you'd take care of me and you know where I
thought we'd go. I thought we'd hunt and fish and eat and read and sleep
together and not worry and love each other and be kind and good" (qtd.
in Comley and Scholes 72).

Thus far, my discussion of Nick and Littless's queer family has focused
on the way that their break with their blood family enables them to pursue the ideals of reciprocal love, care, protection, and community, which
the traditional family lays claim to, yet often falls short of achieving. But
the relationship between Nick and Littless exhibits another characteristic
of the traditional, biological family that this family does not advertise,
indeed typically represses: incestuous desire. To put this another way, the
incest that was imagined in "The Battler" and both imagined and symbolic in *The Garden of Eden* has the potential to become literal in "The
Last Good Country." The existence of this potential reinforces my observation that Nick and Littless are both inside and outside the family,
which is also to say that although the traditional family might be socially
constructed, as my reading of *The Garden of Eden* demonstrates, the lines

forming that construction are not immaterial or infinitely flexible. Because Nick and Littless are brother and sister, and because Nick is sexually mature whereas Littless is not, the potential incest between them raises ethical considerations that the symbolic incest between consenting adults in *The Garden of Eden* does not. It emphasizes that neither queer nor normative families can ignore the ethics of power in relationships.

From one perspective, incestuous feelings queer the relationship between Littless and Nick, especially when Littless, in the same vein as Catherine Bourne, cuts her hair and announces her wish to be both Nick's sister and his brother (96). From another perspective, these feelings normalize their relationship, exposing the circuits of desire that flow among members of the nuclear family. Either way, I find myself unwilling to reconstruct the potential incest between the teenage Nick and the ten- or eleven-year-old Littless as ethical. Further, I believe that this refusal is compatible with the queer paradigm that motivates this paper. If that paradigm consists only of opposing and transgressing the normative, then not only does the normative continue to define the terms of our discussions but also we can actually abrogate responsibility for delineating the ethical grounds of our work. As Steven Seidman notes, queer theorists must be ready to identify the ethical guidelines that would permit sexual innovation "while being attentive to considerations of power and legitimate normative regulation" (136). To state this in terms relevant to the argument at hand, if queer ethics consists only of transgressions, then incest between a teenage brother and his preteen sister would become ethical because it transgresses the idealized norm of exogamous adult heterosexuality.

The queer project to which I subscribe focuses on redefining the quality of relationships that form the social. Sometimes this means challenging the normative; other times, it means accepting it; and many times, it means re-imagining relationships. As many feminist scholars have shown, incest usually involves an inequity of power and a breach of trust within a family relationship. In this context, a major problem with the traditional family is not its form; it's that relationships within this family are constituted inequitably.[13] One of the most inequitable of these relationships is that between older male family members (fathers, uncles, and brothers) and younger female family members (daughters, nieces, and sisters). And one way in which this inequity is too often manifested is through the older male forcing or encouraging the younger female to submit sexually. As Rosaria Champagne observes, "When we understand the brother's power over his sisters as natural (including the power to 'protect' his sisters from other men), we have fallen prey to the complex ideologies of patriarchy, which represent male power as natural because it is institutionalized" (155).

Although I am not prepared to address the ethics of all forms of incest, I strongly resist any implication that incest between a sexually mature brother and his young sister would be acceptable in any current formation of the family. Given this view, I could approach the potential incest of "The Last Good Country" in two ways. I could argue that we should go only so far in approving the queer family that Hemingway depicts. We might admire the loving, reciprocal relationship that Nick and Littless cultivate, but we should pull back at the inference that incest between them might be an acceptable part of that new family arrangement. However, a number of elements in "The Last Good Country" and its manuscripts suggest that I might take a different path. Nick and Littless do seem to recognize that consummating their incestuous feelings would be a mistake. Littless might claim that she is going to be Nick's "common-law wife under the Unwritten Law," that they will have a couple of children while she is still a minor, and that "[o]ur mother will think we're fugitives from justice steeped in sin and iniquity" (104–05), but this is clearly an embellished fantasy. In the manuscript, she distinguishes between the wrong she and Nick are doing and "that kind of wrong [sexual relations] like [he] and Trudy [did]" (qtd. in Comley and Scholes 70–71). Similarly, Nick realizes that he loves "his sister very much and she loved him too much. But, he thought, I guess those things straighten out. At least I hope so" (101). So the queerness that I find in their relationship centers not on the incestuous desire itself but on the fact that Nick and Littless admit to that desire and expect to avoid acting on it. Even more, Nick's inability to know how he will work out his incestuous feelings for his sister exposes another inadequacy of the nuclear family: its habitual repression that makes desire a dirty secret and thus provides its members with no clearer instruction about incest than to hope that "those things straighten out" (101).[14] Similarly, Littless's wish to marry Nick points to the constricted imagination of the traditional family, which offers children only one model—heterosexual marriage—for the adult expression of love, care, and family.

Three narratives are surely not enough to make a compelling case that queer families appear throughout Hemingway's fiction. But other possibilities spring to mind: Brett Ashley and Jake Barnes in *The Sun Also Rises;* Robert Jordan, Maria, and Pilar in *For Whom the Bell Tolls;* Colonel Cantwell and Renata in *Across the River and into the Trees;* Thomas Hudson, Roger Davis, Eddy, and the Hudson sons in *Islands in the Stream;* Mr. and Mrs. Elliot and Mrs. Elliot's friend in "Mr. and Mrs. Elliot"; and Santiago and Manolin in *The Old Man and the Sea.* All these groupings consist of characters who support each other emotionally and sometimes materially. Further, the bond between characters of many of these groupings is sealed with some form of queer desire (the groupings of *Islands* and *Old Man* might stand as exceptions, although one could make a case for homoeroticism in both). Finally, these are all transient families. For the most part, they lack a permanent home, and their connections are temporary, lasting only so long as the love lasts or until one or more members dies.

One could surely propose psycho-biographical reasons for Hemingway's interest in redefining family. As my epigraph indicates and as scholars such as Michael Reynolds, Kenneth Lynn, Gerry Brenner, Bernice Kert, James Mellow, and Mark Spilka have shown, Hemingway had many difficulties, both real and imagined, with his biological family. As Earl Rovit puts it, "To the extent that it was possible, he . . . cut his ties to his family, his childhood religion, and his regional roots" ("American Family" 496). Nor did Hemingway create, in a sustained way, a traditional family with any of his wives or sons. It's not surprising, then, that he might explore alternative family formations in his fiction. Whatever its sources, through this recurrent interest in family and what it means, Hemingway's work engages in a timely debate over what—and who—constitutes a family and which families should be recognized as such by the state.

In the United States, many people still believe strongly that the biological family is the natural, the real, and the indispensable family, with all other family formations viewed as imperfect and fictive substitutes. This belief is not simply a cherished notion but has serious social and psychological implications for us all. Jane Collier, Michelle Rosaldo, and Sylvia Yanagisako point out that because we have typically interpreted the traditional family as a private, autonomous unit, "the punishments imposed on people who commit physical violence [has been] lighter when their victims are their own family members." Consequently, "We are faced with the irony that in [American] society the place where nurturance and noncontingent affection are supposed to be located is simultaneously the place where violence [has been] most tolerated" (43–44). Another effect of naturalizing the family can be seen in the ways that families headed by gays and lesbians are regularly denied both recognition *as* families (for example, until recently they have not been counted as families on the census records) as well as privileges accorded to traditional families (such as adoption and marriage, and all the entitlements that come with these). Not incidentally, in Great Britain such families have been officially designated "pretended families," implying that they are impersonations of the "real" family.[15] But as Kath Weston notes, "The concept of fictive kin lost credibility with the advent of symbolic anthropology and the realization that all kinship is in some sense fictional—that is, meaningfully constituted rather than 'out there' in a positivist sense" (105). As I have argued in this essay, Hemingway's fiction views families in this same light, insisting that family can be formed outside the conventional lines of blood, breeding, and marriage. Some of his fiction even goes so far as to imply that the families we choose have greater success in caring for their members than do the families we are born into.

12

"Go to Sleep, Devil"

The Awakening of Catherine's Feminism in *The Garden of Eden*

Amy Lovell Strong

On 14 May 1947 Ernest Hemingway dyed his hair bright red. Or perhaps "bright red" does not capture the effect he hoped for. In his own words, then:

> [I] started on test piece with just the drab and only tiny bit of mixture and it made fine red in about 35 minutes. . . . Hair as dark as mine has to go through red before can be blond—So I thought, what the hell, I'll make really red for my kitten and did it carefully and good, same as yours, and left on 45 minutes and it came out as red as french polished copper pot or a very new minted penny—not brassy—true bright coppery. (letter to Mary Welsh Hemingway)

Of all the photographs that abound of Hemingway with a slain lion or a fishing rod, in military uniform, at his typewriter, or with the distinctive white beard, we unfortunately have none that show him with hair the color of a new minted penny. Perhaps if a few *Look* photographers had captured Hemingway on film in 1947 with polished copper pot hair, it might have been more obvious how constraining and monolithic his public image had become.

Hemingway's reputation, unlike that of so many other literary figures, has preceded him since the 1930s. Students who have never opened one of his books have an idea about their content simply through the channels of popular culture. People who have never studied twentieth-century literature know what Hemingway looks like and will breezily summarize his reputation as one who defined manhood through his life and his characters. The line between his personal life and his fictional creations has never been carefully drawn; consequently, Hemingway has suffered the slings and arrows of readings absolutely riddled with intentional fallacies. The distinction between his personal life and his writings has always been fine, in part because he wrote so much non-fiction and in part because his composition methods could lead any well-intentioned scholar astray. He blurred distinctions between genres in numerous works: *Green Hills of Africa, Death in the Afternoon, A Moveable Feast, True at First Light;* he included several details about his wives and travels in his works of "fiction," and he wrote with such exact detail about the geographical places of his boyhood and adulthood that Hemingway scholars regularly tour the sites of his short stories and novels.

Such preconceived notions about a writer, or about a writer's typical subject matter, have an inherent danger. It is always possible that we have become so conditioned to reading a writer like Hemingway, and thinking about the persona of Hemingway, that we overlook inconsistencies and deviations from the norm. If we allow the mythos surrounding Hemingway to guide our reading, we will remember and validate the pieces of writing that feel Hemingwayesque and dismiss the rest. In *The Garden of Eden,* for example, the reader meets a very familiar Hemingway character in David Bourne: a virile, sexually active man who makes his living as a writer. His young wife Catherine, however, feels like a character who would be more at home in a Charlotte Perkins Gilman story: newly married, vibrant imagination, yearning for creative outlets, desirous of sexual adventure, increasingly marginalized by her husband's career, then a growing sense of helplessness, fear of madness, and a tendency toward suicide.

In a Hemingway novel, this woman's behavior feels so anomalous, so destructive; the male character, on the other hand, feels so natural and aligned with the author himself that the tendency is to validate his perspective, which leads to the simple conclusion: Catherine must be crazy. In this essay, however, I would like to start from the premise that Catherine is not at all mad; rather, she is a woman who feels trapped within the limitations of her gender and commits seemingly destructive acts as an act of re-vision, in Adrienne Rich's sense: "if the imagination is to transcend and transform experience it has to question, to challenge, to conceive of alternatives, perhaps to the very life you are living at that moment . . . nothing can be too sacred for the imagination to turn into its opposite or to call experimentally by another name" (*On Lies, Secrets, and Silence* 43). What does this mean for David Bourne? Perhaps, for a brief time, we will relegate him to the position of John in "The Yellow Wallpaper," a well-meaning husband who stifles his wife's creativity.[1] Seen in this context, Catherine's inner life becomes worthy of serious analysis and it removes the convenient and tidy desire to dismiss her depressing fate.

Stephen Spender has argued that "making Catherine mad is a fatal weakness in the novel—because it turns her into a case history and acquits David and Marita of moral responsibility for their actions" (6). Indeed, relegating Catherine to the edges of madness is a fatal weakness in the novel, but for even more profound reasons than Spender allows; by rejecting Catherine's way of looking at the world, by judging her view as a skewed one, we devalue her avid desire for multiplicity, complexity, and diversity in human relationships. After all, what is it that Catherine stands for? What makes her transformations, racial and sexual, so dangerous? Very simply, her experiments challenge the very categories upon which we base our identities: race, gender, nationality. The blurring of these categories has historically been at the very heart of our culture's greatest conflicts and fears: dread of miscegenation and homosexuality, wars over national borders, struggles to define ethnicity. Catherine wishes to inhabit the unstable territory between binaries—a place that breeds extreme tension, anxiety, and insecurity.

Critics have described Catherine as destructive, and she undoubtedly does bring destructive tendencies into her marriage with David. But it might be more useful to describe her acts as deconstructive, rather than destructive. By deconstructive, I mean she reads her culture in a way that rejects universals. As a deconstructionist (and a feminist), she believes that one's identity is an invention, not a cultural given. Much of the novel's tension revolves around her desire to prove that gender identity is a dynamic and fluctuating entity, fraught with conflicts and contradictions. Whether her husband decides to accept or reject this notion determines her success or failure as a wife. And once seen in this light, her acts of destruction begin to look a bit more like acts of self-preservation. Why does she burn David's clippings? Why does she bring Marita into her marriage? Why does she want to perform the male role? All of these actions demonstrate her larger desire to subvert fixed notions of gender identity, an effort that she shares with many other literary women of the twentieth century. In short, using both the manuscript versions and Tom Jenks's edited print version of *The Garden of Eden*, I will argue that Hemingway, wittingly or unwittingly, has created a feminist character in Catherine.

Throughout the novel, the pressure that she behave in a "normal," wifely role is a source of frustration for Catherine. As she says in the manuscript, "Who said normal? Who's normal? What's normal? I never went to normal school to be a teacher and teach normal. You don't want me to go to normal school and get a certificate do you?" (ser. 422.1, folder 18, p. 33). Catherine is a woman tortured by definitions of normality, anxious to break beyond uniformity to find a place where her less constrained, personal identity can emerge. Feminist theorist Denise Riley argues in her book *'Am I That Name?': Feminism and the Category of 'Women' in History* that women, as a group, can have unique experiences (pregnancy, for example), but she contends that these experiences in and of themselves do not define womanhood. The category of "woman" is an unstable, fluctuating state of being that can be willfully performed, unwillingly imposed by one's own body (as in menstruation), or imposed by another individual (as in a derisively hissed remark). When we examine critically the rhetoric that exists around these exclusively female experiences (rhetoric that defines what a woman is, or what a woman should be), we will often find a rift exists between discursive representations of "woman" and individuals' experiences of their own identity from moment to moment. If we conceive of Catherine Bourne as a woman who accepts her own identity as a woman, but at times detests the socially imposed category of "woman," then her self-dividedness, her bursts of rage, her desire to enact forbidden sexuality, and even her decision to burn David's manuscripts can make sense.

Catherine, first and foremost, is a divided self. Because she finds the female role an oppressive, predictable, and inexpressive form, she wants to escape. She has a heightened awareness of female stereotypes and tries to make David more conscious of the moments when he himself invokes these stereotypes. In a brief argument with David, he tells her to lower her voice so others in the restaurant would not hear her, and she replies, "Why should I hold it down? You want a girl don't you? Don't you want everything that goes with it? Scenes, hysteria, false accusations, temperament isn't that it?" (*GOE* 70). She is quite aware of the female-as-hysteric stereotype and can easily see how, at any given moment, her conversation can move from a personal interaction to a stereotyped construction. It is in this vein that we can understand what Catherine means when she says, "I'm not a woman. I can't stand how women are and I never could" (ser. 422.1, folder 18, pp. 24, 33). And when Marita accuses her, "You aren't really a woman at all," Catherine responds, "I know it. I've tried to explain it to David often enough" (192). It is not that she despises either herself or other women; rather, she despises the category of women that defines her as hysterical, passive, and weak. In her desire to circumvent constricting categories, Catherine embarks on a series of gender transformations with the hope of liberating herself from the codes of female behavior.[2] Importantly, Catherine performs her experiments only in very small laboratory, the laboratory of her marriage to David. She does not measure herself by other people's standards and says as much to David: "We're not like other people" (27). She simply wants to establish a world without gender stereotypes within the confines of her marriage, and a large part of her success depends on having a willing partner.

It is hard to gauge how much Catherine trusts David, and in fact she probably ought to be very skeptical of his ability to imagine a world devoid of stereotypes. First of all, he does not seem particularly imaginative in his conceptions of her as a woman; she is either his "good girl" or "Devil" (an all too familiar dichotomy). Once she introduces the idea that they could be equals, "the same," he expresses strong reservations:

"I want us to be just the same" [Catherine says].
"We can't be the same."
"Yes we could if you'd let us."
"I really don't want to do it." (176)

Catherine repeatedly decries the standards of normality that determine male and female behavior: "Why do we have to go by everyone else's rules? We're us" (15) and "Why do we have to do other things like everyone does?" (27). David does not see: "We were having a good time and I didn't feel any rules" (15). Catherine must educate David by showing him where the rules exist in terms of gender identity. Not one to tread lightly, she cuts straight to the first lesson and transforms herself into a boy (and asks David to position himself female). He gets the message, and the effect is swift and devastating.

After their very first nighttime gender transformation, the narration enters David's thoughts and we realize it's all over for his young wife: "he held her close and hard and inside himself he said goodbye and then goodbye and goodbye" (18). His forlorn and final farewell seems rather premature (we're only on page eighteen, after all), but it has the effect of alienating the reader from Catherine. Here, he is the sane husband who has been a reluctant participant in his wife's inexplicable and apparently intolerable desires. At once, he privately withdraws from her and from their project. And yet, the novel provides ample evidence that David wants to participate in Catherine's nighttime reversals. He says to himself, "All right. You like it . . . don't say that anyone tempted you or that anyone bitched you" (84). Moreover, when Catherine asks him, "You don't really mind being brothers do you?" he flatly replies: "No" (21). Understandably then, Catherine acts on the assumption that she and David want to be the same, and that together they want to break down gender differences. If she does lose her grip on reality, as many critics believe, then David's disingenuous and misleading remarks certainly contribute to her decline.

For his part, David feels quite comfortable with the benefits he receives from a culturally constructed identity (i.e., his status as author) and this, above all, prevents him from embracing Catherine's mission. The press clippings represent a public identity for David, an identity that (at least Catherine believes) does not represent his authentic self and undermines her desire to create complex identities for them both.

> They both read the clippings and then the girl put the one she was reading down and said, "I'm frightened by them and all the things they say. How can we be us and have the things we have and do what we do and you be this that's in the clippings?"
>
> "I've had them before," the young man said. "They're bad for you but it doesn't last."
>
> "They're terrible," she said. "They could destroy you if you

thought about them or believed them. You don't think I married you because you are what they say you are in these clippings do you?"

"No. I want to read them and then we'll seal them up in the envelope." (24)

Catherine finds the publicly constructed David abhorrent in the same way she finds cultural constructions of "woman" abhorrent. She wants David to know that she married him for his authentic self, not this culturally powerful identity that exists in texts. And perhaps more importantly, she wants David to act on the same principle in his affections toward her. "Please love me David the way I am. Please understand and love me" (17), she says, hoping that he can move beyond static definitions of "woman," "wife," or "bride" to find in her a more complex and complete individual.

In order to create a world where both she and David can be safe from the world's standards or "everyone else's rules," both partners must adopt an internal set of values that need not refer to anything outside of themselves. David, however, has already made it clear to the reader, if not to his wife, that he will not submit to such an enclosed system:

"The book's made some money already," he told her. "That's wonderful. I'm so glad. But we know it's good. If the reviews had said it was worthless and it never made a cent I would have been just as proud and just as happy."

I wouldn't, the young man thought. But he did not say it. He went on reading the reviews, unfolding them and folding them up again and putting them back in the envelope. (25)

Even the repetitiveness of David's motions, "unfolding them and folding them up again," suggests his desire to soak in their cumulative effect in an almost obsessive way. Or, as Steven Roe has pointed out, "David's review-reading is itself a kind of mass-like ceremony . . . he unfolds and refolds the clippings . . . as if they were of sacramental value. David, however, is a poor priest, engaged in a form of self-worship" (54). His unwillingness to admit the deep importance of these reviews contributes enormously to Catherine's growing sense of alienation and dividedness.

While Catherine wants to explode the notion that gendered subjec-

tivity exists as a single, coherent, unified entity, her husband's public career works in total opposition to that notion. The clippings construct a
static and commodified author-figure: "There were hundreds of [clip-
pings] and every one, almost, had his picture and they were all the same
pictures. It's worse than carrying around obscene postcards really. I think
he reads them by himself and is unfaithful to me with them" (215). David,
in effect, has usurped Catherine's role as the cover girl: fetishized, sexualized, commodified.[3] And yet there is a difference. Unlike mass media
images of women and the devaluation that lies therein, male authorship
and authority carries privilege and power. From Catherine's perspective,
David's interest in these cultural constructions of himself stands in direct
opposition to her project; he reveres the cultural image of masculine
authority that perpetuates itself in the public sphere and she strives to
destabilize such monolithic texts.

As Catherine becomes increasingly aware of David's dividedness, she
too becomes torn between the role of "good girl" and her individual desires. She tries to ease his mind by proving that she is committed to
the role of wife: "I've started on my good new life and I'm . . . looking
outward and trying not to think about myself so much" (53). Submissive, dutiful, accommodating, she attempts to live according to the standards of wifeliness. After a short time, she cannot sustain such a divided
self and pleads with David, "Do you want me to wrench myself around
and tear myself in two?" (70). She begins to feel even more desperate once
she realizes that their gender role reversals are having only a limited,
temporary effect. In an ingenious plan, albeit an unconventional one,
Catherine sets up a kind of puppet regime in her marriage, importing the
girl named Marita to fulfill the obligations of "good wife" while she gains
the space to breathe freely and act out her own desires without feeling
self-conscious about her lack of enthusiasm for the wifely ideal.

Accordingly, Marita becomes David's helpmeet, his supporter, his
lover; she gives, she sacrifices, she fulfills, she submits.[4] Her rhetoric fits
the mold of the wifely ideal: "Nothing I do is important" (112). And
she admits to Catherine, "I'm trying to study [David's] needs" (122). She
even reads *Vogue* magazine, a text written explicitly for women, and the
ultimate source of information about codified female behavior. When
Catherine and Marita return to see David after a day spent together,
Marita immediately asks, "Did you work well David?" Catherine re-

sponds, "That's a good wife. I forgot to ask" (109). Marita's submission is so extreme, in fact, it almost becomes a parody of itself. In a conversation with David about a man's giving Madame a black eye, she says, "There's a difference in age and he was within his rights to hit her if she was insulting" (243). Marita's stance contrasts markedly with Catherine's earlier comment to David, "I'm of age and because I'm married to you doesn't make me your slave or your chattel" (225).

Catherine's puppet regime, as it were, fails. What she had neglected to factor into her experiment is the overwhelming power that accompanies a man and a woman who join in a culturally sanctioned union. Once Catherine has resigned her role as "good wife" to Marita, she feels freer to act on her sexual desires and she becomes increasingly marginalized. At the same time, Marita is studying David's needs, reading *Vogue*, and generally trying to fashion herself into an ideal wife, and thus grows increasingly mainstream. In a reversal of Catherine's highest hopes for herself and for her husband, Marita joins David in a conservative and powerful alliance of heterosexuality. They have all the weight of culturally prescribed normalcy on their side, and worse, they subscribe to it. Marita asks David, "Are we the Bournes?" and David replies, "Sure. We're the Bournes. It may take a while to have the papers. But that's what we are. Do you want me to write it out? I think I could write that" (243). David and Marita have psychologically transformed themselves into a married couple, and David's way of legitimizing the union falls back on a familiar source of cultural power—the public, written document that sanctions their union—something Catherine would have despised.

Once Catherine realizes that Marita has joined in a conventional union with David, she has very few options left to preserve the private world she had tried to invent. Once Marita has disrupted that world, David has an easy option—he can start a new life with Marita where they both know their roles and live within the prescribed boundaries of gender. Catherine's final desperate act seeks to eradicate the texts that have transfixed her husband and hindered him from developing a purely private world with her. She burns the clippings as well as the stories that will generate more clippings.

By the time Catherine decides to attack the very texts that enable David to strengthen his role as a powerful cultural producer, he has not only abandoned Catherine, but he divides his time between his conventional union with Marita and an exclusively male world (the world of his African stories) as a source of renewal. He thinks to himself, "Tomorrow he must go back into his own country, the one that Catherine was jealous of and that Marita loved and respected" (193). Marita respects that writerly world by simultaneously revering it, maintaining distance from it, and encouraging David to become even more entrenched in his own manhood. She prods, "I want you to have men friends and friends from the war and to shoot with and to play cards at the club" (245). David refuses to acknowledge that he had once subscribed to Catherine's multiplicity, if indeed he ever did, and he interprets her former attempts to achieve equality between them as plain old selfishness:

> "You only want things for you, Devil."
> "That's not true, David. Anyway I am you and her. That's what I did it for. I'm everybody. You know about that don't you?"
> "Go to sleep, Devil." (196)

Catherine's refusal to embrace a unified and coherent form of female sexuality has now become intolerable to her husband, the ultimate arbiter of her success or failure as a woman and a wife. His stiff response, "Go to sleep, Devil" literally puts to rest the possibility for her to explore and develop the diverse aspects of her own identity within their marriage.

Not unlike the climactic scene in Bronte's novel *Jane Eyre,* where Bertha finally takes her revenge upon Rochester in a release of primal rage, rebellion, and destruction, Catherine Bourne burns the very foundation of David's cultural identity. As though making an allusion to Bronte's novel, David says to Marita, "We've been burned out. . . . Crazy woman burned out the Bournes" (243). Catherine has become Bertha, the overly expressive, libidinal outcast, who—displaced by the good, ministering wife—takes her final revenge. And just as the blinding and maiming of Rochester endows Jane with a new power over him, Marita, too, benefits markedly from the burning of David's stories. In the wake of his destroyed stories, David is stripped of his former authority: "He had never before in his relatively short life been impotent but in an hour standing before the armoire on top of which he wrote he learned what impotence was" (ser. 422.3, folder 44, p. 1). Nothing a good woman can't fix—and Marita does, as we will see.

If Catherine's enterprise could be called deconstructive, then the work of Scribner's editor Tom Jenks must rightly be called reconstructive. Where Catherine strove to emphasize the value of plurality, he tied up loose ends; instead of continuing to challenge the constructedness of gender categories, he reinstates the husband's dominant, creative role in opposition to the wife's passive, submissive position; where ambiguities existed, he resolved them. Most of all, he opted for a neat and tidy ending: the marriage plot, in essence. But a thorough reading of the manuscripts will reveal that Hemingway was hardly looking back to the nineteenth century as a model for his novel's ending; on the contrary, I would argue that he was pushing quite edgily into the postmodern.

It is useless to criticize Tom Jenks, who felt compelled to choose only one ending, but it does leave those who have not had a chance to look at the manuscript completely unaware of the other endings that quite change the story's thrust. According to Jenks's story, Catherine conveniently disappears, leaving behind a letter that is filled with apology; Marita is the good and supportive wife who sleeps softly while David walks into his private room where he works and achieves phenomenal success. With his new pencils and a new cahier, he not only begins the story about his father but finds that "he knew much more about his father than when he had first written the story" (247). Miraculously, the story comes to him complete and entire and "what . . . had taken him five days to write originally" is completed by two o'clock that same afternoon. This is a man who not only recovers his original powers of composition, but finds renewed and enhanced abilities. Jenks's ending glorifies the writer's gift and pushes women off center stage, an arrangement that certainly finds an easy home within the Hemingway oeuvre. What I have tried to show here is that the complete text of *The Garden of Eden* does not have such a comfortable place within our traditional understanding of Hemingway's legacy.

Jenks could have gone with Hemingway's "Provisional Ending," a seven-page piece written as a safeguard in case anything happened to him before he finished the work. In this ending, Catherine and David are together, lying in the sun, carrying on a brittle, unsteady exchange reminiscent of "Hills Like White Elephants." Catherine repeatedly talks about the past, asking David if he remembers how it was then:

Remember when I used to talk about anything and everything and we owned the world?. . . . All we had to do was see it and we owned it. . . . Remember? I could change everything. Change me change you change us both change the seasons change everything for my delight and then it speeded up and speeded up and then it went away and then I went away. (4–5)

David tries to be positive, saying "Then you came back," to which Catherine responds, "Not really."

Their conversation strongly echoes the agonizing exchanges between Jig and her lover:

"We can have everything."
"No we can't" [Jig replies].
"We can have the whole world."
"No we can't."
"We can go everywhere."
"No we can't. It isn't ours anymore." ("Hills" 276)

The world is now a strange and alienating place for these two women who have been emotionally abandoned by their husbands, and both narratives end in irresolution. Catherine concludes a discussion of her thoughts on suicide with the falsely cheerful: "Who knows? Now should we have the nice swim before lunch?" Jig, too, puts on a forced smile in response to her lover's question of whether she feels better: "I feel fine. There's nothing wrong with me. I feel fine" (278). Even the landscapes share similar qualities. In "Hills Like White Elephants," barren countryside is set in opposition to a fertile valley. *The Garden of Eden*'s provisional ending juxtaposes the bright, hot sun and yellow sand where Catherine lies fully exposed against the clear and smooth blue water that refreshes David when the sun and conversation become too much for him. These comparisons are simply meant to point out that Hemingway's "Provisional Ending" fits rather nicely with some of the more provocative, gender-based stories of Hemingway's career; furthermore, the similarities between these two narratives bolster my own sense that our sympathies are ultimately meant to rest with Catherine, as they do with Jig.

A third conclusion to the novel exists, if we simply allow the narrative to end where the manuscript leaves off.[5] In an astonishing development (one that Jenks leaves out in the published version), the manuscript reveals that Marita has her hair cut short to look like an African girl, but the barber cuts off so much she ends up looking like a boy; and yet, David admits quite readily that he is "very excited" by her appearance. Later that evening, Marita proposes that she play the male role at dinner, just as Catherine had done:

> "I'm your girl and your boy too. Do you know it?"
> "If you want."
> "No. If we both want. Can I be at dinner?"
> "Sure." (ser. 422.3, folder 45, p. 27)

Later that night, they enact their gender reversals in bed as well. Marita, in an internal monologue, comforts herself with the knowledge that she is better than Catherine at these gender transformations: "I'm better than she is because I really am both. I'm a better boy because I really am. I don't have to change back and forth and I'm a better girl I hope" (ser. 422.3, folder 46, pp. 36–37). Debra A. Moddelmog has noted the major implications this has for David's character:

> Of all the changes Jenks made, the one that stands out in greatest opposition to the movement of the manuscript is the cauterizing of the pages which reveal that Catherine's departure does not 'cure' David's desire to engage in and enjoy actions that call into question his masculinity as well as his heterosexuality. ("Protecting" 113)

Beyond its implications for David, though, this section of the manuscript absolutely begs the question: what precisely, then, was Catherine's failing as a wife? Is it still fair to call Catherine "mad," given this new information about her husband's complicity? We must assume, at this point, that David does indeed want a wife who will push at the boundaries of gender identity, performing the role of boy and girl. So how can we condemn Catherine?

The narrative, ever so faintly, suggests one difference between Marita and Catherine in their nighttime reversals: Catherine had insisted on being the boy (Peter), and therefore the dominant partner, while David was forced to position himself female. In the provisional ending, Catherine remarks that she cannot remember the name of the product they used "to aid such miracles" (2). Marita, on the other hand, allows David to retain the position of dominance; he remains in the male role, and she positions herself as a boy, presumably the submissive role to his dominant role (Marita thinks to herself, "I must do that part [being a boy] better than she did. It's good I'm just the opposite" [ser. 422.3, folder 45, p. 11]). Catherine's failing as a wife is precisely as she feared and imagined it to be: she wanted to be equals in a marriage where the husband could not relinquish his dominance.[6] In the end, David finally acknowledges his responsibility for the destruction of his young wife: "his changing of allegiance, no matter how sound it had seemed, no matter how it simplified things for him, was a grave and violent thing" (238).

If the novel were to end in such a way as to echo Hemingway's own biography, then Marita's duplication of Catherine's gender experimentation would be quite appropriate. Michael Reynolds has shown that in 1922 Hemingway wanted to let his hair "grow to reach the bobbed length of Hadley's so they could be the same person" (98). And in *A Moveable Feast*, Hemingway says he and Hadley "lived like savages and kept our own tribal rules and had our own customs and our own standards, secrets, taboos, and delights" (4). During his later courtship with Pauline, she repeatedly remarked, "We are one, we are the same guy, I am you" (qtd. in Kert 186). Two decades later, Mary Welsh's autobiography explains that she (Mary) had always wanted to "be a boy" and loved Ernest to "be her girls" (389); moreover, in a handful of letters, Hemingway nicknamed himself "Catherine" and referred to Mary as "Peter."[7] Only his third wife, Martha Gellhorn, seems to have refrained from the gender experimentation Hemingway enjoyed with his other three wives.[8]

It may be that the weight of Hemingway's own "clippings" kept him from publishing such a self-revealing novel during his own lifetime. But for nearly two decades he worked on *The Garden of Eden*, and in it we gain entrance past the carefully cultivated persona of the Hemingway legend. If we are able to distance ourselves from the immediate tendency to label Hemingway as a purely male-centered writer, we may have room to see the awakening of Catherine Bourne, perhaps Hemingway's first— certainly one of his greatest—feminist women.

13

The Light from Hemingway's Garden

Regendering Papa

Nancy R. Comley

The road to my present identity, a woman scholar writing on Hemingway, began with Brett Ashley. This is not surprising, of course, for Brett, until Catherine Bourne was unearthed, was the most interesting woman character in a Hemingway text. In addition, for me, Brett and the novel in which she figured were tinged with the glamor of the 1920s, and of the expatriate life in Paris. That's one of the reasons why, as a graduate student, I chose *The Sun Also Rises* as one of the key texts to be considered in my dissertation, which was also concerned with Henry Adams's legacy to American modernist writers. During the research and writing of this dissertation I began to define myself as a feminist critic, prompted in part by my reactions to the male writers I was dealing with (Adams, Anderson, Eliot, Fitzgerald, Hemingway, and Pynchon), but perhaps to an even greater extent by their (primarily male) critics.

At the time—the mid-1970s—Hemingway criticism was indeed predominantly male, and the prevailing view of Brett Ashley was that she was queen of Hemingway's stable of bitches. With this judgment I did not agree, as indeed, neither did Brett: a bitch was precisely what she refused to be (*SAR* 243). I was then engaged in reading the presentation of women in my selected group of American modernist writers by the light of Adams's Virgin of Chartres. About one of the key scenes in *The Sun Also Rises*, I wrote: "Brett's importance as feminine center of the text is symbolized during the fiesta procession in Pamplona, when she is surrounded by *riau–riau* dancers. . . . Because the fiesta takes place just after

midsummer's eve, it is likely that Brett has been set up as a fertility symbol, for she too is decked with garlic to ward off evil spirits" ("A Critical
Guide" 197). I had agreed in part with Richard Lehan's assessment of
Brett as "an inversion of Adams's Virgin since she fragments rather than
coalesces the group" (198), but I pointed out that Lehan overlooks the fact
that Adams's Virgin is herself an anarchic figure, a descendant of Venus
and other pagan goddesses. As a construct of Adams's modernist mind,
she is the none-too-stable center of *Mont Saint Michel and Chartres.* I had
noted that "Brett is always at the center of all groups, and if at times she's
none too stable a center, the fragmentation of the group is largely caused
by men's reactions *to* her rather than her actions working upon them"
(197). In particular, Robert Cohn projects his fantasies about romantic
love onto Brett, and it is her assessment of their liaison as a merely sexual,
hence transitory, experience that he cannot accept, and that makes him
behave badly.

I had also noted at the time that Carlos Baker, in *Hemingway: The
Writer as Artist,* saw Brett as a "witch," but for reasons I cannot recall, I
chose not to respond to such criticism. However, in rereading Baker recently, I was more forcibly struck by his vituperative treatment of Brett.
After proclaiming Brett's "witch-hood," Baker pounces on Brett's statement, "I've got the wrong type of face" for a religious atmosphere:

> She has indeed. Her face belongs in wide-eyed concentration over
> the tarot pack of Madam Sosostris, or any equivalent soothsayer in
> the gypsy camp outside Pamplona. It is perfectly at home [with the
> dancers, or] in the tavern gloom above the wine cask. For Brett in
> her own way is a lamia with a British accent, a Morgan le Fay of
> Paris and Pamplona, the reigning queen of a paganized wasteland
> with a wounded fisherman as her half-cynical squire. She is, rolled
> into one, the *femme fatale de trente ans damnée.* (90)

It is perhaps wiser to say of Baker that he found T. S. Eliot's misogyny
contagious rather than to speculate on the psychodrama that Brett inspired in him (he ends by calling Brett "an alcoholic nymphomaniac").
We shall simply let his tirade serve as a prime example of a modernist
male's reaction to Brett Ashley as well as the kind of *ad feminam* criticism
that prompted me to examine my own reaction to it. That is, I had finally

reached the moment when I reacted to such criticism as male, and as sexist, and as in need of correction—feminist correction, of course.

For a woman, that is the moment of becoming, under the influence of Judith Fetterley's *The Resisting Reader* (1978), a member of that group. However, I was primarily resisting male critical readings, whose desire to emasculate my mind was, I felt, greater by far than Hemingway's. Yet even such harsh critics of Brett as Baker had to admit, albeit grudgingly, that Brett is sympathetically presented by her creator. Such sympathy becomes evident once one analyzes the value system in *The Sun Also Rises* and groups the characters into those who know the values and have paid for this knowledge, like Brett and Jake, and those who do not, like Robert Cohn. Brett is "one of the chaps," as she likes to call herself, and she seems not to care much for the company of women. Hemingway's sympathies frequently lie with women (and little girls) who have (by Hemingway's standards) masculine characteristics (and are sexy): besides Brett, we have Pilar of *For Whom the Bell Tolls* and Catherine Bourne of *The Garden of Eden*. (As for little girls, there's Krebs's kid sister and Littless of "The Last Good Country.") Perhaps Brett's harshest critics disapprove of her for a similar reason: they consider her sexual adventuring appropriate behavior for males only. Hence, like Pedro Romero, they would prefer a "more womanly" Brett, faithful to her one man.

In teaching and writing about Hemingway in the years between the dissertation and my discovery of and immersion in *The Garden of Eden* manuscript, my critical approach soon evolved from resistance and an emphasis on critique of male writers' treatment of women in literature, a position that characterized the first stage of feminist criticism, as Elaine Showalter has pointed out, to an examination of what we do when we read, and how our subjectivity is structured. This stance was encouraged by the explosion of theory that was going on in the late 1970s and 1980s, especially in the areas of reader response and sexuality and gender. Equally important as a stimulus to interpretation and analysis was teaching, and what I learned in the classroom in discussion and in analyzing my students' responses to Hemingway's texts. Hemingway's short stories are wonderful for teaching narrative, modernism, and of course, gender issues. I continue to be fascinated with the way discussions of "Indian Camp" divide along the lines of gender: how most men in the class reenact the Doctor's role: unlike most women in the class, they do not hear the Indian woman's screams; they pay little attention to the possible reasons for the Indian husband's suicide. I agree with Peter Schwenger's assessment of the message to male readers: "The equation is clear: those who feel emotion die; those who reject it are practical men" (104–05). Some readers make the mistake of assuming that Hemingway is saying this is how real men should behave. Such readings were often produced by those devoted to the concept of the "hero" and the "code" in Hemingway's work. Philip Young's definition of the "code hero" in 1952 proved highly influential:

> It is made of the controls of honor and courage which in a life of tension and pain make a man a man and distinguish him from the people who follow random impulses, let down their hair, and are generally messy, perhaps cowardly, and without inviolable rules for how to live holding tight. (*Reconsideration* 63–64)

Those "messy" people who "let down their hair" sound, well, feminine. Using Young's definition as a guide produces a simplistic reading of "Indian Camp" in which the Doctor is a hero and the Indian father, who "couldn't stand things," is cowardly. (It should be noted that Young ignores the code business in his reading of the story.) Hemingway's men do have feelings and at times they do express them: but mainly to themselves. They operate under a code established by a patriarchal culture, which the author, who has been shaped by it himself, examines in his fiction. The hero is a man who holds on tight to his feelings, believing that if he blabs he will lose everything, meaning, for example in the case of Krebs in "Soldier's Home," the pristine clarity of his memories of his heroic acts.

Hemingway excised the original opening of "Indian Camp" that showed Nick as a child who was afraid of the dark, which he found synonymous with dying. The excision made "Indian Camp" a more modernist story, but the reader's attention tended to focus more on the doctor than on Nick, whose story it really is. While "Indian Camp" is but one of the many Hemingway stories that can be read as commentaries on sexual and cultural differences, it should also be read, as Young has done, as one of the more brutal stories of a boy's premature initiation into "the violence of birth and death" (32).

Consistently, however, the Indian woman's part in the tale was ignored, though her effect was duly noted, as for example, in Joseph DeFalco's assessment in 1963: "The Indian as a primitive has no effective method of dealing with the terror created by the screaming wife" (31). This "primitive" female body, then, whose language of pain is ignored by the white man of science, is there to be colonized, indeed brutally incised, penetrated, and scarred. To be fair, in 1963, no one was considering the body in Hemingway's work; colonization of bodies and cultural differences had not themselves been incised in the critical lexicon. They had, however, by the time *The Garden of Eden* was published, the text that would call into question the consideration of sexuality and gender as a matter of simple binary oppositions in Hemingway's work. I had been looking forward to the publication of *The Garden of Eden* ever since Aaron Latham's article, "A Farewell to Machismo," appeared in the *New York Times Magazine* in 1977. At the time, the description Latham gave of the manuscript material allowed me to provide this neat conclusion to an article I was writing on the economic structure of exchange in Hemingway's fictional value system:

> Hemingway's last and unpublished work reveals the desire to remove the barrier between the sexes. . . . In this late work, androgyny is foregrounded. Androgyny would remove the bargaining and complexity Hemingway associated with male-female relationships. Here, finally, would be the simple exchange system he so greatly desired. ("Hemingway's Economics" 253)

The publication of *The Garden of Eden* in 1986 brought gender issues to the foreground, not simply of that text but of the whole Hemingway text. During this same period, and continuing into the 1990s, biographies of Hemingway by Peter Griffin (1985, 1990), Michael Reynolds (1989), Kenneth Lynn (1987), and Mark Spilka's biographical-critical study, *Hemingway's Quarrel with Androgyny* (1990) appeared. All of these books drew on the unpublished material that was becoming available at the Kennedy Library. Other significant publications of interest to me were Robert Fleming's "The Endings of Hemingway's *Garden of Eden*," (1989) and J. Gerald Kennedy's "Hemingway's Gender Trouble" (1991), both of which helped to seal my conviction that Scribner's *Garden of Eden* differed significantly from Hemingway's in ways that simply could not be ignored.

And it was at this juncture that my identity shifted for a time from "a woman writing on Hemingway" to "a woman collaborating with a man to write on Hemingway." Robert Scholes and I had worked together on a number of projects, most of them textbooks, and were mulling over ideas for a new project. We had both been writing on Hemingway, so why not pull our stuff together and make a book out of it? We realized that the availability of Hemingway's manuscripts, and the *Garden of Eden* manuscript in particular, would very likely make us want to revise any previous work we had done. However, once we settled in among the wealth of material in the Hemingway room at the Kennedy Library, we soon knew that what we would write would be entirely new. The book that evolved from this collaboration, *Hemingway's Genders*, was in large part shaped during our commute between Barrington, Rhode Island and the Kennedy Library in Boston. As in our other collaborations, I can tell only some of the time which ideas were definitely mine or which words I remember writing. The book is very much univoiced, largely the result, as I have suggested, of our highway dialogues.

The *Garden of Eden* manuscript opened up the gender issue in all of Hemingway's work in ways we could not have predicted. In a sense, we started our research with the question, Where did this book come from? The novel as published seemed at first a startling departure from Hemingway's other work. To try to answer our question, we read through unfinished stories and novels, notes, letters, drafts, manuscripts, as well as published work, considering all of his writing as the Hemingway Test. In *The Archaeology of Knowledge*, Michel Foucault had raised the question, What is an *oeuvre*? In using this term, he says, "One is admitting that there must be a level . . . at which the *oeuvre* emerges, in all its fragments, even the smallest, most inessential ones, as the expression of the thought, the experience, the imagination, or the unconscious of the author, or, indeed, of the historical determinations that operated upon him" (24). Foucault repeated this question in his essay, "What Is an Author?" wherein he considers the "problems related to the proper name" (121), problems I'm not going to deal with here, interesting though they may be, given the ubiquity and power of the proper name "Hemingway." Foucault finds the word "work" (*oeuvre*) problematic, along with the notion of unity that it designates. And so did we: we used "text" in the Barthesian sense, as regulated by a metonymic logic, "the activity of associations, contiguities, carryings-over [that] coincides with a liberation of symbolic energy" (158). In pointing out the plurality of the text, Barthes recalls its etymology: "The text is a tissue, a woven fabric" (159), and it is not closed off, as a work is; one can enter through any one of many strands. Rose Marie Burwell applied the concept of the text to Hemingway's posthumous novels, which she read as a "serial sequence," showing the connections between them, connections that have been unrecognized "because of the manuscript deletions made for publication, the order in which the three published works appeared, and the restrictions of archival material that clarifies much about their composition and intentions" (*Postwar Years* 1). In so doing, Burwell had Hemingway's approval. She notes that he reminded Charles Scribner, who had chided him when Hemingway switched from one writing project to another, "All my work is a part of all my work" (51).

From her work then in progress, Burwell generously shared her research on the African book, having managed to read that manuscript at Princeton before legal entanglements closed it to scholars. The African material sheds light on the play with racial changing in *The Garden of Eden*, change that is signified by tanning rituals, and in the manuscript made more obvious by Catherine and Marita's joking about being David's "Somali women." While the Scribner editor left in much of the material on sexual changing, the racial element was completely excised. Yet this racial business, of which tanning is the outward and visible sign, is an integral element of the desire for transformative experimenting that drives this text. The references to Somali women, "kanakas," or "Oklahoma oil Indians" stem from Hemingway's fascination with primitivism. He liked to pose as part Indian in real life, and in Africa, he played his own games with racial transformation, when he shaved his head, dyed his clothes "a rusty Masai color, and began an elaborate courtship of his African 'fiancée,' Debba" (Meyers 502). The connection of Debba to Hemingway's fictional first love, an Indian girl who appears as "Prudie" or "Trudy" in several Michigan stories, is fairly obvious. Nick Adams's sexual initiation with Trudy in "Fathers and Sons" is echoed in David Bourne's initiation with the Wakamba woman in Africa. The "Last Good

Country" manuscript contains a dialogue about Trudy between Nick and his little sister:

> "I thought you were through with her."
> "I was. But I'm not sure now."
> "You wouldn't go and make her another baby would you?"
> "I don't know."
> "They'll put you in the reform school for that if you keep it." (Kennedy Library ser. 542, folder 1, p. 11)

"The Last Good Country" is another piece of Hemingway's later, unfinished work, so that the slippage of concerns (or in this case, fantasies) from one manuscript to another is not surprising. The business of transgression in *Garden* is expressed frequently in terms of "tabus" or "tribal laws." Such language comes directly from the African material, in which the narrator as would-be Masai warrior wants to make a baby with Debba. But as Burwell tells us, "Debba is protected by tribal law that forbids him to make love to her" (144). Nevertheless, the narrator defies the Elders, makes love to Debba, and thus violates a tabu. (The African book, *True at First Light*, edited by Patrick Hemingway, has been published, and the Debba business has of course been of interest to the press.)

As Hemingway is in the process of writing up his African material, he says of it in a letter to his friend Buck Lanham that "some of the stuff I think you'll like unless you have too strong views on mis-cegenation" (*SL* 839). Hemingway must have had them himself, and in *The Garden of Eden* he lets Catherine voice them. In a dialogue with David on the sexual merits of Somali men and women she says, "Then why don't you quit worrying and thinking in terms of Lutherans and Calvinists and St Paul and everything you don't come from" (ser. 422.1, folder 17, 25 bis). The worrying is about having two "Somali wives." But a bit later, Catherine brings up a part of David's African narrative that is not written in the text but is referred to. This narrative concerns David's youth and purported sexual initiation by a Wakamba woman who, as Catherine reports it, apparently gave him the clap at age fourteen (ser. 422.1, folder 20, 14). Such is the price for violating a tabu, and we must note that

David/Hemingway has imposed his own tabu against exposing this particular African narrative to his audience.

Certainly Hemingway conceived of sex and gender as a binary system, and that basic belief underlies the relationships in *The Garden of Eden,* as it does all of his work. However, at the same time, he was fascinated with the possibilities of experiencing a shift in genders, which explains his own experiments with hair and, if we can believe Miss Mary's diary, with sex. But as much as Puritanism is disavowed, a price is exacted nonetheless in this *Garden* for sexual experimentation. Hence, in this text, to try to break the binary system is to transgress. Here Hemingway appears to be incapable of considering variations in sexual positions or any similar experimentation as other than transgressive, or *tabu.* For him, there are certain positions that male heterosexuals assume to perform sex with female heterosexuals, positions sanctified by Western culture (as, for example, the *missionary* position). Other positions and actions are coded as perverse, if not homosexual (the latter implied in David's calling Marita a "Bizerte street urchin" with a "water-front Arab's" hair [ser. 422.1, folder, 36, p. 1]).

The problem of morality is one of the unresolved conflicts in *The Garden of Eden.* It underlies the issue of who one might consider, if one cared to do so, the "good girl" in the text, Catherine or Marita. Following the biblical line, the women are the temptresses in Hemingway's garden, and David is the willing-to-be-led Adam. Catherine, nicknamed "devil" by her Adam, has been subjected to some of the same sort of criticism that Brett has endured, and for similar reasons: both are perceived as destructive temptresses and catalogued in the "bitch" file. If Brett has been excoriated because she has supposedly corrupted a young bullfighter (bullfighters being *numero uno* on the hero scale), so also is Catherine for trying to corrupt a writer (also high on the hero scale), and (worse) for destroying his work. Scribner's certainly took the latter view in tailoring the manuscript to produce a happy ending (in Hemingway!) with the writer rewriting his lost stories with his faithful handmaiden, Marita, by his side. Such a scenario, Scribner's must have thought, was more in keeping with the Hemingway hero code.

It's fair to say that Hemingway was not sure whether David Bourne should remain with Catherine or Marita. He was rewriting his own personal dilemma of being in love with two women at the same time, Hadley

and Pauline, and of having to make a decision, one that seems to have haunted him throughout his life. Many critics have no problem deciding between Marita and Catherine: those who favor David the (Hemingway) Writer choose Marita. She praises David's writing and is not jealous of his writing. Her only occupation is pleasing David, thus appearing to those critics as the ultimate Good Girl. However, Marita is no angel of mercy, like Catherine Barkley; she can be nasty—but is so only to Catherine Bourne, whose position she is artfully usurping. As the manuscript makes clear, Marita is the true bisexual who can switch roles without guilt, and she is proud to be able to do anything that Catherine can do better than she (ser. 422.1, folder 27, p. 32). In the manuscript, Marita reveals herself to be more knowledgeable and experienced in sexual matters than Catherine. Musing on her sameness with David, Marita concludes, "we're darker than she was inside" (ser. 422.1, folder 36, p. 14). In the manuscript, Marita comes to "look like Africa," all right, with a difference, as David points out: "But very far north and you mixed up the genders." Marita is happy to be both his "African girl" and his "street Arab" (ser. 422.1, folder 36, pp. 3, 25). She believes she is a better boy than Catherine because unlike Catherine, who feels driven to change, Marita does not have "to change back and forth," in as much as she feels she is both a girl and a boy. Her attitude toward these sexual adventures is "It's not perversion. It's variety" (ser. 422.1, folder 36, p. 5), and "How could it be bad if it makes you feel so good and wonderful" (ser. 422.1, folder 36, p. 35).

Though David has enjoyed for the most part being shared by two women (and thus realizing a prime male fantasy), he feels "that it is was wrong to love two women and that no good could ever come of it" (132). But if he feels he has suffered a loss of moral fiber, he also realizes he has written better as he has "deteriorated morally" (ser. 422.1, folder 17, p. 9). And so he remains passive, accepting and enjoying sexual favors from each woman. However, he does suggest to Catherine that it's "not normal for any woman to want to share with anyone." To which she replies, "Who said normal? Who's normal? What's normal?" (ser. 422.1, folder 18, p. 33). Catherine's awareness of her incipient madness (she exhibits some of the characteristics of schizophrenia) has made her want to provide a woman to take care of David: she refers to Marita as "heiress" for that reason and also because Marita has plenty of money. Readers who perceive Catherine as vindictively destructive overlook the fact that she is operating within the logic of madness, a condition that allows her to view her most destructive act, burning David's stories, as fully justifiable. If anything, Catherine is more self-destructive than destructive to others. Similarly, the same readers tend to overlook David's willingness to be treated as a sort of semi-helpless prodigy incapable of taking care of himself.

Catherine is the spur to David's creativity, and her edginess, wit, and unpredictability are what move Hemingway's narrative along. In this sense, she most resembles Brett Ashley, who, as we have seen, is the edgy center of *The Sun Also Rises*. Catherine, like Brett, has the best lines. That's why this woman reader was so impressed with *The Garden of Eden:* here at long last was another interesting woman, one who signaled a more complex and interesting Hemingway in this late phase of his career. To be sure, in David Bourne we have a familiar type, the sort of manly man of few words, here fashioned into the writer-as-(dubious)-hero. But David is rather boring, and the reader's attention is mainly focused on its women, who provide good conversation, a feature not to be underestimated in a novel where the major action consists of a man writing or a threesome whose primary endeavors consist of hair appointments, tanning, swimming, eating, drinking, and sex. Indeed, I have not mentioned a third woman in this garden, Barbara Sheldon, whose narrative is entirely missing from the published version. Barbara is married to Nick Sheldon, an artist, and the story of their marriage is being chronicled by Andy, another writer. Like Catherine, Barbara is unstable mentally and has given up her painting because she feels her work is inferior to Nick's. She is strongly attracted to Catherine, but is wary of Catherine's destructive powers. Though nothing comes of this attraction, Barbara does make love with Andy, and during the second of their trysts, she learns that Nick has been killed in an accident. Overcome by guilt, she later commits suicide.

Co-coordinating two triangular relationships was probably more than Hemingway could handle, which no doubt accounts for his summary extermination of the Sheldons, who are a slightly older, artier doubling of the Bournes. Indeed, the Sheldons physically resemble Hadley and Ernest Hemingway, while the blonde Bournes with their perfect bodies recall other fictional (or fantasy) blondes, both male and female, in the

Hemingway Text. I have not stopped to count the times a beautiful blonde-haired woman with long lovely legs has strolled through Hemingway's work, avatars of the movie stars who visit blond Robert Jordan's dreams in *For Whom the Bell Tolls*. (Hemingway, of course, did not have much luck with real long-legged blondes, especially that talented one with brains.) This little blonde excursion is simply an example of the kind of associations a reading of *The Garden of Eden* prompts.

But let me return to my opening statement regarding Catherine Bourne as, along with Brett Ashley, the most interesting of Hemingway's women. My reading of Catherine Bourne was enlightened by recent work in gender theory, with its emphasis on the social construction of the feminine. *Garden* dramatizes the interplay between sexual theory, based on observable biological differences and the binaries of male and female, and gender theory, which is concerned with the social meaning for feminine and masculine. Judith Butler, in contesting "a mimetic relation of gender to sex," points out, "When the constructed status of gender is theorized as radically independent of sex, gender itself becomes a free-floating artifice, with the consequence that *man* and *masculine* might just as easily signify a female body as a male one, and *woman* and *feminine* a male body as easily as a female one" (6). Inexplicably excised from the published version of *Garden* is the object that moves the Bournes and the Sheldons to question their binary conceptions of sex and gender: the Rodin statue that each couple, on separate occasions, has viewed at the Rodin museum in Paris, the Hotel de Biron, "where the changings had started" (ser. 422.1, folder 1, p. 30). The statue is *The Metamorphosis*, but this title is crossed out in the manuscript and the statue is simply identified as "The one there are no photographs of and of which no reproductions are sold" (ser. 422.1, folder 1, p. 21). Just as the statue is neither named nor described, so also do the nocturnal experiments of the two couples remain in the dark, as far as the text is concerned. But for eager scholars, a little research is rewarding. The statue represents an androgynous-looking couple in sensuous embrace, a fine example of Rodin's fascination with the erotic and with sexual fluidity. The statue thus functions as a subversive element, calling sexual binarism into question, because sexual differences are not easily discerned in these figures. Rodin has caught the moment when Iphis, a girl who has been brought up as a boy, is transforming into a male, thus validating her "masculine" love for the girl, Ianthe. But Rodin's boy, poised in the dominant sexual position, has breasts: the transformation is by no means complete, as if Rodin is taunting Ovid, in whose world homosexual love is considered abnormal.

That also holds true in the Hemingway text. Catherine's sexual experiments with Marita prove distasteful to her, and constitute another downward step in her psychic deterioration. Catherine dislikes her sexual self as well as her gendered self. She seems to believe that a woman's primary use is for reproduction, and that if she cannot conceive a child, her body is useless. When she and David are in Madrid, she lets loose a tirade summing up her disgust with what she construes as feminine characteristics, asserting that being a girl is "a god damned bore." When David asks her to "hold it down," she lashes out: "Why should I hold it down? You want a girl don't you. Don't you want everything that goes with it? Scenes, hysteria, false accusations, temperament isn't that it?" Of course, it's that time of the month for Catherine, as David learns when she says she must return briefly to their room: "Because I'm a god damned woman. I thought if I'd be a girl and stay a girl I'd have a baby at least. Not even that." To give David credit, he does say, "That could be my fault" (70–71).

In this scene, Catherine performs feminine hysteria, thus becoming the stereotype she so despises. Her shift to a masculine role in sexual intercourse can thus be seen as a desire to break out of the repetition of performing the feminine, and the Rodin statue has symbolized for her the possibility of doing so. In Butler's terms, "The possibilities of gender transformation are to be found precisely in the arbitrary relation between such acts, in the possibility of a failure to repeat, a de-formity, or a parodic repetition that exposes the phantasmatic effect of abiding identity as a politically tenuous construction" (141). In the game of sexual politics in *Garden,* Catherine takes on a radical approach, while Marita practices a quiet but effective subversion, performing "feminine" docility, catering to the male's belief in his superior sexual and intellectual powers, and winning him over by performing his fantasy of the feminine.

Scribner's would have the story end there, but Hemingway did not wish it to, as his provisional ending makes clear, with its handwritten notation: "Written when thought something might happen before book could be finished. EH" (ser. 422.2, p. 1). Here, Catherine and David are a little bit older, but a good deal wiser. Catherine is sobered by her break-down and her stay in a Swiss sanitarium, the price she has paid for trying to "change everything for my delight" (ser. 422.6, p. 5). This is a subdued, bittersweet ending, with the possibility of Catherine's going "bad" again, and with a suicide pact made if she should. Hemingway's is a mature ending, free of the male fantasy that makes the Scribner's version of a proper manuscript so insipid. Catherine Bourne, as she appears in the manuscript of *The Garden of Eden*, introduces the woman reader to a more complex, more interesting Hemingway, one who plays and questions the masculine role.

2
Mothers, Wives, Sisters

14
Alias Grace

Music and the Feminine Aesthetic
in Hemingway's Early Style

Hilary K. Justice

Art is a manifestation of Imagination, Intuition & Inspiration, but
controlled by laws of design.

Grace Hall Hemingway

The laws of prose writing are as immutable as those of flight, of
mathematics, of physics.

Ernest Hemingway

In 1958 Ernest Hemingway told interviewer George Plimpton that he
had learned "as much from painters about how to write as from writers,"
adding "I should think what one learns from composers and from the
study of harmony and counterpoint would be obvious" ("Art of Fiction"
118).[1] In a 1950 *New Yorker* interview, Hemingway told Lillian Ross that
"In the first paragraphs of 'Farewell,' I used the word 'and' consciously
over and over the way Mr. Johann Sebastian Bach used a note in music
when he was emitting counterpoint. I can almost write like Mr. Johann
sometimes—or, anyway, so he would like it" (*Portrait* 50). Although it is
tempting to consider his claim as just so much Hemingway bluster, the
fact that he knew enough about music to distinguish between "harmony"
and "counterpoint" suggests there may be more substance than shadow in
his statement. As early as 1925, he referred to his stories as though they
were musical compositions, telling editor Horace Liveright not to change
any words, because "the stories are written so tight and so hard that the
alteration of a word can throw an entire story out of key" (*SL* 154). Similarities between music and prose are not as easily ascertained or defined
as those between prose and the visual arts, yet, as Hemingway implied to

Liveright, music and prose may work similarly to achieve similar effects.[2] An examination of his early work through the lens of musical theory offers support for his assertion. Understanding the musical elements of Hemingway's style provides insight into how his texts work, how they achieve their effects, and, at least in part, how they "make people feel something more than they [understand]" (*MF* 75). Further, his admission of a musical influence—an influence that, for him, was inescapably feminine and maternal—can, if properly understood, illuminate a facet of his deeply troubled relationship with his mother, Grace Hall Hemingway. Clearly recognizable musical patterns and forms in Hemingway's early work show his indebtedness to Grace Hemingway as his earliest artistic mentor.

Hemingway once claimed that his mother, a music teacher, composer, and classically trained vocalist, "forced me to play the cello even though I had absolutely no talent and could not even carry a tune. She took me out of school one year so I could concentrate exclusively on the cello" (Hotchner 116). He told George Plimpton that he was "kept . . . out of school a whole year to study music and counterpoint" ("Art of Fiction" 118). Although Hemingway did play cello (well enough to play in his high school orchestra), none of his biographers support the claim regarding a year's absence from school. Grace did, however, keep each of his sisters out of school for a year upon menarche (Spilka, *Quarrel* 47). Hemingway's claim to have suffered similarly, then, is revealing despite—or perhaps because of—being false; it suggests a link in his mind between the musical aesthetic and the feminine (via his sisters' menarches and differently, but especially, via his mother).

He was able to learn the "obvious" from "Mr. Johann" because he had grown up surrounded by and participating in music-making. As Hemingway recalled, "We played chamber music—someone came in to play the violin; my sister played the viola, and my mother the piano" ("Art of Fiction" 28). Bach, being male, long-dead, and acknowledged by posterity as a master, is a much easier mentor to admit to *The New Yorker* than one's mother, whom he instead represented as an unreasonable woman who forced him to do something to which he was unsuited.

This essay will show that Hemingway's sustained early exposure to music in his mother's home, and even his novice experiences playing cello in his school orchestra, provided the young Hemingway with an aural and visceral understanding of this kind of musical patterning, patterns later manifested in his prose.[3] The structures of certain early works strongly suggest identifiable counterpoint forms (the round, canon, ground, and fugue); other works suggest alternative musical forms (the theme and variation, the sonata form).[4] In order to explicate these patterns, I will first present a crash course in music theory to deploy three terms, "harmony," "counterpoint," and "melody," the terms on which the identification and discussion of the specific musical patterns within Hemingway's early works depend. After locating and illustrating these patterns within Hemingway's (and, for comparison, Stein's) prose, I will return to the earlier questions regarding Hemingway's association of music and the feminine, and, finally, his artistic indebtedness to his mother, Grace. Without her influence, whether in inherited talent or in overt instruction, the distinctive Hemingway style would look, sound, and even "feel" very different.

Some understanding of the terms "harmony" and "counterpoint" is necessary in order to see how Hemingway's counterpoint assertion plays out in his early works. The distinction between harmony and counterpoint, especially the Baroque counterpoint to which Hemingway alluded with his reference to Bach, is instantly recognizable aurally. Because Hemingway grew up in a musical household, he was able not only to hear but also to name the difference, yet anyone who has ever listened to Western music (classical, jazz, or rock) already has a basic understanding of the concepts of counterpoint and harmony, if not in those precise terms.

Counterpoint is music comprised entirely of multiple simultaneous melodies. Listeners generally perceive melody as the foreground of a musical piece; harmony, generally speaking, as the background. Melody involves the sounding of one note at a time and operates primarily on the listener's consciousness, whereas harmony involves the sounding of multiple notes together and works, at least on the untrained ear, more subconsciously (perhaps even viscerally). In terms of musical time, melody constitutes the immediate, the "now" of the music. The sense of movement or musical progression, however, is primarily a result of harmony, which creates a sense of resonance with what has come before and a sense of expectation for what will follow.

Harmony's multiple simultaneous notes sound together in chords, the progression of which forms the harmony of a musical piece. Controlling this harmonic progression is what allows a composer to manipulate his audience into knowing exactly where (or "when") they are in a piece. For example, in Beethoven's *Fifth Symphony* (the very end of the first movement, "da da da *dum*—da da da *dum*—da da da *dum* da *dum* da *dum* da *dum* da *dum*—da—*dum!*"), harmonic progression (combined with increasing rhythmic intensity) tells the listener that this movement is ending, several moments before it actually does. The piece is written in the key of c minor ("*dum*"), of which G major ("da") is the dominant (the dominant "feels" penultimate and thus "requires" resolution back to c minor—imagine the piece ending on the last "da" beat, and you will immediately sense the irresolution of the dominant). The alternating G major and c minor chords at the end of this movement increase the listener's tension by repeatedly creating then subverting the expectation that each c minor chord will be the last. The final c minor chord, then, is extremely satisfying to Western listeners—subjectively speaking, this piece does not just end, it *really* ends.[5]

In counterpoint, there are multiple lines, each of which functions *both* melodically and harmonically, simultaneously. As these independent lines interweave, they organically produce the chords that constitute harmonic progression. In other words, in counterpoint there is no distinction between foreground and background.[6] Music written in this style is mathematical, paradoxically intricate and clear. The clarity of counterpoint results from the fact that every note, every rhythm, every line, and every relationship between each of these elements contributes directly and equally to the musical whole. Even an untrained ear (or eye) will perceive counterpoint's multiple individual lines separately, although they occur simultaneously, for several reasons: each line is a melody, each melody is similar to or complementary to the others, each motif and figure of each line is repeated frequently, and because in this style harmony is a *product* of melody rather than a separate and subordinate formal entity. There is nothing to distract, nothing to detract from the experience of this music as music; it is music about music, complicated, yet simple. It is "lean," "spare," and "clean"; its leanness and spareness "make you see" what it is.[7]

A kind of contrapuntal influence is suggested in the work of at least two modern prose stylists: Hemingway and Stein, both of whom received ample music instruction as children.[8] Often their work achieves the cognitive (or visceral) effects of counterpoint style. That Stein influenced Hemingway is a critical commonplace, yet how her influence is actually manifested in his prose remains something of a mystery. When reading Hemingway—especially early Hemingway, such as the *In Our Time* "chapters"—one may sense a small-scale rhythmic cadence similar to that in Stein's prose. Although his familiarity with Stein and her work may have foregrounded for Hemingway the possibilities of rhythmic repetition in prose writing, this device did not originate with Stein. However, an examination of their styles from a musical perspective reveals that both of these authors rely on rhythmic repetition in order to achieve an echo effect, which comes as close to the effect of musical counterpoint as anything in prose.

The paradox of contrapuntal prose is the problem of simultaneity: a musical audience can hear multiple lines simultaneously, whereas a reader of words can only read one "line" at a time. This is possible in music because music has a vertical dimension as well as a horizontal one, while prose has only a horizontal one. Prose should (and often does) function "melodically"—one is always in the "now" of the words one is reading. Reader memory provides the harmony, allowing each line, paragraph, and chapter to inform the next, which somewhat satisfies the simultaneity required by the definition of counterpoint.[9]

However, the term "counterpoint" also refers to certain musical forms that are structured by strictly repeating, recognizable patterns. Several of these forms appear in Stein and early Hemingway, of which I will limit my discussion to four—the round, the canon, the ground, and the fugue. The simplest of these forms is the round (for example, "Three Blind Mice"). The technical definition of a round is "a strict canon at the unison," meaning that one melody is repeated exactly by each voice, that the melody always starts and ends on the same note, and that the entrances of the voices are staggered (i.e., the second voice will always begin the melody before the first voice has completed it). Stein's famous line, "Rose is a rose is a rose is a rose," achieves a perfect prose equivalent of a musical round.[10] With each successive iteration of "rose is a," the reader, expecting different words, will remember, or echo, the previous iterations of the same phrase. The structure of this sentence suggests that it may continue in perpetuity: "Rose is a rose is a rose is a rose is a . . . ."

Much of Stein's writing depends in some way on the round pattern, especially her experimental writing in which she deploys her notion of the "continuous present." Her short piece "As a Wife Has a Cow: A Love Story," like much of her experimental prose, can be linguistically baffling, containing such perplexing lines as "And to in six and another." When it is read aloud, however, its playful nature fully emerges—its linguistic codes may remain opaque, but their importance recedes somewhat as rhythm comes to the fore. In such texts, Stein uses words (and phrases) as though they are musical notes, which combine to form short, repetitive motifs. These motifs combine in turn to form longer phrases that, finally, structure entire works.

The piece begins "Nearly all of it to be as a wife has a cow, a love story. All of it to be as a wife has a cow, all of it to be as a wife has a cow, a love story" (543), in which the round structure operates on the level of the sentence (as it does, more exactly, in "A rose is a rose . . . "). Here, the reader's memory is freed from providing these echoes; Stein provides them for us. Unlike the "Rose" sentence, however, the longer "As a Wife Has a Cow" introduces new, apparently unrelated, material. This new material evokes the round in two ways: it forms roundlike sentences or passages on its own (e.g., "And to in six and another. And to and in and six and another. And to in six and and to and in and six . . . " and "Not and now, now and not, not and now, by and by not and now . . . "), and it allows for the departure from and return to the governing "key" or mood of the piece (the "wife has a cow" motif). The structure of the piece as a whole depends on three statements of that title motif (at the beginning, middle, and end), which provide the reader with a sense that longer phrases also repeat throughout the piece.

Unlike other canons, which must break their patterns in order to end (Kennan 94), rounds simply stop, more or less where they started. The round thus asserts a "continuous present" in music. Stein's extensive experimentation with the continuous present results in many such rounds (or roundlike moments) in her prose, in which words and phrases are repeated so often, and in such juxtaposition, that their rhythms subvert the dominance that linguistic meaning usually has in traditional prose, moving certain of Stein's works beyond the limits of language and into the realm of music.

Without going so far as to assert that Hemingway and Stein actually discussed the possibilities of prose harmony during their conversations about writing (although they may have; we can never know for sure), an examination of "Chapter 1" from *in our time* (1924), one of Hemingway's earliest experimental pieces, reveals at the very least how good his "ear" was.[11] In Stein's more obviously musical style, meaning is often subordinated to sonority, resulting in linguistic opacity; Hemingway's style, less obviously musical, achieves the inverse effect. While his simple declarative sentences create the illusion that one is functioning in a concrete, knowable reality, these sentences are performed according to subtly embedded patterns—patterns that evince a more deeply grounded harmonic resonance than that which is found in the simple round. Hemingway's earliest surviving Paris works reveal an incorporation of, but movement beyond, the strict limitations of the round (or its prose cognate, Stein's continuous present). In "Chapter 1" Hemingway experimented with a relatively freer (and thus more challenging) pattern than that posed by the round, a pattern that bears strong resemblance to the musical canon.

Although, as I will argue in a moment, "Chapter 1" evinces some of the constitutive elements of a musical round (i.e., emphasis on repetition to form at least a thrice-repeated pattern), it also displays two elements that render it more akin to a prose canon: the incorporation of free (but complementary) material within the repeating melodic structure, and a break in the final iteration of the pattern, which brings the piece to a close. This last, the pattern break, constitutes the primary distinction between rounds and other canons; these other canons end in a way that makes harmonic, rather than merely melodic, sense.

In "Chapter 1," Hemingway constructs a pattern consisting of three elements, repeated three times each, in order. By creating with this pattern a continuous past, he capitalizes on reader memory to make readers "sense more than they know." The three elements of the pattern, the continuous conditions of being (a) "drunk," (b) "along the road," and (c) "in the dark," are the constants of the piece; they are introduced and repeated during reading as portrayed in the following schematic (pattern iteration numbered, in brackets; pattern elements lettered, in parentheses):

[1] Everybody was (a) drunk. The whole battery was drunk (b) going along the road (c) in the dark. We were going to Champagne.
[2] The lieutenant kept riding his horse out into the fields and saying to him, "I'm (a) drunk, I tell you, mon vieux. Oh, I am so

soused." (b) We went along the road (c) all night, in the dark and the adjutant kept riding up alongside my kitchen and saying "You must put it out. It is dangerous. It will be observed."

[3] We were fifty kilometers from the front, but (a) the adjutant [because he is drunk] worried about the fire in my kitchen. It was funny (b) going along that road.

That was when I was a kitchen corporal. (*In Our Time* 13)

The three elements, "drunk," "along the road," and "in the dark," constitute the prose melody that repeat aurally, à la Stein; they also continuously inform the piece after they all but disappear from overt statement. All three are conditions that persist throughout, and as such do not seem to need repeating (especially in so short a piece), yet Hemingway does so in order to establish the pattern (a, b, c) that he will then break. The third statement of the pattern does not resolve; element 1, "darkness," is left out. The "drunk-road-dark" pattern lingers, however subliminally, to create a sense of absence—something is missing. The absence of pattern resolution endows the final line, "That was when I was a kitchen corporal" with the potential to stand for more than it says (indeed, the reader already knows that the speaker is a soldier and a cook). If considered even as a possible resolution to the contrapuntal pattern (i.e., as a substitute for element [c], "in the dark"), the line may metaphorically represent the narrator's entire time as kitchen corporal, and perhaps the entire war, as interminably blundering along in the darkness, led by fools. This interpretation is merely a possibility; its existence implies that there may be others—but the incompleteness of the pattern requires consideration and evaluation, providing an echo against which the final line must be read. The need to resolve the pattern, and the simultaneity of distinct thoughts ("darkness"/"kitchen corporal") required to resolve it, raises mere repetition to the prose counterpoint of the canon form.

The story "Cat in the Rain" (1925) represents an increase in the complexity and subtlety of Hemingway's contrapuntal prose. Like "Chapter 1," it suggests a canon. It is sophisticated in that it uses a ground. The first statement of the canon melody (the "leader") is often accompanied by a very simple harmonic bass line that supports but does not necessarily participate in canonic repetition in the upper voices (comprised of the leader and its "follower[s]"). This bass line may, however, repeat of its own accord; when it does, it is called a "ground" or a "ground bass." Ground bass is a bass line repeating its own motif.

The prose equivalent of the ground (or ground bass, the lowest line) plays throughout "Cat in the Rain," and, like "drunk/road/dark" in "Chapter 1," establishes a continuing pattern against which action will occur. In the opening paragraph, Hemingway repeats the words "rain" or "raining" as insistently as he does "drunk" (and its synonyms) in "Chapter 1":

> It [the war monument] was made of bronze and glistened in the rain. It was raining. The rain dripped from the palm trees. Water stood in pools on the gravel paths. The sea broke in a long line in the rain and slipped back down the beach to come up and break again in a long line in the rain. (167)

The rain and its dominant variant, the sea, become the harmonically constitutive elements, the "ground bass" line, against which the endlessness of the wife's boredom and the husband's reading (and their ensuing lack of communication) provide the counterpoint. Once the rain and the surf are set in motion, only a few reminders are necessary to keep it "raining" in the reader's consciousness (the umbrella, the dripping tables); the surf, which the reader is likely to forget, disappears altogether but certainly does not stop. Its influence, if not forgotten, informs the reader's role in the story.

By using the ground pattern of rain and surf, Hemingway underscores and gives a harmonic resonance to a dull, boring, monotonous afternoon and to one episode, at least, in a marriage, whose emotional tone complements the dripping weather, and the future of which may be found in the unremitting "coming up" and "breaking" of the sea. The canonic melody plays out as follows.

The wife is bored and endlessly "wanting"; she is the canonic "leader" in the marriage counterpoint, being the one to initiate both dialogue and physical movement. Her husband George is the melodic "follower," in that he only speaks when spoken to (and, initially, only in an echo of his wife, when he offers to get the cat). He is always reading but seems unable to "read" his wife. It is imperative to the affective achievement of this story that the surf not "pound" or do anything otherwise exciting. In its monotony, it is akin to whatever is really bothering the wife: the rain,

George, desire for a cat, a home, a baby, the *padrone,* anything but what she has.[12] The wife's boredom, like the sea, will "come up" and "break," repeatedly, without getting anywhere. The pattern of the surf is unceasing and will end only when the story ends. Against this background, the pattern of the leader/follower canonic melodies *will* have to break before it can end—which it does, first when George momentarily assumes the "leader" role (when he tells her to "shut up and get something to read" [170]), and finally, when the maid enters with the cat. The "cat in the rain" structures the story; when the cat is no longer in the rain, the story is over. But the story ends, like "Chapter 1," with some work for the curious reader. It demands a re-reading to address certain questions: Whose story is it? What will break? The pattern of the marriage, or the marriage itself? The questions belie definitive answers, but their asking is required.

Although the overall structure of "Cat in the Rain" bears strong similarities to a canon played against a ground, the "sea breaking" sentence constitutes, microcosmically, a fugue (a form that I will explain in more depth momentarily). The fugue is similar to the canon in all aspects save one. In a fugue, the melody (here called the "subject," similar to the "leader") enters unaccompanied, and plays out completely before it is echoed by another voice (called the "answer"), as exactly as possible, but in a different key.[13] Again, the music/prose translation is not intuitively obvious; how does one change keys in prose?

In the subject/answer pattern of a fugue, the subject moves from the primary key (the "tonic") toward a related key (the "dominant"), then, in the answer, the movement is reversed (from dominant back toward tonic). Consider the verbal moods, which change halfway through the sentence: "The sea broke in a long line in the rain and slipped back down the beach to come up and break again in a long line in the rain" (167). The verbal mood "changes keys," in a shift from the indicative ("broke," "slipped") to the infinitive ("to come up and break again"). Additionally, and perhaps more importantly, the action of the sentence moves from breaking to breaking (tonic to tonic), and the question of breaking is the underlying question that resonates throughout the story—in other words, provides the story's "key" or mood.

In a fugue, the subject melody does not return to the tonic key of the piece; rather, it leads away from it. As a result, the fugue form takes on a narrative quality, one that is reflected in the technical terms used to identify the statements of the main melody. The "subject" expresses but does not resolve a musical idea; the "answer" both echoes and harmonically develops the subject. Later statements of the melody tend to echo this subject/answer pattern; melodic variation and elaboration heightens complexity and can provide tremendous harmonic variety. Because of a fugue's melodic and harmonic patterns and structure, hearing one is like listening to a dialogue of which one can only catch the intonations, not the words. Despite its relative harmonic complexity when compared to canons or rounds, the fugue subject sticks in the listener's memory as easily as does the melody of "Three Blind Mice." Whenever the melody reoccurs (as subject or answer), aural recognition is automatic; it is a fixed aural node in the progression of the music. The mind recognizes it as an echo despite the simultaneous presence of other, equally complex, melodic lines. This aural recognition is automatic even when the subject occurs in one of the middle voices, which are the most difficult for the ear to isolate in a piece of any complexity (to illustrate this principle, try to pick out the altos in a chorus or the violas in an orchestra).

Since Hemingway proposed the opening section of *A Farewell to Arms* as exemplary of the similarities between his writing and Bach's counterpoint, I will end with a consideration of that section, gesturing toward the rest of the novel only briefly. Hemingway stated that the word "and" in this opening section functions like a note in counterpoint. Consider the opening paragraph:

> In the late summer of that year we lived in a house in a village that looked across the river and the plain to the mountains. In the bed of the river there were pebbles and boulders, dry and white in the sun, and the water was clear and swiftly moving and blue in the channels. Troops went by the house and down the road and the dust they raised powdered the leaves of the trees. The trunks of the trees too were dusty and the leaves fell early that year and we saw the troops marching along the road and the dust rising and leaves, stirred by the breeze, falling and the soldiers marching and afterward the road bare and white except for the leaves. (3)

Although the word "and" does appear rather more times per sentence than one might expect, how it functions as a contrapuntal note is not immediately evident. The rhythms of this section, however, suggest that there may be something musical about it. Scanning the first two sentences reveals a recurring 7-beat metrical pattern [^^/^^/^] in the phrases

"in a house in a village"
"and the plain to the mountains"
"and the water was clear and,"
and in the last 7 beats of "swiftly moving and blue in the channels."[14]

The use of "and" in this opening section seems rhythmically subordinate to—but grammatically necessitated by—the sequence of prepositional phrases on which the rhythm of the opening section depends. There is enough of an aural pattern in this section to seduce the reader's "ear" and to suggest musicality (indeed, the entire paragraph can be read in a fast 3/8 [waltz time] or slow 4/4 [march time] without sounding forced)—yet the counterpoint of this opening section results from the interplay of these rhythms with the visual patterning he achieves with repeated references to leaves, troops, dust and road.

The changing relative vertical positions of these four elements evokes a progression of three "still" images (a fourth is implied) in which these elements interact and interweave like lines in music. The progression plays out as follows:

TIME	Before march [implied]	During march (1)	During march (2)	"Afterwards"
TOP	leaves (on trees)	leaves (dusty)		
MIDDLE		troops (marching) dust (rising)	dust (rising) leaves (falling) troops (marching)	leaves (fallen)
BOTTOM	road	road (turning to dust)	road (turning to dust)	road (=dust)

The visual counterpoint here is based on relative positioning—effected grammatically (by a strong reliance on prepositions) and visually. Foreground and background shift and exchange; resolution is fragmentary, momentary, and relative.

The marching troops disappear, for a time, after which Hemingway introduces the rain as the catalyst whereby the road (now a mixture of dust and leaves) may reverse the action of covering and coloring the troops (as the dust they raised once covered and colored the then-fertile trees):

> and all the country wet and brown and dead with the autumn. There were mists over the river and clouds on the mountain and the trucks splashed mud on the road and the troops were muddy and wet in their capes; their rifles were wet and under their capes the two leather cartridge-boxes on the front of the belts, gray leather boxes heavy with the packs of clips of thin, long 6.5 mm. cartridges, bulged forward under the capes so that the men, passing on the road, marched as though they were six months gone with child. (4)

In this passage, the word "and" tolls like a note in a dirge and then disappears as the focus moves under the capes of the troops to the death that bulges there. Hemingway herein sets forth a patterned, relative progression of transformation toward decay; the troops return to the road "as though" pregnant with death; this decay takes as its musical "motif" the combination of road and water, which reappear throughout the novel. The counterpoint and poetry of this opening section cement its images as a mnemonic node, the "subject" to which other roads in the novel will "answer" (in related, but progressively lower, keys).

This opening chapter establishes the "key," or central problem, of the novel as one of orientation and relative location: long chains of prepositional phrases that seem so precisely to *locate* do not; they merely *orient*. Throughout the novel, problems of relative location and orientation underscore moments of extreme tension and structure the narrative. During the long retreat, for example, physical orientation is useless; Frederic moves "away" from the front, but the front is also moving. His disorientation reaches its extreme as he dives into the river, having no way of knowing which direction is "away" from the front and which is "toward" Catherine. As Frederic and Catherine cross the lake to Switzerland, they achieve only partial orientation; they navigate by a mountain, which they can barely see in the darkness. Finally, their attempt to mutually constitute some magnetic North by which each may guide the other ultimately fails in the Swiss hospital where Catherine dies. The novel closes with a gesture toward its beginning, with Frederic walking away, back to the hotel, in the rain, toward nothing in particular.

Although *Farewell* reveals only momentary reliance on the contrapuntal style and forms that seem to structure Hemingway's earlier work, such moments and their echoes are crucial. The doubling of relative direction ("away" and "toward"), without the possibility of any fixed reference point, structures the novel as an interwoven duality suggestive of—but not limited to—the interplay of individual lines of counterpoint sounding simultaneously. In the larger thematic concerns of the novel, love and war, the statement of the subject (war) always occurs starkly against the statement of its countersubject (love)—like Frederic and Catherine, the two cannot exist in this novel without each other, and their melodies play out over roads of water and dust, of life and death.

Other recognizable musical patterns appear in several early Hemingway works. "Out of Season" echoes the classical sonata form. "Cross Country Snow" suggests a toccata, "Canary for One," a pavane, and "Hills Like White Elephants," a theme and variation.[15] After his earliest experimentation with the possibilities of musical prose (in the *in our time* chapters), Hemingway seemed to reserve this kind of musical patterning exclusively for the so-called marriage tales (in which *A Farewell to Arms* may reasonably be included). The deployment of these patterns in works concerned with heterosexual relationships supports the biographical link for Hemingway between music and the feminine. By employing an aesthetic that, since early childhood, he had identified with individual women, Hemingway added a dimension of complexity to these already tense works. Gendered communication may break down in these stories, but narrative communication does not. Hemingway's reliance on the reader's willingness to locate, remember, and investigate patterns as they fluctuate under his control results in a narrative voice that is half flirtation, half seduction, and all ego, and does not differentiate its audience by gender.

In 1953, Hemingway wrote in a letter to Bernard Berenson that, during a "curious juxtaposition of Venus, Jupiter, Mars and Mercury," he had been playing Bach records to a mockingbird.

> I have never seen Venus so wonderful in my life and no one will again for a long time. . . . there are ten pairs of mocking birds nested here on the place. I play Bach on the phonograph to one and he learns it very well. We have a pure black lizard at the pool and I have learned to whistle to him soundlessly so that he comes to me any time I call him. I do not know what the magic is in the calling. (*SL* 812)

There was something about Bach and counterpoint and music that held for Hemingway the potential to transcend boundaries, even species boundaries, to be a force akin to the force of the feminine, a force of nature. Any musician or music-lover would agree that there is "magic . . . in the calling." Even, or perhaps especially, Grace Hemingway, whose musical talent and music instruction are both manifest in Hemingway's early style.

Hemingway's brutal and public rejection of all of his once-acknowledged mentors—Sherwood Anderson, Gertrude Stein, and F. Scott Fitzgerald, to name but a few—resolves into a portrait of an author who refused to admit obligation or indebtedness.[16] It is small wonder, then, that Grace Hemingway, who was his earliest artistic instructor and one whose influence he could no more escape than the shape of his ears or the line of his chin, should receive her proportionate share of his ingratitude.

Grace Hall Hemingway, however, cannot be so easily dismissed as her son may have wished. As early as 1928, she began to draw comparisons between painters and composers based on the ends to which they deployed formal principles. In a series of college lectures given toward the end of her life, this singer who became a composer, a painter, and a lecturer engaged in cross-media experimentation of her own, interpreting the "design of pictures" at the piano (Sellroe 2). Although she purported to be "too much a mid-Victorian" to appreciate the then modern art (Downing np), including by extrapolation, the work of her own son, she was staunch in her belief that, in art, form and not content determined greatness.

Her emphasis on form over content renders her a curiously liminal (and conflicted) critic, poised uncomfortably between Victorian sensibility and Modernist intellectual rigor. Although her notes for the October 1928 lecture begin with the derisive statement, "Modernists hold That a picture, to be a great work of art, need not contain any recognizable objects," by the end of the first page, she has argued for that very position, highlighting the similarities between Old Master and Modernist deployment of formal elements to achieve an effect rather than dwelling on the obvious superficial differences between the two periods. The next page begins with something of a manifesto that reads more like an argument with herself than notes for a lecture: "There would be no music if there were no hearers There would be no art if there were no appreciative eyes" Although she seems determined to insist on "taste" as the sine qua non of Art, in the next line she declares the opposite, that "Beauty is anything that is strong of its kind."

This conflict between socially determined taste and innate strength played out in her relationship with her writer son. Despite her objections to the subject matter of his stories (which she found so offensive that she returned her copy of *in our time*), Ernest Hemingway persisted in pointing out which stories he thought she might most appreciate. Were he being truly vindictive, as one might expect given his later reference to her as "a castrating bitch," he might have suggested "A Soldier's Home" (in which he locates a silent domestic tragedy in the chasm between a mother's "provincial" values and her son's experience in World War I). He did not. Rather, he commended to her attention those stories in which he approaches musical formal perfection—foremost among them, "Cat in the Rain" (qtd. in Reynolds, *Paris Years* 278). And one might hope, indeed, Ernest Hemingway probably did, that Grace Hemingway would have seen past the "modern" subject matter to perceive and appreciate her son's formal achievements. But she did not. However, philosophically, these two Hemingways were much closer in their opinions about art than either could probably admit.

In her lecture notes, Grace Hemingway implied that "strength of kind" derives from the quality of design—in visual art, "perfectly posed form in three dimensions," or composition, the search for which "has been the impelling dictate of all great art" (1). She continues:

Giotto, El Greco, Rubens—the greatest of all the old painters strove continually to attain form, as an abstract emotional force. The picture was composed as to line, organized as to masses and spaces. Out of this grew the subject matter (quite accidentally.) The human figure and the recognizable natural object were only auxiliaries, never the sought for result. If in the works of truly significant art, there is a dramatic, narrative or illustrative interest, it will be found to be the incidental, and *not* the important adjunct of the picture. (1)

This is just as her son believed. The impact of his writing lay in his ability to show "both sides—3 dimensions and if possible 4" (*SL* 153), to "do country so that you don't remember the words after you read it but actually have the Country" (123), to displace emotion and content onto details (often onto "the particulars of place") that reveal more than they merely describe (Kennedy 109, 111).

In other words, according to both Hemingways, art depends on form, form dictates effect, and thus the great works of art "make people feel something more than they [understand]" (*MF* 75). Grace Hemingway's criteria for greatness in art nearly matched her son's who, like Nick Adams, "wanted to write like Cézanne painted" ("On Writing" 218). It is unfortunate that her mid-Victorian penchant for "appropriate" subject matter blinded her to the extent to which she and her son were striving toward the same artistic ends, in similar ways.[17] Reading her words, one suspects that she was aware of this conflict and was troubled by the limitations of her sensibilities, the very sensibilities that barred her from appreciating the artistic revolution in which her son participated, but in which he is now thought to be the least radical of figures.

Ernest Hemingway is so-considered, partly because his work, however "shocking" its subject matter, seems so simple. But simple is not simplistic; stylistically, his engagement with the possibilities of cross-media patterning earns him a place among the most experimental, not the least, of the Moderns. While Eliot was blowing the dust off of Grecian urns, Ernest Hemingway was achieving in prose the same (equally dusty) contrapuntal forms heard in every Protestant church in every bourgeois suburb every Sunday—the Bach chorales that have long provided the mainstay of most Protestant hymns. In the 1920s, stolid Protestant Victorian dust of the kind found clinging to apron strings (or, in this case, cello strings) was not, perhaps, as sexy as Grecian dust, but Hemingway's artistic move was concomitant with who he was. The writer who wrote in 1945 that "The laws of prose writing are as immutable as those of flight, of mathematics, of physics" (*SL* 594) was, ineradicably, the son and the legacy of the woman who, in 1928, wrote that "Art is a manifestation of Imagination, Intuition & Inspiration, but controlled by laws of design." On this last point, had they been willing to admit it, mother and son agreed.

A Lifetime of Flower Narratives

Letting the Silenced Voice Speak

Miriam B. Mandel

"'I remember everything we ever did and everything we ever said on the whole trip,' Hadley said. 'I do really.'"

Ernest Hemingway, *A Moveable Feast*

Like most writers, Ernest Hemingway used the same material in more than one place.[1] As Rose Marie Burwell has argued, "reiterated thematic links" recur frequently in the prose Hemingway wrote in the last years of his life, even though the settings of the five books that those years produced range from France to Spain to the Caribbean to Kenya, and the represented events reflect a time span of thirty years. In spite of disparate settings, events, and even genres, these books must be considered together, she claims, because they were written within the same time span. Burwell notes that an image or psychological issue that occupied Hemingway's mind at a certain period was likely to recur in whatever he was writing at that time, be it fiction, nonfiction, or a letter to a friend.[2] Clearly, when a problem or image captured Hemingway, he explored it in a variety of venues.

Such repetition certainly encourages us to link synchronous works. But repetition also joins works written at very different periods of time. We have, for example, the story of Agnes von Kurowsky, told in "A Very Short Story" and partially retold several years later in *A Farewell to Arms;* and the story of the fisherman who lost his large fish, which first showed up in the April 1936 "Gulf Stream Letter" and resurfaced in 1952 as *The Old Man and the Sea.*[3] Readers interested in Hemingway's creative and psychological development are inevitably drawn to a comparative reading of these repetitions.

I would like to trace Hemingway's use of a minor event, which oc-

curred when he was in his early twenties. The event is Ernest and
Hadley's only springtime visit to Chamby-sur-Montreux, near Aigle, in
the Swiss province of Vaud, from 7 to 14 May 1922. Ernest and Hadley
had been married about six months, but the honeymooners were really a
threesome because Hemingway had invited his war-time buddy, Eric
Dorman-Smith (Chink), to come along.

Chink had gone straight from the military academy at Sandhurst to
the battlefields of 1914. By the time Ernest met him in 1918, Chink had
been wounded several times and been mentioned in three dispatches. Recovering from his own wound, Ernest was impressed by the young man,
only four years older than himself, who wore a Military Cross with a star
and carried the rank of Major. The two became fast friends, with a shared
interest in war, military history, and literature. Ernest introduced Chink
to Agnes von Kurowsky, the American nurse he was hoping to marry. A
few years later, the two men met again at Chamby and decided to cap
their two-week vacation with a mountain trek over militarily important ground (Chink loved such walks), and to visit again the Milanese
cafes where they had last sipped cappuccino with Agnes. They wanted to
renew their friendship, to drink and talk as they had in 1918. Again,
Ernest would introduce Chink to the new woman in his life.

Like most of the events of Hemingway's early life, this springtime visit
to Chamby and Aigle was transformed into literature. Over the next
thirty-five years, the flowers of that setting and the activities of that
May—the fishing, drinking, talking, and mountain trekking—surfaced in
at least four different pieces of writing, in which the three principals (or
four, if we count the memory of Agnes) are variously configured. The
narratives are linked by clusters of flowers—an unusual motif for Hemingway, who is more likely to use animal than plant imagery. But in these
narratives, he employs the narcissus, the blooms of the horse chestnut
tree, and a flowering wisteria vine. All three plants produce showy clusters of flowers, and all produce white flowers. Most interestingly, these
romantic flowers do not appear in any of his short stories, not in those
that are synchronous with these narratives, nor in those that deal with the
same subjects: fishing, drinking, love, and marriage. The flower narratives
are thus more closely related to each other than they are to any other
narrative. And although they are most fully developed in pieces we label
as journalism or nonfiction, they are so artfully imaged and so variously

framed that they confirm what we have long suspected: that Hemingway blurred the boundaries between fiction and nonfiction as much as he blurred those between life and art.

Flowers are, of course, traditional markers for the feminine, and white flowers in particular connect to feminine virtue and innocence and are traditionally carried by brides. But Hemingway's treatment of these flowers, like so much of his work, breaks the rules: he connects the flowers to men as well as to women and uses them to examine same-sex as well as heterosexual relationships. The narcissus is closely connected to the Ernest-Chink relationship: two tipsy show-offs talking about literature. It is the simplest, most obvious use of flower imagery, and it appears only once. Attached to the feminine sphere, the flowers gain in complexity. The original happy connotations (innocence, virtue, and young marriage) are undercut with unease, denial, and guilt-ridden subversion. The wisteria vine, a climbing shrub that requires support and rises by twining itself around a stronger structure, is associated with love; so is the white-flowering horse chestnut whose perfume enters the lovers' bedroom. The horse chestnut is also connected to luck—"For luck you carried a horse chestnut and a rabbit's foot in your right pocket" (*MF* 91)—a necessary element not only for good writing, but also for good marriage. Because he has betrayed love, the narrator sometimes suppresses or forgets details related to these flowers.

The Ernest-Hadley marriage has the reputation of being the happiest of Hemingway's four marital ventures. Hadley's first biographer insists that "for Hadley . . . the years with Ernest never lost their aura of enchantment. Many, many years later she would recall Ernest and all they did together and would become gay and animated at the recollection. And often she would say, "he gave me the key to the world" (qtd. in Sokoloff 102). Another biographer identifies Hadley as "a bright reflection of everything fine and noble in himself" (Diliberto 282). What the flower narratives reveal, however, is that Ernest and Hadley's marriage was in desperate trouble as early as May 1922.

In all the flower narratives, Hadley is excluded and marginalized, her voice silenced by the guilt-ridden narrator. The four passages are like the layers of a palimpsest, in which we can see the artist's distortions, erasures, and false starts. But we can also mark the repetitions that clarify the constants and make visible the basic pattern of abandonment, denial, betrayal, guilt, and an attempt at self-justification. The discomfort, which had only been sensed vaguely in May 1922, became clearer as Hemingway's life unfolded and as, at widely spaced intervals, he returned to the earliest of the occasions when he had felt it. These repeated narrations of exclusion and silence, which obviously focus on absence, necessarily make us aware of presence and thus raise an interesting question: if we are made aware of the voice that has been silenced, are we not in fact invited to hear it?

The First Flower Narrative: "Fishing the Rhone Canal," *The Toronto Daily Star* (10 June 1922)

Hemingway's first version of the fishing and hiking vacation was a feature story published in the *Star* about three weeks after the actual events. Curiously, Hemingway chose to excise both Chink and Hadley from this account of a pleasurable day spent fishing for trout in the Rhone canal. In other travel articles for the *Star,* at least those not in second person, he either identifies his companions or indicates that he has companions. Here, however, the young journalist is emphatically alone as he fishes, then escapes the heat of the day by reading under a pine tree, eating cherries from a paper bag, and admiring the countryside. At sundown, he moves down stream, fishing, until evening when he walks in to Aigle. As he walks, he thinks about "Napoleon's Grand Army, marching along" the same road, and he speculates that "Napoleon's batman" or "some Helvetian in the road gang probably used to sneak away" to fish for trout in the canal. He follows the road to a cafe across from the station:

> There are horse chestnut trees along the road with their flowers that look like wax candles . . . and very soon I was in Aigle [where] . . . there is a cafe that has . . . a great wisteria vine as thick through as a young tree that branches out and shades the porch with hanging bunches of purple flowers that bees go in and out of all day long and that glistens after a rain. . . . the beer comes foaming out in great glass mugs . . . and the barmaid smiles and asks about your luck. (*BL* 35).

Four details recall Chink's contribution to the May 1922 vacation: the St. Bernard Pass, which he suggested they cross; its military history, which he recounted to Ernest and Hadley; the Melvillean simile about the wax candles, which he discussed with Ernest; and the good beer that they consumed.[4] But in this insistently first-person singular narrative, there are no fellow drinkers: Chink and Hadley are absent. The bees' activity and the wisteria's thick trunk and heavy, wet branches offer strong sexual connotations, further underscoring Hadley's absence. The pleasures are those of a man who relishes unencumbered freedom—the warm weather, the refreshing breeze, the satisfying fishing, the beautiful scenery, the dark beer, the flirtatious barmaid. Not only does Hemingway deny Chink and Hadley by not mentioning them, he justifies this glorification of solitary pleasure by subtly suggesting that it is universally held, that the "very good place" of Aigle is so desirable that all its visitors, himself included, wish they could stay there forever: "Trains are always at least two hours apart in Aigle, and those waiting in the station buffet, this cafe with the golden horse and the wisteria hung porch is a station buffet, mind you, wish they would never come" (35).

But the narrative is complicated by an unspoken yet clearly present system of values. The narrator, like Napoleon's batman and the Roman roadman, has sneaked away from responsibilities and commitments. In his native Oak Park, such behavior would be considered antisocial, irresponsible, self-indulgent and childish, and his awareness of this makes the narrator uneasy. This discomfort is suggested by his awkward expansion of the single self into "those waiting in the station buffet," clearly an attempt to validate his behavior by vaguely positing other unidentified, similarly inclined individuals. And his frequent use of the second person ("you fish up-stream with the breeze at your back") makes the reader complicit in and therefore approving of his guilty solitary pleasures. The first flower narrative is, implicitly, a self-justifying narrative. To rid himself of the complications and compromises of commitment, the young journalist excises Hadley, attempting, in silencing her voice, to quell the voice of his own conscience.

The Second Flower Narrative: *Green Hills of Africa*
(composed 1934)

Written about a dozen years later, the second version of the Chamby vacation focuses on the friendship between the narrator and Chink. This flower narrative is a flashback embedded in *Green Hills of Africa,* the work that Hemingway shaped from his experiences in Africa in 1933–34. The passage is framed by a story that further indicates that the flowers and activities of that vacation elicit in the narrator a sense of uneasy guilt. In the frame story, the Hemingway character is a successful writer on safari in Africa. Competitive by nature, he is irritated at having been out shot by his friend Karl: "I don't want that guy to beat me," he complains to Pop (*GHOA* 153). He looks at a sable hunt as his last chance to pull ahead but is hindered in his quest by a tracker whom the narrator calls Garrick because of his overwrought manner and dramatic gesticulations. Quick with advice yet singularly inept, Garrick makes the narrator nervous by urging him to shoot at what the tracker assures him are sable bulls. The narrator shoots badly but finally hits a target with his third shot, only to discover that he has shot a cow. As the episode ends, he is nervous, angry, and distressed: he blames Garrick for his woeful error, loses his temper, hits Garrick, and calls for a bottle of beer, the dregs of which he shares with M'Cola. The beer, an important element in the first flower narrative as well, triggers the memory of the events of May 1922:

> I was thinking about beer and in my mind was back to that year in the spring when we walked on the mountain road to the Bains de Alliez and the beer-drinking contest where we failed to win the calf and came home that night around the mountain with the moonlight in the fields of narcissus . . . and how we were drunk and talked about how you would describe that light on that paleness, and the brown beer sitting at the wood tables under the wisteria vine at Aigle when we came in across the Rhone Valley from fishing the Stockalper with the horse chestnut trees in bloom and Chink and I again discussing writing and whether you could call them waxen candelabras [*sic*]. God, what bloody literary discussions we had; we were literary as hell then. (*GHOA* 279–80)

The connection between literary talk and beer is cemented by a literary quote from Robert Graves: "Flags for the Fusilier, / Crags for the Mountaineer, / For English poets beer, / Strong beer for me." As the narrator returns to the present, he remarks upon his beer-based bond with M'Cola: "beer was still a bloody marvel. The old man [M'Cola] knew it too. I had seen it in his eye . . . 'Beer,' said M'Cola" (280), proffering an open bottle. The flashback has alleviated the narrator's guilt for shooting the cow, which is illegal, and hitting the servant, which is despicable. Once again, the narrator has found himself at odds with the value system within which he functions, and once again, he has attempted to assuage his guilt and discomfort through a flower narrative. This version emphasizes Dorman-Smith, whom he connects with beer and with literary discussion about the landscape ("Now if he were there we could discuss how to describe this deer park country" [281]). The flowers, "the fields of narcissus" through which Chink and Ernest had strolled together a dozen years ago, are a proper correlative for narcissistic male bonding. Remembering the bibulous amity of the past, the narrator of *Green Hills of Africa* soon expands the Chink-Ernest fellowship to include Pop: "Pop and Chink were much alike. Pop was . . . the same sort of company" (281). Temporal and geographic boundaries are dissolved to join three mutually approving white men of different ages, professions, and nationalities. And beer is a strong enough bonding agent to permit a black man, M'Cola, entry into the group: when M'Cola offers the narrator a second bottle of beer, he is allowed to drink the "good two fingers of beer . . . left in the bottom of the bottle" (287).

Hadley, however, is excluded from this second flower narrative. The narcissus, the wisteria vine, the horse chestnuts in bloom, the hiking, the fishing, the drinking, and, indeed, the whole Aigle experience of May 1922 are recalled only in terms of "Chink and I."[5] The presence of Chink makes Hadley's absence even more striking. Yet, while she has been repressed in the flower narrative, Hemingway's concomitant guilt finds expression in the frame story, which posits a narrator at odds with the dominant set of values. His anxiety at having acted in a manner inconsistent with his self-picture is reflected in an internal debate: "Why did I miss on that cow? Hell, everybody is off sometime. You've got no bloody business to be off. Who the hell are you? My conscience?" (281). He attempts to justify his actions, forms an alternative social group of mutually approving men, and yearns for a different life, for a simpler world, free of marital complications and guilty consciences.

The careful framing, the increased reliance on memory, the enlarged cast of characters, and the focus on literary concerns all mark this as a more intense effort. In this second narrative, Hemingway has again attached to the flowers and activities of that spring vacation, the same discomfort that accompanied them in the first narrative: they have become objective correlatives for guilt, unease, and betrayal.

The Third Flower Narrative: *African Journal*
(composed 1954–56)

Hemingway's third flower narrative is a dream sequence written about twenty years after *Green Hills of Africa*.[6] It appears in the third part of the posthumously published *African Journal,* when the narrator is alone in the hunting camp while his wife, Mary, undergoes medical treatment in Nairobi. Like the *Green Hills of Africa* version, this passage in *African Journal* is a retrospective narrative. But this African flower narrative is even more distanced, separated from the original events by about thirty years. And where the second flower narrative (*GHOA*) was presented as a waking memory, the passage in *African Journal* is presented as a remembered dream. It, too, is carefully framed, but now the frame focuses on women. The focus is, once again, on an alternative value, this time, polygamy. And once again, the narrative posits a social system that supports the narrator in his unconventional desires: the norm in Africa permits him not only his two good wives (the absent Miss Mary and the African bride, Debba, who is sleeping elsewhere), but encourages him to expand upon his former and presumed wives. Another character, Ngui, has five wives, bringing the total to about twelve women for two men.

The dream itself is monogamous, about the narrator and "[t]he wife I had loved first and best." The wisteria vine and the horse chestnut blooms take center stage. The wisteria has been moved from the train station, where the barmaid flirts with the unattached narrator, to the inn where the narrator sleeps with his wife:

> I dreamed I was in an inn, or *Gasthaus* rather, in the canton of Vaud in Switzerland. The wife I had loved first and best and who was the mother of my oldest son was with me and we were sleeping close together to keep warm and because that was the best way to sleep if both people love each other and it is a cold night. There was a wistaria [*sic*] tree, or vine, that grew up on the face of the hotel and over an arbor and the horse-chestnut trees in bloom were like waxen candelabra. We were going to fish the Rhône canal and the

day before the dream we had fished the Stockalper. Both streams were milky with snow water and it was early spring. My first and best wife was sleeping soundly, as always, and I could smell every scent of her body and the chestnut trees as well and she was warm in my arms and her head was under my chin and we were sleeping as close and as trusting as kittens sleep. . . . tonight, in the dream, I slept happily with my true love in my arms and her head firmly under my chin. (*AJ* 52)[7]

In this sensuous, heterosexual version of the May 1922 visit to Chamby-sur-Montreux, the implied (historical) antecedents for the "we" are Ernest and Hadley, and it is "we" who are going fishing. Clearly all activities, whether nighttime lovemaking or daytime fishing, are shared by two newlyweds completely in tune with each other. The innocence and purity suggested by the white flowers are echoed in the "streams [which] were milky with snow" and in the image describing the lovers "sleeping as close and as trusting as kittens sleep" (*AJ* 52).[8]

In this poetic flower narrative, carefully framed to emphasize that this is a marriage story, the wisteria is described fully, and the Melvillean connection between horse chestnuts and waxen candelabra recurs unobtrusively, without the self-congratulatory fanfare that dominates the first, self-centered version or the exclusively masculine version presented in *Green Hills of Africa*. Indeed, there are no other men here; even Chink has been excised. Missing also are the drinking, the hiking, the self-conscious discussion about literature and, most significantly, the obvious image of the narcissus. In this 1950s version, the wisteria and the horse-chestnut blooms are closely associated with the sleeping figure, the beloved wife. The passage seems to focus strongly on Hadley, but I shall argue that here, too, she is silenced, distanced, and denied to the reader. First of all, she is nameless, identified only by her roles as wife and mother.[9] Second, she exists only in a dream, and thus becomes a figure of fantasy or imagination. And third, she is asleep in that dream, motionless and silent. Notice that the narrator, who dreams that they are both asleep, is able to smell and to feel warmth and cold: he claims to be sleeping, but his lively sensual perceptions suggest he is more awake than asleep, and by remembering the dream he further bridges the distance between sleep and wakefulness. His wife, however, is sleeping soundly, completely motionless, absent. While the first two flower narratives excluded Hadley simply by effacing her presence, this version denies her even more pointedly by making her a nameless, silenced, sleeping dream figure, a passive portrait of remembered perfection, a dream within a dream within a narrative.

Upon awakening, the narrator turns his thoughts to his present situation. His speculations concerning the boundaries of marital fidelity and the variations in moral standards reveal both his sense of guilt for having betrayed Hadley and his desire to escape from that guilt into a more comfortable alternative value system, one that will accommodate many and even concurrent wives: "I wondered about how many true loves to which you were faithful, until you were unfaithful a man could have and I thought about the strange strictures of morality in different countries and who it was that could make a sin a sin" (*AJ* 52). While Ngui, his gun bearer, has five wives, Papa—who because of his position would have been accorded at least twelve by tribal law—is limited by his culture to "one legal wife." Nevertheless, he intends to take Debba as his second wife.[10] Although Bwana Papa may have found a way to sanction his present behavior, he cannot obviate past wrongs, and, to silence his guilt, he must silence Hadley. Still, although she is denied in the passage and diminished in the frame, Hadley has at least entered the narrative.

The Fourth Flower Narrative: *A Moveable Feast* (composed 1957–61)

The fourth narrative which recalls the springtime trip to Chamby is the only one of the flower narratives to be dramatized and the only one to name all three of the principals. Hadley and Ernest are in the foreground, walking and talking. Among other things, they remember "the inn at Aigle," "the horse-chestnut trees . . . in bloom," and "a wisteria vine" (*MF* 54); they discuss Chink and mention several other people, such as Jim Gamble and Gertrude Stein. But a careful reading of the passage reveals that Hadley has once again been shunted aside.

In this narrative, written in the knowledge that three marriages had failed and that the fourth was disintegrating, the despairing author creates a first-person narrator who tries to believe that Ernest and Hadley are happy together. After a fine meal at Pruniers, they walk through the Tuileries, look through the Arc du Carrousel and then toward the Arc de Triomphe, and wonder if the two arches really are in line with the Sermione in Milan. This speculation leads them to recall the hike into Italy, which ended their Swiss vacation at Chamby, a hike that Chink called "across the St. Bernard in street shoes" (*MF* 53).

When, at Chink's suggestion, he, Ernest, and Hadley climbed the Dent du Jaman and traversed the St. Bernard Pass in deep snow, Hadley had worn a pair of flimsy shoes, "a rather neat pair of tan American Ox-fords" that were not designed for trekking in the snow. By the time they arrived in Aosta, she had turned into a "human blister" (qtd. in Baker, *Life* 92). Clearly, such a hike could not have been pleasant for her, but in *A Moveable Feast* her discomfort is silenced, and she is allowed only one remark, "My poor shoes," before the talk turns to the pleasure of the fruit cup in the fashionable Biffi. Going further back in time, Ernest recalls "the inn at Aigle" where the three of them had stayed before embarking upon the uncomfortable hike. The fishing expeditions mentioned in *African Journal* reappear, but in this fourth version, as in the first one, it is Ernest alone, and not "we," who enjoy the fishing.

The focus of the dialogue in *A Moveable Feast* is consistently on Ernest and *his* memories of *his* solitary pleasures; he dominates the reader's at-tention just as he controls the conversation, which clearly brings him more pleasure than it does her. He recalls "the inn at Aigle," where the three of them had stayed before embarking upon the uncomfortable hike and the two trout streams he fished while Hadley and Chink "sat in the garden . . . and read." He then introduces the next memory by recalling the "wisteria vine" and "the horse-chestnut trees . . . in bloom," which, according to *African Journal*, had perfumed their bedroom at night. Tell-ingly, in *A Moveable Feast* the flowers are connected to "a story" attributed to Jim Gamble (Hemingway's war-time friend); the vine is now the sub-ject of masculine conversation.[11] Hemingway has replaced their shared private experience with public, masculine story-telling, and the man he names is not only unknown to Hadley, he dates back to Ernest's army days and his romance with Agnes von Kurowsky. The trip down memory lane has gone beyond Ernest's shared past with Hadley, whom he met in 1920, to the past Ernest shared with Agnes and Jim Gamble in 1918.[12] Here Hadley is not only completely irrelevant to any narrative about the vine (the story is Gamble's, not Hemingway's), but she is also excluded from conversation about it: Ernest cannot tell her the story, because he has forgotten it. His talk of this absent flower narrative reminds her of other stories and discussions from which she was excluded. Suddenly, she assumes control of the conversation, and her tone is bitter:

> "Yes, Tatie, and *you and Chink always talking* about how to make things true, writing them, and put them rightly and not describe. *I remember everything.* Sometimes he was right and sometimes you were right. I remember the lights and textures and the shapes *you* argued about." (my emphasis, *MF* 54)

If Hadley remembers everything, then her memories are not pleasant. In 1922, married only a few months, she had been alone in Paris for most of April while her husband covered a conference in Genoa, and another long separation was looming (he was scheduled to go to Russia)—so the prospect of having to share her May vacation with her husband's wartime friend Chink could not have been a welcome one. Chink, who, like Jim Gamble, had known Hemingway before she had; who had known him when he was in love with Agnes; who had known Agnes herself, now proposed a nostalgic return to those places in Milan where he, Ernest, and Agnes had enjoyed themselves. Even if she eventually came to like Dorman-Smith as much as she insisted to her biographers, he was on several counts an unwelcome addition.[13]

If she remembers everything, she remembers silent days spent reading while Ernest fished, and evenings during which Ernest and Chink were "always talking" while she listened to their reminiscences and literary discussions. Furthermore, Chink's response to Hadley was as uneasy as hers to him. Chink recalls that every morning, Ernest would report the previous night's sexual events. His discomfort with these intimate reports, which "disturb[ed] my bachelorhood" and betrayed Hadley's privacy, as well as his obvious attachment to Ernest—"Hem seemed to make up for all the friends I'd lost in the World War"—suuggest that Hadley's presence was an uncomfortable new element in his relationship with Ernest (qtd. in Reynolds, *Paris Years* 50–51; and in Diliberto 117). Only Ernest, the object of all affection and attention, would have unreservedly enjoyed the threesome, especially since he was quite adept at denying and silencing any dissenting opinion. With his powerful prose, he was also able to convince the public at large that his version, even when too saccharine to be realistic, was accurate.

If Hadley remembers everything, she remembers their heated argument over whether or not she was to be allowed to take her toilet articles on the trans-Alpine trek, an argument that reduced her to tears. If she remembers everything, she remembers the cold, blistered feet on which she tried to keep up with Ernest and Chink on the difficult, snowy mountain climb. Her outburst elicits silence from her husband. He does not deny her version of the events or her claim that she remembers everything. Yet, while his silence confirms his wife's recollection that Ernest and Chink's conversation had excluded her, the length of that silence denies her the right to speak about her memory of the event. He maintains this punishing silence from the Arc du Carrousel to the bridge where they stand "looking down at the river." Clearly, while seeming to paint an idyllic portrait, the passage reveals the husband's neglect of his wife and his method of punishing her when she accuses him. Hadley knows that she can alleviate the attendant guilt and tension only by offering a conciliatory revision of her previous remarks:

> "We *all three* argued about everything and always *specific things* and we made fun of *each other.* I remember *everything we ever did* and *everything we ever said* on the whole trip," Hadley said. "I do really. About *everything.* When you and Chink talked I was included. It wasn't like being a wife at Miss Stein's." (my emphasis, *MF* 54)

The appeasing untruths, "We all three argued," rewrite the original script. Hadley is denied the right to remember and to speak about her experience and forced to suppress what she knows in order to validate the version he prefers. In this passage, Ernest's silence forces Hadley not only to accept her exclusion from Ernest's life, but also to suppress her knowledge (and her resentment) at being marginalized. If she wants to speak, she must speak *his* version of the events.[14] However, her remarks, which were written by the master dialogist himself, actually reveal further miseries. Her claim that "We all three argued about everything and *always specific things* and we made fun of *each other*" suggests remarks about the vanity of women who "refused to be parted from . . . toilet bottles" or who insisted on wearing flimsy shoes.[15] Her remark that "we made fun of each other" suggests taunts aimed in one direction, and her insistence that "It wasn't like being a wife at Miss Stein's" suggests that it may have been just as bad, if not worse. At least she could complain about the exclusion she endured at Miss Stein's.

Ernest's response is, once again, withdrawal—he moves back beyond their shared memory: "I wish I could remember the story about the wisteria vine." The oxymoronic play of speaking/silencing is perhaps most concentrated in this forgotten and therefore, it seems, untellable story about the wisteria vine. Hemingway posits a narrator who tries "to remember a story . . . about a wisteria vine," which "Jim Gamble, *I think,* had told me" (my emphasis, *MF* 54). We seem to have a three-fold betrayal: first he betrayed her by talking of the vine with another man, then by forgetting who really told the story of the vine, and finally by forgetting what was said. What our reading reveals is that in May 1922, at Chamby, Ernest repeatedly excluded and marginalized Hadley, that he needed to forget or deny that he had done so, that she was aware of the betrayal, and that she remembered the undistorted, unfictionalized original events quite well: "'I remember everything we ever did and everything we ever said on the whole trip,' Hadley said. 'I do really. About everything.'"

The chapter in *A Moveable Feast* that tells the story of this betrayal is aptly titled "A False Spring," and it ends just as aptly with talk of hunger—a hunger not to be appeased by food or by sex—and of memory. Hadley says, "There are so many sorts of hunger. In the spring there are more. But that's gone now. Memory is hunger" (56–57). What she remembers is her unsatisfied hunger, the hunger she felt in the first spring of her marriage, the hunger for the undivided commitment that her husband could not give her, because he had a greater commitment to himself, to solitary fishing and thinking, to the fellowship of other men, to the salving of his conscience through the telling of stories. Her hunger for his love and commitment slowly faded when she realized that he was incapable of satisfying it, and she says, with heart-rending simplicity, "But that's gone now," handwritten words that Hemingway added to a late typescript. But she remembers that hunger, which is why, for her, "Memory is hunger." The narrator does not understand. He "was being stupid . . . I knew I was hungry in a simple way," hungry for the steaks he sees in the restaurant (57).

In the chapter's final scene, so reminiscent of the dream sequence in *African Journal*, the narrator wakes, looks at his wise, sleeping wife, and tries again to understand: "I had to try to think it out and I was too stupid." But he knows that "nothing was simple . . . not even . . . right and wrong, nor the breathing of someone who lay beside you in the moonlight" (58).

A Moveable Feast, which seemed to idealize Hemingway's years with Hadley, was accepted as accurate biography for two decades. In 1983, however, Gerry Brenner perceptively argued that Hemingway's "exaggerated portrait of himself" as a virtuous, responsible artist and husband reveals that "he felt vulnerable" in these areas. Brenner asked, "What irresponsibility is he reluctant to own up to, and who did he feel he had to justify himself to when he wrote *Feast*? The obvious answer to both questions points to the first Mrs. Ernest Hemingway, Hadley, the betrayed wife" (*Concealments* 224). More recently, Burwell expands upon Brenner's thesis to include Hemingway's abandonment of his second wife as well. She writes that as he was writing *Feast* Hemingway "was experiencing remorse for what he had done to others. . . . In the summer of 1960, Hemingway was beginning to lose his notorious and protective ability to blame others for whatever went wrong in his own life" (*Postwar Years* 183). In writing *A Moveable Feast* he had been forced to acknowledge to himself that it was he who had destroyed his first two marriages, "the two personal relationships that had been most sustaining of him as a writer and most indicative of his integrity as a man" (183). Both these critics focus upon Hemingway's guilt about his adultery and abandonment of his wives. But the flower narratives reveal that Hemingway's awareness of his psychological mistreatment of Hadley began just a few months after their wedding.

If the behavior itself was unattractive, the continued concern with it was admirable. By not abandoning the painful flower narratives, Hemingway reveals what Mark Spilka calls "the writer's better self—whereby most writers can be said to relate better to their own fictions than to other people, and to aspire to and generally be more honest in their creative efforts than in their private lives" (*Lessons* 15). Hemingway returns repeatedly to the same uncomfortable episode, attempting to reconcile two mutually contradictory needs: to soothe his personal conscience through denial, and to soothe his artistic conscience by writing truthfully. As he came closer and closer to acknowledging Hadley's point of view, he became increasingly desperate until, in terminal despair, he refused to publish *A Moveable Feast*.[16] But by then his artistic integrity had produced such rich writing that even the voice he silenced in the first three narratives could finally be heard in the fourth. It speaks indirectly and sometimes it is forced to deny itself, but it is there, and we can hear it.

The flower narratives show us once again that Hemingway demands careful reading, especially when we think we already know the story or the characters. Although Hemingway uses the same material repeatedly, he does not repeat himself. The variations are instructive. We are first given the material as unvoiced or indirect discourse (*Toronto Star*); then as a flashback, which shatters the boundaries between itself and its frame (*Green Hills of Africa*); then as a dream sequence, which denies while it seems to affirm (*African Journal*); and finally as a dramatized dialogue, which allows Hadley to speak, then silences her, then reveals the method of silencing her, and finally enables us to resurrect her unspoken thoughts about a misattributed, forgotten, but oft-told story (*A Moveable Feast*).

In the various narratives, the denial of the one significant Other was masked by a variety of activities—fishing, flirting, literary talk with Chink, beer-drinking with hunting companions, and dreamy myth-making—but none assuaged the discomfort that permeates all the flower narratives. As the failed marriages piled up and as his defenses became weaker, Hemingway finally understood the unease that had, from the beginning, been attached to the flowers of the Chamby episode.

A Moveable Feast not only gives us the last flower narrative, it gives us its most sophisticated version, burying marital betrayal in a forgotten, unspoken and presumably unspeakable flower narrative attributed to someone else. But Hemingway permits Hadley to brush that irrelevancy away, to claim not just that she remembers "everything"—the fact that she was excluded and forced to deny her exclusion—but to insist that the red herring, the displaced, forgotten, misattributed "story about the wisteria vine," was not important. That particular evasion is not the issue, and she will not be sidetracked. She insists that "It was the vine that was important," the flowers themselves, the situation in which the flowers played a central role, both romantically (perfuming the bedroom at night) and intellectually (as subjects for discussion). Thus Hemingway empowers her to guide us to a more careful reading of all the flower narratives, to enable us to see not only that she had been silenced and excluded in the bedroom, but that she had been excluded and even betrayed in conversation—not allowed to speak her own experiences, memories, and feelings, while others spoke and wrote about them as they pleased. Very indirectly, Hemingway enables us to resurrect the voice he had so desperately needed to silence, the voice that leads us to understand the flower narratives as consistently and painfully self-incriminating.

16
Rivalry, Romance, and War Reporters

Martha Gellhorn's *Love Goes to Press*
and the *Collier's* Files

Sandra Whipple Spanier

In the spring of 1945 as the war in Europe was coming to an end, Martha Gellhorn and fellow war correspondent Virginia Cowles were in London, "feeling aimless like millions of others." "Though no one spoke of it, sorrow affected me; now there was time to think of the heart-sickening cost of war," Gellhorn recalled. "Nothing seemed worth the effort of doing it. Ginny, more energetic, dreamed up this brilliant idea. We would write a jokey play about war correspondents. After a successful run in London, the play would be bought by the movies, bringing us pots of money, of which neither of us had much. I said no, it's silly, we don't know how to write a play, not even how to begin. Ginny observed that I might as well try it, since I was clearly unemployed" (Introduction viii).

A madcap romantic comedy set in a press camp in Italy in 1944, Gellhorn and Cowles's *Love Goes to Press* was a hit on the London stage in the summer of 1946. The play features a pair of sexy, quick-witted women war correspondents who try to juggle their careers and their love lives and find it easier to deal with war than with men. Action on the Italian front picks up when one of our heroines unexpectedly encounters at the press camp her ex-husband, himself a famous writer, whom she had divorced—twice—on the grounds of plagiarism. Our other heroine falls in love with the Public Relations Officer, a proper Englishman whose angry objection to women at the front turns to fantasies of hunting, fishing, and tending dairy cows together on his country estate, assuming that once they are married she will give up the nonsense of writing.

The London run was so successful that play and cast were moved to New York. It opened on Broadway on New Year's Day 1947 and folded after four performances, earning, as Gellhorn's hometown paper, the St. Louis *Post-Dispatch,* put it, "the combined doubtful honor of being the first play and the first flop of the year." Gellhorn later wrote that for the English audiences, laughter was a vital escape. Those who had experienced war on their own soil and were living in the ruins felt free to laugh at "this comic unreal version of war." The American response ranged from yawns to moral indignation. One critic was downright offended, calling the play "a libel on the profession":

> If this is the way Martha Gellhorn and Virginia Cowles themselves behaved in the pursuit of their newspaper assignments, it would seem wise for the high command to banish all women journalists from the next war. Presumably the whole affair was supposed to be funny but since their writing lacks wit and their plotting any elements of conviction one is driven back to a criticism of the content of the play and the strange ethics as well as the incredible human callousness exhibited by the characters they portrayed. (Gilder 18)

As Martha Gellhorn later said, "There you are: some jokes, like some white wines, do not travel" (xi).

Like any newsroom comedy, the play is rife with rivalries. The opening scene is a conversation between correspondents Hank and Tex, who scoff at the "eyewitness stuff" of their "poor dumb ambitious colleagues wading around those roads near Mount Sorello" while they get their stories hot off the typewriter of a diligent dupe the minute he goes off to the bathroom (8). But however competitive they are among themselves, when the men hear they are about to be joined by "internationally known, glamourous war-correspondent" Jane Mason, we witness instant male bonding (10). The Public Relations Officer is incensed: "Dressed up in Molyneux uniforms. Cooing at all the men. They act as if the war was some sort of special coming-out party. Want to go to the front, and scream when they get there. Any decent woman would stay at home" (10) Newsman Joe Rogers remarks: "I'm allergic to newspaper women. I married one once. They never stop trying to scoop you, and when you scoop them they divorce you" (10). Imagine the surprise when a second newspaperwoman turns up: Annabelle Jones, Jane's old war buddy and Rogers's ex-wife. To add to the merriment, a third woman joins the crowd—a dizzy blonde English actress named Daphne, who is in Italy not only to entertain the troops but to marry Joe Rogers.

Annabelle's version of their marriage is rather different from her ex-husband's: "He married me to silence the opposition" (19). "What would you think if your husband's first conscious act after the honeymoon was to steal your stories?" she asks Jane. When Jane replies, "I'd steal his," Annabelle explains: "He never had any. He just waited around until I dug something up, and then he pinched it." Not only had he stolen a trip to the front in Russia that she had labored to arrange, he offered the "unforgivable" excuse that "he did it because he loved me so much he couldn't bear to have me in danger" (19).

The *New Yorker* reviewer commented that "Much of 'Love Goes to Press' was said to be autobiographical, and it is quite possible that Miss Gellhorn and Miss Cowles were indeed able to commandeer ambulances and even airplanes to take them behind the enemy lines practically at will. I can only say that it seemed a little silly to me, almost as if somebody had been tinkering around with an idea for a moving picture" (47). It would be a serious exaggeration to say that "Collier's girl correspondent," as Martha Gellhorn was sometimes billed, could commandeer airplanes at will (although she *did*, in fact, fly a number of military missions, including a harrowing night flight over Germany in the glass bulb between the twin tails of a P-61 "Black Widow" fighter plane in pursuit of enemy aircraft).[1] And we now know that a "moving picture" is precisely what the playwrights had in mind.

Whatever else they had to say about the play, nearly every reviewer on both sides of the Atlantic remarked on its autobiographical aspects. At the time the play opened in London in June 1946,[2] Virginia Cowles was newly married to Aidan Crawley, a well-born English journalist who later would serve as a member of Parliament. Martha Gellhorn was newly divorced from Ernest Hemingway.

"Funny how it should take one war to start a woman in your damn heart and another to finish her," Hemingway wrote of Martha Gellhorn to their mutual editor and friend Max Perkins in October 1944, as their marriage had fallen apart (*SL* 574).[3] The Spanish Civil War marked the beginning of their relationship, and Gellhorn and Hemingway were married in November 1940. Their "honeymoon" was a grueling adventure in the Far East as Gellhorn set off on assignment for *Collier's* magazine to report on the Sino-Japanese war—reluctantly accompanied by Hemingway (identified in her memoirs of the trip only as "U. C.": "Unwilling Companion").[4] Between their first meeting in December 1936 and their divorce in December 1945, Gellhorn filed stories from Spain, Finland, China, Singapore, Java, the Caribbean, Italy, Holland, France, England, and Germany. Lonely back home in Cuba, where he and his "Crook Factory" had been patrolling the Caribbean for German submarines in his fishing boat, the *Pilar,* Hemingway cabled her at the Italian front in 1944: "ARE YOU A WAR CORRESPONDENT OR WIFE IN MY BED?" (qtd. in Kert 391). In turn, Gellhorn begged him to abandon what she considered his "Q-boat play-acting" and join her in Europe where he could do some real good.[5]

Finally he obliged. In the spring of 1944, Hemingway became the front-line correspondent for *Collier's* magazine and Gellhorn, a *Collier's* correspondent since 1937, took "second place" on her magazine, in her words, "forbidden to work where the war was being fought." She called the situation "absurd and intolerable" (Afterword 329). In *Hemingway: The Final Years,* Michael Reynolds notes that Gellhorn "forgot to remember the War Department ruling that female correspondents 'could go no farther forward than women's services go,' restricting Martha and fellow female correspondents to hospital areas." Had *Collier's* editor Charles Colebaugh not hired Hemingway to cover the combat zone, he would have hired another man (Reynolds 92). But in Gellhorn's view, Hemingway stole her job. Famous enough to have had his pick of any magazine in the world, he chose *Collier's*. He did it "to fix me," she told me in 1990: nothing could beat it for "sheer bitchery."

In the summer of 1992, I suggested to Martha Gellhorn, then eighty-three years old and living in London and Wales, that the play, never published, really ought to be in print, available to contemporary audiences. After nearly fifty years and multiple moves (she counted eleven residences in seven countries), she did not own a copy. I sent her a second-generation photocopy of the blurry carbon typescript on file at the U.S. Copyright Office in the Library of Congress. A few weeks later, on 24 August, she replied on a picture postcard of St. Petersburg, Russia: "The play made me laugh out loud 3 times to my vast surprise." She would be willing to write an introduction. I would write an afterword. I knew it would be a gamble as to whether her journalist's devotion to getting the facts straight, her deep regard for the "record," would outweigh Gellhorn's known antipathy toward any mention of Hemingway's name in association with hers. But I decided to write it straight and hope that the journalist in her would prevail. The play was published for the first time in 1995 by the University of Nebraska Press with an Introduction by Martha Gellhorn and an Afterword by me—"Hemingway-cleansed," as directed by the author.

To be sure, the interest of the play does not rest on the Hemingway connection. As I did write in the Afterword, nearly fifty years before Susan Sarandon and Geena Davis hit the road in *Thelma and Louise*, Martha Gellhorn and Virginia Cowles had created a similar pair of daring, sexy, quick-witted (though entirely non-violent) heroines in *Love Goes to Press*. The critical controversy surrounding the 1991 movie hit testifies to just how far ahead of their time Gellhorn and Cowles were in portraying two women road buddies making it on their own decidedly female terms.[6] Yet the play is also close kin to its contemporaries, such 1940s screen classics as *His Girl Friday* (1940) and Katharine Hepburn and Spencer Tracy's *Woman of the Year* (1942) and *Adam's Rib* (1949)—Battle of the Sexes comedies in which a "New Woman," good looking as well as ultracompetent in her profession, threatens to outman her mate at his own game, whether in the newsroom or the courtroom. Both ahead of its time and *of* its time, *Love Goes to Press* is an important piece of women's literary history, still fresh and funny after half a century. The source of its humor—men and women at war (particularly within the military)—is still news.

Love Goes to Press reverses the male gaze. In the play we watch our heroines cold-creaming their faces, folding their khaki laundry, and admiring each other's hairstyles while discussing the charms of various men about camp. But they have their priorities straight. When Annabelle asks Jane "How's your love life?" she replies, "Bad. I got slightly involved with a Frenchman in Tunis last summer, but then we invaded Sicily, and I had to leave him" (18). Hemingway famously titled his 1928 story collection *Men Without Women;* in their 1940s wartime comedy, Gellhorn and Cowles had created a world of women without men.

Our heroines are indeed glamourous women, but they are at the same time crack war correspondents, legendarily fearless, and, in the eyes of their competitors, maddeningly successful. As one newsman warns another: "Don't be deceived by Miss Mason. She and her pal Miss Jones sail around looking like Vogue illustrations and they get the stories before you've even heard of them" (12). When the ranking officer learns that Annabelle has arranged transport to the Polish front, he exclaims that it is not possible. "It sure is, pal," Annabelle's plagiaristic ex-husband cynically responds. "Didn't you know this war was run on sex-appeal? No other correspondent has ever gone to Poland but then most correspondents don't look like Miss Jones" (49).

Despite the cries of foul play from the rivals they threaten to outshine, the fact is, of course, that being female is a definite occupational handicap for a war correspondent. (Co-author Virginia Cowles, who "got awfully bored doing the sort of articles you have to do in New York—fashions, love, marriage, and stuff about college boys and girls," explained the indirect method by which she persuaded the manager of the Hearst papers to let her go to Spain in 1936: "The only way a girl can cover the War is to tell the paper of her choice that she is going anyway and would they like some stories" [qtd. in *Current Biography*]). As a running gag in the play, whenever Jane attempts to place a call to headquarters, she must insist repeatedly to the invisible person on the other end of the line, "No, I'm not a nurse." As our heroines commiserate about the perpetual battle to stay ahead of Public Relations Officers bent on obstructing their plans, Annabelle seethes: "If I'm told once more I can't do something because I'm a woman." Jane mockingly recites in reply: "What if you got wounded, Miss Jones? All the forces on land, sea and air would stop fighting the war and take care of you. Not good for the war effort." Annabelle replies: "And considering the number of times we couldn't even get out of a car when a shelling started because the men pinned us down with their elbows while they stepped over us. It makes me sick with rage." She adds: "Darling, your hair's wonderful cut short like that" (17).

To today's reader, that last line is startling if not embarrassing. The fact is that Annabelle *has* arranged the trip to Poland by flirting with a smitten pilot, and when she does not fancy riding around in freezing weather in a jeep, she can dial up General Pinkerton ("Pinkie dear" to her), and a closed staff car with driver is at her disposal. At first consideration, the play's exploitation of such female stereotypes for comic effect seems dated, if not downright politically incorrect. But viewed from another angle, it illustrates why *Love Goes to Press* is still a revolutionary play. Like their controversial 1990s counterparts Thelma and Louise, who sip Wild Turkey from miniature airplane bottles and look fabulous even after throwing their lipstick to the wind, Jane and Annabelle get ahead in a man's world acting unapologetically if not extravagantly like *women*. (For the record, Martha Gellhorn, ever an avid moviegoer, told me she saw *Thelma and Louise* and thought it "great fun, wonderful—two pissed-off women going off and having some fun" [9 July 1992]). Because their gender is something that they have never been allowed to forget, Jane and Annabelle have great fun flaunting it, subversively turning a handicap to their own advantage. These feminist heroines literally do wear combat boots, but they bring silk stockings to the front as well, and they never lack for an "errand brigade" of willing men to carry their luggage. But while they can play traditional female roles to the hilt when it serves their purposes, they do find all that listening and nurturing to be exhausting. After being stranded with a group of soldiers, Annabelle sighs to Jane, "Oh, the pictures of wives I had to look at last night. Wives, children, girl friends, and dogs. They're all angels, but I'm worn to the nub" (65).

Our female leads defy stereotypes from every direction. They are not victims, but they are sometimes vulnerable. And as much satisfaction as they take in their work, they also need love. Jane claims to be sick and tired of the rigors of her chosen career: "I *hate* this ghastly life," she says to Annabelle. "Everything about it. The discomfort, the red tape, the people you have to be nice to, and frankly I'm even tired of being shot at." "Millions of women do something else," she says (18). ("But it's so deadly," Annabelle reminds her.) Jane's fantasy is "a house with ten bathrooms all full of hot water, and a husband who never stops saying, 'Are you comfortable, my sweet?'" (19). When Jane asks Annabelle why she had ever fallen in love with Joe Rogers in the first place, Annabelle replies, "You can't tell from the outside that he's got the character of a cobra. From the outside he's a beautiful, funny, fascinating man" (20). Yet when Jane suspects that her friend might still be "a little in love with this beautiful, funny, fascinating man," Annabelle is hard-pressed to deny it. Annabelle's ex-husband Joe can render her speechless by telling her that her nose is shiny. And when Annabelle is forced to choose on the spot between her coveted trip to Poland and the chance to win Joe back in the critical twenty-four hours remaining before his scheduled wedding to the ditsy Daphne, she agonizes briefly, then gives up the trip.

Joe Rogers changes his mind about wanting to marry the actress the minute he lays eyes on Annabelle again. Jumping to the false conclusion that there's another man in his ex-wife's life, he blurts out: "Does he love you the way I do? The way you talk, the things you say, how mad you get, the lost causes. Or does he just think you're a beautiful woman—like any other beautiful woman?" (67). For the first time ever, he tells Annabelle how much he admires her competence and courage: "No other girl would have dared fly that mission. That's what I mean about you. You're everything. You're pretty and funny and brave. I think being so brave is one of the things I'm proudest of." He begs her to give him another chance and promises never again to interfere with her work: "I'll sit at home and sew purple hearts all over your uniforms," he vows (67). What girl could resist? "Joe! You've never talked like this," Annabelle exclaims, and she falls for him again. As Joe makes plans to sweep her off with him to Capri, she coos, "I do *love* being arranged for" (68). However, she *is* wiser this time. When Jane asks, "Will you marry him?" Annabelle replies, "No, it's too dangerous. You risk ruining everything with marriage" (69).

But in Gellhorn and Cowles's play, for the woman who wants it all, there can be no happy ending. While their intelligence and independence are our heroines' most alluring attributes, each learns that as soon as she commits to marrying her man, his pride in her turns proprietary. Although he was initially hostile to the women, Philip Brooke-Jervaux, the camp's Public Relations Officer, gallantly defends Jane when the brass threaten to take away her credentials for attempting to get to the front by ambulance. He values her for her difference from other women: "I've never met one I could talk to before," he claims (54). They fall into one another's arms, and the next time we see them they are engaged to be married. One attraction for Jane in sitting out the war at Philip's farm in England is the prospect of finally having the time to work on a novel. But when she makes the mistake of expressing her joy, he brushes off the idea as nonsense: "I don't want you sitting in a stuffy room typing all day. . . . All that business of writing and earning money is over. I'm looking after you now" (72). Fearless on the war front, Jane is terror-struck as she imag-

ines the rigors of life on the home front: sitting in wet duck blinds at four
A.M., being thrown by horses on fox hunts, getting stung while keeping
bees, and catching mastitis from dairy cows.

As Annabelle is packing for her third honeymoon with Joe, she discovers a note saying *he* has gone to Poland: "[The pilot] sent for you, but
it's too dangerous. I love you too much. It doesn't matter for a man. P.S.
Back tomorrow" (73). Not only has Joe stood her up *and* stolen her trip—
to add insult to injury, he claims to have done it to protect her. Worst of
all, unlike Annabelle, who has a strong social conscience, he does not
even *care* about the Poles. When the General calls to offer Annabelle an
opportunity to cover the "forgotten army" in Burma, she jumps at the
chance. When Jane tells Philip she is afraid she will feel like a "slacker"
in Yorkshire, he reassures her that as a member of the "land army," plow-
ing fields with his sister at five A.M., she would not even have to give up
wearing a uniform (76). Seconds later, she is racing to catch up with
Annabelle to join the trip to Burma.

Even the dizzy Daphne is more interested in making a name for herself than in making a home for a man. Her initial enthusiasm for marrying Joe and waiting out the war at home with his mother may have had
a lot to do with the fact that his mother lives in Hollywood. She ditches
Joe as soon as she gets a better offer: an exclusive contract for the story
of her adventures on the front and a starring role in a Powermint Studios
picture. At this, Philip concludes that Daphne is a "dreadful woman" who
thinks only about her "silly career" (63). But Jane has to admit she is really
growing fond of Daphne and says it's not the career that's silly: "She *is* an
actress, even if she's a fool. It's her job" (63). Our heroines' dearest fantasy
is to find satisfaction in both love *and* work, those basic dual requisites
for mental health and happiness. But if they have to choose, work seems
the safer bet.

Thelma and Louise has been described as "'9 to 5' meets 'Easy Rider'"
(Rohrter C21).[7] *Love Goes to Press* might be described as *9 to 5* meets *Huck
Finn* with scenes from *A Room of One's Own*. In the end, when the chase
party closes in, the only way Thelma and Louise can maintain their
autonomy is to clasp hands and drive their car off a cliff. The only way
Annabelle and Jane can escape the clutches of domesticity and keep their
freedom is to light out for the Territory—in this case, Burma. But they
will not make a clean getaway, either. The punch line of the play comes

after our heroines have left the stage. Messages arrive independently for each of the male leads, neither of them aware yet that his woman has ditched him. Both men have been ordered to Burma.

The reviewer for *The New York Times* conceded that the authors "know the racket as well as a few of the most celebrated operators whom they satirize." However, he charges: "*Love Goes to Press* is not the cartoon that two frisky artists ought to draw of the typewriter soldiers. As the title indicates, they waste most of the evening on some dull and profitless love affairs. But love will have to fly out the window when the real satire of war correspondents gets written" (Atkinson 22). What he did not get was that the play is not so much a satire of war correspondents as a satire of the war between the sexes.

"War throws gender into sharp relief," in the words of one historian (Riley 260). To some degree, the gender war depicted in Gellhorn and Cowles's play can be seen as a product of the cultural climate of the Second World War. In her essay "This is My Rifle, This is My Gun: World War II and the Blitz on Women," Susan Gubar demonstrates through visual as well as literary examples how images of women were exaggerated and codified in the popular and literary imagination during the Second World War. Women were represented variously as victims of enemy rape and pillage, as mothers exhorting the nations's sons to do their duty, as alluring vamps who could entice unwary soldiers to reveal military secrets or kill them with VD, or as fresh-faced, buxom pinups hanging in lockers and reproduced on the sides of airplanes as mascots. (Sometimes, with grid lines superimposed, the pinups served as bombing targets in pilot training.) Gubar observes that "a menacing hostility, as well as a curious unreality, permeates both positive and negative images of women in these works. They are viewed almost entirely as ladies-in-waiting, solacing outsiders or resented beneficiaries of suffering. Even the women who represent the values that men are struggling to retain amidst barbaric, death-dealing circumstances are often identified as the cause of the fighting" (240).[8]

In *Love Goes to Press,* after her introductory spat with the Public Relations Officer, Annabelle fumes that if she had to spend three days with the "handsome major," she'd "kick his teeth in" (25). But a male reporter assures her he is "not a bad chap really" and begs her tolerance: "The poor guy's been away from England for three years, fighting to protect womankind from the horrors of war. And then the womankind walks in on him. He might as well have spared himself the trouble. You can see it would upset him for a while." Like the work of a number of women writers of the Second World War, Gellhorn and Cowles's play serves as an exposé of gender myths.[9] But *Love Goes to Press* may be unique in the body of women's war writing in employing the genre of dramatic farce as the vehicle of its critique.

In her introduction to the published play, Martha Gellhorn acknowledges that the two female leads "were caricatures of Ginny and me," recalling that "Ginny wrote most of Annabelle (me) and I wrote most of Jane (Ginny)." She also declares: "The male characters were not caricatures of anybody, pure and improbable figments of the imagination" (ix). Gellhorn's disclaimer notwithstanding, *Love Goes to Press* is delicious from the standpoint of literary gossip. The very name of one of our heroines is either a wild coincidence or a wickedly funny in-joke, given Hemingway's romantic relationship in the 1930s with the beautiful Havana socialite Jane Mason.

In *Love Goes to Press,* the coupled correspondents kept their marriage secret: "We didn't want our Editors to think marriage would interfere with the cut-throat competition," according to Annabelle (19). The November 1940 marriage of Martha Gellhorn and Ernest Hemingway was hardly a secret (The 6 January 1941 issue of *Life* magazine marked the event with a photo spread shot in Sun Valley by Robert Capa [49–51]), and one editor, at least, was alert to the possibility of any breach of the "cut-throat competition." Like the couple in the play, Gellhorn and Hemingway took a working honeymoon. In February 1941 Martha Gellhorn set off on assignment to *Collier's* to report on the Sino-Japanese war, accompanied by Hemingway, who had arranged an assignment for himself with Ralph Ingersoll's short-lived New York tabloid, *PM.*

The archives of *Collier's* magazine contain an interesting item: a cable from Editor William L. Chenery to "Martha Gellhorn Hemingway," San Francisco de Paula, Cuba, dated 18 June 1941—the same day Hemingway's China piece, "Chinese Build Air Field," appeared in *PM.* It reads: "MISTER HEMINGWAY PM JUNE EIGHTEENTH SCOOPS MISS GELLHORN COLLIERS JUNE TWENTYEIGHT STOP CANT YOU WRITERS PROTECT YOUR STORIES BETTER STOP PLEASE REASSURE RELATIVE EAST INDIES." Hemingway was incensed. He fired back a letter the same day to *Collier's* editor

Charles Colebaugh (since he did not know Chenery, he said) vigorously denying the charge: "In order not to interfere with Martha's pieces I did not write a line about China that some son of a bitch from any fifth rate staff college graduate wouldn't write and put in a box somewhere on page II." "Tell Mister Chenery for me that Mister Hemingway does not scoop friends or relatives," he continued, and he reminded Colebaugh that "Mister Hemingway has a certain unremunerated (or unremunerative rather) by Colliers value as a courier, bed-bug sprayer, and safari organizer. Also tell him that this trip was run for Colliers not for us and the only reason I went along and wrote any pieces *at all* was to look after Martha on a son of a bitching dangerous assignment in a shit-filled country. To be called a scooper gets me." He concluded that "if it isn't too much like walking in to the Pope with a tray of blood sausage on Friday," Colebaugh should show the letter to Chenery "just so he will see how well writers try to get together sometimes for his best interests. That is what Marty and I were doing in the east."[10]

A letter from Martha Gellhorn to William Chenery apparently enclosed with Hemingway's corroborates her husband's and exonerates him completely from any charges of "scooping." Hemingway had written an article about the construction of the Chengtu airfield (built in six weeks by 100,000 men and a steam shovel); *her* story, "These, Our Mountains," was about the China front with one paragraph (out of about fifty) about Chengtu. "This is very funny actually, and only goes to prove something or other," Gellhorn says. "I never went to Chengtu: Ernest did. It was his pigeon. (I was seeing Madame Chiang and writing on the China front story.) When he came back I picked his brains and stole from him. He was very decent about it; and in his article he goes into all the technical detail on Chengtu; but I used the best color. He, on the other hand, was offered six thousand plunks to write a piece about the China front and would not, for fear of stealing my thunder." Both she and Hemingway had thought the front was the story; the Chengtu airfield had already appeared in *Time*. Yet what Chenery liked was Chengtu. "Whereas no one at all has ever visited the fronts of Chiang Kai-Shek's armies; not even our military observers. So there you are. What it proves I do not know."[11]

Hemingway's "scoop" of Gellhorn on the Chengtu story appears to have been a misunderstanding. Colebaugh wrote a conciliatory letter, and in his reply on 25 June, Hemingway apologized for blowing up about the wire, explaining that the fact he was being sued for $5,200,000 by a man claiming the writer had stolen *For Whom the Bell Tolls* from a movie script of his that Hemingway had never seen "embittered me on the day I wrote you." Yet the incident shows that even if the newly wed Gellhorn and Hemingway did not consider each other competitors, others did. In a follow-up letter of 28 June, William Chenery explains to Gellhorn the "curious fact" that *Collier's* publicity department elected to focus on precisely the same news item in her forthcoming article that was emphasized in Hemingway's *PM* piece. And he offered Gellhorn some advice: "What I seriously did want to suggest is the need that every two reporters whether husband or wife or legmen for rival sheets have to consider. When I was a reporter in Chicago, we hunted in packs and in order to keep the peace between our city editors, we had to plot very carefully to give twists to our stories. I thought that you would like to know that your story boiled into newspaperese color litmus paper to the same tone your husband's story produced and that was all."

From China Martha Gellhorn went on alone to Java and Singapore. In August and September of 1942 she set off for six weeks (in hurricane season and amid German submarine activity) in a thirty-foot potato boat to report on Allied military operations in the Caribbean, ending her journey in the jungles of Surinam.[12] In November 1943 she returned to England, and from there, as she says, "followed the war wherever I could reach it" (*Face* 86), including a stint at the press camp in the ruined village near Cassino that serves as a model for the camp in *Love Goes to Press*.

Whether or not Hemingway can be said to have stolen her job when he became the front-line correspondent for *Collier's* in the spring of 1944, Gellhorn's lack of credentials did not keep her from "where the war was being fought." She smuggled herself to the D-day invasion by locking herself in the toilet of an unarmed hospital ship. (The hospital ship, a white target amid the other grey and camouflaged boats of the invasion armada, was the third to attempt the crossing—the two before had hit mines.) While Hemingway and the official press viewed the operations from a landing craft, Gellhorn went ashore with the stretcher bearers, an achievement for which, Carlos Baker says, "he never forgave her" (395). Bernice Kert reports that "This so infuriated Ernest that he convinced himself it never happened, explaining that Martha could not have made the landing because she did not have the proper credentials" (406).

"From D-Day until the war ended, I was on the run from those London desk officers who had threatened to deport me to the U.S. if I again disobeyed their orders as I had by smuggling myself to the Normandy invasion," Gellhorn later recalled (Afterword 329). After the hospital ship, she was banished to a nurse's camp in Essex, "where these poor women were trundling around in steel helmets, something I'd never had on in my life," Gellhorn said in a 1997 interview. "And so I just rolled under the barbed wire and got to the nearest airfield where two guys in a fighter bomber were going to Italy. I told them a sad story about I had to get to Italy because my fiancé was wounded and sat on a sort of ledge behind their seats with my legs hanging between them, and got to Italy. And from then on I spent the whole war as a nomad." As far as she was concerned, there were two enemies in the war: the Germans and the American Public Relations Office. Avoiding American units, she moved from one outfit to another, joining up for a while in Italy with the Polish Carpathian Lancers, who regarded her as a sort of mascot. Later, near the Dutch town of Nijmegen, out of uniform and riding a liberated bicycle, she was picked up as a spy by an American MP and taken to the commander of the eighty-second Airborne Division, General James Gavin, who said, "If you're fool enough to be here, I haven't seen you." But she got word from Virginia Cowles that the American Public Relations Office knew where she was and she had better move on (Interviews 1992, 1997). By "bumming lifts" across Germany as the Allied troops advanced, she got to Dachau a week after American soldiers discovered the prison camp at the end of the village street: "It was a special justice to hear the news of Germany's defeat in the Dachau infirmary," she later wrote (Afterword 329).

The 22 July 1944 issue of *Collier's* featured as its cover story Hemingway's D-day report, a five-page illustrated spread entitled "Voyage to Victory." That same issue contains a one-page piece by Gellhorn entitled "Over and Back," a home-front view of D-day bearing no indication that its author had ever left the shores of England. It was not until a week later, when her piece about German prisoners called "Hangdog Herrenvolk" appeared in the 29 July issue, that *Collier's* readers would have had any inkling that Martha Gellhorn actually had been part of the invasion armada.

A dig through the *Collier's* magazine archives sheds light on the matter. Jammed in cardboard boxes and never completely catalogued are the raw materials of the magazine—correspondence, manuscripts, galley proofs—filed in manila folders long bound together, issue-by-issue, with ancient twine. (When I first saw them in 1991, a librarian had to be summoned to snip the bundles open.) Among the papers are the original cablegrams of Hemingway's and Gellhorn's *Collier's* reports—long, narrow strips of yellowed paper sliced off a teletype machine in varying lengths. Razored cut-outs and purple dated stamps testify to the work of military censors. But Martha Gellhorn's reports underwent a second round of censorship in her own magazine's New York offices.

The original cablegram reveals that "Over and Back," published with Hemingway's cover spread in the 22 July 1944 issue, was not the first Gellhorn piece radioed from London after the invasion. It was sent in on 14 June. "Hangdog Herrenvolk," the timelier and more newsworthy report that clearly places Gellhorn on a ship in the midst of the invasion, was wired a day earlier, on 13 June—the same day that Hemingway wired his D-day report. Yet "Hangdog Herrenvolk" did not appear in *Collier's* until the following week, in the 29 July issue.

Scrawled in pencil across the top of Hemingway's 13 June D-day cable is the editorial order "Lead All *Hemingway*." Clipped to Gellhorn's 13 June cable about German prisoners is this typewritten note:

> Hank: Okay. By the time this gets printed, tho, D-day will be five or six weeks old and maybe we had better fix the lead a little so as not to date it too definitely. Prisoners will be going ashore in England for weeks yet. I hope.

"Fix the lead" they did, although the editors had not considered D-day old news when they chose Hemingway's report—dated *very* "definitely" on D-day—as the cover story for the 22 July 1944 issue, five weeks after the invasion began.

The opening line of Gellhorn's cable reads: "THE FIRST OF THE MASTER RACE ARRIVED ON THE SHORES OF ENGLAND AT NIGHT" (my emphasis). But the lead sentence of the published story reads simply, "The Master Race arrived on the shores of England at night." A few lines down, Gellhorn's original radiogram reads: "EARLIER IN THE DAY COMMA AND THIS WAS D PLUS ONE COMMA A FEW GERMAN WOUNDED HAD BEEN BROUGHT OVER ON LIGHT CRAFT COMMA BUT NOBODY HERE HAD YET SEEN SO MANY GERMANS COLLECTED IN ONE PLACE." In the published piece the reference to "D plus one" is gone, and with several other crucial editorial excisions, all evidence that Gellhorn actually was on the scene in the critical first days of the invasion is erased ("Hangdog Herrenvolk" 24). Not only did the editors at *Collier's* hold back Martha Gellhorn's eyewitness invasion story for a week, but they gutted it when it *was* finally published—possibly because she had broken rules to get there; more probably to avoid any embarrassment caused by her upstaging the magazine's newly acquired superstar.

Collier's readers would have to wait for the 5 August 1944 issue to learn from her piece "The Wounded Come Home" that Gellhorn actually had set foot on French soil. And even then it was not at all clear that she had gone ashore in the first waves of the D-day operations. In the original typescript of that story, Gellhorn describes the awesome sight:

> Then we saw the coast of France which we had all been waiting for and suddenly we were in the midst of the great armada of the invasion. People will be writing about this sight for a hundred years and whoever saw it will never forget it. First it seemed incredible; there were simply not so many ships in the world. Then it seemed incredible as a feat of planning; if there were so many ships, what genius it required to get them here, what amazing and unimaginable genius. After the first shock of wonder and admiration, one began to look about and see separate details. There were destroyers and battleships and transports, a Sargasso sea of huge vessels lying at anchor on the hard green water out from the green cliffs of Normandy. Occasionally you would see a gun flash or perhaps only hear a distant roar, as naval guns fired far over that hill. Small craft beetled around in a curiously jolly way. It looked like a lot of fun to race from shore to ships in snub-nosed boats beating up the spray. It was no fun at all considering the obstacles and mines that remained in the water, the sunken tanks with only their radio antennae showing, above water, the drowned bodies that still floated past.

Gellhorn's vivid eyewitness description of the "great armada of the invasion" is X-ed out in editorial pencil. It does not appear in *Collier's*. In the published version, any reference that would date the report definitely, placing Martha Gellhorn square in the midst of the historic D-day invasion, was again erased.

Each page of the archival copy of Gellhorn's "The Wounded Come Home" bears the oval stamp of the Field Press Censor of SHAEF (Supreme Headquarters Allied Expeditionary Forces) certifying the story "Passed for Publication as Censored" and dated "21 JUN 44." The story was published in the 5 August issue. Why the delay? To be sure, the publication of a weekly magazine like *Collier's* involved considerable lead time. Beyond that we can only speculate. When asked about it in 1992, Martha Gellhorn, who admitted to having been casual about filing her reports, recalled that she had given that story to Hemingway: he had said he had a friend who would send it in for her. Certainly it is possible that Gellhorn's recollection could have been prompted by the question. But the situation resonates with a scene in *Love Goes to Press*. Annabelle tells Jane that on her second honeymoon with Joe Rogers in Mexico (after she had forgiven him for stealing her trip to Russia on their first one), he did it again: "There was a classy international murder in one of the villas and I got the story as usual. Rogers popped back from a day's fishing and said he'd file it for me. I was supposedly too tired. So he sent it the slowest rate he could find and wrote himself a fine piece and telephoned it through." The original copy in the *Collier's* files of Gellhorn's "The Wounded Come Home" is not a radiogram, like the originals of her two previously published D-day articles. Rather, it is a sixteen-page typescript corrected in her own hand and signed, "Martha Gellhorn, Dorchester Hotel." The typescript appears to have been folded and sent to the New York office by mail.

The temptation to read the rival reporters in *Love Goes to Press* as comic caricatures of Martha Gellhorn and Ernest Hemingway is hard to resist. But Gellhorn herself discouraged that game. She later recalled that during the war she never saw her published pieces in *Collier's* magazine. "And I can't tell you how indifferent I was," she insisted. "Because as far as I was concerned, selfishly, I wanted to know, and then I wrote it the best I could, and if anybody wanted to take it in, that was up to them. I had done my job by seeing or learning and writing it the best I knew and getting it in. And from then on, it was somebody else's show, and not mine" (Interview 9 July 1992).

Still, for anyone keeping score (and certainly Hemingway did), a close inspection of the original cables of Hemingway's "Voyage to Victory" and Gellhorn's first D-day report, both sent from London on the night of 13 June, reveals one more detail of interest apropos of the professional rivalry depicted so colorfully in the play *Love Goes to Press*. The radiogram of Hemingway's D-day report is stamped in purple in the upper right corner with the date and time it was filed: "1944 JUN 13 P.M. 10 20."[13] Gellhorn's report is stamped "1944 JUN 13 P.M. 9 55." Not only had Martha Gellhorn witnessed the Allied invasion firsthand and set foot on French soil before Hemingway or, to my knowledge, any other American journalist, her D-day story was filed first: twenty-five minutes earlier, to be exact. Even if it was just on a technicality, and even if she claimed not to care, Martha Gellhorn *had* scooped Ernest Hemingway at the single most important event of the Second World War.

In September 1993, with some trepidation, I sent Martha Gellhorn a draft of an afterword to her play in which I had touched upon its apparent autobiographical aspects and these archival finds with what I hoped was adequate circumspection while still being true to the record. She responded promptly, in a two-page typed letter of 22 September 1993 that begins: "Good for you, such work and research. I had no idea that Collier's had done the dirty on me on the hospital ship piece and have been reprinting it in 'The Face of War' as it must have been printed in Collier's. Old stuff. I'm not sure I'd have cared even then though I wish I could see the full mailed article."[14]

"I'm sorry about all the Hemingway stuff," she continued. "Do you absolutely need it. I'd be happier without any of it and the competition angle doesn't matter really." Two paragraphs later, after providing information about photographs for the volume, she revisits the subject: "I do wish though that you'd cut everything about Hemingway that you feel you can. I've suffered professionally wickedly from being always noted as his third wife, as if that was my high point, not my work." After she typed the letter, her feelings apparently intensified: "Actually, I hate it," she wrote in the margin in her bold hand. "Do we need him at all?" "And he was gone and finished by 1945." Still, she graciously included an invitation to her eighty-fifth birthday party, to be held in London that November eighth (and I was thrilled to attend).

In another letter written the following day, having had a night to sleep on the matter, she did not mince words: "I really hate the whole Hemingway bit." Neither she nor her co-author was thinking about him and competition with her, she assured me: "In fact it did not occur to me for years that E. H. did feel competitive—the idea being too absurd." The D-day saga, she said, was needless and irrelevant, and it was distasteful to her to have the Hemingway competition bit thrown in. "We had NO real men in mind and I repeat, no reporters acted like those dopes in our play," she insisted. "It strikes me as again using him and his fame—and thus demeaning me. It is NOT his play, had nothing to do with any common past (he was never in Italy for the war)." "I really loathe it all and feel as if again Hemingway is being used to make his (odious) light shine on me," she added. She asked that I please send her a "shorter, Hemingway cleansed version." "I am unhappy having him intrude where he does not belong," she concluded. "I have a right to stand on my own for God's sake."

I did and do understand. Emotions that fresh after fifty years demand respect. I will not recount in excruciating detail the ups and downs of the correspondence that continued for several months concerning what could and could not be said in the notes and afterword to the play. Gellhorn's objections expanded to include biographical details that she already had edited to her satisfaction in earlier drafts I had sent her or that she herself had put into print: for example, Franklin Roosevelt's invitation to Gellhorn to come live at the White House until she sorted herself out after she was fired from the Federal Emergency Relief Administration for inciting dole "clients" to throw an overnight brick through a relief office window in Coeur d'Alene, Idaho (*View* 70–71). Across the left and top margins of one letter she wrote: "How do you know I got [to Dachau] a week after its liberation? *I* don't know. They were unloading the trains. They could not have waited a week because they found some living people. Where do you get these facts?" In that case, I had gotten them from her own Afterword to her novel *Point of No Return*, originally published in 1948 as *The Wine of Astonishment* and republished in 1989 with her original choice of title restored. In the end, the understanding publisher and I agreed there was nothing to do but "cleanse" the play's Afterword as requested. Gellhorn was right: it was her book. Hemingway's name does not appear in the published volume.

The time seems ripe for a wider recognition of Martha Gellhorn's achievement. When I wrote to her to this effect in 1990, she responded: "Dear girl, people are always 'rediscovering' me, you'd be amazed. Everybody does it and nothing works; I am never going to be a great saleable property. But the way it operates is: someone finds me for the first time and is astounded that everyone around him/her has not heard of me, and so sets about re-discovering me. I think it is sweet and funny. . . . I always said I was going to wait for posthumous fame and glory, suits me fine. I've been found and lost and found again for a long time; all that matters to me is that I can still do reporting when I want to, about what I want. As for fiction, nobody stops me, I stop myself." Martha Gellhorn died in London on 15 February 1998 at the age of eighty-nine. Despite her professed indifference, I think she would be pleased to be found again, the record of her accomplishments fully restored. I hope the time for her posthumous fame and glory is at hand.

17
Hemingway's Literary Sisters

The Author through the Eyes of Women Writers

Rena Sanderson

Ernest Hemingway's complex and ambivalent relationship with Gertrude Stein has been widely discussed. Relatively little has been said, however, about Hemingway's relationships with other women writers. Among those who played important roles in Hemingway's life and works were his wives, all of whom except Hadley Richardson were professional writers (and even Hadley proofread his stories before he submitted them). In addition, a number of other women writers participated in the making of Hemingway's public image and reputation. Three such women were Dorothy Parker, Lillian Hellman, and Hemingway's third wife, Martha Gellhorn. The way these three responded to Hemingway and incidentally to each other is the focus of the present exploration.

In writings that span the years from 1926 to 1981, those women writers drew attention to certain features in his character and his works, and thus they functioned as unofficial publicity agents during and after his lifetime. This study will examine Parker's role in constructing the Hemingway legend, Hellman's questioning of that legend, and Gellhorn's surprising defense of it. In addition, this study will show that all of these writers, including Hemingway, served as mirrors for each other that helped them to define themselves and their work. In other words, this analysis offers fresh insights into the gender dynamics at the center of Hemingway's literary reputation. What emerges is a better understanding of women's complicity in modernist aesthetics that privileged male writers and writings over female ones.

Especially important are Parker's writings on Hemingway during the formative stage of his career when, according to Daniel J. Boorstin, the graphic revolution of the media resulted in the manufacturing of media celebrities chiefly famous for being famous (288). At this time, as Margaret Lawrence claimed in *The School of Femininity* (1936), Parker was one of those media figures who exercised "a public influence far out of proportion" to her actual book publications (175). Without a doubt, Parker's two early pieces on Hemingway in *The New Yorker* (29 October 1927 and 30 November 1929) helped to confirm and advance Hemingway's reputation as a major American writer. The point, however, is not only that Parker deserves credit for promoting Hemingway, but also that she drew special attention to certain characteristics of his work and personality.

Having first met Hemingway in 1926, Parker, who was six years his senior, admired him from the start. When he sailed back to France aboard the *President Roosevelt,* she and her friends Seward Collins and Robert Benchley joined him. It was that "golden summer" when everyone who counted was in France; in Paris, Parker met Sara and Gerald Murphy (who became her lifelong friends), the MacLeishes, the Seldeses, and the Fitzgeralds. She spent time at the Murphys' Villa America at Antibes on the French Riviera, she spent time in the Alps, and she joined the Hemingways in Spain to watch the bulls run in Pamplona.

During this European stay, Parker had ample reason to form a grudge against Hemingway. According to some, "Hemingway resented Dorothy Parker's celebrity status" (Frewin 133). Whereas F. Scott Fitzgerald admired her and, as he had done for Hemingway, urged his editor Max Perkins at Scribner's to sign her up, Hemingway publicly insulted Parker at a party hosted by Ada and Archibald MacLeish in Paris in October of that year. In his long poem, which eventually appeared in his *Complete Poems* under the title "To a Tragic Poetess," Hemingway in passing ridiculed Parker's Jewishness and appearance ("the Jewish cheeks of your plump ass"). Most of all though, he derided in detail her suicide attempts, her abortion, and her love of "dogs and other people's children" as expressions of her self-indulgence and sentimentality in contrast to the extensive suffering and loss endured by Spanish men (*Poems* 87). As Jeffrey Berman notes, the poem expresses "suicideophobia, misogyny, and anti-Semitism" and suggests that male suffering is superior to female suffering (121).

Nevertheless, Parker's report of the trip, published in the January 1927 issue of *Vanity Fair,* revealed no resentment. Indeed, Donald Ogden Stewart accused her of "sucking up" to Hemingway (Frewin 217). More importantly, on 29 October 1927, she published a positive review of *Men Without Women* in the *New Yorker,* a review that helped to establish the parameters and set the tone for Hemingway's reception during this early phase.

The review presented Hemingway as "a young American living on the left bank of the Seine in Paris, France," hanging out at the bars and cafés with the likes of Pound, Joyce, and Gertrude Stein. "There is something a little—well, a little *you*-know—in all of those things. You wouldn't catch Bruce Barton or Mary Roberts Rinehart doing them. No, sir" ("Book" 459). In other words, Parker highlighted the Romantic image of Hemingway, the expatriate non-conformist Bohemian, i.e., the antithesis to the popular writers of the mass market (Barton and Rinehart).

Most of all this review was a defense of the short story form and of Hemingway as master of that form. With ridicule for the critical acclaim granted his novel *The Sun Also Rises,* Parker objected to the critics' disregard of his short story collection *In Our Time.* The problem was one of literary genre, she suggested: "*In Our Time* was a book of short stories. That's no way to start off. People don't like that; they feel cheated" ("Book" 459).

Hemingway, she noted, was a masterful craftsman who knew how to transform actual experience into tight stories. She credited him with a "reportorial talent" comparable to Sinclair Lewis's, but she insisted that Lewis was just a reporter while Hemingway was "a genius . . . [with] an unerring sense of selection. He discards details . . . ; he keeps his words to their short path" ("Book" 461). She regarded his "style, this prose stripped to its firm young bones" as "far more effective, far more moving, in the short story than in the novel" and called him "the greatest living writer of short stories" ("Book" 460). His was "a dangerous influence," she concluded ("Book" 461).

In future articles, she would identify the debts that writers owed to Hemingway. In March 1928, for example, she specified Claude McKay's "debt—part of what is rapidly assuming the proportions of a National Debt—to the manner of Ernest Hemingway" ("Bungler" 503). One cannot help but wonder, however, if she was not also comparing herself with Hemingway. She was, after all, cultivating her own public image as a Romantic rebel, and she was perfecting her own short story form. Since her first published story had appeared in *Smart Set* in 1922, she had already produced several fine pieces, and in 1929 "Big Blonde" gained Parker the five hundred dollar O. Henry prize as the best story of the year. The early 1930s saw the publication of such masterpieces as "Horsie" and "The Waltz," and her collection of short stories *Laments for the Living* (1930) sold well.

On 30 November 1929, *The New Yorker* published Parker's long and flattering profile of Hemingway entitled "The Artist's Reward." It revised and elaborated points already raised in the earlier review—Hemingway's individualism, artistic genius, and craftsmanship—but they were now transformed into Hemingway's persona.

The image of Hemingway that Parker developed already resembles the legendary celebrity figure that eventually became as well or even better known than his work. In presenting the biographical "facts" (a runaway kid, prize-fighter, war correspondent, and wounded soldier sporting an aluminum kneecap), Parker exercised considerable poetic license. In truth, there were other discrepancies besides the extra touch of the aluminum kneecap, but then, of course, this was obviously not an exercise in accuracy but rather the creation of a larger-than-life mythical figure that "intrigues the imagination" ("Reward" 583). As John Raeburn has observed, Parker's rendition of Hemingway's life simply answered what she herself recognized as the public's desire for Hemingway "to be a figure out of a saga" ("Reward" 583). Parker was "not averse to a little saga-making herself" (Raeburn, *Fame* 27).

In some respects, Parker simply exaggerated Hemingway's assets, especially his male appeal—his physical attractiveness, his infectious charisma, and his irresistibility to women:

> He is in his early thirties, he weighs about two hundred pounds, and he is even better than those photographs. The effect upon women is such that they want to go right out and get him and bring him home, stuffed. ("Reward" 584)

Indeed Parker, who frequently uses gender imagery tending toward the stereotypical and sexist, stressed Hemingway's masculinity. Her Hemingway was endowed with "the most profound bravery": "He has had pain, ill-health, and the kind of poverty that you don't believe—the kind of which actual hunger is the attendant; he has had about eight times the normal allotment of responsibilities." Moreover, Hemingway used no prissy euphemisms but simply called his courage "guts." When asked to define "guts," he replied "grace under pressure" ("Reward" 588). Parker's report thus initiated the most widely quoted tag-line associated with the name Hemingway.

There was also nothing effeminate about Hemingway's profession: "He works like hell, and through it. Nothing comes easily to him; he struggles, sets down a word, scratches it out, and begins all over. He regards his art as hard and dirty work" ("Reward" 586).

Hemingway did, however, have a soft spot, she said: "He is outrageously sensitive to criticism," but for good reason since most criticism misunderstands him ("Reward" 586). But then, of course, there was Parker, rushing to the job to do it right and in the process defining her own role as understanding critic.

In descriptions of her role as critic, Parker again used strong gender imagery, mostly to poke fun at herself. She suggested that her assessment of Hemingway was like the response of a klutzy "lady tourist" who at the sight of the Grand Canyon cannot contain herself: "And woman's world-old need of speech seized her, and seemed as if it would rack her very tweeds apart. 'Well!' she said, 'He certainly *is* attractive'" ("Reward" 582). Insisting that it was "no misses' size assignment to dash off a description of Ernest Hemingway," she distanced herself from critical approaches associated with female inadequacy. She did not want to be associated with biographical criticism of a sentimental nature: "The present vogue to rip off sketches of the famous in a sort of delicate blend of the Anecdotal, or Brightest-Things-Our-Baby-Ever-Said, manner, and the Tender, or Lavender-and-Old-Rubbers, school. As a subject, Mr. Hemingway does not lend himself to the style" ("Reward" 583).

She did not want to be confused with either "the sabre-toothed ladies of stage, pen, salon, and suburb who throng the local Bohemian gatherings" in New York or with the provincial "Miss Harriet McBlease, who does 'Book-Looks' for the Middletown *Observer-Companion*" and who, of course, would "not find the new Hemingway book to her taste" ("Reward" 587). Dorothy Parker was, after all, one of the very few women reviewers and critics who wrote on Hemingway during his own time.

In other words, she was defining herself as one of the boys, someone who appreciated and practiced the qualities she ascribed to Hemingway.

She cultivated a public image as an eccentric and developed her own distinct style. Lacking any pretentiousness associated with the genteel, she was known for her outspokenness and for her dry, understated wit. Her method as reviewer was, as she had said of Hemingway, that of "a slow worker" ("Reward" 588). Also like Hemingway, she saw herself as an exposer of sham, and sharing his contempt for criticism of the wrong kind, she set out to correct "the bilge" and "tripe" ("Reward" 583).

As Raeburn points out, Parker's profile of Hemingway in 1929 had special "developmental importance" since it "codified prevalent attitudes held by literary critics and the intellectual elite during the 1920s," attitudes that changed during the next decade (*Fame* 27).

In the 1930s Hemingway's legend grew to extraordinary dimensions, but it came under scrutiny even as it evolved. Possibly in response to his private circumstances and partly in defense against perceived attacks, Hemingway himself cultivated a public image of masculinity and male authority. He engaged in manly sports. And he wrote about manly topics in *Death in the Afternoon* (bullfighting), *Green Hills of Africa* (safari hunting), and the *Esquire* essays (bullfighting, fishing, boxing, hunting, and politics) that appeared in the new men's magazine from 1933 to 1936. By 1933, Clifton Fadiman observed that Hemingway "triumphed more as a hero than as an artist," because his projection of "violence, waywardness, and independence" satisfied the public's need for a Romantic hero myth during a critical period ("Byron" 125, 128). What Fadiman celebrated, others ridiculed. Max Eastman, in a 1933 review of *Death in the Afternoon*, suggested that Hemingway's "red-blooded masculinity" and "literary style of wearing false hair on his chest" covered up his fear that he was not "a full-sized man" ("Bull" 131). By the mid-thirties, magazines featured caricatures of the manly Hemingway including a "paper doll satire in *Vanity Fair*" (Raeburn, *Fame* 59).

Hemingway's construction of a more virile public image may have expressed his increasingly defensive reaction to women during the early 1930s due to his father's suicide (which he blamed on his mother's dominance and his father's passivity), his own troubled second marriage to Pauline, and his affair with Jane Mason. In addition, Hemingway felt himself targeted by several women writers. Already in 1927, he found a review by Virginia Woolf "damn irritating" (*SL* 264), and he was outraged when Margaret Anderson, in her autobiography *My Thirty Years' War*

(1930), suggested that "his interest in the bullring was simulated" (*SL* 388). Finally, Gertrude Stein's well-known questioning of his artistic courage in *The Autobiography of Alice B. Toklas* provoked numerous counterattacks in private comments and in several of his writings including *Green Hills of Africa, For Whom the Bell Tolls,* and *A Moveable Feast.*

During a decade that called for proletarian literature, critics grew disenchanted with Hemingway, whose public image became better known than his work, and his one proletarian novel *To Have and Have Not* (1937) received mixed reviews. His involvement in the Spanish Civil War, therefore, assumed special importance since it could either legitimize his stature or expose him as a swaggering fraud. At this critical stage in his career, the paths of Hemingway, Parker, Lillian Hellman, and Martha Gellhorn crossed. Although the extent of their involvement in the Civil War varied, Parker, Hellman, and Gellhorn witnessed Hemingway's role in the events and subsequently provided very different evaluations of his performance.

Parker (b. 1893) was six years older than Hemingway while Hellman (b. 1905) and Gellhorn (b. 1908) were respectively six and nine years younger than him. Although they differed in many ways, all three women were, of course, serious professional writers who hoped to become just as successful as Hemingway. Most of all, the three women shared strong political convictions and an antifascist position.

Lillian Hellman first met Parker in 1931 when Parker's behavior toward Dashiell Hammett (who never came to like Parker) sent Hellman into a fit of jealousy. After their second meeting in 1935, however, they became good friends and together were active in leftist politics.

Back in 1927 Parker had marched in protest (along with Edna St. Vincent Millay and Katherine A. Porter) against the execution of Sacco and Vanzetti and was duly arrested. Subsequently, she became a committed political activist and organizer. In 1934 she became, along with Hellman, the chief organizer of the Screen Writers Guild, and in June 1936, she helped to found the Anti-Nazi League (Kinney 60). In January 1937, while Hemingway was in New York City, he joined Parker, Hellman, John Dos Passos, and Archibald MacLeish in founding Contemporary Historians to raise funds for Joris Ivens's documentary on the Spanish Civil War, one of several films intended to raise American awareness of the situation (Baker, *Life* 300). According to some sources, Hellman collaborated with MacLeish in writing the story for *The Spanish Earth* but quit the project because of illness (Riordan xv–xvi; Rollyson 106), so that Hemingway ended up writing the script. In July 1937, in California Parker helped to set up a private screening of a silent version of *The Spanish Earth* that Hemingway accompanied with a speech, an event that Hellman also attended. The screening was meant to raise funds for ambulances, and Parker herself contributed one thousand dollars and invited everyone to her place for a late party.

On 19 August 1937, Parker, her husband Alan Campbell, and Hellman sailed from New York to France on the *Normandie*. On board ship Parker and Hellman first met Martha Gellhorn, whose purpose was to join up with Hemingway, who had sailed on the *Champlain* two days earlier. After an extended stay in Paris, Hemingway, Herbert Matthews, and Gellhorn went to Spain in early September while Parker, her husband, and Hellman followed later that month.

Parker's loyalty to the legendary Hemingway she had helped to create withstood the test of the events. Although she spent only ten days in Spain, what she saw deeply moved her and made her a committed Loyalist. Upon her return to the States, the public media, including *Newsweek* and *Time,* poked fun at the "startling conversion to the Loyalist cause of hitherto class-unconscious intellectuals" and specifically attacked "the bitter-sweet wit and poetess" (Keats 220–23). Nevertheless, she was tireless in her efforts to alert the public to the Fascist threat and participated in numerous fund-raising activities. For example, she delivered speeches for the North American Committee to Aid Spanish Democracy and thereby "helped to raise an estimated $1.5 million for refugees from Franco" (Meade 286–87, illus. 20).

She wrote a detailed, emotional report on the war, "The Siege of Madrid," for *The New Masses* (23 November 1937). She wrote that she felt "bewildered. While I was in Valencia, the Fascists raided it four times" ("Siege" 592). A fictional narrative set in Valencia during the war, "Soldiers of the Republic," appeared in *The New Yorker* on 5 February 1938. Biographer Keats has commented on the similarities between this story and Hemingway's "Old Man at the Bridge":

[S]he did what Hemingway tried all his life to do: she created literature more true than fact. . . . Both stories are examples of an attitude and a technique employed by two contemporary and very similar masters during the golden age of the short story. (220)

In addition to the pieces concentrating on the Spanish Civil War, Parker also wrote proletarian stories, such as "Clothe the Naked" (*Scribner's,* January 1938). However, she transformed neither her political convictions nor her experiences into a book-length work.

Nevertheless, in 1940, she wrote a glowing review of Hemingway's Spanish Civil War novel *For Whom the Bell Tolls.* Although Hemingway was known to have attacked her "more than once" for her "puerile journalism" (Frewin 133), she praised Hemingway's novel as an expression of the author's maturity and "wisdom." She, whose love of animals and children Hemingway used to satirize, credited him for a book "written with an understanding that rips the heart with compassion for those who live, who do the best they can, just so that they may go on living" ("Finest" 42).

Although Hemingway's handling of love relations was an easy target for other critics, Parker, whose stories specialize in depicting male/female relations, made a special point of praising Hemingway's skillfulness in showing "a man and a woman together, their completion and their fulfillment" ("Finest" 42).

She also noted a new stylistic method in this, Hemingway's "finest book": "It is not written in his staccato manner. The pack of little Hemingways who ran along after his old style cannot hope to copy the swell and flow of his new one" ("Finest" 42). And yet Parker herself, in discussing her own rhetorical strategies in writing the review, at once advocated and adopted Hemingway's well-known principles:

> *For Whom the Bell Tolls* is nothing to warrant a display of adjectives. Adjectives are dug from soil too long worked, and they make sickly praise and stumbling reading. I think that what you do about this book of Ernest Hemingway's is point to it and say, "Here is a book." As you would stand below Everest and say, "Here is a mountain." ("Finest" 42)

Interestingly enough, as she had done ten years earlier when she compared Hemingway to the Grand Canyon (in "The Artist's Reward"),

Parker once again equated Hemingway's work with a sublime natural wonder.

Before the bombing of Pearl Harbor and America's official entry into World War Two, Parker, Hellman, and Hemingway continued their joint efforts to warn the world of Fascism. In fall of 1941, for example, Hellman co-chaired with Hemingway a fund-raising dinner, "Europe Today," to benefit antifascist refugees. The dinner was sponsored by the Joint Anti-Fascist Refugee Committee, of which Parker was the national chairperson. When Governor Lehman of New York rescinded his participation in the dinner, charging that the committee was a Communist organization, Hellman defended the dinner's antifascist cause in a response published in the *New York Times* on 4 October 1941. And in August 1942, the committee published an illustrated, limited edition of Hellman's antifascist play, *Watch on the Rhine*, for which Parker wrote a special foreword.

With the onset of the Cold War, Parker and Hellman, like many other leftists, found that there was a price to be paid for their "premature anti-Fascism." In the late 1940s, both women were blacklisted as alleged Communist sympathizers and subpoenaed to appear before the California State Senate Committee on Un-American activities (while the FBI tracked Hemingway and Gellhorn for years). In September 1951 Parker and Campbell were included in a list of Hollywood communists that the screenwriter Martin Berkeley gave to the House Committee on Un-American Activities, and the Joint Anti-Fascist Refuge Committee was identified as a communist-front organization (Kinney 70). The events triggered a series of unfortunate developments and initiated Dorothy Parker's general personal and professional decline as documented in her biographies.

Nevertheless, even during her last years, Parker continued to promote Hemingway's reputation. The preface of *Short Story: A Thematic Anthology* (1965), which Parker co-edited with Frederick B. Shroyer, included a lengthy restatement of the "principle of the iceberg," which Hemingway had earlier explained to George Plimpton in an interview for the *Paris Review* (125). Although the preface did not credit Hemingway with the idea, it nevertheless advanced and popularized the concept itself and thus Hemingway's literary influence.

After Parker's death of a heart attack on 7 June 1967, there appeared two different accounts of the interaction between Hemingway, Parker, and Hellman during the Spanish Civil War. The first one, Hellman's attack on Hemingway, appeared in 1969 in *An Unfinished Woman: A Memoir.*

Hellman's biographical focus on Hemingway is part of the predominantly biographical approach that began in his lifetime and accelerated after his suicide in 1961. In 1948, Hemingway provided information about his life to Malcolm Cowly and to Lillian Ross. As a result, in 1949, Cowly depicted Hemingway in most flattering terms as a man of action in an illustrated article that appeared in *Life* (five million subscribers). Less flattering was the profile by Ross, "How Do You Like It Now, Gentlemen?," which appeared in 1950 in *The New Yorker* and presented a caricaturelike Hemingway bragging about his war heroics, sporting feats, sexual conquests, and psychic wounds. During the 1960s, following his suicide, Hemingway's reputation suffered. In 1966, however, Philip Young published *Ernest Hemingway: A Reconsideration* (a revised version of the book originally published in 1952). Young's influential study helped to redeem the Hemingway Hero outlined by Parker and by others including Cowley. In a psychological analysis of Hemingway's fictional males, and to some degree of Hemingway himself, Young defined the Hemingway code as "'grace under pressure' . . . made of the controls of honor and courage which in a life of tension and pain make a man a man and distinguish him from the people who follow random impulses" (*Reconsideration* 63). In other words, Young, like Parker before him, equated substance of character with manliness.

In *An Unfinished Woman* Hellman questioned precisely that substance of character in depicting, somewhat like Lillian Ross before her, a swaggering, strutting Hemingway—a caricature and parody of everything Parker admired in him. What emerges is a picture of Hemingway, the bully with the big ego who displays bravado rather than real courage; Hemingway, the womanizer; and Hemingway, the chauvinist throwing a fit over unfavorable criticism.

Whatever their validity, Hellman's attacks deserve attention for the way they promoted particular views of Hemingway and his work. It is no secret that the caricature of a swaggering, macho Hemingway remains a matter of debate among literary scholars and continues to rule the popular imagination so that some women readers even refuse to read him.

There are hints of a feminist sensitivity in Hellman's perception of Hemingway. She records that Hemingway, made defensive by her response to his manuscript, used "a tone one would use with an annoying child," and she reports that he made a half-hearted pass at her (66). When Hemingway gives her the compliment, "So you have *cojones*, after all," she tells him to "[g]o to hell with what you think" (88). She is clearly insulted by Hemingway's treatment of her as a child or as sex object rather than as an equal writer. Interestingly enough, however, she does not hesitate to belittle Martha Gellhorn in a similar way when she describes her not as a serious war correspondent but as Hemingway's bride-to-be who spends too much time in the gym and on her fashionable clothes (63, 83).

To appreciate the response to Hellman's account and the defense of Hemingway that Martha Gellhorn delivered eleven years later, one needs to recall the competitive nature of Hemingway's third marriage. Initially, Gellhorn's entrance into Hemingway's life was the direct result of her admiration for his writing. Before they ever met, she had used a line from *A Farewell to Arms* as the epigraph for her first novel *What Mad Pursuit* (1934), and, according to her (unauthorized) biographer, when she set out to win Hemingway away from Pauline, the famous author "held a peculiar fascination for her just then because she was going through a tremendous crisis of confidence in her own work" (Rollyson 93).

When Gellhorn married Hemingway on 21 November 1940, she was thirty-two and he was forty-one. She was young, beautiful, and intelligent, and he was in his prime, at his physical and professional best. Indeed, they were such a handsome couple that they stayed free at the newly established Sun Valley Lodge in Idaho in return for promotional pictures for the new resort. In these pictures, taken by house photographer Lloyd Arnold, Gellhorn, as Hemingway's radiant third wife, helped to promote his public image of success. But the fact that she was his third wife and had broken up his marriage to Pauline, the mother of two of his sons, also advanced his public image as a womanizer who needed a new woman for each new book he wrote.

During their five years of marriage Gellhorn's independence and professional seriousness developed into a problem that drew attention to Hemingway's sexism. Neither during nor after their marriage did Gellhorn want to make a career out of being Mrs. Hemingway, but she could not get an unbiased hearing on her own terms. In 1944, Hemingway wrote his son Patrick that he was tired of being married to a wife who "want[ed] to be in different war theatre that stories not compete. Going to get me somebody who wants to stick around with me and let me be the writer of the family" (*SL* 576). After her divorce from Hemingway in 1945, it was well known that Gellhorn did not like to be asked any questions about him. Herself the author of numerous novels, collections of short stories, and articles, she preferred to talk about her own work. At the same time, she must have known that her own fame had been linked to Hemingway's. Even Carl Rollyson's 1990 biography of Gellhorn, which superficially supports her desire to be free of the Hemingway mystique, takes its own title, *Nothing Ever Happens to the Brave,* from *A Farewell to Arms.* And the biography's thesis is that, in her very independence and love of adventure, Gellhorn, who came to hate Hemingway, "modeled herself after his early characters. . . . She wanted her life to be the Hemingway fiction she had read" (xvi–xvii).

In light of her hostility to Hemingway, it was a surprise when, in 1981, Gellhorn came to his defense. Her article, "On Apocryphism," appeared in the *Paris Review,* paired with an article by Stephen Spender, under the heading "Guerre de Plume." She used the piece to attack Stephen Spender and Lillian Hellman for misrepresenting (on separate occasions) the involvement of Hemingway and herself in the Spanish Civil War. Both Spender and Hellman were guilty of "*apocryphism,*" a neologism Gellhorn applies when a story and its teller ("apocryphiar") are inauthentic and false (281).

She acknowledged that Hemingway "became a shameful embarrassing apocryphiar about himself" in his later life and that "his own boastful apocryphisms" perhaps spawned those by others. But "he was not like that in Spain," she insisted (301).

Displaying her typical disdain for scholars (comparable to Hemingway and Parker's contempt for critics), she announced that she would set the record straight and make it clear that Hemingway's motivation in the Spanish Civil War was beyond reproach:

> I mean to nail that good and hard, so no forthcoming Hemingway scholar picks it up. And then another and another repeats it until, in the evil manner of apocryphism, this trash turns to truth, and the Republic of Spain and that noble lost war become merely an athletic exercise for Hemingway's nerve. There was plenty wrong with Hemingway but nothing wrong with his honest commitment to the Republic of Spain. (284)

Of course, in defending Hemingway's role in the Spanish Civil War she was also defending her own part against Hellman's charges. Just as Hemingway cared deeply for the men of the Brigades and of the Spanish Divisions and for the Spanish people, she herself still found "the memory of the suffering of others and the defeat and the aftermath for the losers . . . unendurable" (284).

She claimed for Hemingway and herself the courage of those who stayed the longest and stayed in the most dangerous spots. While Hellman, Parker, and her husband, "like most visitors, were based in Valencia, in every way a more comfortable city," Hemingway and Gellhorn were in dangerous Madrid (292). In other respects, however, Gellhorn contrasted Hellman's cowardice with Parker's courage as well. Parker "preceded" Hellman and "safely blazing the trail . . . survived several weeks in Spain without fuss or mishap" (291–92).

Indeed, Gellhorn ascribed to Hellman weaknesses that were exactly opposite to the strengths she ascribed to Hemingway, herself, and Parker. "Unlike Dottie she [Hellman] was not funny," Gellhorn reports, being sure to claim a good sense of humor for Hemingway (who "made good jokes") and for herself (292; 301). Also, while "no hint of conceit marred Mrs. Parker's acts and attitudes in Spain," Hellman is accused of taking herself all too seriously by imagining that her "clippings and fame had preceded her" (292).

According to Gellhorn, it was neither Hemingway nor herself but Hellman who was guilty of self-aggrandizement. It was Hellman, after all, who told lies simply to enhance her self-importance (295):

> Mrs. H. has written a great part for herself throughout AUW [*An Unfinished Woman*], with special skill in her Spanish War scenes. She is the shining heroine who overcomes hardship, hunger, fear, danger—down stage center—in a tormented country. . . . Self-serving apocryphisms on the war in Spain are more repellent to me than any others. (300)

Finally then, Gellhorn contrasts Hellman's falsehoods with her own professional accuracy. Gellhorn was not the first to accuse Hellman of lying. There were others before and after Gellhorn, including Mary McCarthy, Stephen Spender, Samuel McCracken, William Philips, and Diana Trilling, who questioned the trustworthiness of Hellman's autobiographical writings. Part of the turmoil over Hellman's alleged false-hoods, as Timothy Dow Adams has suggested, arose perhaps from "a problem in defining literary . . . terms." Not everyone shared Diana Trilling's respect for Hellman's autobiographies as works of a vivid imagination (Adams 128–29). In 1978, Hellman acknowledged that she "did not fool with facts" but that she tried to tell the truth, nevertheless, yet found that truth to be highly subjective and ever-changing (*Three* 9). Gellhorn, however, insisted on the difference between fact and fiction. As possibly "the sole surviving witness," and thus an authority on the topic, she wrote to tell the Truth (281).

Gellhorn's insistence on truthful facts and her respect for firsthand accounts may reflect her professional pride as a war correspondent. In the 1940s she had seen journalism "as a 'guiding light,' a beacon of truth" (Orsagh 245), and she covered seven wars as a foreign correspondent. And yet, there are also reports that she once "fictionalized and dramatized her experience, including her 'eyewitness' account of a lynching that (she confessed to Mrs. Roosevelt) she made up" (Rollyson xiv).

Of interest in this feud, and justifying this look at it, is the question of authority. However differently Parker, Hellman, Gellhorn, and Hemingway defined truth, they all believed, with modernist naiveté, in the possibility of an artistic Truth grounded in the artist's substantial character and experience. Parker not only identified Hemingway as an embodiment of such artistic mastery, but she used a gendered rhetoric that privileged male experience over female experience and equated artistic mastery with maleness. Although he had met with charges, such as those by Stein, Anderson, and Hellman, that he was all show and no substance, i.e., a fraudulent impostor, Hemingway typically claimed for himself the position of authority that Parker had granted him. Even when he praised "Cry Shame," Gellhorn's article on the House Un-American Activities Committee (*New Republic* 1947), Hemingway credited himself with having "spent a lot of time trying to help her to write well, in her own way and not like me" (*SL* 630–31). In the same letter, he admitted that she had by then "hung about enough wars to know something about that," but he immediately undercut the validity of her war experiences: "after Spain, I think she took war to be a sort of very highly organised tribute to her own beauty and charm in which, unfortunately, people were killed and wounded; in which there was a satanic enemy fought by Our Side, and the chronicalling of the trials and victories of Our Side was something that produced a sizeable and very pleasant amount of tax free money" (*SL* 630). The implication is, of course, that Hemingway's own attitude toward war was never this superficial and self-serving.

In her attack on Hellman, Gellhorn adopted a strategy similar to Hemingway's. Thus her attack functioned not only as a double-edged defense of both Hemingway and herself but also as a means for defining herself in opposition to Hellman and for establishing her superiority over a professional rival. Her points of attack even recall Hemingway's particular charges of narcissistic self-centeredness levelled against Gellhorn herself.

In a *Paris Review* interview in 1965, Hellman had declared that writers are "often mean and petty. Competing with each other and ungenerous about each other. Hemingway was ungenerous about other writers. Most writers are" (qtd. in Plimpton, *Women Writers* 142). Indeed, the same Hemingway who belittled Gellhorn's war experiences and insisted that he had taught her to write, apparently felt threatened by her potential as a competitor. In a letter of 1949, he warned Charles Scribner: "If Miss Martha publishes a book [on Italy] . . . before you publish my book [*Across the River and into the Trees*] I give you straight word that I will turn in my suit. You can really count on this. Seriously. And double seriously" (*SL* 669).

Gellhorn charged Hellman with directing "venom" against Hemingway, but she herself also sprayed venom. Acknowledging Hellman's "bitchery" in describing Gellhorn as the "best-dressed woman at a war," Gellhorn, in "a spirit of fun," returned it. She ridiculed Hellman's appearance ("if Miss H's beauty had matched her brains, she would have been a more cuddly personality" [297]), and she suggested that Hellman perhaps attacked Hemingway because she never "charmed" him (299). "Miss H. is a crazy mixed-up kid about Hemingway; she wants us to think she was great buddies with him and that he danced attendance on her yet she cannot stop knifing him" (298).

In attacking each other's appearance, and in discrediting each other's professional function at the front, both Hellman and Gellhorn showed that they adopted and even promoted certain assumptions that equated female nature with the superficial, with vanity, and with cattiness. In a similar display of bias against her own sex, Katherine Anne Porter wrote in a letter of 1932 that Hemingway's point of view was "as false and in-complete as any memoirs of an ex-wife" (qtd. in Boyle). Such use of misogynistic weapons by women attests to the pervasiveness of gender stereotypes in literary battles.

Hemingway's interaction with Parker, Hellman, and Gellhorn during the Spanish Civil War resembled his response to other women such as Stein and Cather in that he cast himself in the role of expert, teacher, mentor, or father initiating the inexperienced pupil. Kirk Curnutt, draw-ing on Harold Bloom, suggests that Hemingway re-enacted or misread his apprenticeship with Stein so that he could cast her in the role of student and himself in the role of teacher, thereby gaining artistic au-tonomy.

It has not been noted sufficiently, however, that Hemingway typically responded to women competitors *as women*. When he felt attacked by Virginia Woolf in 1927, he fantasized of humiliating her by taking her clothes off and parading her "down the Avenue de l'Opera" (*SL* 265). When he insisted that Gertrude Stein had changed, he blamed the per-ceived change on her menopause and on her lesbian preference (*SL* 384, 387, 395).

He tended to interweave into his commentary on women writers ex-pressions of his personal feelings ("I liked"; "I loved") and even of sexual attraction. He recalled telling Stein in 1944 that "I had always loved her and she said she loved me too. . . . I always wanted to fuck her and she knew it" (*SL* 650). His display of sexual attraction naturally shifts atten-tion away from the woman's work; it is, of course, a way of not taking her seriously as an equal.

Nevertheless, Parker, Hellman, and Gellhorn confirm that Heming-way's approval was in fact important to them. A week before her death, Parker asked Don Stewart's wife Beatrice Ames, "'Did Ernest really like me?'. . . It was important to her to have Hemingway's good opinion" (qtd. in Keats 296). Even Hellman, who brags at one point that she did not care what Hemingway thought of her, more than once seems preoccupied with their mutual feelings for each other (88). She admits that she herself "liked Ernest" and that "it would have been hard for a woman not to like him if he wanted you to; tried for it"; a few pages later, however, she worries that he never liked her again after their interaction in Madrid and announces that "I'm not sure what I felt about him, either" (64, 88).

Unlike Parker who helped to shape the Hemingway persona, Gellhorn saw that saga as a burden: "The Hemingway saga, probably swelling with each new book on Hemingway, is bad news. His work sinks beneath the personality cult and the work alone counts." Thinking it "sad that the man's handmade falsehoods—worthless junk, demeaning to the writer's reputation—survive him," she called for a shift of attention from the myth of Hemingway back to his work (301). Like Parker fifty years earlier, Gellhorn identified his influence as stylistic originator: "All writers, after him, owe Hemingway a debt for their freedom whether the debt is acknowledged or not" (301). Nevertheless, except for this passing reference to his stylistic innovation, Gellhorn's own article concentrated on his character rather than on his work and thus further contributed to the personality cult.

Gellhorn's piece "attracted attention beyond the narrow audience of the *Paris Review*" and sent Hellman into rage (Wright 399). In terms of Hemingway's reputation, Gellhorn's defense of Hemingway in 1981 perhaps partly compensated for the fact that in other ways her affiliation with him had raised new questions about him and had clouded his public image.

While Hemingway's reputation as a serious writer was redeemed by the one critical success that *For Whom the Bell Tolls* brought him midway in a twenty-year lull, Parker's career declined after the late 1940s. Although Hellman certainly was set back by the political turn of events in the late 1940s, she made excellent use of her experiences in her articles, plays, and memoirs. After the publication of her memoirs—*An Unfinished Woman* (1969), *Pentimento* (1973), *Scoundrel Time* (1976), and *Maybe* (1980)—her career soared. Gellhorn's impressive productivity as writer, not only of nonfiction but also of six short story collections and several novels, has yet to gain adequate critical attention.

Much has been said about the "anxiety of influence" that Harold Bloom says male writers experience toward their male precursors. Claims regarding a women's literary tradition of mutual inspiration and collaboration remain a matter of debate.[1] The interaction of male and female authors, however, deserves further attention. Although this study certainly adds to the growing evidence that male modernists such as H. L. Mencken, Edmund Wilson, Joseph Hergesheimer, F. Scott Fitzgerald, and Ernest Hemingway feared the competition of female writers, the interactions of male and female modernists were at once more complicated and more productive than that.[2]

This study confirms Shari Benstock's assertion, expressed in *Women of the Left Bank*, that women as well as men helped to shape our understanding of modernism. Parker, Hellman, and Gellhorn acted as literary sisters to Hemingway. Whether they were adoring (Parker), critical (Hellman), or begrudging (like Gellhorn), they helped to identify and advertise Hemingway's message, style, method, and persona.

But they did more than that. Eager to prove themselves worthy of membership in the exclusive circle of serious writers, Parker, Hellman, and Gellhorn joined the modernist voices that equated feminine cultural work with the mediocre and blamed the inferiority of American intellectual life on the feminization of American culture, belles letters, and the mass market. Their work in promoting both Hemingway and themselves thus validates the theory that gender dynamics played a central role in the formation of modernism.[3] Both in what they rejected and in what they embraced, Parker, Hellman, and Gellhorn helped to define the aesthetics of twentieth-century American literature in gender-specific terms that privileged male work over female work.

Thus, we must acknowledge the formative influence that Hemingway, however inadvertently, exercised over the women's lives, works, and careers. All three women participated in the sexism of their youth. The characteristics that Parker, Hellman, and Gellhorn ascribed to Hemingway and his writings expressed their own values of non-conformist individualism and bravery, political idealism, artistic genius and craftsmanship, and disdain for literary criticism. If they were "feminists," they were the kind who looked for equality by adopting male ways—by becoming good sports, drinking buddies, and artistic competitors.

Notes

Introduction

1. We do not mean to slight the pioneering efforts of such obviously important male critics as Carl Eby, Mark Spilka, Gerry Brenner, and Robert Scholes in reevaluating the role of women and gender in Hemingway's fiction. Our essayists recognize the inestimable contributions of these and other male scholars in encouraging closer, more sensitive treatment of issues pertinent to women readers.

2. We intend the work of the notable scholars represented here to reflect the contributions of Hemingway's female critics in general, many of whom appear in our bibliography.

3. While the connotation of loving Hemingway may confound readers, we suggest that the idea of love as used in Miller's essay does not refer naively or sentimentally to the writer's relationship to her subject but refers to the personal identification with Hemingway that some women (and men) readers have always felt. This is as important a response to the Hemingway canon as the formally academic ones more characteristic of this collection. Many readers respond personally to Hemingway as surely as they answer to his art. They applaud the vitality that underlies the elemental intensity of his work. In other words, caught and held by that intensity, men and women alike will fall "in love" with Hemingway. Miller's acknowledgments of Hemingway's personal failings and the fact that female readers feel a bit betrayed by Hemingway's inability to sustain relationships—his driving women to bitchery—move her observations as a whole to objectivity.

Chapter 1

1. I presented earlier versions of this essay as talks at the Michigan Hemingway Society "Hemingway in Michigan Weekend," (Petoskey, Michigan, 20 October

1996), and at the University of North Carolina, Chapel Hill, as part of their symposium "Hemingway at 100," (22–24 July 1999).

2. See my earlier essay, "Hemingway's Women: A Reassessment," for further discussion of the possible causes for a misreading over time of Hemingway's women.

3. Since the publication of *The Sun Also Rises* in 1926, readers and critics have derogated Brett Ashley as Hemingway's ultimate bitch. Whether labeling her a drunkard, a nymphomaniac, or a modern-day Circe who turns men into swine, these interpretations ignore the complexity of Brett's character and the intricate role she plays in the novel, particularly with regard to her beauty. "Take Brett out" of the novel, says critic Harold Bloom, "and vitality would depart." He adds that only when the critic puts aside "the vision of Hemingway's heroine as a Circe" will he discover "there is more inwardness to Lady Brett" (Introduction 1–2). That many critics still do not see beyond that "vision" helps to illustrate Brett's dilemma as a beautiful woman whose appearance both identifies and traps her. Bloom's 1991 collection of reprinted articles focuses on Brett and attempts to redress some of the critical neglect and malignment of Hemingway's heroines. When critics have not dismissed Hemingway's female characters as less interesting or less complex than their male counterparts, they have tended to categorize them as either goddesses, such as Catherine Barkley, or bitches, such as Brett Ashley. Edmund Wilson, in *The Wound and the Bow*, describes Brett as "an exclusively destructive force" (238) and is usually credited with initiating what Roger Whitlow calls in *Cassandra's Daughters* the "Brett-the-bitch" school of criticism (51). Whitlow provides an excellent overview of the critical reaction to Hemingway's women, including Brett (10–15). He focuses more directly on Brett as a character and the critical reaction to her in his chapter called "Bitches and Other Simplistic Assumptions" (*Cassandra's* 49–58). Whitlow believes that critics "almost to a person . . . rely on Brett's own pronouncements for their interpretation, particularly the assertion that Brett makes to Jake after she leaves Romero: "You know it makes one feel rather good deciding not to be a bitch" (51). The 1980s marked a significant shift in Hemingway criticism, as scholars began to reassess Hemingway's fictional treatment of women, particularly in the short stories. Wagner-Martin's groundbreaking article "'Proud and Friendly and Gently': Women in Hemingway's Early Fiction" argues that Hemingway's female characters demonstrate a greater complexity and strength of character than their weaker male counterparts, thus overshadowing them (63–71). Charles J. Nolan Jr. continues this revisionist trend in his "Hemingway's Women's Movement," pointing out the degree to which "Hemingway the writer is much more sympathetic to women and their plight than readers have generally recognized" (22). Nevertheless, such revisionist readings have not prevailed. Brett continues to be judged more than understood by critics, something that Delbert E. Wylder attributes to the residual Victorian attitudes of many male critics ("Two Faces of Brett" 28).

4. Sam S. Baskett sees Brett as an "uncertain image of great value" to her several lovers (45). Although Baskett implies that Brett is trapped within this image, he does not analyze the implications for Brett so much as focus on the male characters in

relation to her. Baskett suggests that Jake is the only one of her lovers who recognizes both her mysterious, almost spiritual, power and her "ordinary, human dimension," and Baskett allows for a more "complicated characterization" of Brett because of her "symbolic beauty" than have most critics to date (45–48). In part because many critics persist in regarding Brett as belonging to an "insider" group, they fail to recognize her aloneness and isolation. H. R. Stoneback points out that for all of Brett's "facile assumption of an insider's 'code' knowledge or style," she is actually "quite alone and quite without the values that sustain such characters as Jake, the Count, Montoya, Romero" (22).

5. Jenks's remarks were later published as "Editing Hemingway: *The Garden of Eden*" in the *Hemingway Review*.

6. For a fuller analysis of Dorothy Parker's intense but essentially short-lived relationship with Hemingway during 1926, see my article "Ernest Hemingway and Dorothy Parker: 'Nothing in her life became her like her almost leaving of it.'"

Chapter 2

1. For Part 1 of "Re-Reading Women," see Jamie Barlowe (-Kayes), "Re-Reading Women: The Example of Catherine Barkley."

2. During Susan Beegel's editorship of *The Hemingway Review*, women's scholarship has been valued and honored, as it also is in Wagner-Martin's most recent collection, *Hemingway: Seven Decades of Criticism*. The collection in which this essay appears seeks as well to bring women's scholarship to the foreground.

3. To make this kind of trivialization clearer, can we even imagine a scholarly book in which someone refers to a man's beautiful upturned penis?

4. See also Cathy N. Davidson.

5. See also Josephine Z. Knopf.

6. I am not claiming that male critics and scholars, following Robert Cohn's lead in the novel, have not also referred to Brett Ashley as Circe or as a bitch; many of them have. For male takes on Brett as bitch or as Circelike, see, for example, Edmund Wilson, *The Wound and the Bow;* Mark Spilka, "The Death of Love in *The Sun Also Rises*"; Carlos Baker, *Hemingway: The Writer as Artist;* Roger Whitlow, *Cassandra's Daughters: The Women in Hemingway;* Milton Cohen, "Circe and Her Swine"; E. Roger Stephenson, "Hemingway's Women: Cats Don't Live in the Mainstream."

7. See also Judy Hen and Ellen Andrews Knodt.

8. See also Mary Katherine Grant, Elizabeth Hyde, Kathleen L. Nichols, Janet Lynne Pearson, Emily Stipes Watts, and Sarah P. Unfried.

9. Even critics and biographers who have named Jake's condition as "lesbian" have, according to Moddelmog, "maintain[ed] Hemingway's identity as a heterosexual; under this ideology, it is safer to make Jake a lesbian because he can never really be one" ("Reconstructing" 191).

10. See also Bernice Kert.

11. See also Joyce Carol Oates.

Chapter 3

1. In "Brett's Problem" Wolfgang E. H. Rudat sees Brett as pivotal to interpreting much of the novel. In "Roles and the Masculine Writer," Jackson J. Benson says that Lady Brett is "to a great extent . . . not only the center of the conflict but the central character in the novel" (81).

2. While in "A Supplement to Hemingway's Reading" Michael Reynolds speaks of Hemingway's interest in Ellis's *Erotic Symbolism,* no mention is made of another Ellis text, *The Soul of Spain,* but given Hemingway's interest in both Spain and Ellis, it is hard to imagine that he was unaware of such a work.

Chapter 4

1. Reynolds also calls Hemingway "an historical artifact, a representative man." See also Reynolds's *Hemingway's Reading, 1910–1940, An Inventory.* In his *The Young Hemingway,* he discusses the "national debate" over sex education (119–20); and James R. McGovern applies the term "Sex O'clock in America" to this period (346). Along with Ellis's writing, Weininger's *Sex and Character* in 1906 and Edward Carpenter's *Love's Coming of Age* (published in the United States in 1911) helped introduce concepts of sexuality, androgyny, and eroticism to the middle class. As Ann Snitow, Christine Stansell, and Sharon Thompson discuss in their introduction to *Powers of Desire,* Carpenter along with Emma Goldman "took sex radicalism out of its enclaves and brought it closer to mainstream sexual politics. . . . Throughout the middle class, a growing acceptance of contraception (within marriage) allowed men and particularly women to disassociate sexual pleasure from conception" (16–17).

2. Among their shared reading was August Strindberg's collection of bleak stories, *Married,* in which "love" is inexplicable and boring and marriage is random; Conrad's *Victory,* with Lena subservient to Axel Heyst; Sinclair Lewis's *Main Street;* Anatole France's *The Red Lily;* Thomas Hardy's *Tess of the D'Urbervilles;* Gabriele D'Annunzio's *The Flame;* Somerset Maugham's *Of Human Bondage* and others by Maugham; Edward Fitzgerald's translation of *The Rubaiyat of Oman Khayyam;* F. Scott Fitzgerald's *This Side of Paradise;* Frederick O'Brien's *White Shadows in the South Seas;* Siegfried L. Sassoon's *Counter-Attack;* James Stephens, *Crock of Gold;* and Kipling ("Supplement" 102–07).

Reflective of the hair fetishism in much of Weininger and Ellis, Peter Griffin records that Hadley sent Hemingway a lock of her hair and notes that in the nine months of their courtship, each wrote a thousand pages to the other (*Along with Youth* 144). Reynolds comments that through his reading and his correspondence with Hadley, Hemingway is clearly creating a persona of himself that reflects those of his heroes—D. H. Lawrence, T. E. Lawrence, and Byron. Reynolds thinks Hemingway is attracted to not only these men's "Foreign travel" but by their "Sexual extravagance" (*Hemingway's Reading* 25). Griffin notes, in oblique confirmation, that

Hadley in one of her letters refers to Hemingway, quoting from the *Prologue to the Canterbury Tales,* as a "verry, perfect, gentile knight" (*Along with Youth* 154).

3. See Spilka, "Victorian Keys to the Early Hemingway: Part I—*John Halifax, Gentleman*"; "Part II—*Fauntleroy* and *Finn*"; "Hemingway and Fauntleroy: An Androgynous Pursuit"; "Victorian Keys to the Early Hemingway: Captain Marryat"; Stein, *The Autobiography of Alice B. Toklas;* William Adair, "*A Farewell to Arms:* A Dream Book"; Kim Moreland, *The Medievalist Impulse in American Literature.*

4. For material about Agnes von Kurowsky, one of the models for Catherine, see Villard and Nagel's *Hemingway in Love and War: The Lost Diary of Agnes von Kurowsky.*

5. For discussion about the order and composition of this collection of memoirs, see Gerry Brenner, "Are We Going to Hemingway's *Feast?*" For comments about Hemingway's tactics in the memoir, see Raeburn, *Fame Became of Him,* 195–98.

Chapter 5

1. See Nadine DeVost's article, "Hemingway's Girls," on Hemingway's intentional use of "girl."

2. This study was inspired, in part, by Pamela Smiley's fascinating essay "Gender-Linked Communication in 'Hills Like White Elephants.'" I am also grateful to the anonymous reviewers for the University of Alabama Press, whose comments have helped me strengthen this essay.

3. Warren Bennett observes of George: "His egocentricity is so concentrated that he expects his wife to deny her own desires, model herself on her husband, and do as he does" ("Poor Kitty" 31). Of their difference of opinion over her hair, Bennett adds, "He wants and expects her to suppress her female sexuality and create the appearance of being like him, a male. But she is female and wants him to see her as such" ("Poor Kitty" 33). Nancy R. Comley and Robert Scholes also refer to the "wife's desire to be a woman rather than a girl (or a boy)" (13).

4. See, for example, J. Barbour (101), Brenner ("From 'Sepi Jingan'" 162), Hagopian (221), Magee, and to a lesser extent Holmesland (232).

5. "All we know about the cat from this description is that it does not want to be dripped on and that it is female" (Lindsay 18).

6. DeVost interprets this change of terminology differently, arguing that "as soon as she discovers that the cat has vanished, she is referred to as 'the American *girl,*' indicating that through this loss, she has suffered a diminution" (my emphasis, 52).

7. Wendolyn E. Tetlow points out that Hemingway named her "Kitty" at one point in the drafts but later deleted the name (79).

8. John V. Hagopian was the first to suggest that the big tortoise-shell is "probably not" the same cat (222). Lodge concurs, noting that the cat's size indicates it is a different animal: "We might infer that the padrone, trying to humor a client, sends up the first cat he can lay hands on, which is in fact quite inappropriate to the wife's needs. This would make the reversal an ironic one at the wife's expense" (11). Warren

Bennett also takes this position ("Poor Kitty" 27). Clarence Lindsay contends that the cat is male (24).

It is both amusing and telling that Oddvar Holmesland asserts, "The tortoise-shell cat, with its animal sensuality, ultimately serves as a metaphor for the dynamic sensuality required to reconcile nature to *man's* desire" (my emphasis, 233). The fact that woman is linked with the second cat indicates that even some of the critics see the female character as purely a reflection of masculine desires.

9. Bennett makes a similar point: "The fact is that Phil has exercised authority over her by virtue of his masculine power, but she is also insinuating that Phil's sexual preferences have taken priority and Phil has been preventing her, in one way or another, from fulfilling her own sexuality" ("That's Not Very Polite" 230).

10. Steven Carter makes a similar comparison (132).

11. If such a scenario of female hypocrisy seems unlikely, it might be useful to read (or reread) Dorothy Parker's often-anthologized short story "The Waltz" as an entertaining reminder of how thoroughly society brainwashed "girls" into praising their male partners regardless of whether they merited such praise. Parker, who was born in 1893 and died in 1967, was a contemporary of Hemingway (1899–1961).

12. Hemingway's use of the term was not idiosyncratic. In Chapter 18 of *The Maltese Falcon*, Sam Spade tells Gutman's henchman (and possible lover), Wilmer, "Put your paw on me and I'm going to make you use your gun," before saying to Gutman, "I told you I didn't like that punk" (149).

13. Robert E. Fleming offers an alternate explanation in his discussion of the story in *The Face in the Mirror: Hemingway's Writers* (48–53), contending that Phil's "vice" is not homosexuality but his use of human beings as material for his work as a writer—his identity as a writer being the omitted information required by Hemingway's famous "iceberg principle." Fleming sees Phil's confrontation with his own image in the mirror as a dramatization of his (and Hemingway's) "moment of self-recognition" (53).

Chapter 6

1. See, for example, Stuart B. McIver, *Hemingway's Key West*, 75–77, and Carlos Baker, *Ernest Hemingway: A Life Story*, 375–76; for an interesting twist on this perspective, see Robert E. Fleming's "The Libel of Dos Passos in *To Have and Have Not.*"

2. See, for example, Rose Marie Burwell, *Hemingway: The Postwar Years and the Posthumous Novels*, 31; Richard S. Pressman, "Individualists or Collectivists?: Steinbeck's *In Dubious Battle* and Hemingway's *To Have and Have Not*"; Keneth Kinnamon, "Hemingway and Politics," 149, 153, and 163–64; Baker, *Life*, 400; and Maxwell Geismar, "No Man Alone Now."

3. See Robert W. Lewis Jr., *Hemingway on Love*, 113–14, for an overview of the discussion of this novel as a turning point in Hemingway's writing.

4. For such a discussion, see Rena Sanderson, "Hemingway and Gender History," 186; and Baker, *The Writer as Artist*, 216.

5. Delbert E. Wylder and Lawrence R. Broer represent two ends of the critical spectrum with regard to Harry Morgan's characterization. In *Hemingway's Heroes*, Wylder argues that *To Have and Have Not* is "the final work in which the anti-hero is the central character" (96). In *Hemingway's Spanish Tragedy*, Broer argues that "Harry is the first major Hemingway protagonist to act out dramatically the author's vision of the majestic life and death of the matador" (80).

6. The complicated history of the novel's composition may account in part for the appearance of the female characters, however marginalized, in part 3. Part 1 was written in 1933 and published in 1934 as the short story "One Trip Across" in *Cosmopolitan* magazine. Part 2 was completed in December 1935 and published in 1936 as "The Tradesman's Return" in *Esquire* magazine. Hemingway initially conceived part 3 as a third story, then was persuaded to link it to the other two Morgan stories, weaving them together so as to make a novel, which was published in October 1937.

7. Lisa Tyler draws a parallel between Richard's misinterpretation of Marie and Marie's later misinterpretation of Richard as "some poor rummy" (255), perceptively noting that "the parallel misreadings are ultimately *not* parallel, for Richard, as the writer, has the power to foist his misinterpretation onto others . . . the power to represent—or, more accurately, *mis*represent—Marie to thousands, perhaps hundreds of thousands, of unsuspecting readers, whereas Marie's misinterpretation—which is surely more reasonable, less extravagant, than Richard's—is purely a personal one" (61).

8. See Mark Spilka, "Dying," for a provocative discussion of abusive marriages in Hemingway's fiction, including *To Have and Have Not*.

9. Nancy R. Comley and Robert Scholes offer a somewhat sympathetic reading of Dorothy: "Poor Dorothy is left to masturbate her evening away. . . . She expects she'll end up as one [a bitch]. In this world—or is it in this [Hemingway] Text?—she can find little else to do" (41). Similarly, in their discussion of Helen's angry monologue—"one of the strongest monologues allowed a woman in the Hemingway Text"—they note "how Hemingway can move toward more interesting female characterization by working a transformation of his standard model of bitchery, a transformation that preserves the ego strength of the bitches but justifies their anger or complicates their sexual appetite with other feelings" (42–43).

10. Robert W. Lewis Jr., for example, notes of Dorothy: "She wonders if she ought to masturbate, and she does, and eros has . . . [become] a tool of inversion (the masturbation of the loveless, lonely beautiful bitch). Masturbation, the final surrender of the eros that must live in two bodies or not at all, the demise of the eros that led to agape" (138–39). Employing a climactic ordering of telling adjectives, he describes this scene as "the final, the female, the most horrible of the scenes that contrast with Harry's death" (138). Lisa Tyler astutely asks: "Why is a scene of a woman masturbating more horrible than one that depicts a man guilty of both evading his

income taxes and driving other men to suicide, a man who has prostituted himself and will soon kill himself, or a smugly well-off family who have profited outrageously from a simple product?" and she concludes, "Lewis's misogyny is showing" (59).

Chapter 7

1. Robert Martin points out in endnote two of his article "Robert Jordan and the 'Spanish Country'" that Hemingway had twenty-six considered titles and 'The Undiscovered Country' comes from Hamlet's "to be or not to be" soliloquy (63):

> But that the dread of something after death,
> The undiscovered country, from whose bourn
> No traveller returns, puzzles the will. (*Hamlet* 3.1.78–80)

2. Pamela Boker discusses Pilar as a "powerful and dominating woman," yet one toward whose maternal qualities Robert Jordan gravitates because of his "unconscious yearning to be rescued by the archaic mother" (87). Robert Gajdusek argues for Pilar's power as a storyteller in her recanting Pablo's execution of the fascists ("Pilar's Tale" 113). Nancy R. Comley and Robert Scholes see Pilar's power as a combining of "masculine massiveness with feminine qualities" (46).

3. Whitlow's list also incorporates a variation of the pejorative dichotomy. For a full discussion, see his chapter, "The Critics on the Women" in *Cassandra's Daughters: The Women in Hemingway* (10–15).

4. This view of Catherine Barkley is a standard one offered by most traditional readings of *A Farewell to Arms*. In "Catherine Barkley and the Hemingway Code," Sandra Whipple Spanier cites several critics fostering this position. She then refutes their stance with a bold, but highly cogent and convincing thesis, presenting Catherine as the true code hero for the novel. Again, Roger Whitlow provides supportive readings for previously maligned female characters in his chapter, "Bitches and Other Simplistic Assumptions" (Cassandra's 49–82).

5. Linda Miller offers two essays supporting Brett as a misunderstood and ultimately positive figure: "Brett Ashley: The Beauty of It All" and "Hemingway's Women: A Reassessment." Spanier suggests that only Joyce Wexler shares her view that Catherine Barkley is a positive character because she possesses strength ("Catherine Barkley" 132).

6. Philip Young has defined this figure as one who possesses "honor and courage which in a life of tension and pain make a man a man and distinguish him from the people who follow random impulses, let down their hair, and are generally messy, perhaps cowardly, and without inviolable rules for how to live holding tight" (*Reconsideration* 63). Young agrees with Earl Rovit's earlier description and both men believe that distinctions exist between that model and the hero figure (Young, *Hemingway* 63–66). The latter, which Rovit calls "tyro," is a complex character tortured,

thoughtful, and a novice initiated in a nihilistic world. The former, the "tutor," is the model through which the "tyro" learns the necessary skills for survival, the "grace under pressure" that comes naturally, instinctually, because it has been ingrained as habit. The tutor is simplistic and professional in the sense that he follows the rules of his trade (53–67).

7. While I quibble with Moddelmog on this small point, her basic argument is sound and stresses a different point than mine. For a thorough discussion of the wound's symbolic importance, see Moddelmog's chapter "The Disabled Able Body and White Heteromasculinity" (*Reading Desire* 119–30).

8. Leo Gurko and John J. Teunissen both point out Arturo Barea's observations that Hemingway does not have a clear understanding of young Spanish girls. Two points are at issue: no Spanish girl would go so easily to a man's bed, nor would she be so naive about kissing as Maria seems to be (Gurko 119; Teunissen 22).

9. Moddelmog discusses gaze in terms of gender in Hemingway. She writes that "the body is identified as female (and simultaneously feminized) in part by the intensity of the male gaze, a pattern that mirrors a dynamic of the larger society" (*Reading Desire* 128). This visual gesture generally represents male power and female submission.

10. Carl P. Eby identifies Aaron Latham's 1977 *New York Times* article, "A Farewell to Machismo," as the turning point for critical studies. Though the general public still maintains its man's man image of Hemingway, increasing numbers of critics are shedding new light on his complex and more inclusive vision. I have already mentioned Spilka, Comley, and Scholes, and would add Moddelmog. Eby also lists Kenneth Lynn and Peter Messent's book-length studies (*Hemingway's Fetishism* 3). Articles are too numerous to mention specifically, but suffice it to say that gender issues have become arguably the hottest topic in current Hemingway scholarship.

11. Maria is also paired as a sibling with Joaquín who tells her she is pretty now that her hair is growing out. Maria's response is, "You'd be pretty with a haircut" (131). (Jordan has also been told earlier by General Goltz that he needs to visit a barber as well.)

12. Though I am among those who believe that Freudian symbolism sometimes goes too far, and as Freud said, "sometimes a cigar is just a cigar," still in gender discussion the phallus is central. And for Hemingway, certainly, hair does have sexual significance.

13. Eby furthers his point beyond the text of *For Whom the Bell Tolls* by relating an incident occurring shortly after completing the manuscript. Carlos Baker's biography suggests that Hemingway, his third wife, Martha, and his sons, Patrick and Gregory, went on a jackrabbit hunt in which reportedly more than four hundred rabbits were killed. Eby interprets this slaughter as masked aggression against Martha; he further points to Maria as likely modeled after her, so therefore, Hemingway as intentionally aggressive against Maria in the novel's text (*Hemingway's Fetishism* 117). This seems stretching a point without clear factual backup.

Chapter 8

1. Kolodny's *The Lay of the Land* traces ways American writers have depicted the American landscape as feminine—as both bountiful mother, as mirror of the self and as the seductive Other who must be mastered. She details the costs of that sense to protagonists who find they can no longer merge "passively with the maternal landscape" but finally succumb to the desire to "master and act upon that same femininity." The cost is nothing less than "psychological separation" from nature itself.

In her essay "Melodramas of Beset Manhood: How Theories of American Fiction Exclude Women Authors," Nina Baym, extending Kolodny's work, suggests that the feminine is present in works by American males in two significant ways: as entrappers inextricably bound up in cultural entanglements and as the very landscape to which male protagonists flee. For nature itself is characterized as feminine in two ways at once: as the mistress (lover) who waits to be taken—the virgin who awaits this male mastery—and the all-nurturing mother who provides succor and respite. Baym's work ultimately seeks to explain how this theory has shaped the American canon and how it necessarily excludes women writers. She traces the development of the canon in its privileging of the romance over the novel, the howling wilderness over the sewing circle, and how that privileging excludes those works by women who find what happens around the hearth or the campfire as compelling and legitimate a narrative as what happens in the forest; and she examines the problematic nature of taking female characters beyond the boundaries of the town and traditional female settings. According to these readings, the feminine presence in most canonical works by American writers is either essentially "pared away" completely (in Westling's words); or the feminine is represented by everything that is entangling, complicating, an other to be avoided at all costs. It is what the hero is always running from, the presence against which the male protagonist must prove his manhood, his worthiness, and out of which he carves his very identity. See Kolodny (28, 4), Baym, Westling, and Glen A. Love. See also *Hemingway and the Natural World*, edited by Robert Fleming. The essays in this volume came out of the 1997 International Hemingway Conference whose theme was Hemingway's relationship to the natural world.

2. This echoes Love's belief that Hemingway's "aggressive and isolated individualism" competes and "wars against those natural manifestations he claims to love." Love also says that the fact that Hemingway "may have repented does not change the fact that in most of his fiction there is no room to maneuver except at the edge of death."

3. Cowley, of course, extends Edmund Wilson's reading five years earlier (see "Ernest Hemingway: Bourdon Gauge of Morale"). Recent biographical criticism has called into question whether or not it is the *war* that is the "thing left out." See for example Kenneth Lynn's interpretation of the story (102–08).

4. For a representative example see Carrabine. See Summerhayes for an interesting interpretation that plays off this premise.

5. Again, the difficulty with Lynn's premise that the thing left out is in conflict

with Hemingway's mother is that there is no more *textual* evidence for this than for the war.

6. For example, see William Bysshe Stein, and for the idea that the entrapment of marriage is what is in the swamp, see Moddelmog, "Unifying Consciousness."

7. The term comes from Leo Marx's *The Machine in the Garden,* in which he describes that midpoint between savage nature and civilization, an oasis and temporary stay against the encroachments from either side. In this, "River" fits into the romantic tradition in American literature of Cooper, Hawthorne, Melville, and Thoreau. It is a "Walden" of sorts, part natural order, part created order. On one side is civilization with its ambiguous sometimes evil complexities; on the other is that sense of "unhandseled" nature that Thoreau found on Mt. Ktaadan. "River" fits nicely into this tradition, with civilization on one side—with its railroad and blackened town of Seney—and the swamp on the other. Most of the story takes place in the area of the *green:* the middle position.

8. See Pamela Smiley's "Gender-Linked Miscommunication" and Darrel Mansell's "Words Lost in *In Our Time*" for an intriguing discussion of the role of wordlessness and silence.

9. See especially Fiedler's chapter, "The Failure of Sentiment and the Evasion of Love," in *Love and Death in the American Novel* (337–90).

10. See also the discussion of the gathering metaphor of the monster in Gilbert and Gubar, *Madwomen in the Attic,* 187–247.

11. A fuller discussion of the concept of the spirit animal and what it means to slay it can be found in my essays, "Across the River and into the Stream" and "Memory, Grief, and the Terrain of Desire."

Chapter 9

1. This essay will refer to works Hemingway read (*Moby-Dick,* the poetry of Whitman, Thor Heyerdahl's *Kon-Tiki*) before composing *The Old Man and the Sea,* as well as books that he may have read during its composition (Carson's *The Sea Around Us* and *Under the Sea Wind,* Steinbeck and Ricketts's *The Log from the Sea of Cortez*). Hemingway drafted his novella in January and February 1951 (Baker, *Life* 489–90) but did not publish the story until 1 September 1952, in a single installment of *Life* magazine. The long lag between the initial composition of the story and its publication has interesting implications for understanding how Hemingway's reading might have influenced *The Old Man and the Sea* and its ecological ethics. During this period, Hemingway was reading Carson, Steinbeck, and Ricketts and was probably rereading *Moby-Dick,* celebrating its centennial year in 1951. The John F. Kennedy Library holds two typescripts of *The Old Man and the Sea* with corrections in ink; however, Mary Hemingway recalled that her husband "did the whole thing by hand and then I typed it" (qtd. in Bruccoli 191). No longhand draft of *The Old Man and the Sea* has yet been located, making a study of Hemingway's possible revisions based on his 1951 reading impossible.

2. When Hemingway won the Nobel Prize, in part for his achievement in *The Old Man and the Sea,* he gave his medal to the Virgin of Cobre, to be kept in her sanctuary at Santiago de Cuba (Baker, *Life* 528).

3. Originally published in 1941 as *Sea of Cortez: A Leisurely Journal of Travel and Research,* this book was reissued in 1951 as *The Log from the Sea of Cortez,* with its scientific apparatus (an appendix including a phyletic catalogue on the marine animals of the Panamic faunal province) removed.

4. Hemingway owned a copy of the 1951 edition (Brasch and Sigman).

5. Hemingway owned a copy of *Kon-Tiki,* a nonfiction bestseller of 1950, the year before he wrote *The Old Man and the Sea* (Brasch and Sigman).

6. Santiago also admires the loggerheads because they are "strange in their lovemaking" (36), and in *To Have and Have Not,* Hemingway refers to the widely held belief that loggerheads copulate for three days—"Do they really do it three days? Coot for three days?" Marie asks Harry (113). For this reason, the loggerhead eggs that Santiago eats to "give himself strength" (37) are considered an aphrodisiac (Dennis), and some of this folklore may resonate in his three-day battle with the fish.

Hemingway's description of the loggerhead turtle eating jellyfish with its eyes closed is probably drawn from Thomas Barbour's *A Naturalist in Cuba,* a book in Hemingway's library (Brasch and Sigman). Barbour writes:

> I saw an enormous loggerhead ease up to a Portuguese man-of-war, close its eyes, and nip at the beast. Physalia is well provided with stinging cells and its tentacles are dangerous things to touch. It was amusing to see the old turtle close his eyes as he made his dab at the jellyfish. I have no doubt that the membranes surrounding his eyeballs were the only place where the stinging cells of the siphonophore's arms would have been effective. All other regions were protected by heavy armor. (76)

7. Malcolm Cowley notes that when *The Old Man and the Sea* was published, it was widely referred to as "the poor man's *Moby-Dick*" ("Hemingway's Novel" 106).

8. In Caribbean Spanish, the word *galano,* when applied to an animal, simply means having a dappled or mottled skin (Mandel, e-mail to Beegel). Hence, the Cuban common name for this shark helps with identification. Shark expert Dr. Perry Gilbert notes that near the village of Cojimar a "grande Galano" may be a bull shark (in Farrington 32), or *Carcharhinus leucas.* However, this species, which can inhabit fresh and brackish water as well as saltwater, is never found far from land (R. Ellis 139) and hence cannot be Santiago's deepwater *galano.* Miriam B. Mandel located among Hemingway's papers a 1936 list of commercially valuable fish published by the Cuban secretary of agriculture giving for a *galano* the scientific name of *Charcharias limbatus* (*Reading Hemingway* 352), probably an error for *Carcharhinus limbatus.* But the characteristic black-tipped fins of *C. limbatus* (R. Ellis 302) mean it cannot be Santiago's *galano,* which has "white-tipped wide pectoral fins" (107). Mandel's corre-

spondence with Dr. José I. Castro, senior research scientist of the National Marine Fisheries Service, Miami Branch, identifies the *galano* as the oceanic whitetip, *Carcharhinus longimanus* (*Reading Hemingway* 352, 522). In my opinion, this is the only identification that satisfactorily covers the shark's deepwater habitat, mottled skin, white-tipped fins, aggressive scavenging behavior, and notoriety as a man-eater.

9. Rachel Carson first published *Under the Sea Wind* in 1941. The book was republished in April 1952, when it joined *The Sea Around Us* on the *New York Times* bestseller list (Lear 226). Hemingway owned a copy of the 1952 edition (Brasch and Sigman).

Chapter 10

1. For a brief summary of Hemingway's regard for Wister and his recognition of the bond between Wister's commitment to style and his own, see Baker's note in *Ernest Hemingway: Selected Letters, 1917–1961*, 255. In response to Wister's praise of plain speech, Hemingway wrote: "All we can do is to restore the old language—as it is spoken it should be written or it dies—is to the good" (*SL* 301).

2. See Michael Reynolds's "Hemingway's West: Another Country of the Heart."

3. The remainder of this essay incorporates some material I used in chapter 3 of *Hemingway: The Postwar Years and the Posthumous Novels*.

4. In a letter dated 31 December 1948 to Charles Scribner, Hemingway says of what he referred to as the "Land, Sea and Air" novel: "[it] starts with the sea in 1936" (Princeton University Library). In a later letter to Scribner he asks him to not mention to anyone that his present "old man story" is related to an unnamed 1936 piece. In April 1936 he had published "On the Blue Water: A Gulf Stream Letter" in *Esquire*, a short version of what became *The Old Man and the Sea*. That Hemingway did further work on *The Old Man and the Sea* during that period is supported by the facts that there is no known holograph manuscript of the work and that word counts on the virtually clean typescript at the John F. Kennedy Library (files 190–91 and 190–92) go as high as 1,805 per day, nearly double Hemingway's usual production. This strongly suggests that he was working with material he had written previously.

See also Darrel Mansell's "When Did Ernest Hemingway Write *The Old Man and the Sea?*"

5. Consider how many variations there are on the adage, "A man with nothing to lose makes a bad enemy."

6. In a 9 July 1976? letter to Mary Hemingway from Charles Scribner Jr., discussing Mary's suggested list of future publications, Scribner says that it is going to be very difficult to disentangle the elephant story from the remainder of the novel. This is the first evidence I have seen that Hemingway's publisher recognized the connection between the damaged children and the troubled adults who populate his fiction.

7. Torpex is an explosive powder used in making torpedoes, hence part of the submarine hunting that Hudson has chosen.

Chapter 11

1. I would like to thank Debian Marty for her perceptive comments on various drafts of this essay and especially for her help in working out some of the complexities of my argument.

2. Both *The Garden of Eden* and "The Last Good Country" were unfinished at Hemingway's death and therefore published posthumously. In *Hemingway's Quarrel with Androgyny,* Mark Spilka notes that the last date on the unfinished manuscript for "The Last Good Country" is 20 July 1958, about the time Hemingway began revising earlier drafts of *The Garden of Eden* (277). Not incidentally, Hemingway's more explicit representations of transgressive behaviors and relationships are to be found in works not published in his time. However, I believe, as do many other Hemingway critics, that these works draw our attention to concerns and issues that have always been present in Hemingway's fiction.

3. Several critics, including Toni Morrison, interpret Bugs's thumping of Ad more severely. Morrison points to Kenneth Lynn's claim that Bugs might be solicitous but he is also a sadist and a prophet, thus playing a dual role of nurturer and destroyer (Lynn 272). While I admit that Bugs's conduct has this element of ambiguity—an element that prevents the white men he encounters from knowing whether his gestures and comments are threats or kindhearted directions—I also believe that Bugs demonstrates true affection for Ad. In fact, his drama with Ad might be staged to keep Nick from hanging around too long, thus scaring off the white man who underestimates his intelligence and fails to see his humanity. Reading Bugs's actions accurately is made difficult by the fact that we see him through Nick, who does not really see Bugs at all. As Morrison notes, the typical role of Hemingway's black men is to disturb the reality of the white male protagonist, not to set forth an agenda of their own: "No matter if [Hemingway's black male characters] are loyal or resistant nurses, nourishing *and* bashing the master's body, these black men articulate the narrator's doom and gainsay the protagonist-narrator's construction of himself" (83–84).

4. Nick Adams will suffer a similar mental instability during his enlistment in World War I. In "A Way You'll Never Be," he attempts to hold back hostile outbreaks during conversations with others but is often unable to keep "it" from coming on. For instance, while speaking to Captain Paravicini, Nick thinks, "He felt it coming on again" and tries to hold it in but finally knows "he could not stop it now" (*NAS* 146).

5. According to Barrie Thorne, in 1986, "nationally the most common household, nearly half of the total, now has an adult male and an adult female wage earner, with or without children; the next most common types of household are single-parent families and unmarried couples living together; then come individuals living

alone. Gay and lesbian couples, some with children, are increasingly visible, although census takers do not count them as a separate category" (9).

6. For a description of these changes in the family, see Fass, *The Damned and the Beautiful* and Hawley, *The Great War and the Search for a Modern Order.*

7. References to *The Garden of Eden* manuscripts denote series, folder numbers, and pages as they were classified at the John F. Kennedy Library in the summer of 1993.

8. Although David is more reticent about his feelings regarding the multiple implications of the change, in the manuscript we also see him expressing some openness to incest. When Marita tells him that her brother, who died in the war, was in love with her, David repeats the weak joke told to him once by "a girl" that he "never minded incest if it was in the same family" (ser. 422, folder 133, second p. 22).

9. Consider David's musing after finishing his writing for the day: "His thoughts turned to the two girls and he wondered if he should go find them and see what they wanted to do or if they wanted to go off and swim. After all, it was Marita's and his day and she might be waiting" (211). Here it is clear that David has accepted Catherine and Marita's arrangement to share him.

10. Robert E. Fleming explores this provisional ending in his essay "The Endings of Hemingway's *Garden of Eden.*" He is more cynical about the state of Catherine and David's marriage, claiming that David has basically become Catherine's caretaker: "David and Catherine's relationship has become a parody of the one they shared in the early pages of the novel, furthering the theme that the discovery of evil makes it impossible to dwell in the Garden of Eden" (268).

11. Consider, for example, Robert Jordan's thoughts about his parents. His father, Jordan claims, was "just a coward. . . . Because if he wasn't a coward he would have stood up to that woman [Jordan's mother] and not let her bully him" (*FWTBT* 365).

12. In "Fathers and Sons" we get another hint of the connection between Nick and Littless when an adult Nick thinks back on his childhood: "There was only one person in his family that he liked the smell of, one sister. All the others he avoided all contact with" (*NAS* 243). Although Nick does not identify the sister here, it makes sense, given what happens in "The Last Good Country," to presume that he is referring to Littless.

13. The inequities of the traditional (also called the patriarchal) family are delineated in much feminist scholarship on the family, including Thorne and Yalom's *Rethinking the Family.* More recently, Stuart Aitken proposes new forms of community that "justly reflect the diverse and continuously changing lives of men, women, and children" (196).

14. Similarly, in "Fathers and Sons," Nick recalls the insufficiency with which his father answered his questions about sexual matters: "His father had summed up the whole matter by stating that masturbation produced blindness, insanity, and death, while a man who went with prostitutes would contract hideous venereal diseases and that the thing to do was to keep your hands off of people" (*NAS* 237).

15. As Kate Chedgzoy explains, "the Conservative Government's 1988 attack on

lesbian and gay rights in Section 28 of the Local Government . . . stigmatised households headed by lesbians or gay men as 'pretended family relationships.' "

Chapter 12

1. Kathy G. Willingham, in her essay "Hemingway's *The Garden of Eden:* Writing with the Body," has argued that Catherine wants to be an artist but cannot succeed because of her feelings of inadequacy and her need for David to "act as scribe" (47). I argue that Catherine does not so much need David as a scribe for her artistic expression; but as a partner in her invention of a world without restrictive gender roles.

2. John Raeburn makes a similar point in his essay "Sex and Art in *The Garden of Eden.*" He writes, "Catherine's reversals of erotic and sexual roles derive in part from her sense of powerlessness in the world, her perception that women's lives are constrained by rigid cultural definitions of appropriate behavior and that men are freer to construct their identities" (114). Raeburn goes on to argue that the novel is also very much concerned with the inviolability of writing as a professional discipline and the "supreme importance of art itself" (121).

3. David admits that his ability to write or not to write is wrapped up in his sexual identity. Once the manuscripts are burned, he makes a few aborted attempts at rewriting the original texts. The clippings represent a male-centered world of power and authority; without them he feels creatively and sexually powerless.

4. In his essay on the British critical reception of *The Garden of Eden,* Roy Simmonds points out that many critics find Marita "a major flaw in the book's emotional structure" (18). John Raeburn describes her as "mostly pasteboard" ("Sex and Art" 112). Paul Taylor feels "Marita never really begins to exist" (5). Steven Roe writes that "her abject subservience bespeaks a fanatical, soul-less longing for self-abasement" (56). If we see Marita as consciously and determinedly amorphous, taking on the role of "good wife" once she realizes this is what Catherine and David expect, then her shallowness may seem more crafted and deliberate.

5. The manuscript offers a third conclusion that involves the subplot of Nick and Barbara. Since I have not discussed the Andy/Nick/Barbara subplot here, I would simply refer the reader to Robert E. Fleming's article, "The Endings of Hemingway's *The Garden of Eden,*" which offers a thorough explanation of this parallel plot and its tentative conclusion.

6. Catherine A. MacKinnon has summarized why it is so crucial for Marita to transform herself into the passive boy: "Vulnerability means the appearance/reality of easy sexual access; passivity means receptivity and disabled resistance; softness means pregnability by something hard" (530–31). By maintaining the qualities of the female stereotype, staying in the role of "penetrated," Marita allows David to structure their encounter on his own terms.

7. In a letter to Mary dated 5 May 1947, Hemingway describes how much he looks forward to having his "dearest wife and partner and friend and Pete home." In

a letter dated 2 May 1947, Hemingway tells his wife that he has dyed his hair red as a special surprise for her and, in parentheses, "also for Pete and for Catherine."

8. In "Hemingway's *The Garden of Eden*" Burwell offers a thorough discussion of the women in Hemingway's life who serve as models for Catherine Bourne: his four wives, Zelda Fitzgerald, and Jane Mason.

Chapter 14

The epigraph containing the Grace Hall Hemingway quote is taken from "Notes for Art Talk," October 1928, from the private collection of John E. Sanford (used with permission). Here and throughout I have preserved the capitalization and punctuation of the original. I am deeply grateful to John Sanford for his willingness to share his personal recollections of his grandmother, Grace Hall Hemingway, as well as for the generosity with which he made available various family scrapbook items pertaining to her artistic careers.

1. For the complete list of "literary forebears" Hemingway acknowledges, see the Plimpton interview, 118. For a similar, although less formal, list, see Ross's *Portrait of Hemingway* 47, 50–52.

2. Many critics have considered the influence of the visual arts on Hemingway's style. See especially Josephs's "How did Hemingway Write" and Hays's "Wright, Cézanne, and Hemingway" (Cézanne), Spilka's *Hemingway's Quarrel with Androgyny* (Rodin), and Brogan (the Cubists). This essay is particularly informed by Brogan's discussion of *In Our Time* as a "cubist anatomy" and Hays's consideration of the disappearance of the foreground/background distinction in Cézanne's landscapes.

3. It is likely, although by no means certain, that he played in chamber groups at home as well. His elder sister, Marcelline, played the viola; he played the cello. In choosing instruments for her children, Grace Hemingway was very likely creating a Hemingway family chamber group.

4. In editing his father's work, *True at First Light*, Patrick Hemingway notes that "this book is organized more on a sort of musical basis. It rises and falls, rises and falls, rises and falls" (10) and says "Almost everything that a writer writes if he is a writer of fiction has gone through his memory and imagination and comes out a little more structured and a little bit more interesting" (15).

5. I strongly recommend that the reader unfamiliar with the musical terms I discuss listen to recordings of the specific pieces recommended below. Accessing a website such as Classical MIDI Archives will allow readers to listen to these pieces as they read. Ludwig Van Beethoven's *Symphony no. 5* (1st movement) illustrates the expectation created by harmonic progression. An example of a ground bass may be found in the opening measures of Johann Pachelbel's *Canon in D* (original version, for strings). The "subject" and the "answer," which both echoes and develops it harmonically, may be heard in J. S. Bach's "Fugue #2 in cm" (BWV 847) from *The Well-Tempered Clavier, Books I and II.*

6. I have borrowed the application of the visual terms "foreground" and "back-

ground" as descriptors for contrapuntal effects from Douglas Hofstadter's *Gödel, Escher, Bach.* Hofstadter constructs an analogy between this contrapuntal feature and the effect of contemplating Escher's "tiling" works. For a visual example of this effect, see, in Hofstadter, the reproduction of Escher's "Tiling of the plane using birds" (68).

7. This description of counterpoint is adapted from *The New York Times Book Review* and *Kansas City Star* reviews of *In Our Time.* See Michael Reynolds's "Hemingway as American Icon" in Voss.

8. Many children of their class and time had musical training. When Stein left high school, her brother Michael "thought she should become a musician . . . but the idea did not excite her" (Mellow, *Charmed Circle* 26). She could, however, sing from sheet music (see photograph, Mellow 436a).

9. For an elaboration of the possibilities of dialogism, or polychronous prose, and the audience's role in constructing that aspect of prose discourse, see Bakhtin's "Discourse in the Novel," in which he states that "every word is directed toward an answer and cannot escape the profound influence of the answering word that it anticipates" and that despite being "monologic in their structure," "[a]ll rhetorical forms . . . are oriented toward the listener and his answer" (*The Dialogic Imagination* 280). Although Bakhtin's approach does not directly state that prose can thus evince simultaneous polyvocalism—nor that this simultaneity depends to a great extent on reader memory—these ideas are implicit in, and extensions of, his discussion.

10. This line also works as a pictoral round; Alice Toklas chose this line, printed in a circle, as their household's symbol. A proficient pianist (Simon 9, 14; Stendhal 61), Toklas once said that in order to type Stein's *The Making of Americans,* she had to develop "a Gertrude Stein technique, like playing Bach" (Simon 72).

11. Many years later, when asked what one needs in order to be a writer, Hemingway began his answer with "All you need is a perfect ear, [and] absolute pitch" (Hotchner 200). His "ear" and "pitch" are evident in *Torrents of Spring,* his parody of Sherwood Anderson's *Dark Laughter.* A good ear and perfect pitch may be desirable in a writer, but they are essential to the parodist.

12. Critical opinion regarding what the wife wants varies widely. See Paul Smith 46–48.

13. For a more detailed explanation of the differences between canon and fugue, see Hofstadter 8–9. For a more technical discussion, with musical examples, see Kennan 90–113 (canon), and 201–48 (fugue).

14. In scansion, "^" indicates an unstressed syllable and "/" indicates a stressed syllable. For an excellent discussion of how Hemingway crafted the poetics (or musicality) of the opening of *A Farewell to Arms,* see Michael Reynolds's *Hemingway's First War* 54-57, in which he reprints the opening section as a poem.

15. For a detailed description of "Hills Like White Elephants" as a "theme and variation," see Justice.

16. For a more complete list of Hemingway's broken artistic friendships, see, e.g., Bruccoli, *Fitzgerald and Hemingway* 4.

17. Grace Hemingway's paintings, which have been shown in The Art Institute

of Chicago (Sellroe 2), reveal her preoccupation with form and composition. One in particular that depicts a Taos street scene "won her an award," and is "probably her finest" (Sanford 6); it bears more than passing resemblance to the Cézanne landscapes of the sort Hemingway found so resonant with his own work ("On Writing" 218; see also Hays, "Wright, Cézanne and Hemingway"). (This untitled painting is privately owned by Carol Sanford Coolidge.) Art critic Adah Robinson located Grace Hemingway's "universal appeal" in her achieving "the interpretation of the old masters combined with the technique of the moderns" (Sellroe 2).

Chapter 15

1. This essay evolved out of a larger project, an annotation of Hemingway's nonfiction, which is supported by a generous three-year grant from the National Endowment for the Humanities.

2. Burwell provides a schematized summary of these "reiterated thematic links" at the beginning of her book (xxiv–xxv).

3. There are many other such repetitions in Hemingway. In nine years, he wrote several times about the animals sacrificed at Smyrna: they appear in a journalistic essay (27 January 1923, *Toronto Daily Star;* rpt. *Dateline: Toronto,* 249–52), in interchapter 2 of *In Our Time* (1925); in "On the Quai at Smyrna," added as an introduction to *In Our Time* (1930); and twice in *Death in the Afternoon* (1932; 2, 135). When the Old Lady complains about the repetition, he apologizes, "I know it and I'm sorry. . . . I won't write about them again. I promise" (*DIA* 135).

4. Trogdon suggests that Dorman-Smith and Hemingway's argument is based on Melville's description of New Bedford, Massachusetts, where "the beautiful and bountiful horse-chestnuts, candelabra-wise, proffer the passer-by their tapering upright cones of congregated blossoms." The image appears only once in *Moby Dick,* in the penultimate paragraph of chapter 6.

5. Pauline was similarly excised from much of *A Moveable Feast* and is just as easily retrievable. In the racing episode, for example, "Pauline and I" was changed to a "we" for which "Hadley" can be read as a referent (Tavernier-Courbin 188). And Pauline, though not named, is obviously one of the unnamed rich who destroyed the happy relationship between Ernest and Hadley.

6. According to Carlos Baker, Hemingway wrote his impressions of his second African safari in the fall of 1954 (*Life* 526). According to Mary Hemingway, he was still "[w]riting every morning about Africa and his native friends there" in September 1955 (408, 426).

7. Although the three-part serial was not paginated, I have numbered the pages consecutively. In the penultimate page of part 3 of the *Sports Illustrated* version of *African Journal,* there is only one cut. This cut material, identified by Carl P. Eby as "Cut 83," refers to Hemingway's typescript p. 550 (Firestone Library, Scribner Archives; Ernest Hemingway, African Book, box 1, folder 4) and mentions the African bride Debba who, like Mary, is considered in a positive light. The British, the Dutch,

and "bible-punching" Protestants—both men and women—come under brief attack, after which the published version continues with "And I remember that more than half of my life had been spent at night." After one short paragraph, we get the long paragraph that presents the flower narrative. (I am grateful to Professor Eby, who generously shared his notes with me.)

8. The brief reference to "Western Wind" ("I slept happily with my true love in my arms") also recalls *A Farewell to Arms,* when Henry wishes "that my love were in my arms and I in my bed again" (189). It is interesting that flower imagery also surfaces, albeit briefly, in this novel. The chestnut and the wisteria appear in the first chapter:

> The mountain that was beyond the valley and the hillside where the chestnut forest grew was captured and . . . we crossed the river in August and lived in a house in Gorizia that had a fountain and many thick shady trees in a walled garden and a wistaria vine purple on the side of the house. (*AFTA* 5)

A Farewell to Arms is, of course, a retrospective narrative about desertion from war and the death of a woman in childbirth. It is, in many ways, a self-justifying narrative in which the narrator reveals his flaws and his guilt. The flowers that appear in this short passage of *A Farewell to Arms* are unremarkable in themselves, but connecting them to their counterparts in the other narratives indicates how firmly Hemingway had connected the flowers to the pain that attends betrayal.

9. In May 1922, Hadley was not yet "the mother of my oldest son": John Hadley Nicanor Hemingway (Bumby) was born in 1923.

10. Although *True at First Light* (1999), edited by Patrick Hemingway from the same manuscript that yielded the *African Journal,* excludes the flower narrative that I discuss in this essay, it offers more details about the relationship between Papa and Debba. In *True at First Light,* as Papa lies on his cot, his pistol between his legs, his shotgun "rigidly comfortable" at his side, he considers one of the problems a man with two wives faces: how to spend the remainder of the night: "it was both my duty and my great and lovely pleasure to be in camp when Miss Mary should return. It was also my duty and my wonderful pleasure to be with Debba" (281). He is, nevertheless, a happy man: "how lucky I was to know Miss Mary and have her do me the great honor of being married to me and to Miss Debba the Queen of the Ngomas" (281). He feels no moral compunctions, explaining, "Now that we had religion it was easy. Ngui, Mthuka and I could decide what was a sin and what was not" (*TAFL* 282). According to Mary, "Papa makes up the religion. . . . He and Ngui and the others" (*TAFL* 79).

11. The story was attributed to Jim Gamble late in the process of composition. The chapter was already in typescript when Hemingway decided to cut a section that begins, "We remembered that same spring with the horse chestnuts in bloom . . . and the heavy wisteria vine in the garden of the inn at Aigle." He replaced this with

a handwritten section that attributes the vine to Jim Gamble and adds much of the sharp, pointed dialogue that appears in the published version. This same typescript contains the handwritten addition of Hadley's remark, "But that's gone now" (Kennedy Library, file 144).

12. Hadley knew about Agnes von Kurowsky and about the wealthy Jim Gamble. And just as in 1918 Agnes had urged Ernest to resist Gamble's lavish hospitality, which she thought might turn him into a "sponger, a floater, and a bum" (qtd. in Baker, *Life* 54), so in 1920 Hadley urged Ernest to resist Gamble's all-expense-paid trip to Rome "unless . . . it was going to be great gain to your work" (qtd. in Diliberto 48).

13. As a reporter for the *Toronto Star,* Hemingway had been in Genoa for three weeks, from 6 to 27 April 1922, and was scheduled to go to Russia. Although that assignment never materialized, it was a real possibility in May, and Hadley dreaded it. Even in Paris, before the Genoa trip, Hadley was often alone. Sokoloff writes, "Brides are notoriously lonely the first year or so of marriage, but Hadley was especially so, torn out of context, as it were, in a strange city, and with Ernest absorbed and away, busy with his work so much of every day" (51). The Genoa trip had been particularly stressful for her. According to Sokoloff, "Hadley was lonely and a little frightened without Ernest" (53). Another long separation threatened, and Hadley resisted it. Michael Reynolds suggests that "[T]he prospect of an even longer Russian trip may have triggered the first serious argument of their marriage" (*Paris Years* 53).

14. It turns the victim who dares to speak into the guilty. The situation is reminiscent of Ernest's anger when Hadley spoke of his affair with Pauline; by voicing the event, he argued, she (and not his infidelity) destroyed their marriage.

15. Dorman-Smith wrote to Carlos Baker that "Hadley had refused to be parted from her toilet bottles. A furious Hemingway declined to carry them. For the sake of peace I stuffed them into my already heavy rucksack. Hemingway had developed a form of mountain sickness and Hadley had to help him on. . . . The journey became something of a nightmare with Hem sick, Hadley worried and myself carrying two packs forward at a time and returning for the odd one" (qtd. in Diliberto 118).

16. According to Burwell, "On 18 April 1961 Hemingway wrote Charles Scribner, telling him that the book [*A Moveable Feast*] should not be published" and that "Mary withheld the letter," which forbade publication (*Postwar Years* 2, 155, 161, 183–84, 186).

Chapter 16

1. For a vivid account of the experience, see Martha Gellhorn, "Night Life in the Sky" 18–19, 31 revised and republished as "The Black Widow" in her collection of war journalism, *The Face of War* 153–61.

2. The play opened for a weeklong preliminary run on 10 June 1946 at the Devonshire Park in Eastbourne before its premiere on 18 June 1946 at the Embassy Thea-

ter in Swiss Cottage, North London (which Gellhorn described as the equivalent of Off-Broadway). It then moved to the Duchess Theater in London's West End and ran for forty performances from 22 July to 24 August, 1946.

3. The divorce decree, granted in Cuba to Hemingway on the grounds of desertion, was issued on 21 December 1945.

4. For an account, see Martha Gellhorn, "Mr. Ma's Tigers," chapter 2 in *Travels with Myself and Another* 19–63.

5. See Bernice Kert's landmark book, *The Hemingway Women: Those Who Loved Him—The Wives and Others* 385–92 and 397–98. Michael Reynolds's *Hemingway: The Final Years* offers new and meticulously documented information on the scope and nature of Hemingway's patrol operations. Dan Simmons's novel *The Crook Factory* also draws from a wealth of archival sources, including FBI documents, in its fictional portrayal of Hemingway's submarine-hunting activities during World War II.

6. At one extreme, John Leo of *U.S. News and World Reports* called *Thelma and Louise* "toxic feminism" and found in its "paean to transformative violence" an "explicit fascist theme" (20). On the other hand, film critic Janet Maslin suggested that what really rankled some about the movie was "something as simple as it is powerful: the fact that the men in this story don't really matter." She wrote of the film's heroines: "Their adventures, while tinged with the fatalism that attends any crime spree, have the thrilling, life-affirming energy for which the best road movies are remembered (C1).

7. The film's producer, Callie Khouri, credits her husband, David Warfield, with what she thinks is the most accurate description of the movie (Rohrter).

8. A revised version of Gubar's essay appears as "Charred Skirts and Deathmask: World War II and the Blitz on Women" in Sandra M. Gilbert and Susan Gubar's *No Man's Land*.

9. Critical studies of gender, war, and twentieth-century literature have burgeoned in the past decade and a half. Important works include Gilbert and Gubar, *No Man's Land;* Shari Benstock, *Women of the Left Bank;* Margaret Randolph Higonnet et al., eds., *Behind the Lines;* Helen M. Cooper, Adrienne Auslander Munich, and Susan Merrill Squier, eds., *Arms and the Woman;* Susan Schweik, *A Gulf So Deeply Cut;* Jean Gallagher, *The World Wars through the Female Gaze;* and Sayre P. Sheldon, ed., *Her War Story*.

10. I am grateful to Michael Reynolds and the Hemingway Foundation for permission to quote from the two letters from Hemingway to Colebaugh cited in this essay. Letters from Chenery to Hemingway, Gellhorn to Chenery, and Hemingway to Colebaugh are located in the Crowell-Collier Publishing Company Records, Manuscripts and Archives Division, the New York Public Library, Astor, Lenox and Tilden foundations.

11. I am grateful to Dr. Alexander Matthews for permission to quote from the Gellhorn letters and manuscript materials cited in this essay. A revised version of Gellhorn's article (without the paragraph on the Chengtu airfield) is republished as "The Canton Front" in *The Face of War* 71–83.

12. See Martha Gellhorn, "Messing About in Boats" in *Travels with Myself and Another* 64–108.

13. Loose in the manila file folder containing the raw materials for *Collier's* 22 July 1944 issue may be found a small slip of white paper, a standard editor's note bearing a title and lead-in for the story, apparently once pasted on the upper right corner of the radiogram of Hemingway's D-day report. Judging from the swath of yellowed glue remaining on the radiogram, the note would have obscured the purple stamp indicating the date and time that the report was filed. Whether this was done intentionally or accidentally, it is impossible to know.

14. In fact, Gellhorn must have kept a carbon of her typescript of the hospital piece. The version reprinted in *The Face of War* includes some of the material omitted from the piece published in the 5 November 1944 issue of *Collier's*, including portions razored out of the manuscript in the *Collier's* files by military censors—details such as the fact that the two hospital ships preceding hers had hit mines as well as the exact names of "those now famous and unhealthy beaches"—"Easy Red" and "Dog Red." The paragraph describing the "armada of the invasion" that was missing in the published magazine piece is included in *The Face of War*.

Chapter 17

1. See Gilbert and Gubar, *The Madwoman in the Attic*; see also Showalter, *A Literature of Their Own* and Erkkila, *The Wicked Sisters*.

2. See Erkkila, *The Wicked Sisters*.

3. See Ammons, *Conflicting Stories*; Guy Reynolds, *Willa Cather in Context*; Rado, *Rereading Modernism*; Kerr, "Feeling 'Half Feminine'"; and Minter, "The Fear of Feminization." See also Gilbert and Gubar, *No Man's Land*, Ammons, G. Reynolds, Rado, and Kerr.

Works Cited

Achuff, Louise R. "'Nice' and 'Pleasant' in *The Sun Also Rises*." *Hemingway Review* 10.2 (1991): 42–46.

Adair, William. "*For Whom the Bell Tolls* as Family Romance." *Arizona Quarterly* 41.4 (1985): 329–37.

———. "*A Farewell to Arms:* A Dream Book." *Journal of Narrative Technique* 5.1 (1975): 40–56.

Adams, Timothy Dow. *Telling Lies in Modern American Autobiography.* Chapel Hill: U of North Carolina P, 1990.

Aitken, Stuart C. *Family Fantasies and Community Space.* New Brunswick: Rutgers UP, 1998.

Ammons, Elizabeth. *Conflicting Stories: American Women Writers at the Turn into the Twentieth Century.* New York: Oxford UP, 1992.

Angelou, Maya. *I Know Why the Caged Bird Sings.* New York: Bantam, 1971.

Atkinson, Brooks. Rev. of *Love Goes to Press. New York Times* 2 Jan. 1947, 22.

Bach, J. S. Fugue 2, C minor (BWV 847). *The Well-Tempered Clavier, Books I and II, Complete.* New York: Dover, 1983.

Backman, Melvin. "Hemingway: The Matador and the Crucified." *Modern Fiction Studies* 1 (1955): 2–11.

Baker, Carlos. *Ernest Hemingway: A Life Story.* New York: Scribner's, 1969.

———. *Hemingway: The Writer as Artist.* 4th ed. Princeton: Princeton UP, 1972.

———, ed. *Ernest Hemingway: Selected Letters, 1917–1961.* New York: Scribner's, 1981.

Bakhtin, M. M. *The Dialogic Imagination.* Trans. Michael Holquist. Austin: U of Texas P, 1981.

Balassi, William. "The Trail to *The Sun Also Rises:* The First Week of Writing." *Hemingway: Essays of Reassessment.* Ed. Frank Scafella. New York: Oxford UP, 1991. 33–51.

Barbour, James. "Fugue State as a Literary Device in 'Cat in the Rain' and 'Hills Like White Elephants.'" *Arizona Quarterly* 44.3 (1988): 98–106.

Barbour, Thomas. *A Naturalist in Cuba.* Boston: Little, 1945.

Barea, Arturo. "Not Spain but Hemingway." *Horizon* 3 (May 1941): 350–61.

Barlowe (-Kayes), Jamie. "Re-Reading Women: The Example of Catherine Barkley." *Hemingway Review* 12.2 (1993): 24–35.

Barlowe, Jamie. "Rereading Women: Hester Prynne-ism and the Scarlet Mob of Scribblers." *American Literary History* 9 (1997): 197–225.

——. "Response to the Responses." *American Literary History* 9 (1997): 238–43.

Barnett, Louise K. "The Dialect of Discourse in *The Sun Also Rises.*" *Authority and Speech: Language, Society, and Self in the American Novel.* Athens: U of Georgia P, 1993. 149–64.

Barthes, Roland. *Image, Music, Text.* New York: Hill, 1977.

Barton, Edwin J. "The Story as It Should Be: Epistemological Uncertainty in 'Cat in the Rain.'" *Hemingway Review* 14.1 (1994): 72–78.

Baskett, Sam S. "An Image to Dance Around: Brett and Her Lovers." *Centennial Review* 22 (1978): 45–69.

Bataille, Georges. "Hemingway in Light of Hegel." *Semiotexte* 2.2 (1976): 4–13. Rpt. of "Hemingway à la Lumière." *Critique: Révue Générale* IX (1953): 195–210.

Baym, Nina. "Melodramas of Beset Manhood: How Theories of American Fiction Exclude Women Authors." *American Quarterly* 33 (1980): 315–30.

Beegel, Susan F. "Conclusion: The Critical Reputation of Ernest Hemingway." *Cambridge Companion to Ernest Hemingway.* Ed. Scott Donaldson. New York: Cambridge UP, 1996. 269–99.

——. "The Journal in the Jungle: *The Hemingway Review* and the Contemporary Academy." *Hemingway Review* 17.2 (1998): 5–17.

——. "'The Undefeated' and Sangre y Arena: Hemingway's Mano a Mano with Blasco Ibáñez." *Hemingway Repossessed.* Ed. Kenneth Rosen. Westport, CT.: Praeger, 1994. 71–85.

van Beethoven, Ludwig. *Symphony no. 5, op. 67. Symphonies Nos. 5, 6, and 7 in Full Score.* New York: Dover, 1989.

Benjamin, Jessica. *The Bonds of Love: Psychoanalysis, Feminism, and the Problem of Domination.* New York: Pantheon, 1988.

Bennett, Warren. "The Poor Kitty and the Padrone and the Tortoise-shell Cat in 'Cat in the Rain.'" *Hemingway Review* 8.1 (1988): 26–36.

——. "'That's Not Very Polite': Sexual Identity in Hemingway's 'The Sea Change.'" *Hemingway's Neglected Short Fiction: New Perspectives.* Ed. Susan F. Beegel. Ann Arbor: UMI, 1988. 225–45.

Benson, Jackson J. "Roles and the Masculine Writer." *Brett Ashley.* Major Literary Characters. Ed. Harold Bloom. New York: Chelsea, 1991. 76–85.

Benstock, Shari. *Women of the Left Bank: Paris, 1900–1940.* Austin: U of Texas P, 1986.

Berman, Jeffrey. *Surviving Literary Suicide.* Amherst: U of Massachusetts P, 1999.

Betancourt, Cecilia. "Reaction Paper: El Viejo y La Mar." Unpublished essay, 1997.

Bigelow, Henry B., and William C. Schroeder. *Fishes of the Gulf of Maine.* Fishery Bulletin of the Fish and Wildlife Service. Washington DC: GPO, 1953.

Bloom, Harold. *The Anxiety of Influence.* New York: Oxford UP, 1973.

———. Introduction. *Brett Ashley.* Major Literary Characters. Ed. Harold Bloom. New York: Chelsea, 1991. 1–3.

Boker, Pamela. "Negotiating the Heroic Paternal Ideal: Historical Fiction as Transference in Hemingway's *For Whom the Bell Tolls.*" *Literature and Psychology* 41.1–2 (1995): 85–112.

The Book of Common Prayer and Administration of the Sacraments. 1662. Cambridge: Cambridge UP, 1968.

Boorstin, Daniel J. *Hidden History.* New York: Harper, 1987.

Bradstreet, Anne. "The Author to Her Book." *Norton Anthology of American Literature.* 4th ed. Vol. I. New York: Norton, 1994. 88.

Brasch, James, and Joseph Sigman, comps. *Hemingway's Library: A Composite Record.* New York: Garland, 1981.

Brenner, Gerry. "Are We Going to Hemingway's *Feast*?" *Ernest Hemingway: Six Decades of Criticism.* Ed. Linda W. Wagner. East Lansing: Michigan State UP, 1987. 297–311.

———. *Concealments in Hemingway's Works.* Columbus: Ohio State UP, 1983.

———. "From 'Sepi Jingan' to 'The Mother of a Queen': Hemingway's Three Epistemologic Formulas for Short Fiction." *New Critical Approaches to the Short Stories of Ernest Hemingway.* Ed. Jackson J. Benson. Durham, NC: Duke UP, 1990. 156–71.

———. The Old Man and the Sea: *Story of a Common Man.* New York: Twayne, 1991.

———. "Once a Rabbit, Always? A Feminist Interview with Maria." *Blowing the Bridge: Essays on Hemingway and "For Whom the Bell Tolls."* Ed. Rena Sanderson. Westport, CT: Greenwood, 1992. 131–42.

Broer, Lawrence R. *Hemingway's Spanish Tragedy.* Tuscaloosa: U of Alabama P, 1973.

Brogan, Jacqueline Vaught. "Hemingway's *In Our Time* as Cubist Anatomy." *Hemingway Review* 17.2 (1998): 31–46.

Bronte, Charlotte. *Jane Eyre.* New York: Penguin, 1966.

Bruccoli, Matthew J. *Fitzgerald and Hemingway: A Dangerous Friendship.* New York: Carroll, 1994.

———. "Interview with Mary Welsh Hemingway." *Conversations with Writers.* Detroit: Gale, 1977. 180–91.

Budick, Emily Miller. "*The Sun Also Rises:* Hemingway and the Art of Repetition." *University of Toronto Quarterly* 56.2 (1986–87): 319–37.

Burwell, Rose Marie. "Hemingway's *The Garden of Eden:* Resistance of Things Past and Protecting the Masculine Text." *Texas Studies in Literature and Language* 35.2 (1993): 198–225.

———. *Hemingway: The Postwar Years and the Posthumous Novels.* Cambridge: Cambridge UP, 1996.

Busch, Frederick. "Reading Hemingway without Guilt." *New York Times Book Review.* 12 Jan. 1992: 3, 17–19.

Butler, Judith. *Gender Trouble.* New York: Routledge, 1990.

Carpenter, Edward. *Love's Coming-of-Age.* Chicago: Progress Company, 1911.

Carrabine, Keith. "'Big Two-Hearted River': A Re-interpretation." *Hemingway Review* 1.2 (1982): 39–44.

Carson, Rachel. *The Sea Around Us.* 1951. New York: Mentor, 1989.

———. *Under the Sea Wind.* 1941, 1952. New York: Penguin, 1996.

Carter, Steven. *Bearing Across: Studies in Science and Literature.* Bethesda, MD: International Scholars, 1998.

Cass, Colin G. "The Love Story in *For Whom the Bell Tolls.*" *Fitzgerald/Hemingway Annual: 1972.* Ed. Matthew J. Bruccoli and E. Frazer Clark Jr. 225–35.

Cawelti, John. *Adventure, Mystery, and Romance.* Chicago: U of Chicago P, 1976.

Champagne, Rosaria. *The Politics of Survivorship: Incest, Women's Literature, and Feminist Theory.* New York: New York UP, 1996.

Charney, Maurice. "Sexual Fiction in America, 1955–80." *The Sexual Dimension in Literature.* Ed. Alan Bold. Totowa, NJ: Barnes and Noble, 1983. 122–42.

Chedgzoy, Kate. *Shakespeare's Queer Children: Sexual Politics and Contemporary Culture.* Manchester, Eng: Manchester UP, 1995.

Chenery, William L. Telegram to Martha Gellhorn. 18 June 1941. Crowell-Collier Publishing Company Records. Manuscripts and Archives Division. New York Public Lib. Astor, Lenox and Tilden Foundations.

———. Letter to Martha Gellhorn. 28 June 1941. Crowell-Collier Publishing Company Records. Manuscripts and Archives Division. New York Public Lib. Astor, Lenox and Tilden Foundations.

Chevalier, Jean, and Alain Gheerbrant. *The Dictionary of Symbols.* Trans. John Buchanan-Brown. New York: Penguin, 1996.

Chivers, C. J. "Empty Waves: Have Spotter Planes and Satellites Made Fishermen Too Good at Practicing Their Art?" *Wildlife Conservation* July–Aug. 1998: 37–44. Abstract. Infotrac Search Bank. Article A20910538. <http://web2.searchbank.com>.

Chodorow, Nancy. *The Reproduction of Mothering: Psychoanalysis and the Sociology of Gender.* Berkeley: U of California P, 1978.

Cohen, Milton A. "Circe and Her Swine: Domination and Debasement in *The Sun Also Rises.*" *Arizona Quarterly* 41 (1985): 293–305.

Collier, Jane, Michelle Rosaldo, and Sylvia Yanagisako. "Is There a Family? New Anthropological Views." *Rethinking the Family: Some Feminist Questions.* Ed. Barrie Thorne and Marilyn Yalom. Rev. ed. Boston: Northeastern UP, 1991. 31–48.

Comley, Nancy R. "A Critical Guide to the Literary Journey in Henry Adams's Mont-Saint-Michel and Chartres." Diss. Brown U, 1978.

———. "Hemingway: The Economics of Survival." *Novel* 12 (1979): 244–53.

Comley, Nancy R., and Robert Scholes. *Hemingway's Genders: Rereading the Hemingway Text.* New Haven: Yale UP, 1994.

Cooper, Helen M., Adrienne Auslander Munich, and Susan Merrill Squier, eds. *Arms and the Woman: War, Gender, and Literary Representation.* Chapel Hill: U of North Carolina P, 1989.

Cousteau, Jacques-Yves, and Philippe Cousteau. *The Shark: Splendid Savage of the Sea.* Trans. Francis Price. Garden City, NY: Doubleday, 1970.

"Cowles, Virginia." *Current Biography: Who's News and Why* 3 (1942): 61.

Cowley, Malcolm. "Hemingway's Novel Has the Rich Simplicity of a Classic." Rev. of *The Old Man and the Sea. New York Herald Tribune Book Review* 7 Sept. 1952. Rpt. in *Twentieth Century Interpretations of "The Old Man and the Sea."* Ed. Katherine T. Jobes. Englewood Cliffs, NJ: Prentice Hall, 1968. 106–08.

———. "Hemingway: The Image and the Shadow." *Horizon* (Winter 1973): 112–17.

———. "Nightmare and Ritual in Hemingway." *Hemingway: Collection of Critical Essays.* Ed. Robert P. Weeks. Englewood Cliffs, NJ: Prentice Hall, 1962. 40–51.

Crozier, Robert D. "The Mask of Death, The Face of Life: Hemingway's Feminique." *Ernest Hemingway: Six Decades of Criticism.* Ed. Linda Wagner-Martin. East Lansing: Michigan State UP, 1987. 239–55.

Curnutt, Kirk. "In the temps de Gertrude": Hemingway, Stein, and the Scene of Instruction at 27, rue de Fleurus." *French Connections: Hemingway and Fitzgerald Abroad.* Ed. J. Gerald Kennedy and Jackson R. Bryer. New York: St. Martin's, 1998, 121–39.

Curtis, Mary Ann C. "*The Sun Also Rises:* Its Relation to The Song of Roland." *American Literature* 60 (1988): 274–80.

Davidson, Cathy N. "Death in the Morning: The Role of Vincente Girones in *The Sun Also Rises.*" *Hemingway Notes* 5:1 (1979): 11–13.

Davidson, Cathy N., and Arnold Davidson. "Decoding the Hemingway Hero in *The Sun Also Rises.*" *New Essays on "The Sun Also Rises."* Ed. Linda Wagner-Martin. Cambridge: Cambridge UP, 1987. 83–107.

DeFalco, Joseph. *The Hero in Hemingway's Short Stories.* Pittsburgh: U of Pittsburgh P, 1963.

Dennis, Jerry. "Tracks in the Sand." *Wildlife Conservation* 99.1 (1996): 60–63. Abstract. Infotrac Search Bank. Article A17971853. <http://web2.searchbank.com>.

DeVost, Nadine. "Hemingway's Girls: Unnaming and Renaming Hemingway's Female Characters." *Hemingway Review* 14.1 (1994): 46–59.

Diliberto, Gioia. *Hadley.* New York: Ticknor, 1992.

Donaldson, Scott. "Hemingway's Morality of Compensation." *American Literature* 43 (1971): 399–420.

Downing, Margot. "He Wrote Better in School, Says Hemingway's Mother." *Detroit News* 19 June 1949. N. pag.

Eastman, Max. "Bull in the Afternoon." *New Republic* 7 June 1933: 94–97. Rpt. in *Ernest Hemingway: The Critical Reception.* Ed. Robert O. Stephens. New York: Burt Franklin, 1977. 130–32.

Eby, Carl P. *Hemingway's Fetishism: Psychoanalysis and the Mirror of Manhood.* Albany: State U of New York P, 1999.

——. "Rabbit Stew and Blowing Dorothy's Bridges: Love, Aggression, and Fetishism in *For Whom the Bell Tolls*." *Twentieth Century Literature* 44.2 (1998): 204–18.

——. Unpublished Notes on *African Journal*.

Ellis, Havelock. *The Soul of Spain*. New York: Houghton, 1915.

Ellis, Richard. *The Book of Sharks*. New York: Grosset, 1975.

Erkkila, Betsy. *The Wicked Sisters: Women Poets, Literary History, and Discord*. New York: Oxford UP, 1992.

Fadiman, Clifton. "Ernest Hemingway: An American Byron." *Nation* 18 Jan. 1933: 63–64. Rpt. in *Ernest Hemingway: The Critical Reception*. Ed. Robert O. Stephens. New York: Burt Franklin, 1977. 124–28.

Farrington, S. Kip. *Fishing with Hemingway and Glassell*. New York: David McKay, 1971.

Fass, Paula. *The Damned and the Beautiful: American Youth in the 1920s*. New York: Oxford UP, 1977.

Fetterley, Judith. *The Resisting Reader: A Feminist Approach to American Fiction*. Bloomington: Indiana UP, 1978.

Fiedler, Leslie A. "Adolescence and Maturity in the American Novel." *An End to Innocence: Essays on Culture and Politics*. Boston: Beacon, 1955. Rpt. in *Twentieth Century Interpretations* of The Old Man and the Sea. Ed. Katherine T. Jobes. Englewood Cliffs, NJ: Prentice Hall, 1968. 108.

——. *Love and Death in the American Novel*. New York: Stein, 1982.

Fitzgerald, F. Scott. To Ernest Hemingway. June 1929. *Correspondence of F. Scott Fitzgerald*. Ed. Matthew J. Bruccoli and Margaret M. Duggan. New York: Random, 1980. 225–28.

Fleming, Robert E. "The Endings of Hemingway's *The Garden of Eden*." *American Literature* 61 (1989): 261–70.

——. *The Face in the Mirror: Hemingway's Writers*. Tuscaloosa: U of Alabama P, 1994.

——, ed. *Hemingway and the Natural World*. Moscow: U of Idaho P, 1999.

——. "The Libel of Dos Passos in *To Have and Have Not*." *Journal of Modern Literature* 15 (1989): 597–601.

Flora, Joseph M. *The Nick Adams Stories*. Baton Rouge: Louisiana State UP, 1982.

Foucault, Michel. *The Archaeology of Knowledge*. Trans. A. M. Sheridan Smith. New York: Harper, 1972.

——. "What Is an Author?" *Language, Counter-Memory, Practice*. Trans. Donald F. Bouchard. Ithaca: Cornell UP, 1977.

Frank, Waldo. *Virgin Spain: The Drama of a Great People*. New York: Duell, Sloan and Pierce, 1942.

Frazer, James G. *The Golden Bough*. New York: Avenel, 1981.

Frewin, Leslie. *The Late Mrs. Dorothy Parker*. New York: Macmillan, 1986.

Friedman, Bonnie. *Writing Past Dark: Envy, Fear, Distraction, and Other Dilemmas in the Writer's Life*. Harper, 1993.

Gajdusek, Robert E. "The Mad Sad Bad Misreading of Hemingway's Gender Politics/Aesthetics." *North Dakota Quarterly.* 64.3 (1997): 36–48.

——. "Pilar's Tale: The Myth and the Message." *Blowing the Bridge: Essays on Hemingway and "For Whom the Bell Tolls."* Ed. Rena Sanderson. New York: Greenwood, 1992. 113–30.

Gallagher, Jean. *The World Wars Through the Female Gaze.* Carbondale: Southern Illinois UP, 1998.

Garcia, Wilma. *Mothers and Others: Myths of the Female in the Works of Melville, Twain, and Hemingway.* New York: Lang, 1984.

Geismar, Maxwell. "No Man Alone Now." *Virginia Quarterly Review* 17 (1941): 517–34.

Gellhorn, Martha. Afterword. *Point of No Return.* New York: New American Library. Lincoln: U of Nebraska P, 1995. 326–32. Rpt. of *The Wine of Astonishment.* New York: Scribner's, 1948.

——. *The Face of War.* New York: Atlantic Monthly P, 1988.

——. "Guerre de Plume: Martha Gellhorn: *On Apocryphism.*" *Paris Review* 79 (1981): 280–301.

——. "Hangdog Herrenvolk." *Collier's* 29 July 1944.

——. Interview with Sandra Spanier. Chepstow, Wales. 19 Aug. 1990.

——. Interview with Sandra Spanier. Chepstow, Wales. 9 July 1992.

——. Interview with Sandra Spanier. London. 21 May 1997.

——. Introduction. *Love Goes to Press: A Comedy in Three Acts,* by Martha Gellhorn and Virgina Cowles. Ed. Sandra Spanier. Lincoln: U of Nebraska P, 1995. vii–xi.

——. Letter to William Chenery. 18 June 1941. Crowell-Collier Publishing Company Records. Manuscript and Archives Division. New York Public Lib. Astor, Lenox and Tilden Foundations.

——. Letter to Sandra Spanier. 23 Nov. 1990.

——. Letter to Sandra Spanier. 23 Sept. 1993.

——. "Night Life in the Sky." *Collier's* 17 Mar. 1945: 18–19, 31.

——. Postcard to Sandra Spanier. 24 Aug. 1992.

——. "These, Our Mountains." *Collier's* 28 June 1941: 16–17, 38, 40–41, 44.

——. *Travels with Myself and Another.* London: Eland Books, 1978.

——. *The View from the Ground.* New York: Atlantic Monthly P, 1988.

——. *What Mad Pursuit.* New York: Stokes, 1934.

Gellhorn, Martha, and Virginia Cowles. *Love Goes to Press: A Comedy in Three Acts.* Ed. Sandra Spanier. Lincoln: U of Nebraska P, 1995.

Gensler, Mindy. "Response Paper: *The Old Man and the Sea.*" Unpublished essay, 1997.

Gilbert, Sandra, and Susan Gubar. *The Madwoman in the Attic: The Woman Writer and the Nineteenth-Century Literary Imagination.* New Haven: Yale UP, 1979.

——. *No Man's Land: The Place of the Woman Writer in the Twentieth Century.* 3 vols. New Haven: Yale UP, 1988, 1989, 1994.

Gilder, Rosamond. "Rainbow Over Broadway." Rev. of *Love Goes to Press*. *Theater Arts* 31 (Mar. 1947): 18.

Gladstein, Mimi Reisel. *The Indestructible Woman in Faulkner, Hemingway, and Steinbeck*. Ann Arbor: UMI, 1986.

Godwin, Gail, "Becoming a Writer." *The Writer on Her Work: Contemporary Women Writers Reflect on Their Art and Their Situation*. Ed. Janet Sternburg. New York: Norton, 1981.

Gordon, Mary, and Frank McCourt. *Seattle Arts and Lectures*. Fifth Avenue Theater. Seattle. Mar. 1968.

Grace, Nancy McCampbell. *The Feminized Male Character in Twentieth-Century Literature*. Lewiston, NY: Mellen, 1995.

Grant, Mary Kathryn, R.S.M. "The Search for Celebration in *The Sun Also Rises* and *The Great Gatsby*." *Arizona Quarterly* 33.2 (1977): 181–92.

Grant, Naomi M. "The Role of Women in the Fiction of Ernest Hemingway." Diss. U of Denver, 1968. *DA* 29 (1968): 4456A.

Graves, Robert. "Strong Beer." *Fairies and Fusiliers*. New York: Knopf, 1918.

Greenacre, Phyllis. *Emotional Growth: Psychoanalytic Studies of the Gifted and a Great Variety of Other Individuals*. 2 vols. New York: International Universities P, 1971.

Greenlaw, Linda. *The Hungry Ocean: A Swordboat Captain's Journey*. New York: Hyperion, 1999.

Griffin, Peter. *Along with Youth: Hemingway, The Early Years*. New York: Oxford UP, 1985.

———. *Less Than a Treason: Hemingway in Paris*. New York: Oxford UP, 1990.

Gubar, Susan. "'This is My Rifle, This is My Gun': World War II and the Blitz on Women." Ed. Margaret Randolph Higonnet et al. *Behind the Lines: Gender and the Two World Wars*. New Haven: Yale UP, 1987. 227–59.

Gurko, Leo. *Ernest Hemingway and the Pursuit of Heroism*. New York: Crowell, 1968.

Hagopian, John V. "Symmetry in 'Cat in the Rain.'" *College English* 24 (1962): 220–22.

Hammett, Dashiell. *The Maltese Falcon*. 1929. Franklin Center, PA: Franklin, 1987.

Hasbany, Richard. "The Shock of Vision: An Imagist Reading of *In Our Time*." *Ernest Hemingway: Five Decades of Criticism*. Ed. Linda Welshimer Wagner. East Lansing: Michigan State UP, 1974. 224–40.

Hawley, Ellis W. *The Great War and the Search for a Modern Order: A History of the American People and Their Institutions, 1917–1933*. New York: St. Martin's, 1979.

Hays, Peter L. "Hemingway, Nick Adams, and David Bourne: Sons and Writers." *Arizona Quarterly* 44.2 (1988): 28–38.

———. "Wright, Cézanne and Hemingway." Hemingway Centennial Conference. Oak Park, IL. 20 July 1999.

Helbig, Doris A. "Confession, Charity, and Community in *The Sun Also Rises*." *South Atlantic Review* 58.2 (1993): 85–110.

Hellman, Lillian. *Three*. Boston: Little, 1979.

———. *An Unfinished Woman: A Memoir*. Boston: Little, 1969.

"Hemingway Dead of Shotgun Wound; Wife Says He Was Cleaning Weapon." *New York Times* 3 July 1961: 1, 6.

Hemingway, Clarence Edmonds. "Forceps." Unpublished essay, 1913. Archives of the Ernest Hemingway Foundation of Oak Park, Illinois.

Hemingway, Ernest. *African Journal.* Ed. and intro. Ray Cave. Illus. Jack Brusca. "Part One: Miss Mary's Lion." *Sports Illustrated* 20 Dec. 1971: n. pag.; "Part Two: Miss Mary's Lion." *Sports Illustrated* 3 Jan. 1972: n. pag.; "Part Three: Imperiled Flanks." *Sports Illustrated* 10 Jan. 1972: n. pag.

——. *African Journal.* Mss. Scribner Archives, Firestone Library, Princeton University. Princeton, NJ.

——. "The Art of Fiction XXI: Ernest Hemingway." Interview with George Plimpton. *Paris Review* 5 (1958): 60–89. Rpt. in *Conversations with Ernest Hemingway.* Ed. Matthew J. Brucolli. Jackson: UP of Mississippi, 1986. 109–29.

——. "The Battler." *In Our Time.* 1925. New York: Scribner's, 1970. 53–62.

——. "Big Two-Hearted River: Part I." *Short Stories.* 1938. New York: Scribner's, 1966. 207–18.

——. "Big Two-Hearted River: Part II." *Short Stories.* 1938. New York: Scribner's, 1966. 219–32.

——. "Cat in the Rain." *Short Stories.* 1938. New York: Scribner's, 1966. 167–70.

——. "Chapter 1." *In Our Time.* 1925. New York: Scribner's, 1970, 13.

——. "Chinese Build Air Field." *PM* 18 June 1941. Rpt. in *By-Line.* Ed. William White. New York: Scribner's, 1967. 335–39.

——. *Complete Poems.* Rev. ed. Lincoln: U of Nebraska P, 1992.

——. Correspondence with Adriana Ivancich. 1950–54. Harry Ransom Humanities Research Center. University of Texas at Austin.

——. *Death in the Afternoon.* 1932. New York: Scribner's, 1960.

——. "The End of Something." *Short Stories.* 1938. New York: Scribner's, 1966. 107–11.

——. *Ernest Hemingway: Selected Letters, 1917–1961.* Ed. Carlos Baker. New York: Scribner's, 1981.

——. *Ernest Hemingway Reading.* LP. Caedmon, 1965.

——. *A Farewell to Arms.* 1929. New York: Scribner's, 1957.

——. "Fathers and Sons." *The Nick Adam Stories.* New York: Bantam, 1973. 234–45.

——. "Fishing the Rhone Canal." *Toronto Daily Star* 10 June 1922. Rpt. *By-Line.* Ed. William White. New York: Scribner's, 1967. 33–35.

——. *For Whom the Bell Tolls.* New York: Scribner's, 1940.

——. *For Whom the Bell Tolls.* Mss. Hemingway Collection. John F. Kennedy Library, Boston.

——. *The Garden of Eden.* New York: Scribner's, 1986.

——. *The Garden of Eden.* Mss. Hemingway Collection. John F. Kennedy Library, Boston.

——. *Green Hills of Africa.* New York: Scribner's, 1935.

———. "Hemingway's Introduction to Atlantic Game Fishing." Farrington. *Fishing with Hemingway and Glassell.* New York: David McKay, 1971. 9–14.

———. "Hills Like White Elephants." *Men without Women.* New York: Scribner's, 1997. 50–55.

———. *in our time.* Paris: Three Mountains P, 1924.

———. *In Our Time.* 1925. New York: Scribner's, 1970.

———. *Islands in the Stream.* New York: Scribner's, 1970.

———. *Islands in the Stream.* Firestone Library, Princeton University, Princeton, NJ.

———. *Islands in the Stream.* Hemingway Collection. John F. Kennedy Library, Boston.

———. "The Last Good Country." *The Nick Adams Stories.* New York: Bantam, 1973. 56–114.

———. Letter to Charles Colebaugh. 18 June 1941. Crowell-Collier Publishing Company Records. Manuscript and Archives Division. New Your Public Lib. Astor, Lenox and Tilden Foundations.

———. Letter to Charles Colebaugh. 25 June [1941]. Crowell-Collier Publishing Company Records. Manuscript and Archives Division. New York Public Lib. Astor, Lenox and Tilden Foundations.

———. Letter to Mary Hemingway. 2 May 1947. Hemingway Collection. John F. Kennedy Library, Boston.

———. Letter to Mary Hemingway. 5 May 1947. Hemingway Collection. John F. Kennedy Library, Boston.

———. Letter to Mary Hemingway. 14 May 1947. Hemingway Collection. John F. Kennedy Library, Boston.

———. Letter to Maxwell Perkins. 28 Jan. 1940. Firestone Library, Princeton University, Princeton, NJ.

———. Letter to Charles Scribner. 31 Dec. 1948. Firestone Library, Princeton University, Princeton, NJ.

———. "Monologue to the Maestro: A High Seas Letter." *Esquire* Oct. 1935. Rpt. in *By-Line.* Ed. William White. New York: Scribner's, 1967, 213–20.

———. *A Moveable Feast.* New York: Scribner's, 1964.

———. *A Moveable Feast.* Mss. Hemingway Collection. John F. Kennedy Library, Boston.

———. *The Nick Adams Stories.* New York: Bantam, 1973.

———. "On the Blue Water: A Gulf Stream Letter." *Esquire* Apr. 1936. Rpt. in *By-Line.* Ed. William White. New York: Scribner's, 1967, 236–44.

———. "On Writing." *The Nick Adams Stories.* New York: Bantam, 1973, 213–20.

———. *The Old Man and the Sea.* New York: Scribner's, 1952.

———. *The Old Man and the Sea.* Mss. Hemingway Collection. John F. Kennedy Library, Boston.

———. "A Room on the Garden Side." Harry Ransom Humanities Research Center. University of Texas at Austin.

------. "Sea Change." *Short Stories*. 1938. New York: Scribner's, 1966, 397–401.

------. *To Have and Have Not*. New York: Scribner's, 1937.

------. "To Bernard Berenson." 20–22 Mar. 1953. Baker, *Letters*. 808–15.

------. "To F. Scott Fitzgerald." 15 Dec. 1925. Baker, *Letters*. 176–77.

------. "To Janet Flanner." 8 Apr. 1933. Baker, *Letters*. 386–89.

------. "To Arnold Gingrich." 3 Apr. 1933. Baker, *Letters*. 384–86.

------. "To Dr. C. E. Hemingway." 20 Mar. 1925. Baker, *Letters*. 153–54.

------. "To Patrick Hemingway." 19 Nov. 1944. Baker, *Letters*. 576–77.

------. "To Edward J. O'Brien." 12 Sept. 1924. Baker, *Letters*. 123–24.

------. "To Maxwell Perkins." 1 Nov. 1927. Baker, *Letters*. 264–65.

------. "To Maxwell Perkins." 26 July 1933. Baker, *Letters*. 395–96.

------. "To Maxwell Perkins." 15 Oct. 1944. Baker, *Letters*. 574–75.

------. "To Maxwell Perkins." 23 July 1945. Baker, *Letters*. 593–94.

------. "To W. G. Rogers." 29 July 1948. Baker, *Letters*. 649–50.

------. "To Lillian Ross." 28 July 1948. Baker, *Letters*. 646–49.

------. "To Charles Scribner." 29 Oct. 1947. Baker, *Letters*. 629–31.

------. "To Charles Scribner." 25–26 Aug. 1949. Baker, *Letters*. 667–69.

------. "To Owen Wister." 25 July 1929. Baker, *Letters*. 301.

------. *The Short Stories of Ernest Hemingway*. 1938. New York: Scribner's, 1966.

------. *The Sun Also Rises*. 1926. New York: Scribner's, 1954.

------. *The Torrents of Spring*. New York: Scribner's, 1926.

------. *True at First Light*. Ed. Patrick Hemingway. New York: Scribner's, 1999.

------. "A Way You'll Never Be." *The Nick Adams Stories*. New York: Bantam, 1973. 135–48.

Hemingway, Grace Hall. Notes for Art Talk, Oct. 1928. Private collection, John Sanford.

Hemingway, Gregory. *Papa: A Personal Memoir*. Boston: Houghton, 1976.

Hemingway, Mary Welsh. *How It Was*. New York: Knopf, 1976.

Hemingway, Patrick. "An Evening with Patrick Hemingway." *Hemingway Review* 19.1 (1999): 8–16.

"The Hemingways in Sun Valley: The Novelist Takes a Wife." *Life* 8 Jan. 1941: 49–51.

Hen, Judy. "'Working on the Farm': Hemingway's Work Ethic in *The Sun Also Rises*." *Ernest Hemingway: The Oak Park Legacy*. Ed. James Nagel. Tuscaloosa: U of Alabama P, 1996. 165–78.

Hergesheimer, Joseph. "The Feminine Nuisance in American Literature." *Yale Review* 10 (1921): 716–25.

Herodotus. *The History*. The Great Books of the Western World. Ed. Robert Maynard Hutchins. Chicago: U of Chicago P, 1952.

Heyerdahl, Thor. *Kon-Tiki: Across the Pacific by Raft*. Trans. F. H. Lyon. Chicago: Rand McNally, 1950.

Higonnet, Margaret Randolph et al., eds. *Behind the Lines: Gender and the Two World Wars*. New Haven: Yale UP, 1987.

Hinkle, Jim. Letter to Linda Patterson Miller. 13 Dec. 1986.

Hofstadter, Douglas R. *Gödel, Escher, Bach: an Eternal Golden Braid.* New York: Basic, 1979.

Holmesland, Oddvar. "Structuralism and Interpretation: Ernest Hemingway's 'Cat in the Rain.'" *English Studies* 3 (1986): 221–33.

Hotchner, A. E. *Papa Hemingway: A Personal Memoir.* New York: Carroll, 1999.

Hyde, Elizabeth Walden. "Aficionado Fishes Worms: A Study of Hemingway and Jake."*American Fly Fisher* 9.2 (1982): 2–7.

Ibánez, Vincente Blasco. *Blood and Sand.* Trans. Frances Partridge. New York: Frederick Ungar, 1996.

Jenks, Tom. "Editing Hemingway: *The Garden of Eden.*" *Hemingway Review* 7.1 (1987): 30–33.

Jobes, Katharine T. Introduction. *Twentieth Century Interpretations of* The Old Man and the Sea. Ed. Katharine T. Jobes. Englewood Cliffs, NJ: Prentice Hall, 1968. 1–17.

Johnson, Elizabeth A. Rev. of *Mary Through the Centuries: Her Place in the History of Culture. Theological Studies* 58 (1997): 372–74. Infotrac Search Bank. Article A19540892. <http://web2.searchbank.com>.

Josephs, Allen. "Hemingway's Out of Body Experience." *Hemingway Review* 2 (1983): 11–17.

———. "Hemingway's Poor "Spanish: Chauvinism and Loss of Credibility in *For Whom the Bell Tolls.*" *Hemingway: A Revaluation.* Ed. Donald R. Noble. Troy, NY: Whitson, 1983: 205–23.

———. "How Did Hemingway Write?" *North Dakota Quarterly* 63.3 (1996): 50–64.

———. "*La Plaza de Toros:* Where Culture and Nature Meet." *North Dakota Quarterly* 64.3 (1977): 60–80.

Justice, Hilary K. "'Well, well, well': Cross-gendered Autobiography and the Manuscript of 'Hills Like White Elephants.'" *Hemingway Review.* 18:1 (1998): 17–32.

Katainen, V. Louise. Rev. of *Mary Through the Centuries: Her Place in History. National Forum* Winter 1998: 44–46. Infotrac Search Bank. Article A53644242. <http://web2.searchbank.com>.

Kauffman, Linda S. *Discourses of Desire: Gender, Genre, and Epistolary Fictions.* Ithaca, NY: Cornell UP, 1986.

Keats, John. *You Might as Well Live: The Life and Times of Dorothy Parker.* New York: Simon, 1970.

Kennan, Kent. *Counterpoint: Based on Eighteenth-Century Practice.* 3rd ed. Englewood Cliffs, NJ: Prentice Hall, 1987.

Kennedy, J. Gerald. *Imagining Paris: Exile, Writing, and American Identity.* New Haven: Yale UP, 1993.

Kennelly, Eleanor. "Rediscovering the Madonna: Virtue as an Icon for the Ages." *Insight on the News* 23 Jan. 1995: 26–28. Infotrac Search Bank. Article A16679524. <http://web2.searchbank.com>.

Kerasote, Ted. "A Talk about Ethics." *Heart of Home: People, Wildlife, Place*. New York: Villard, 1997. 179–92.

Kerr, Frances. "Feeling 'Half Feminine': Modernism and the Politics of Emotion in *The Great Gatsby*." *American Literature* 68 (1996): 405–31.

Kert, Bernice. *The Hemingway Women: Those Who Loved Him—The Wives and Others*. New York: Norton, 1983.

Killinger, John. *Hemingway and the Dead Gods: A Study in Existentialism*. Lexington: U of Kentucky P, 1960.

Kinnamon, Keneth. "Hemingway and Politics." *The Cambridge Companion to Hemingway*. Ed. Scott Donaldson. Cambridge: Cambridge UP, 1996. 149–69.

——. "Hemingway, The Corrida, and Spain." *Ernest Hemingway: Five Decades of Criticism*. Ed. Linda Welshimer Wagner. East Lansing: Michigan State UP, 1974. 57–74.

Kinney, Arthur F. *Dorothy Parker*. Boston: Twayne, 1978.

Knodt, Ellen Andrews. "Diving Deep: Jake's Moment of Truth at San Sebastian." *Hemingway Review* 17.1 (1997): 28–37.

Knopf, Josephine Z. "Meyer Wolfsheim and Robert Cohn: A Study of a Jewish Type and Stereotype." *Tradition: A Journal of Orthodox Jewish Thought* 10.3 (1969). Rpt. in *Ernest Hemingway's "The Sun Also Rises."* Ed. Harold Bloom. New York: Chelsea, 1987. 61–70.

Kobler, J. F. "Hemingway's 'The Sea Change': A Sympathetic View of Homosexuality." *Arizona Quarterly* 26 (1970): 318–24.

Kolodny, Annette. *The Lay of the Land: Metaphor as Experience and History in American Life and Letters*. Chapel Hill: U North Carolina P, 1975.

L'Amour, Louis. *Heller with a Gun*. Greenwich, CT.: Fawcett, 1955.

Lawrence, Margaret. *The School of Femininity*. Toronto: Thomas Nelson, 1936.

Lear, Linda. *Rachel Carson: Witness for Nature*. New York: Holt, 1997.

Lehan, Richard. "Hemingway among the Moderns." *Hemingway in Our Time*. Ed. Richard Astro and Jackson J. Benson. Corvallis: Oregon State UP, 1974. 191–212.

Leo, John. Rev. of *Thelma and Louise*. *U.S. News and World Reports* 10 June 1991: 20.

Leopold, Aldo. "The Land Ethic." *A Sand County Almanac, with Essays on Conservation from Round River*. 1953. New York: Ballantine, 1970. 237–64.

Lewis, Robert W., Jr. *Hemingway on Love*. Austin: U of Texas P, 1965.

Lindsay, Clarence. "Risking Nothing: American Romantics in 'Cat in the Rain.'" *Hemingway Review* 17.1 (1997): 15–27.

Lodge, David. "Analysis and Interpretation of the Realist Text: A Pluralistic Approach to Ernest Hemingway's 'Cat in the Rain.'" *Poetics Today* 1–4 (1980): 5–22.

Lounsberry, Barbara. "*Green Hills of Africa*: Hemingway's Celebration of Memory." *Hemingway Review* 2.2 (1983): 23–31.

Love, Glen A. "Hemingway's Indian Virtues: An Ecological Reconsideration." *Western American Literature* 22 (1987): 202–13.

Lurie, E. "Brandy (You're a Fine Girl)." Perf. Looking Glass. Rec. Sony Music Entertainment, 1972.

Lynn, Kenneth. *Hemingway.* New York: Fawcett, 1987.

MacKinnon, Catherine A. "Feminism, Marxism, Method, and the State: An Agenda for Theory." *Signs* 7 (1982): 515–44.

MacLeish, Archibald. "Hemingway." *New and Collected Poems 1917–1976.* Boston: Houghton, 1976. 482.

Magee, John D. "Hemingway's 'Cat in the Rain.'" *Explicator* 26.1 (1967): no. 8.

Mandel, Miriam B. E-mail to Susan Beegel. 6 June 1999.

———. *Reading Hemingway: The Facts in the Fictions.* Metuchen, NJ: Scarecrow, 1995.

Mansell, Darrel. "When Did Ernest Hemingway Write *The Old Man and the Sea?*" *Fitzgerald/Hemingway Annual.* Ed. Matthew J. Bruccoli and C. E. Frazer Clark Jr. Colorado: Englewood, 1975. 311–24.

———. "Words Lost in *In Our Time.*" *Hemingway Review* 17.1 (1997): 5–14.

"Martha Gellhorn's Play to Close after Four Days." *St. Louis Post-Dispatch* 4 Jan. 1947.

Martin, Robert A. "Robert Jordan and the Spanish Country: Learning to Live in It 'Truly and Well.'" *Hemingway Review* 16.1 (l996): 56–64.

Martin, Wendy. "Brett Ashley as New Woman in *The Sun Also Rises.*" *New Essays on "The Sun Also Rises.*" Ed. Linda Wagner-Martin. Cambridge: Cambridge UP, 1987. 65–82.

Marx, Leo. *The Machine in the Garden: Technology and the Pastoral Ideal in America.* New York: Oxford UP, 1964.

Maslin, Janet. "On the Run with 2 Buddies and a Gun." *New York Times* 24 May 1991, C1.

Matthiessen, Peter. *Blue Meridian: The Search for the Great White Shark.* New York: Random, 1971.

McAlmon, Robert, and Kay Boyle. *Being Geniuses Together.* Rev. ed. London: Hogarth, 1984.

McCormick, John. *The Complete Aficionado.* Cleveland: World, 1967.

McGovern, James R. "The American Woman's Pre–World War I Freedom in Manners and Morals." *Women's Experience in America: An Historical Anthology.* Ed. Esther Katz and Anita Rapone. New Brunswick: Transaction, 1980.

McIver, Stuart B. *Hemingway's Key West.* Sarasota: Pineapple, 1993.

Meade, Marion. *Dorothy Parker: What Fresh Hell Is This?* New York: Villard, 1988.

Mellow, James R. *Charmed Circle: Gertrude Stein and Company.* New York: Praeger, 1974.

———. *Hemingway: A Life without Consequences.* New York: Addison-Wesley, 1992.

Melville, Herman. *Moby-Dick; or, The Whale.* 1851. Berkeley: U of California P, 1979.

Merchant, Carolyn. *The Death of Nature: Women, Ecology and the Scientific Revolution.* San Francisco: Harper, 1983.

Meyers, Jeffrey. *Hemingway: A Biography.* New York: Harper, 1985.

Miller, James E., Jr., ed. *Complete Poetry and Selected Prose of Walt Whitman.* Boston: Riverside, 1959.

Miller, Linda Patterson. "Brett Ashley: The Beauty of It All." *Critical Essays on Ernest Hemingway's "The Sun Also Rises."* Ed. James Nagel. New York: G. K. Hall, 1995. 170–84.

———. "Ernest Hemingway and Dorothy Parker: 'Nothing in her life became her like her almost leaving of it.'" *North Dakota Quarterly* 66.2 (1999): 101–12.

———. "Hemingway's Women: A Reassessment." *Hemingway in Italy and Other Essays.* Ed. Robert W. Lewis. New York: Praeger, 1990. 3–9.

———, ed. *Letters from the Lost Generation: Gerald and Sara Murphy and Friends.* New Brunswick: Rutgers UP, 1991.

Minter, David. "The Fear of Feminization and the Logic of Modest Ambition." *A Cultural History of the American Novel.* New York: Cambridge UP, 1994. 117–24.

Mirales, Laurie Welsh. Final Exam in English 400: Authors, Tests, Contests/ Fitzgerald, Hemingway and the Lost Generation. Fall 1998. Professor Linda Patterson Miller. Penn State Abington.

Moddelmog, Debra A. "Protecting the Hemingway Myth: Casting Out Forbidden Desires from *The Garden of Eden.*" *Prospects: An Annual of American Cultural Studies* 21 (1996): 89–122.

———. *Reading Desire: In Pursuit of Ernest Hemingway.* Ithaca: Cornell UP, 1999.

———. "Reconstructing Hemingway's Identity: Sexual Politics, the Author, and the Multicultural Classroom." *Narrative* 1 (1993): 187–206.

———. "The Unifying Consciousness of a Divided Conscience: Nick Adams as Author of *In Our Time.*" *American Literature* 60 (1988): 591–610.

Moreland, Kim. *The Medievalist Impulse in American Literature: Twain, Adams, Fitzgerald, and Hemingway.* Charlottesville: UP of Virginia, 1996.

Morgan, Kathleen. "Between Two Worlds: Hemingway's Brett Ashley and Homer's Helen of Troy." *Classical and Modern Literature: A Quarterly* 11:2 (1991): 169–80.

Morrison, Toni. *Playing in the Dark: Whiteness and the Literary Imagination.* 1992. New York: Vintage, 1993.

Nichols, Kathleen L. "The Morality of Asceticism in *The Sun Also Rises:* A Structural Reinterpretation." *Fitzgerald/Hemingway Annual: 1978.* 321–30.

Nolan, Charles J., Jr., "Hemingway's Women's Movement." *Hemingway Review* 3.2 (1984): 14–22.

Oates, Joyce Carol. "The Hemingway Mystique." *(Woman) Writer: Occasions and Opportunities.* New York: E. P. Dutton, 1988. 304–09; excerpted in *Brett Ashley.* Major Literary Characters. Ed. Harold Bloom. New York: Chelsea, 1991. 48–51.

Orsagh, Jacqueline E. "Martha Gellhorn." *Dictionary of Literary Biography Yearbook 1983.* Detroit: Bruccoli Clark Layman, 1984. 244–50.

O'Sullivan, Sibbie. "Love and Friendship/Man and Woman in *The Sun Also Rises.*" *Arizona Quarterly* 44.2 (1988): 76–97.

Pachelbel, Johann. *Canon in D.* Cond. Jean-François Paillard. *Pachelbel: Canon and Gigue in D.* Wea/Atlantic/Erato, 1995.

Parker, Dorothy. "The Artist's Reward." *New Yorker* 30 Nov. 1929: 28–31. Rpt. in *The Portable Dorothy Parker.* Rev. and enl. ed. New York: Penguin, 1976. 582–88.

———. "Clothe the Naked." *Scribner's Magazine.* Jan. 1938: 31–35. Rpt. in *The Portable Dorothy Parker.* Rev. and enl. ed. New York: Penguin, 1976. 360–69.

———. "The Compleat Bungler." *New Yorker* 17 Mar. 1928. Rpt. in *The Portable Dorothy Parker.* Rev. and enl. ed. New York: Penguin, 1976. 501–03.

———. "A Book of Great Short Stories." *New Yorker* 29 Oct. 1927: 92–94. Rpt. in *The Portable Dorothy Parker.* Rev. and enl. ed. New York: Penguin, 1976. 458–61.

———. Letter to Alexander Woollcott. Dec. 1940. Alexander Woollcott Papers. Houghton Library, Harvard University.

———. "Mr. Hemingway's Finest Story Yet." *PM* 20 Oct., 1940: 42.

———. "The Siege of Madrid." *New Masses* 23 Nov. 1937. Rpt. in *The Portable Dorothy Parker.* Rev. and enl. ed. New York: Penguin, 1976. 589–94.

———. "Soldiers of the Republic." *New Yorker* 5. Feb. 1938: 13–14. New York: Penguin, 1976. 165–69.

Parker, Dorothy, and Frederick B. Shroyer, eds. *Short Story: A Thematic Anthology.* New York: Scribner's, 1965.

Pearson, Janet Lynne. "Hemingway's Women." *Lost Generation Journal* 1.1 (1973): 16–19.

Peters, K. J. "The Thematic Integrity of *The Garden of Eden.*" *Hemingway Review* 11 (1991): 17–29.

Plimpton, George. "The Art of Fiction: Ernest Hemingway." Interview. *Paris Review* 5 (1958): 60–89. Rpt. in *Conversations with Ernest Hemingway.* Ed. Matthew J. Bruccoli. Jackson: UP of Mississippi, 1986. 109–29.

———. "An Interview with Ernest Hemingway." *Hemingway and His Critics: An International Anthology.* Ed. Carlos Baker. New York: Hill and Wang, 1961. 19–37.

———. *Women Writers at Work: The Paris Review Interviews.* New York: Penguin, 1989.

Prescott, Jeryl J. "Women and Minorities in *To Have and Have Not.*" *Readings on Ernest Hemingway.* Ed. Katie de Koster. San Diego: Greenhaven, 1997. 155–61.

Pressman, Richard S. "Individualists or Collectivists?: Steinbeck's *In Dubious Battle* and Hemingway's *To Have and Have Not.*" *Steinbeck Quarterly* 25.3–4 (1992): 119–33.

Pribram, E. Deidre, ed. *Female Spectators: Looking at Film and Television.* London: Verso, 1988.

Proust, Marcel. *Remembrance of Things Past.* Trans. C. K. Scott Moncrieff. Vol. 1. New York: Random, 1934.

"Punk." *Webster's New Collegiate Dictionary.* 1977 ed.

Putnam, Ann. "Across the River and into the Stream: Journey of the Divided Heart." *North Dakota Quarterly.* 63.3 (1996): 90–98.

———. "Memory, Grief, and the Terrain of Desire." *Hemingway and the Natural World.* Ed. Robert Fleming. Moscow: U of Idaho P, 1999. 99–110.

Rado, Lisa, ed. *Rereading Modernism: New Directions in Feminist Criticism.* New York: Garland, 1994.

Raeburn, John. *Fame Became of Him: Hemingway as Public Writer.* Bloomington: Indiana UP, 1984.

———. "Sex and Art in *The Garden of Eden.*" *Michigan Quarterly Review* 29 (1990): 111–22.

Reynolds, Guy. *Willa Cather in Context: Progress, Race, Empire.* New York: St. Martin's, 1996.

Reynolds, Michael. "Hemingway as American Icon." *Picturing Hemingway: A Writer in His Time.* Frederick Voss. New Haven: Yale UP, 1999. 1–9.

———. *Hemingway: The Final Years.* New York: Norton, 1999.

———. *Hemingway: The Paris Years.* New York: Blackwell, 1989.

———. *Hemingway's First War: The Making of* A Farewell to Arms. Princeton: Princeton UP, 1976.

———. *Hemingway's Reading, 1910–1940, An Inventory.* Princeton: Princeton UP, 1981.

———. "Hemingway's West: Another Country of the Heart." *Blowing the Bridge: Essays on Hemingway and "For Whom the Bell Tolls."* Ed. Rena Sanderson. New York: Greenwood, 1992. 27–37.

———. "Ring the Changes: Hemingway's 'Bell' Tolls Fifty." *Virginia Quarterly Review* 67.1 (1991): 1–18.

———. "A Supplement to Hemingway's Reading, 1910–1940." *Studies in American Fiction.* 14.1 (1986): 99–108.

———. *The Young Hemingway.* New York: Blackwell, 1986.

Rich, Adrienne. "Compulsory Heterosexuality and Lesbian Existence." *Blood, Bread, and Poetry: Selected Prose 1979–85.* New York: Norton, 1986. 23–75.

———. *On Lies, Secrets, and Silence.* New York: Norton, 1979.

Riley, Denise. *'Am I That Name?': Feminism and the Category of 'Women' in History.* London: Macmillan, 1988.

———. "Some Peculiarities of Social Policy Concerning Women in Wartime and Postwar Britain." *Behind the Lines.* Ed. Higonnet et al. New Haven: Yale UP, 1987.

Riordan, Mary Marguerite. *Lillian Hellman: A Bibliography: 1926–1978.* Metuchen, NJ: Scarecrow, 1980.

Roe, Steven C. "Opening Bluebeard's Closet: Writing and Aggression in Hemingway's *The Garden of Eden* Manuscript." *Hemingway Review* 12.1 (1992): 52–66.

Rohrter, Larry. "The Third Woman of 'Thelma and Louise.'" *New York Times* 5 June 1991, C21.

Rollyson, Carl. *Nothing Ever Happens to the Brave: The Story of Martha Gellhorn.* New York: St. Martin's, 1990.

Roof, Judith. "The Match in the Crocus: Representations of Lesbian Sexuality." *Discontented Discourses: Feminism/Textual Intervention/Psychoanalysis.* Ed. Marleen S. Barr and Richard Feldstein. Urbana: U of Illinois P, 1989. 100–116.

Rosenfield, Claire. "New World, Old Myths." *Twentieth Century Interpretations of "The Old Man and the Sea."* Ed. Katharine T. Jobes. Englewood Cliffs, NJ: Prentice Hall, 1968. 41–55.

Ross, Lillian. "How Do You Like It Now, Gentlemen?" *The New Yorker* 13 May 1950: 36–62.

——. *Portrait of Hemingway.* 1950. New York: Modern Library, 1999.

Rovit, Earl. *Ernest Hemingway.* Boston: Twayne, 1963.

——. "Faulkner, Hemingway, and the American Family." *Mississippi Quarterly* 29 (1976): 483–97.

Rudat, Wolfgang E. H. "Brett's Problem." *Brett Ashley.* Major Literary Characters. Ed. Harold Bloom. New York: Chelsea, 1991. 166–74.

——. "Hemingway's Rabbit: Slips of the Tongue and Other Linguistic Games in *For Whom the Bell Tolls.*" *Hemingway Review* 10.1 (1990): 34–51.

——. "The Other War in *For Whom the Bell Tolls:* Maria and Miltonic Gender-Role Battles." *Hemingway Review* 11.1 (1991): 8–24.

Safina, Carl. "Song for the Swordfish." *Audubon* May-June 1998: 58–68. Infotrac Searchbank. Article A20958948. <http://web2.searchbank.com>.

Sanderson, Rena. "Hemingway and Gender History." *The Cambridge Companion to Ernest Hemingway.* Ed. Scott Donaldson. Cambridge: Cambridge UP, 1996. 170–96.

Sanford, John E. "Hemingway's Painting Legacy: Grace's Paintings." 9th International Hemingway Conference. Bimini. 6 Jan. 2000.

Schmidt, Dolores Barracano. "The Great American Bitch." *College English* 32 (1971): 900–905.

Schroer, Silvia. "Mary's Foremothers." *National Catholic Reporter* 25 Dec. 1992: 3. Infotrac Searchbank. Article A1332397. <http://web2.searchbank.com>.

Schwartz, Nina. "Lovers' Discourse in *The Sun Also Rises:* A Cock and Bull Story." *Criticism* 26.1 (1984): 49–69. Excerpted in *Brett Ashley.* Major Literary Characters. Ed. Harold Bloom. New York: Chelsea House, 1991. 51–54.

Schweik, Susan. *A Gulf So Deeply Cut: American Women Poets and the Second World War.* Madison: U of Wisconsin P, 1991.

Schwenger, Peter. "The Masculine Mode." *Speaking of Gender.* Ed. Elaine Showalter. New York: Routledge, 1989. 101–12.

Seidman, Steven. "Deconstructing Queer Theory or the Under-Theorization of the Social and the Ethical." *Social Postmodernism: Beyond Identity Politics.* Ed. Linda Nicholson and Steven Seidman. Cambridge: Cambridge UP, 1995. 116–41.

Sellroe, Edna. "Grace Hall Hemingway—River Forest Woman Whose Interesting Career Embraces Four Arts." *Artistry* (Apr. 1937): 2, 11.

Shaughnessy, Susan. *Walking on Alligators: A Book of Meditations for Writers.* San Francisco: Harper, 1993.

Shelley, Mary. *Frankenstein.* Ed. Johanna M. Smith. Boston: St. Martin's, 1992.

Sheldon, Sayre P., ed. *Her War Story: Twentieth-Century Women Write About War.* Carbondale: Southern Illinois UP, 1999.

Shelton, Frank. "The Family in Hemingway's Nick Adams Stories." *Studies in Short Fiction* 9 (1974): 303–05.

Showalter, Elaine. *A Literature of Their Own: British Women Novelists from Brontë to Lessing.* Princeton: Princeton UP, 1977.

——. "Towards a Feminist Poetics." *The New Feminist Criticism.* Ed. Elaine Showalter. New York: Pantheon, 1985. 125–43.

Simmonds, Roy. "The British Critical Reception of Hemingway's *The Garden of Eden.*" *Hemingway Review* 8.2 (1989): 14–21.

Simmons, Dan. *The Crook Factory.* New York: Avon, 1999.

Simon, Linda. *The Biography of Alice B. Toklas.* New York: Doubleday, 1977.

Smiley, Pamela. "Gender-Linked Communication in 'Hills Like White Elephants.'" *Hemingway Review* 8.1 (1988): 2–12.

Smith, Carol H. "Women and the Loss of Eden." *Ernest Hemingway: The Writer in Context.* Ed. James Nagel. Madison: U of Wisconsin P, 1984. 129–44.

Smith, Paul. *A Reader's Guide to the Short Stories of Ernest Hemingway.* Boston: G. K. Hall, 1989.

Snitow, Ann, Christine Stansell, and Sharon Thompson. Introduction. *Powers of Desire: The Politics of Sexuality.* Ed. Ann Snitow, et al. New York: Monthly Review P, 1983. 9–47.

Sokoloff, Alice Hunt. *Hadley: The First Mrs. Hemingway.* New York: Dodd, 1973.

Spanier, Sandra Whipple. Afterword. *Love Goes to Press: A Comedy in Three Acts.* Martha Gellhorn and Virginia Cowles. Ed. Sandra Whipple Spanier. Lincoln: U of Nebraska P, 1995. 79–90.

——. "Catherine Barkley and the Hemingway Code: Ritual and Survival in *A Farewell to Arms.*" *Ernest Hemingway's "A Farewell to Arms."* Ed. Harold Bloom. New York: Chelsea, 1987. 131–48.

——. "Hemingway's Unknown Soldier: Catherine Barkley, the Critics, and the Great War." *New Essays on "A Farewell to Arms."* Ed. Scott Donaldson. Cambridge: Cambridge UP, 1990. 75–108.

Spender, Stephen. "An American's Eden." *Sunday Telegraph,* 8 Feb. 1987, 5–6.

Spilka, Mark. "Abusive and Nonabusive Dying in Hemingway's Fiction." *Eight Lessons in Love: A Domestic Violence Reader.* Columbia: U of Missouri P, 1997. 210–22.

——. "The Death of Love in *The Sun Also Rises.*" *Hemingway and His Critics: An International Anthology.* Ed. Carlos Baker. New York: Hill and Wang, 1961. 80–92.

——. *Eight Lessons in Love: A Domestic Violence Reader.* Columbia: U of Missouri P, 1997.

——. "Hemingway and Fauntleroy: An Androgynous Pursuit." *American Novelists Revisited: Essays in Feminist Criticism.* Ed. Fritz Fleischmann. Boston: G. K. Hall, 1983. 339–70.

——. *Hemingway's Quarrel with Androgyny.* Lincoln: U of Nebraska P, 1990.

——. "Victorian Keys to the Early Hemingway: Captain Marryat." *Novel* 17.2 (1984): 116–40.

——. "Victorian Keys to the Early Hemingway: Part I—*John Halifax, Gentleman.*" *Journal of Modern Literature* 10 (1983): 125–50.

———. "Victorian Keys to the Early Hemingway: Part II—*Fauntleroy* and *Finn*." *Journal of Modern Literature* 10 (1983): 289–310.

Stearns, Harold E. "The Intellectual Life." *Civilization in the United States: An Inquiry by Thirty Americans.* New York: Harcourt, 1922. 135–50.

Stein, Gertrude. "As a Wife Has a Cow: A Love Story." 1926. *Selected Writings of Gertrude Stein.* Ed. Carl van Vechten. New York: Vintage, 1990. 543–45.

———. *The Autobiography of Alice B. Toklas.* New York: Random, 1933.

Stein, William Bysshe. "Ritual in Hemingway's 'Big Two-Hearted River.'" *Texas Studies in Literature and Language* 1 (1960): 555–61.

Steinbeck, John, and Edward F. Ricketts. *The Log from the Sea of Cortez.* 1951. New York: Penguin, 1986.

Stendhal, Renate, ed. *Gertrude Stein in Words and Pictures.* London: Thames & Hudson, 1994.

Stevens, Mick. Hemingway Book Group Cartoon. *Missouri Review* 21.2 (1998).

Stolzfus, Ben. *Gide and Hemingway: Rebels Against God.* Port Washington, NY: Kennikat, 1978.

Stoneback, H. R. "From the rue Saint-Jacques to the Pass of Roland to the 'Unfinished Church on the Edge of the Cliff.'" *Hemingway Review* 6.1 (1986): 2–29.

Strychacz, Thomas. "In Our Time, Out of Season." *Cambridge Companion to Hemingway.* Ed. Scott Donaldson. Cambridge: Cambridge UP, 1996. 55–86.

Sugg, Richard. "Hemingway, Money, and *The Sun Also Rises*." *Fitzgerald/Hemingway Annual: 1972.* 257–67.

Summerhayes, Don. "Fish Story: Ways of Telling in 'Big Two-Hearted River.'" *Hemingway Review* 15.1 (1995): 10–26.

Sylvester, Bickford. "The Cuban Context of *The Old Man and the Sea*." *Cambridge Companion to Hemingway.* Ed. Scott Donaldson. Cambridge: Cambridge UP, 1996. 243–68.

———. "Hemingway's Extended Vision: *The Old Man and the Sea*." *PMLA* (Mar. 1966): 130–38.

———. "The Sexual Impasse to Romantic Order in Hemingway's Fiction: *A Farewell to Arms, Othello,* 'Orpen,' and the Hemingway Canon." *Hemingway: Up in Michigan Perspectives.* Ed. Frederic J. Svoboda and Joseph J. Waldmeir. East Lansing: Michigan State UP, 1995. 177–87.

Tannen, Deborah. *You Just Don't Understand: Women and Men in Conversation.* New York: Ballantine, 1990.

Tanner, Tony. *The Reign of Wonder: Naivety and Reality in American Literature.* Cambridge: Cambridge UP, 1965.

Tavernier-Courbin, Jacqueline. *Ernest Hemingway's "A Moveable Feast": The Making of Myth.* Boston: Northeastern UP, 1991.

Taylor, Paul. "A Long Post-Mortem." *Literary Review* (1987): 5–6.

Tetlow, Wendolyn E. *Hemingway's "In Our Time": Lyrical Dimensions.* Lewisburg, PA: Bucknell UP, 1992.

Teunissen, John J. "*For Whom the Bell Tolls* as Mythic Narrative." *Ernest Hemingway: Six Decades of Criticism.* Ed. Linda W. Wagner. Lansing: Michigan State UP, 1987. 221–37.

Thomas, Dylan. "Do Not Go Gentle Into That Good Night." *The New Oxford Book of English Verse.* Ed. Helen Gardner. New York: Oxford UP, 1972. 942.

Thorne, Barrie, and Marilyn Yalom. *Rethinking the Family: Some Feminist Questions.* Boston: Northeastern UP, 1992.

Thorne, Barrie. "Feminism and the Family: Two Decades of Thought." *Rethinking the Family: Some Feminist Questions.* Rev. ed. Ed. Barrie Thorne and Marilyn Yalom. Boston: Northeastern UP, 1992. 3–30.

Tintner, Adeline R. "Ernest and Henry: Hemingway's Lover's Quarrel with James." *Ernest Hemingway: The Writer in Context.* Ed. James Nagel. Madison: U of Wisconsin P, 1984. 171–72.

Tompkins, Jane. *West of Everything: The Inner Life of Westerns.* New York: Oxford UP, 1992.

Trogdon, Robert. "Pursuit Reconsidered: *Green Hills of Africa* as Hemingway's Experiment in Prose." Master's thesis. North Carolina State University, 1992.

Tyler, Lisa. "'Women Have a Bad Time Really': Gender and Interpretation in *To Have and Have Not.*" *Marjorie Kinnan Rawlings Journal of Florida Literature* 7 (1996): 57–66.

Unfried, Sarah P. *Man's Place in the Natural Order: A Study of Hemingway's Works.* New York: Gordon Press, 1976.

Villard, Henry S., and James Nagel. *Hemingway in Love and War, The Lost Diary of Agnes von Kurowsky.* Boston: Northeastern UP, 1989.

Vopat, Carole Gottlieb. "The End of *The Sun Also Rises:* A New Beginning." *Fitzgerald/Hemingway Annual: 1972.* 245–55.

Voss, Frederick. *Picturing Hemingway: A Writer in His Time.* New Haven: Yale UP, 1999.

Waggoner, Eric. "Inside the Current: A Taoist Reading of *The Old Man and the Sea.*" *Hemingway Review* 17.2 (1998): 88–104.

Wagner-Martin, Linda. "Hemingway's Search for Heroes, Once Again." *Arizona Quarterly* 44.2 (1988): 58–68.

———. Introduction. *New Essays on "The Sun Also Rises."* Ed. Linda Wagner-Martin. Cambridge: Cambridge UP, 1987. 1–12.

———. "Juxtaposition in Hemingway's *In Our Time.*" *Studies in Short Fiction* 12 (1975): 243–52. Rpt. in *Critical Essays on Ernest Hemingway's "In Our Time."* Ed. Michael S. Reynolds. Boston: G. K. Hall, 1988. 120–29.

———. "'Proud and Friendly and Gently': Women in Hemingway's Early Fiction." *Ernest Hemingway: The Papers of a Writer.* Ed. Bernard Oldsey. New York: Garland, 1981. 63–71.

———. "Racial and Sexual Coding in Hemingway's *The Sun Also Rises.*" *Hemingway Review* 10.2 (1991): 39–41.

Watts, Emily Stipes. *Ernest Hemingway and the Arts.* Urbana: U of Illinois P, 1971.

Westling, Louise H. *The Green Breast of the World: Landscape, Gender, and American Fiction.* Athens: U of Georgia P, 1996.

Weston, Kath. *Families We Choose: Lesbians, Gays, Kinship.* New York: Columbia UP, 1991.

White, Gertrude M. "We're All 'Cats in the Rain.'" *Fitzgerald/Hemingway Annual 1978.* Ed. Matthew J. Bruccoli and Richard Layman. Detroit: Gale, 1979. 241–46.

White, William, ed. *By-Line: Ernest Hemingway: Selected Articles and Dispatches of Four Decades.* New York: Scribner's, 1967.

———, ed. *Dateline: Toronto: Hemingway's Complete Dispatches for The Toronto Star, 1920–1924.* New York: Scribner's, 1985.

Whitlow, Roger. *Cassandra's Daughters: The Women in Hemingway.* Westport, CT: Greenwood, 1984.

———. "The Destruction/Prevention of the Family Relationship in Hemingway's Fiction." *Literary Review* 20.1 (1976): 5–16.

Whitman, Walt. "As I Ebb'd with the Ocean of Life." Ed. James E. Miller Jr. *Complete Poetry and Selected Prose of Walt Whitman.* Boston: Riverside, 1959. 184–86.

———. "Out of the Cradle Endlessly Rocking." Ed. James E. Miller Jr. *Complete Poetry and Selected Prose of Walt Whitman.* Boston: Riverside, 1959. 180–84.

Wilentz, Gay. "(Re)Teaching Hemingway: Anti-Semitism as a Thematic Device in *The Sun Also Rises.*" *College English* 52 (1990): 186–93.

Williams, Terry Tempest. *An Unspoken Hunger: Stories from the Field.* New York: Pantheon, 1994. 81–87.

Willingham, Kathy G. "Hemingway's *The Garden of Eden:* Writing with the Body." *Hemingway Review* 12.2 (1993): 46–61.

Wilson, Edmund. "Bourdon Gauge of Morale." *Atlantic Monthly* July 1939.

———. *The Wound and the Bow.* Cambridge: Houghton, 1941.

Wilson, Jane E. "Good Old Harris in *The Sun Also Rises.*" *Critical Essays on Ernest Hemingway's "The Sun Also Rises."* Ed. James Nagel. New York: G. K. Hall, 1995. 185–90.

Woolf, Virginia. "An Essay in Criticism by Virginia Woolf." *New York Herald Tribune* 9 Oct. 1927: 1, 8.

———. *A Room of One's Own.* 1929. New York: Harcourt, 1981.

Wright, William. *Lillian Hellman: The Image, the Woman.* New York: Simon, 1986.

Wycherly, H. Alan. "Hemingway's 'The Sea Change.'" *American Notes & Queries* 7 (1969): 67–68.

Wylder, Delbert E. *Hemingway's Heroes.* Albuquerque: U of New Mexico P, 1969.

———. "The Two Faces of Brett: The Role of the New Woman in *The Sun Also Rises.*" *Kentucky Philological Association Bulletin* (1980): 27–33.

Young, Philip. *Ernest Hemingway.* New York: Holt, 1952.

———. *Ernest Hemingway: A Reconsideration.* University Park: Pennsylvania State UP, 1966.

Contributors

Jamie Barlowe is Associate Professor of English and Chair of Women's and Gender Studies at the University of Toledo. She is the author of *The Scarlet Mob of Scribblers: Rereading Hester Prynne* and regularly publishes scholarly essays on Ernest Hemingway, Nathaniel Hawthorne, American women writers, film, feminist theory and pedagogy, and women's scholarship. Her current book project is titled *Viewer, I Married Him: Cinematic Adaptations of Novels by 19th and 20th Century American and British Women Writers*.

Susan F. Beegel holds a PhD in English from Yale University and is a Professor in the Williams College-Mystic Seaport Maritime Studies Program, where she teaches "Literature of the Sea." She is editor of *The Hemingway Review*, a scholarly journal devoted to the life and work of Ernest Hemingway, and her books include *Hemingway's Craft of Omission, Hemingway's Neglected Short Fiction*, and *Steinbeck and the Environment: Interdisciplinary Approaches*. She lives at the University of Massachusetts Field Station on Nantucket Island, where she serves as a member of the boards of the Nantucket Atheneum and the Maria Mitchell Science Center.

Rose Marie Burwell is Professor of Modern Literature at Northern Illinois University and author of *Hemingway: The Postwar Years and the Posthumous Novels* (1996). She is currently editing the travel journals of Mary Welsh Hemingway and has just received an NEH grant for a biography of Mary.

Nancy R. Comley is Chair and Professor of English at Queens College of the City University of New York. She is coauthor with Robert Scholes of *Hemingway's Genders: Rereading the Hemingway Text* and author of articles on Hemingway, Fitzgerald, and other modernist writers. She is also coauthor and coeditor of four writing textbooks.

Hilary K. Justice holds a BA in Music from Dartmouth College, an MA in English from Trinity College, and is currently completing her doctoral dissertation in English on textuality and constructions of authorship and iconicity at the University of Chicago. In addition to being a professional pianist and novice violist, she is the author of several articles on Hemingway (appearing in *The Hemingway Review* and *North Dakota Quarterly*). She has lectured on music and literature at various academic and public venues in the Midwest and at the American Literature Association Conference (2000) in California.

Miriam B. Mandel is the author of *Reading Hemingway: The Facts in the Fictions* (1995), *Reading Ernest Hemingway's "Death in the Afternoon,"* and *Reading Ernest Hemingway's "The Dangerous Summer"* (forthcoming). In addition to her ongoing work on Hemingway, she has translated critical essays on the fiction of Ramón del Valle-Inclán and published articles on Jane Austen, Joseph Conrad, F. Scott Fitzgerald, A. E. Housman, and Katherine Mansfield. She has also read papers before learned societies in Australia, Canada, France, Spain, and the United States. She is Senior Lecturer in the English Department of Tel Aviv University.

Linda Patterson Miller is Professor of English at Penn State Abignton. She was a Danforth Foundation Associate as well as a Lilly Foundation Post-Doctoral Fellow, and she has served as a scholarly consultant (on expatriate American writers and artists) for American Playhouse, PBS. Miller publishes in all areas of American studies, but her specialty is early twentieth-century American literature and art. Her articles on the Lost Generation writers, including Ernest Hemingway, have appeared in such journals as *Mosaic, North Dakota Quarterly, Journal of Modern Literature, Studies in American Fiction,* and *The Hemingway Review,* and in several edited book collections. Her books include *Letters from the Lost Generation: Gerald and Sara Murphy and Friends,* and (with Randall M. Miller) *The Book of American Diaries.* She is presently completing another book on American expatriate artists in France to be called *The Summer of '26.* Professor Miller has lectured nationally and internationally on modernist art and on American writing, including American diarists. She has been a Pennsylvania Humanities Council speaker and is a board member of the Hemingway Foundation.

Debra A. Moddelmog is Associate Professor of English and an associated faculty member of both the Women's Studies and the Comparative Studies departments at Ohio State University. She is the author of *Reading Desire: In Pursuit of Ernest Hemingway* (1999) and *Readers and Mythic Signs* (1993). She has also published articles on Hemingway, Porter, Faulkner, Pynchon, and multiculturalism.

Kim Moreland is Associate Professor of English at the George Washington University, where she is also an Associate Dean for Undergraduate Studies. She is the author of *The Medievalist Impulse in American Literature: Twain, Adams, Fitzgerald, and Hemingway*. She recently published "Just the Tip of the Iceberg Theory: Hemingway and Anderson's 'Loneliness'" in the *Hemingway Review*.

Ann Putnam teaches creative writing and American literature at the University of Puget Sound in Tacoma, Washington. She has published fiction, personal essays, and scholarly articles in a number of journals and collections and has presented papers at Hemingway conferences in Pamplona, Havana, and Sun Valley.

Rena Sanderson, Associate Professor of English, teaches American Literature at Boise State University. Her specialization is in early twentieth-century modernism. She edited *Blowing the Bridge: Essays on Hemingway and "For Whom the Bell Tolls"* (1992), and she has published several studies of Hemingway, including "Hemingway and Gender History," a chapter in *The Cambridge Companion to Ernest Hemingway* (1996).

Gail D. Sinclair is a Visiting Assistant Professor at the University of South Florida, where she teaches modern literature. She has published in such journals as *Mississippi Quarterly* and *Studies in the Novel* and is a regular participant at meetings of the Hemingway and Fitzgerald Societies, as well as other academic conferences. In addition, her article "Fitzgerald and the Play of Language" is to be published in the Modern Language Association's series *New Approaches to Teaching Fitzgerald's "The Great Gatsby."* She is presently at work on a book-length critical study of suicide as a thematic force in twentieth-century fiction by females.

Sandra Whipple Spanier, Associate Professor of English at Pennsylvania State University, has frequently taught courses on Hemingway, presented papers at international Hemingway conferences, and serves on the editorial board on *The Hemingway Review*. Her publications include "Catherine Barkley and the Hemingway Code: Ritual and Survival in *A Farewell to Arms*" and "Hemingway's Unknown Soldier: Catherine Barkley, the Critics, and the Great War." She is the author of *Kay Boyle: Artist and Activist* (1986), and she edited and introduced *Life Being the Best and Other Stories* by Kay Boyle (1988), *Love Goes to Press: A Comedy in Three Acts* by Martha Gellhorn and Virginia Cowles (1995), and *American Fiction, American Myth: Essays by Philip Young* (with David Morrell, 2000). Current projects include the authorized edition of the letters of Kay Boyle, supported in part by an NEH Fellowship, and a study of Martha Gellhorn and her work.

Amy Lovell Strong is completing her PhD in twentieth-century American literature at the University of North Carolina at Chapel Hill. Her dissertation examines the ways that race and racial conflicts structure many of Hemingway's works, from the earliest stories of *In Our Time* to the posthumously published *True at First Light*.

Lisa Tyler is Associate Professor of English at Sinclair Community College in Dayton, Ohio. She has published essays in *Studies in Short Fiction, Hemingway Review, Woolf Studies Annual, Pinter Review*, and *Teaching English in the Two-Year College* and is presently completing a book on Hemingway for the Student Companions to Classic Writers series published by Greenwood Press.

Linda Wagner-Martin is Hanes Professor of English at the University of North Carolina, Chapel Hill. She recently served a three-year term as president of the Ernest Hemingway Foundation and Society and has long been active in Hemingway affairs. Besides books on other American modernists such as William Faulkner, John Dos Passos, Gertrude Stein, William Carlos Williams, and others, she has published a number of books and essays on Hemingway's writing. The recipient of grants from the Guggenheim Foundation, the Rockefeller Foundation, the Bunting Institute, and the National Endowment for the Humanities, she has won teaching awards from both UNC and Michigan State University.

Kathy G. Willingham is Associate Professor of English at Tougaloo College, Mississippi. She is author of various notes and articles on Ernest Hemingway and William Faulkner. In addition to modern American literature, her research interests include art history and literary theory, and she has delivered papers on such topics at numerous conferences.

Index